ONE STEP AHEAD IN CONTEMPORARY ECONOMIC ANALYSES

Suggested by the Turkish Experience

Zeyyat HATİBOĞLU
(Professor of Economics)

İstanbul, 2009

Beta

Yayın No : 2162
İşletme-Ekonomi Dizisi : 333

1. Edition - June 2009- İSTANBUL

ISBN: 978-605-377-070-1

Dizgi : Kurtiş Matbaacılık San. ve Tic. Ltd. Şti.
Baskı - Cilt : Kurtiş Matbaacılık San. ve Tic. Ltd. Şti.
Maltepe Mahallesi, Litros Yolu, Fatih Sanayi Sitesi
No:12/74 Topkapı, İstanbul-Turkey
Tel: +90 (212) 613 68 94 Fax: +90 (212) 613 68 96

Beta BASIM YAYIM DAĞITIM A.Ş.
Himaye-i Etfal Sokak Talas Han No. 13-15
Cağaloğlu - İSTANBUL
Tel: (0-212) 511 54 32 - 519 01 77
Fax: (0-212) 511 36 50
www.betayayincilik.com

PREFACE

The development and the last version of my challenging and innovative ideas on economic analysis are summarized in this book. In additon, I tried to support my unconventional ideas expressed in this book (1) by an extension of the theoretical reasoning; 2) by giving more information about the backgound (the Turkish economy) which suggested them, and (3) by reviewing critically the writings of well known economists on the same issues which are discussed in this book.

Although the title of the book might induce any reader to think that this book is about the economy of Turkey, it is not. Yet the information on the Turkish economy (although short as it is) is considered necessary for convincing the reader that the theoretical analysis in the book is not a product of the imagination of the author (an a priory speculation) but the actual operation of this economy has suggested them and the analysis has been validated by observations in this economy.

The first innovative and challenging ideas are found in my book entitled AN UNCONVENTIONAL ANALYSIS OF THE TURKISH ECONOMY published in 1978. Yet, all of them were crude and needed refinement. I improved them in the years ensuing that book in some 50 books each following the other.

The motive of my streneous efforts to write 50 books could be summarized as follows. When I started writing original books, the goal was to analyze the Turkish economy and to spot the inadequacies in the existing analyses of this economy. But the by-product of those efforts has proved to be much more important. The analyses I was interested in were those which were based on the principles of contemporary economics. That meant that by doing so I was underlining the inadequacies in contemporary economics. And that was not all; while I was trying to correct them I was replacing them by findings based on a new methodology, new ideas and new analyses not known in contemporary economics. Again, all those challenging and innovating ideas could be used in the analysis of any country in the world. Moreover, the validation of them by the Turkish experience of the last 60 years encouraged me: what I was doing was right and meaningful for the advance of contemporary economics.

The Turkish experience is in the background. That suggested my analyses and I also validated my challenging and innovative ideas by it. Although some chapters of the book are in the form of pure theory, most of them start with the rendition of the Turkish experience and critical analyses based on them. It should not be thought that this is a book on the Turkish economy. I wrote several books dealing with the history and problems of that economy. The present one is different.

One of the reasons why I publish this book is to present the path I traversed before I reached the final stage of my unconventional theory of economic growth. In fact, when my first writings on economic growth were published, I qualified them as unconventional. Yet, I feel now that this qualification is more appropriate for the present version of my work which is a more developed version of the original essay.

The adventure began in 1978 when my book entitled AN UNCONVENTIONAL ANALYSIS OF THE TURKISH ECONOMY was published. The first two chapters of the books are a summarized reproduction of Chapter V of the 1978 book and the rendition of my comments about the reviews of that book which appeared in leading international journals.

AN UNCONVENTIONAL ANALYSIS OF THE TURKISH ECONOMY (UATE) was concerned with the problems of the Turkish economy and they were analyzed unconventionally. The starting point was a critical examination of import substitution policy which had been adopted since the 1930 s. I tried to show that this could not be stuck to anymore and although the growth rate so far sustained was an end result of this policy, it could not be sustained in future years. What was more important was my efforts to suggest that the officially calculated growth rate of the national income for 1950-1975 was an illusion, i.e., it was much lower than that. While doing it, I developed a different analysis of growth. In the ensuing years I tried to develop the ideas put forward in this book by reversing my approach in the sense that I expressed them theoretically first and validated them by the Turkish experience. The initial theoretical groundwork is in Chapter I. The present state of the unconventional approach to economic growth and its validation are found in the ensuing chapters.

By developing the views launched in UATE I put forward important innovative and challenging ideas and validated them by the Turkish experience.

Here is a very short summary of what I have achieved. The growth theory summarized in elementary textbooks and in those intermediate level is supposed to be known. What did I add to them and why is it unconventional?

In my 1978 work I concentrated upon the per capita earning differences of agricultural and nonagricultural sectors of a dual economy. The rather high per capita incomes in nonagricultural sectors compared to those in agriculture and the shift of accumulating resources from agriculture to nonagricultural sectors would create a higher growth rate; this was known in the literature. But in the 1978 work, I perceived the fact that earnings in nonagricultural sectors should not be taken as they were: the reason of that belief was the main concern of UATE. Once this was explained, the reason why the growth rate in Turkey between 1950 and 1975 was calculated as high as that could be discovered. But this had to decrease whether the country switched to an outward looking policy or not. And my predictions have come true.

In the later work the idea developed in UATE was transported to nonagricultural sectors. But then relative prices of labor and nonlabor intensive goods were in question. As relative prices of labor intensive goods were lower after 1975, this would make the growth rate lower even if the level of production in the country was the same. The end-result of this discovery was the conclusion that pre-and post-1975 growth rates, each calculated by different constant prices, could not be compared. Part of the difference in growth rates should be due to changes in relative prices, an idea that was not found in the literature. In fact, traditionally, when national incomes were deflated in various years in order to compare them with each other, relative prices were kept the same. This brought in the necessity to think over the deflation of two national income figures of a country when the growth rate had to be calculated over time.

The inadequacy of the traditional economic analysis to explain the rather high growth rate in the Turkish economy in 1950-1975 period induced me to seek an alternative analysis. After streneous efforts continuing long years (from 1978 to 2007) the present version of the growth theory came to life. In this book the iteneary of this long voyage is told. The first discovery was an innovative explanation of the rather high income level of the nonagricultural sectors of the economy and its growth. The starting point was a critical examination of the traditional neoclassical theory of economic growth (the source of growth analysis).

In this theory when the is an increase in inputs (capital and labor) the marginal productivity of each factor of production is multiplied by its increase, then they were added up to find out their relative contribution to growth. Again, the increase of productivity had to be added to it in order to come with the observed growth rate.

I started pointing out that the valuation dimension might be lacking in this approach. In order to remedy it, I introduced the differentiation of labor and nonlabor intensive goods, which might take care of the change of the use of inputs, their relative prices and also the productivity change along with the introducing the lost valuation dimension.

Suppose we try to measure the growth of national income between 1950 and 2000. Again, suppose that we divide it into two subperiods, 1950-1975 and 1975-2000. In each sub-period we use a different constant price series to measure the growth rate. We suppose that in each series relative prices of labor and nonlabor intensive goods are kept the same. But relative prices are different in two periods, i.e., in the first one constant prices are those of 1965 and in the second the constant prices are those of 1990.

I attracted attention to three problems. One is the comparison of the national income of 1975 measured by 1965 prices and that one (again 1975) measured by 1990 prices. The second problem is the comparison of growth rates in two subperiods, each calculated by a different constant price series in which relative prices are different. The third problem is the calculation of the growth rate in the grand period, 1950-2000.

Let us look into each of those problems. Firstly the comparison of the level of two national incomes in 1975. Suppose apples and pears only are produced in the country. The first good is labor intensive and the second is a nonlabor intensive good. If at the beginning of the second period the relative apple prices are lower and if the production of each good is the same, I contend that national income in the second period is lower. I call this level effect. I shall return to it in a moment. Now let us look into the second problem. If labor intensive goods prices are relatively lower in the 1975-2000 subperiod and its growth is higher, this should make the growth rate lower. I call it growth effect and I contend that a part of the difference of growth rate in different subperiods should be the change of relative prices.

Now the third problem. We set out to measure the growth rate of 1950-2000 period. If the growth rates of two subperiods are added up, we would come up with a figure which is misleading. For example if the growth rate of 1950-1975 period is 7 percent and that of the second period is 4 percent, we are tempted to say that the growth rate of the grand period is 5.5 percent. This is misleading. If relative prices of the period ensuing 2000 stay as they were in 1990, we cannot say that the trend rate of growth would be 5.5 percent. This is related to the level effect. If the level of the national income measured in 1990 prices is lower than when it was measured by 1965 prices, this should also affect the growth rate of the grand period. The lower level of national income in

1975 should make the growth rate of the grand period less than 5.5 percent. It would be a better guess that the future national income growth rate trend would be around 4 percent.

A few words about how to quantify the lowering the national income when measured by 1990 prices. This is a difficult problem and my solution is problematic. I contend that the prices of labor intensive goods should be the measuring rod. This is because of the fact that if national income is measured by this standard, its sustainability would be projected better. All these questions are addressed in this book.

I realize now that I tried to find a method to compare the growth rate of the national income of two remote years such as 1950 and 2000 when there were substantial changes in the relative prices of labor and nonlabor intensive goods, and while doing it I tried to add together both the growth and level effects. But this was not all, i.e., the problem was not a mere calculation: it had welfare implications. The main idea was as follows. Suppose that national income consists of apples and pears and suppose again that the relative prices of apples are lower in the second period and the production of all goods was the same. Wouldn't that be a lower income level? This is what I called level effect.

The important analyses are related to economic growth. They are at the beginning of the book. Yet the main idea existing there seems to have shaded the whole book. It is the relative prices of nonlabor and labor intensive commodities. I supposed that the nonlabor intensive good prices are more related to international prices compared to those labor intensive goods prices in any country. I think this is observed almost everywhere in the world. What I did was to draw out important consequences of that observation. I tried to show the close relationship between labor prices and economic growth. The most important discovery was the differentiation of growth and level effects (different from what was found in the literature) given rise by the impact of labor prices on national income.

Almost every important topic in economics is analyzed and what is important is that in some of them interesting and in others less interesting ideas were launched.

In the beginning chapters of the book my challenging and innovating analyses on economic growth are found. In the rest of the book almost every problem constituting the topic of economic analyses is studied. Each chapter can be read independently from one another. In addition, they complete each other in the sense that if all of them are read, 4 aims are reached. 1- The inadequacy of contemporary economic analyses in several topics. 2-A replacement and/or a completion of them by new ones. 3- One can have a good idea about how a country economic analysis could be carried out. 4- A fairly good image would be obtained about the growth, structure and problems of the Turkish economy, which could be useful for people interested in this economy.

Note: *Dr. Zeyyat Hatiboğlu was professor of economics at Istanbul University and Istanbul Technical University. He was educated at Istanbul University, Harvard Business School and the London School of Economics. He is 85 years old.*

The address is: *Selim Ragıp Emeç Sokak No: 17, B 8, Suadiye, İstanbul - Turkey.*

Tel: 0212 362 55 41 - Fax: 0212 416 70 61

CONTENTS

PAGE

CHAPTER I

AN UNCONVENTIONAL ANALYSIS OF THE TURKISH ECONOMY

CHAPTER II

MORE ON THE BOOK ENTITLED ‘AN UNCONVENTIONAL ANALYSIS OF THE TURKISH ECONOMY

CHAPTER III

EARNING DIFFERENCES AND THE GROWTH OF NATIONAL INCOME

CHAPTER IV

THE EARLY UNCONVENTIONAL THEORETICAL WRITINGS: THE MAGNIFICATION OF THE LOSS DUE TO DETERIORATING TERMS OF TRADE (PARTLY ORIGINAL VERSION)

CHAPTER V

THE DEVELOPMENT OF UATE

CHAPTER VI

A CONTRIBUTION TO THE THEORY OF GROWTH AND ITS IMPLICATIONS FOR ECONOMIC ANALYSIS

CHAPTER VII
A SHORT HISTORY AND STRUCTURE OF THE TURKISH ECONOMY

APPENDICE CHAPTER VII
AGRICULTURE AND INDUSTRY IN TURKEY

CHAPTER VIII
THE VALIDATION OF THE UNCONVENTIONAL APPROACH BY THE TURKISH EXPERIENCE

CHAPTER IX
FLUCTUATIONS OF NATIONAL INCOME AND MACROANALYSES

CHAPTER X
MACROMODELS

CHAPTER XI

A CRITICAL SURVEY OF CONVENTIONAL ANALYSES OF GROWTH AND DEVELOPMENT IN TURKEY

CHAPTER XII

TWO PAPERS BY CHENERY AND YENAL

CHAPTER XIII

A TEST OF THE METHOD OF THE PURCHASING POWER PARITY (PPP) IN MEASURING NATIONAL INCOME

CHAPTER XIV

EMPLOYMENT

CHAPTER XV

THE ANALYSIS OF INCOME DISTRIBUTION IN TURKEY LEADING TO UNCONVENTIONAL COMMENTS

CHAPTER XVI

THE ANALYSIS OF INFLATION AND THE FINANCIAL SECTOR IN TURKEY LEADING TO UNCONVENTIONAL COMMENTS

CHAPTER XVII

MORE ON INFLATION AND REPRESSIVE FINANCE

CHAPTER XVIII

INTERNATIONAL TRADE

CHAPTER XIX

THE DETERMINATION OF EXCHANGE RATES

CHAPTER XX

THE SWITCH TO OUTWARD AND GLOBALIZATION POLICIES

CHAPTER XXI

MARKET ECONOMY OR SOCIALISM

CHAPTER I

AN UNCONVENTIONAL ANALYSIS OF THE TURKISH ECONOMY

§ 1 - INTRODUCTION

AN UNCONVENTIONAL ANALYSIS OF THE TURKISH ECONOMY(to be noted as UATE) is the vanguard of my unconventional and innovating writings.A short summary of the book is presented in this chapter. I included also a few extracts from UATE in order to show where I started from.

In the years ensuing its publication (30 years) I tried to improve and refine the original ideas expounded in this book.This book was concerned with the economy of Turkey.But the methodology I developed was general and could be used in any country.In addition,important inadequacies of the contemporary analysis of economic growth were noted and clues to enrich the theory of growth could be found in this book.

§ 2 - A SHORT SUMMARY OF THE UNCONVENTIONAL ANALYSIS OF THE TURKISH ECONOMY

In this section of this chapter my book entitled AN UNCONVENTIONAL ANALYSIS OF THE TURKISH ECONOMY (1978, to be noted as UATE) is summarized.This book was the vanguard of my challenging and innovative books.It was a book dealing with the Turkish economy.Yet, the challenging analyses expressed in that book were promising in dealing with any economy;in other words, a new general theory of growth seemed to be on the road.Therefore in this book, while underlining the inadequate aspects of traditional analyses, I tried to open new avenues for research.

The scrutinization of this book could give a clue from where the innovating analysis had started and from where to where it could go.It is also probable that a chapter could be devoted to this book in a book entitled as the development of economic thoughts.

The average yearly growth of the Turkish economy was calculated as 6.4 percent for 1950-1975 period and per capita national income for 1975 was estimated as $ 833, whereas I tried to show that the yearly growth rate in this period should be around 4-5 percent and per capita income was not above $600-650.These conclusions were reached by using newly devoloped economic analyses which were not known in introductory books as well as in economic literature.

The analysis was based on the idea of the sustainability of national income,both its level and growth.According to my analysis if that criterion is used, both its level and growth had to be calculated lower.In fact, the growth of this economy decreased,exactly parellel to my expectations, in the years following the appearance of this book. Could the decrease in national income be explained by means of the analysis developed in this book or was it related only to what happened after the appearance of this book? This question was not asked,and it was not answered by any economist.I do so.

In the background was the duality in the Turkish economy: it was the main basis of the analysis,a poor agricultural and richer nonagricultural sectors (richer than suggested by the world experience when the level of development of the country was taken into consideration). As time passed by, the accumulated resources were shifted to relatively richer nonagricultural sector;as a result, a higher growth rate was materialized for the whole period. In fact, the agricultural sector, which was some 45 percent of the national income at the beginning, had came down to 25 percent at the end of the period.As a result,the growth rate materialized as high as observed figures.But all these were known in the literature.Yet,my main innovation was a result of the understanding of the reason why the income level of nonagricultural sectors were so very high. I could explain it by drawing upon the import substitution policy adopted in the country. It is again known in the literature that this policy could make growth rate higher at the beginning. My original contribution was to show that if costs and as a result the prices of import substituted industries were higher than what they were when measured in terms of the official exchange rate, the price of any good produced in the nonagricultural sector should be high in order that those expensive goods could be sold in domestic markets. This would not mean that labor prices were higher than those in developed countries, yet they were higher than what they should be. As a great proportion of exports were originating from agricultural sector, those high prices in nonagricultural sector could be sustained even if prices in terms of dollars in nonagricultural sectors were higher than what they should be.Would high prices give rise to high income levels? It was apparent that if the exchange rate was based on selling agricultural prices, national income in terms of dollar would ,of course, be higher than it would be when calculated in terms of the national currency,lira.But would that amount to a higher national income in terms of national currency? The main thesis of the book was that it would. Why? As will be shown below, if the rate of growth in terms of national currency in nonagricultural sectors was greater in nonagricultural sectors compared to that in agricultural sector (this was the case,they were 8.3 and 3.3 percent,respectively, for the whole period),the shift of resources from agriculture to nonagriculture would make the growth rate higher in terms the lira.The problem was to explain why the growth rate in nonagricultural sectors was so very high (8.3 percent while that of agriculture was 3.3 percent). New methods were developed to explain this fact (as would be summarized below), yet its full explanation had to wait for some twenty years.

How did I measure the high level of national income and its growth? I used 3 methods;2 of them were more realistic.One of them was to start from high earning differences between nongricultural and agricultural sectors.According to the world experience the multiplier between them should be 2.5; whereas in Turkey it was 4-5. I supposed that if nonagricultural goods could not be exported by an exchange rate determined by the selling possibility of agricultural commodities, the only way would be to decrease nonagricultural price level relatively to agricultural goods.In order to do it I supposed that earning differences between them should be 2.5 (which should be the case according to world experience) rather than 4 or 5 ,the actual case.When I made my calculation on that base, I came up with some 30 percent lower figures for both the level and growth of national income.

The second calculation was based on the reaserch work dealing with the change of some structural magnitudes through economic development.In the 50 s and 60 s several economists calculated them.I compared the Turkish figures with them and drew interesting conclusions not imagined by economists carrying out such research.In fact, my analysis supported the previous expectation,i.e.,the decrease of the national income. It was apparent that the share of the agricultural sector in national income and the rate of people working there was much higher than what it should be for a country having the per capita income of the Turkish economy. It (per capita income) should be lower. The only way to imagine making it lower was to measure nonagricultural per capita incomes lower. In addition to that, when export levels compared to national income they were much lower and it was apparent that it was due to small amount exports originating from nonagricultural sectors.That meant that prices were high in nonagricultural sectors in terms of dollars.In fact, this conclusion was the end result of the first argument summarized above.

I examined factors making earning differences between nongricultural and agricultural sectors high in the literature. They were classified as genuine and nongenuine, perhaps economic or non-economic. Genuine differences are related to better technical knowledge, better education and capital intensity in nonagricultural sectors. Nongenuine differences are mostly connected with institutional arrangements such as powerful trade unions, favorable attitude of the government for labor movement, the ability of foreign investors to pay high wages, etc. There are factors, the classificastion of which under genuine and nongenuine differences is difficult. The first is the difference caused by higher living expenses in towns compared to rural areas and higher wages to attract rural people to immigrate. The second is the high prices caused by the protection policy or import substitution. Thirdly, the relatively rapid increase of demand for products of nonagricultural sectors could also cause earning differences.

I have also observed the parallelism between the adoption an import substitution policy and the level of earning differences,i.e.,their higher level in countries adopting that policy,Turkey being one of them.After all those findings I tried to show that all those factors were not enough to explain them (earning differences and I underlined the conditions which would sustain that level,as shown above.This was the novelty of UATE.

I tried to show that all these factors were not enough to explain big earning differences between two sectors of the dual Turkish economy. A more important factor in addition to existing ones in the literature was the swollen prices in nonagricultural sectors. They were a result of imitative prices increases in nonimport substituting sectors in the nonagricultural sector. In order to buy high cost products of import substitution industries prices in the whole sector had to be high without any relation to productivity level in this sector. As a great proportion of exports were originating from agricultural sector, this could permit high prices in the nonagricultural sector to be sustained. That meant high factor prices in this sector, and this amounted to a greater earning differences between the two sectors. Let us also remember that exchange rates were determined according to saleability of agricultural products, and this would also give rise to a higher national income in terms of dollars. In other words prices in the nonagricultural sectors would not mean much in the fixing of exchange rates.

Earning differences were important in 1930-1980 period. This was because of high share of agriculture in national income. As time went by this decreased and the impact of earning differences became less important in the determination of nation income.

In my posterior work I transported this idea to the nonagricultural sector. I tried to talk about relative prices of labor and nonlabor intensive goods prices rather than prices in nonagricultural and agricultural sectors of the economy. The analysis was the same, i.e., the fall in the prices of labor intensive goods should make both the growth and level of national income lower exactly for the same reason, i.e., higher prices in nonagriculture should make the growth and level of national income higher.

§ 3- CONVERSION OF TURKISH PER CAPITA INCOMES INTO DOLLARS, THE RATE OF GROWTH AND THE LEVEL OF INCOME (An extract from UATE)

Two different methods used in UATE to analyze the growth of the economy and to re-estimate the per capita GNP are summarized in the periveous section. Results reached by both methods suggest that the growth rate of the economy should be less than what figures show and per capita GNP is about two thirds of accepted figures ($ 550-600 against $ 833 for 1975).

This conclusion is strengthened if per capita figures in TL are converted into dollars by a rational method rather than by current exchange rates.

However uncertainties brought about by the official rates of exchange are great, it is still necessary to compile a series of national income figures expressed in dollars in order to make the most vital comparisons necessary to see and evaluate some characteristics of the Turkish economy. The results of an attempt in this direction are depicted in Table I-1. In the second column per capita GNP figures in current prices at factor cost are listed. In the third column, current GNP figures are converted into dollars by official exchange rates prevalent in respective years. But it is quite clear that domestic price increases and devaluations effected in 1958 and 1970 distort dollar figures and produce insignificant results. When inflation accelerates, dollar figures increase very rapidly without respect to real national income, and when devaluations are made per capita national income figures decrease without any real decrease. In order to correct this, a method is devised to remove the abnormalities created by inflations and devaluations. In the fourth column of the table, real per capita national income (GNP) growth is listed. In the fifth column, the per capita income calculated by converting current income in 1950 by the official exchange rate, and then dollar figures for the next years are calculated by increasing those years' figures by the growth of real per capita income relating to the particular year. In the sixth column, GNP deflators in the US are shown. In the seventh column figures so far calculated are increased by the national income deflator in the U.S. and thus a figure showing the current national income is found.

There may be several objections to this calculation, but the author firmly believes that this series is better than the series that is based on official exchange rates.

It is quite apparent that abnormalities created by inflations and devaluations have been removed; the rate of increase of per capita GNP reflects only its growth rate; or, to express the same idea otherwise, it can be said that the change of the GNP figures in dollars is parallel to the real rate of increase in real per capita GNP figures. On the other hand, the figures in the new series are higher than those in the series based on current exchange rates, with the exception of the years 1951 to 1957, when the figures in the new series are less. The difference widens as we approach the terminal years. In fact, the per capita GNP in 1975 in the new series is $ 872 while in the series based on current exchange rates it is $ 833.

Although abnormalities created by inflations and devaluations are removed in the new series, the level of per capita GNP in this series seems to be higher than its real level. As a matter of fact, the level of the series based on actual exchange rates is high anyway with the possible exception of devaluation years and short periods following these years. And the new series is even higher than this series.

TABLE I - 1

PER CAPITA $ GNP'S AT CURRENT PRICES AND CALCULATED BY MEANS OF GROWTH RATES

	Per Capita GNP at Current Prices (Factor Cost, TL)	$ Equivalent of Column II in Prevalent Rates	Per Capita GNP Growth at Constant Prices	$ Per Capita GNP'S Calculated by GNP Growth (at 1950 Prices)	USA GNP Deflators	$ Equivalent at Current Prices
I	II	III	IV	V	VI	VII
1950	420	150	6.5	150	100.00	150
1951	494	176	9.9	165	106.73	176
1952	547	195	9.0	180	109.10	196
1953	624	223	8.3	195	110.10	215
1954	815	220	6.0	183	111.72	204
1955	722	257	5.0	192	113.34	213
1956	818	294	0.3	193	117.21	226
1957	1,060	378	4.9	203	119.00	241
1958	1,231	229	1.6	206	124.68	257
1959	1,482	165	1.2	208	126.80	264
1960	1,549	172	0.5	209	128.80	269
1961	1,598	177	0.5	208	130.42	271
1962	1,813	201	3.7	216	133.16	288
1963	2,052	228	7.2	231	133.66	309
1964	2,128	236	1.6	235	135.78	319
1965	2,222	247	0.6	236	138.27	326
1966	2,596	288	9.4	258	142.14	367
1967	2,773	308	1.6	262	146.63	384
1968	3,013	334	4.1	273	152.69	417
1969	3,256	361	2.8	280	159.72	449
1970	3,753	326	3.0	289	168.70	488
1971	4,773	341	7.7	311	176.96	550
1972	5,681	406	5.1	327	183.15	599
1973	7,350	525	3.0	337	193.95	654
1974	9,909	708	5.0	354	213.92	757
1975	12,086	833	5.6	374	233.17	872

Source : SPO and see Text.

There are several reasons to believe that the level of per capita national income in these two series (Columns III and VII) is higher than the actual per capita incomes are. Firstly, throughout the whole period the trade balance showed a deficit, always very high by any standard. It can therefore be judged that the Turkish currency was overvalued throughout the whole period. If GNP figures in TL were converted by a higher exchange rate, their value in dollars would be less. But when it is attempted to determine equilibrium exchange rates in Turkey, all sorts of problems would arise. There is first of all the problem of determining the exact level of rates of exchange which would equilibrate the balance of trade in various periods. Even if they are found, which is very difficult task, the use of such rates in the calculation of GNP figures might be quite misleading. The reasons are listed as follows.

The very high volume of workers' remittances and the capital inflow (resource inflow) should be taken into consideration in the determination of the equilibrium rate of exchange. But the capital inflow is an ex-post figure; it depends, to a certain extent, on the balance of payment deficits of the country. As for the workers' remittances, it is not correct to consider the revenue obtained from this source on an equal basis with exports earnings. This revenue does not originate from the foreign exchange creating characteristics of the economy; it is not a permanent revenue, and its further development has nothing much to do with the characteristics of the Turkish economy. Therefore, the exact role of workers' remittances and capital inflow in the calculation of an equilibrium exchange rate is highly uncertain.

There is also the fact that the Turkish economy is distorted by several factors. It will be shown later that these distortions have created such disproportional (and in some sectors swollen) demand levels that with such demand characteristics the determination of an equilibrium rate of exchange is impossible. In addition to that, if disincentives created for exports are considered, the idea of an equilibrium rate of exchange cannot be determined.

There is also the further problem created by the practice of judging from past import levels when it is thought that there have always been import controls and a very high level of protection in the country. It is quite natural that the equilibrium rate of exchange would depend of the degree of import controls and on the level of protection. When import controls and the level of protection are high the equilibrium rate of exchange would be low, or vice versa.

If it is concluded that an equilibrium rate of exchange to be used in converting TL figures into dollar figures should be found by another method, the method used above seems to have an economic rationale. But here there is the problem of determination of the base year. The overvaluation of the currency in the base year should be at its minimum if the determination of an equilibrium rate of exchange is sought. Years following devaluations in Turkey possess this characteristic; 1950, 1959 and 1971 are the years following major devaluations.

TABLE I - 2

PER CAPITA GNP'S CALCULATED BY DIFFERENT METHODS

Year	Per Capita $ GNP at Prevalent Exchange Rates	Per Capita $ GNP, 1950 as Base Year	Per Capita $ GNP, 1959 as Base Year	Per Capita $ GNP, 1971 as Base Year
1950	150	150	94	93
1951	176	176	110	109
1952	195	196	123	122
1953	223	215	135	134
1954	220	204	128	127
1955	257	218	137	136
1956	292	226	142	141
1957	387	241	151	150
1958	229	257	161	160
1959	165	264	165	164
1960	172	269	169	168
1961	177	271	169	168
1962	201	288	180	178
1963	228	309	193	191
1964	236	319	199	198
1965	247	326	203	202
1966	288	367	228	227
1967	308	384	239	238
1968	334	417	258	258
1969	361	449	279	277
1970	326	488	303	302
1971	341	550	342	341
1972	406	599	372	371
1973	525	654	406	405
1974	708	757	470	469
1975	833	872	541	540

The method based on real growth rates with 1950 as the base year was used in the first series of this section. 1959 and 1971 are also taken as base years, and two more series are calculated by the same method (see Table I-2). It is quite apparent that the GNP figures based on 1959 and 1971 are almost the same, but they are widely different from GNP figures based on 1950 prices. In fact the GNP figures in the later series are almost sixty percent of the figures calculated by the 1950 base year. It is also noteworthy that calculations based on 1959 and 1971 show that per capita GNP figures are some 60-65 percent of figures calculated by prevalent rates of exchange: the same as figures calculated in the last section.

Before leaving this difference between the series based on 1950 and 1959-1971 figures a point should be emphasized. The possibility that the 1950 exchange rate is an equilibrium rate is the same as it was for the 1959 and 1971 rates. But as time passed, the economic characteristics of the country changed so rapidly that the level of the exchange rate consistent with these characteristics changed. The fastest transformation occurred in the period 1950-1960. The characteristics were so different by 1958; that required a big change in exchange rates. Although the changes after this date were in the same direction, the spread was less. There is, therefore, a big difference between the series based on 1950 exchange rates and the one based on 1959 prices. On the other hand, as the transformation in the 1959-1975 period was slower, the difference between these two series is less.

It can be concluded that if official exchange rates in 1950, 1959 and 1971 are equilibrium rates of the same degree (this seems true), real national income growth rates should be lower.

§ 4- STRUCTURAL CHARACTERISTICS OF TURKEY AS A DEVELOPING COUNTRY AND COMPARSIONS WITH THE WORLD EXPERIENCE *(An extract from UATE)*

Developing countries show certain characteristics, and international observations indicate that these characteristics are very much the same in every developing country. Moreover, as countries develop, the changes in each characteristic show a certain trend. The aim of this section is to find out whether observations in Turkey confirm international trends.

Several attempts have been made to quantify the structural characteristics of developing countries and their time trends. H. Chenery has tried several times to find out such structural characteristics. His most comprehensive research comparing 101 countries for the period 1950-1970 was published in 1975 and it was entitled "Patterns of Development, 1950-1970". He and M. Syrquin gathered more than 10.000 observations for this period, involving 101 countries (Chenery and Syrquin, 1975).

An attempt will be made here to see if structural characteristics revealed in this research on 101 countries for a 20 year period and time trends of these characteristics are comparable to those in Turkey.

Chenery and M. Syrquin think that economic development can be defined by 27 structural characteristics, each exhibiting a certain time trend. The authors calculated these figures by bringing together cross section and time series observations by means of two regression equations. One of them is shown below.

$$X = \varphi + \beta_1 \text{ in } Y + \beta_2 (\text{in } Y)^2 + \gamma_1 \text{ in } N + \gamma_2 (\text{in } N)^2 + \Sigma\, \delta_j T_j$$

where X is the dependent variable

Y = GNP per capita in 1964 U.S. dollars

N = population in millions

T_j = time periods ($_j$ = 1, 2, 3, 4).

An attempt has been made here to find expected structural characteristics in Turkey using the time series data concerning Turkey by means of the above equation, and then comparing them with actual values of these characteristics in Turkey. First, the method used will be described; then results obtained will be exhibited.

Expected values of the 27 Chenery characteristics in Turkey are calculated by the following methods. The Turkish per capita GNP figures in current dollars are first expressed in 1964 dollar prices using U.S.A. GNP deflators, as Chenery calculations are based on 1964 dollar figures. These figures stand in the first column of Table I-3. In the second column of the same table the population of Turkey is listed. These figures are applied to the Chenery regression equation and the expected values of the variables are found. Expected values and their counterpart actual values are depicted in tables below.

The series based on the 1950 exchange rate is used to find expected figures because of following reasons.

TABLE I - 3

$ PER CAPITA GNP IN 1964 PRICES AND POPULATION

Year	$ Per Capita GNP Based on 1950, in 1964 Prices	Mid-Year Population (000)
1950	204.3	20,809
1951	224.7	21,352
1952	245.2	21,953
1953	265.6	22,571
1954	249.2	23,206
1955	261.5	23,859
1956	261.6	24,442
1957	275.2	25,252
1958	279.2	25,983
1959	282.0	26,735
1960	283.4	27,509
1961	282.1	28,237
1962	293.1	28,933
1963	313.5	29,655
1964	319.0	30,394
1965	319.6	31,151
1966	349.8	31,394
1967	355.2	32,750
1968	370.1	33,585
1969	380.9	34,442
1970	391.7	35,321
1971	421.5	36,221
1972	443.1	37,146
1973	456.7	38,094
1974	479.8	39,066
1975	506.9	40,066

Source : See text; mid-year population, censuses.

1- If the actual figures are converted into dollars by using current exchange rates, great disruptions will arise as a result of devaluations in 1958 (The rate increased from $ 1 = 2.80 to 9.00) and 1970 (The rate increased from 9.00 to 15.00), and expected figures would lose all their significance, for at least half to the period.

2- Once it is decided to prepare a series not influenced by devaluations there are three possibilities: (a) a series based on the 1950 exchange rate; (b) a series based on the 1958 exchange rate; (c) a series based on the 1971 exchange rate. Among those three series the nearest official figure to the 1975 per capita income level is given by the 1950 series. The smaller difference in the last year is very important in view of the fact that difficulties making the rate of growth unsustainable are connected with conditions in the last years. Moreover, the 1950 series is also nearest to the series based on actual exchange rates. This characteristic of the series is also very important. It will be shown below that one of the very reasons for the smooth working of the economy was the exchange rates which had prevailed in past years. As a matter of fact, among the three series the 1950 one corresponds most nearly to the actual exchange rates. Therefore, the series based on 1950 is taken to find expected structural relations.

TABLE I - 4

THE SHARE OF THE PRIMARY SECTOR IN GDP AND ALLOCATION OF LABOR (%)

Year	Expected Primary Share	Actual Primary Share	Expected Allocation of Labor in Primary Sectors	Actual Allocation of Labor in Primary Sectors
1950	32.37	47.13	55.40	80.00
1955	28.52	44.71	51.45	77.91
1960	27.10	42.80	49.93	75.57
1965	25.21	35.82	47.71	72.55
1970	22.40	31.90	43.94	66.83
1975	19.66	30.40	39.72	63.00

Source : See text; actual primary share, national income statistics; actual allocation of labor, population censuses.

An examination of these tables reveals the peculiar place of Turkey among 101 nations examined in this comprehensive study. There are usually wide discrepancies between expected values and actual values, but in most strategic variables discrepancies are so wide that they must be very carefully looked into, and their economic significance must be studied at length. It will be shown that (1) the most strategic four structural characteristics, i.e., capital inflow, primary output as percent of GDP, exports as percent of GDP and share of primary labor are closely interconnected; (2) the widest discrepancies between actual figures and expected ones are found in them; (3) these interconnected variables are the result of distortions in Turkey and (4) the discrepancies of these four variables have far reaching consequences, in the sense of creating actual problems for the country and that their close examination is theoretically very interesting. These wide discrepancies in four strategic variables are the most important and most interesting aspect of the Turkish economy.

At the beginning of the period, the share of primary production in GDP was 47.13 percent; whereas the expected value was only 32.37 percent, a very great discrepancy (See Table I - 4). At the end of the period (1975) the relative figures were 30.40 and 19.66, respectively; while the rate of the actual to the expected was 1.44 at the beginning; it was 1.58 in the terminal year. The share of labor in primary production was 80.00 percent for the beginning period, whereas the expected rate was only 55.40 percent. For the terminal period figures are 62.96 percent and 39.72 percent, the ratio of the expected to the actual values are 1.43 and 1.78 respectively.

These wide discrepancies suggest that GNP per capita should be much less than actual computations made in Turkey. As will be seen in a table calculated by Chenery and Syrquin (p. 21-22), countries having a 47 percent primary share of their national products have a per capita income of $ 100, whereas for this year per capita income of Turkey at 1964 prices was calculated to be $ 203.6. In the terminal year the actual primary share was 30.74 percent and the expected per capita income for countries having this primary share is somewhat less than $ 200, whereas actual per capita income in 1964 prices was $ 506.9 in 1975. The figures on the labor share in primary production give an even more distorted picture. In the beginning period, the expected per capita GNP is less than 100, whereas it was calculated to be $ 204.3. At the terminal year it is expected to be somewhere around $ 150, whereas it was calculated to be $ 509.0.

TABLE I - 5

EXPECTED AND ACTUAL EXPORTS

Year	Expected Exports/GDP	Actual Exports/GDP
1950	0.172	0.0877
1951	0.173	0.0896
1952	0.174	0.0901
1953	0.175	0.0830
1954	0.171	0.0690
1955	0.172	0.0623
1956	0.170	0.0614
1957	0.171	0.0496
1958	0.169	0.0305
1959	0.168	0.0304
1960	0.167	0.0450
1961	0.165	0.0741
1962	0.165	0.0697
1963	0.165	0.0589
1964	0.164	0.0780
1965	0.163	0.0645
1966	0.164	0.0574
1967	0.163	0.0550
1968	0.163	0.0475
1969	0.162	0.0464
1970	0.162	0.0515
1971	0.162	0.0630
1972	0.162	0.0700
1973	0.161	0.0810
1974	0.161	0.0740
1975	0.160	0.0590

Source : See text; actual exports, Ödemeler Dengesi Rakamları 1950 - 1970; Maliye Bakanlığı, Ankara 1971, and Annual Programs by SPO.

If there were no other indicators to suggest that Turkish national income figures are much less than actual computations, one could have said that such discrepancies might have occurred and it would be imprudent to jump to the conclusion that actual Turkish income levels, and with them growth rates of income, are much less than computed figures. There are two additional indicators to strengthen the belief that Turkish figures of per capita GNP are much higher than the actual ones.

The first indicator is the low level of Turkish exports, as will be seen in Table I - 5. The share of actual exports is less than fifty percent in the beginning of the period and nearly one third of expected value (perhaps unique in the world). The second indicator is the very high level of capital inflow (or resource inflow) in Turkey. It is three times more than the expected level.Almost everybody was of the opionion that the main reason why exports were so low was related to the import substitution policy adopted in the country and overvalued Turkish currency.That might be true to some extent; but I tried to show that the main factor was the overvalued nonagricultural sectors in which exports were almost nonexistent.This was another reason supporting my argument that the level of national income should be less than what was revealed by statistics.

In that book I calculated the actual and expected 27 structural charecteristics determined by Chenery.There was not much discrepancy in others.Yet that was not important for my analysis (see UATE and chapter II, bellow).

§ 5- THE IMPACT OF EARNING DIFFERENCES ON NATIONAL INCOME

In UATE I used an original method to calculate the impact of the earning differences between nonagricultural and agricultural sectors of the economy.A long passage taken from UATE is found in the rest of this section.

"The Impact of Labor Allocation on the Growth of Turkish National Income and Level of Income

It has been shown previously that the allocation of increasing labor inputs in nonagricultural sectors rather than in agriculture must have created a strong influence on the growth of national income and the present level of the national income.

In order to see the impact of this productivity difference on growth a new series as to the growth of national income is calculated.

In the calculation of a new GNP, the per capita value added in nonagricultural sectors is taken to be two and a-half times higher than in agriculture. It was shown earlier that figures in countries having per capita income at the level of Turkey's, per capita labor input income in nonagricultural sectors is 1.60-2.36 times (Kuznets, 1966 and 1972) that in agriculture, whereas in Turkey it is around 4. The maximum figure is thought to be not more than 2.50.

The new national income series is prepared by multiplying value added per labor input in nonagricultural sectors by 2.50 instead of actual figures, which are between 4-5. This method can be illustrated by the actual computation of 1950 national income. In 1950 the value added per working population in agriculture by current prices was 460.50 TL. This is multiplied by 2.5. The product is 1,151.3 TL which is the supposed value added per labor input in nonagricultural sectors. This figure is multiplied by 2,260,000 which is the number of people working in nonagricultural sectors. The product is 2,607.8 Million (TL). This is added to the actual value added by agriculture. The total is 6,670.3 Million TL, which is the new GNP figure. The actual GNP calculated for 1950 was 9,694.2 Million (TL).

The new GNP is divided by the population of 1950. The quotient is 320.54 TL, which is per capita GNP in 1950. The per capita income calculated by the method described above is converted into its dollar equivalent by using the prevailing exchange rate. The per capita GNP calculated by this method for 1950 is $114.48 (see Table V-19 UATE, here I-6).

TABLE I - 6

OUTPUT PER LABOR INPUT IN NONAGRICULTURAL SECTORS 2.5 TIMES MORE THAN IN AGRICULTURE

Year	Per Capita $ GDP at 1950 Prices (Income growing 2.834 % Annually)	USA National Income Deflators (1950=100)	Per Capita $ GDP at Current Prices
1950	114.48	100.00	114.48
1951	117.72	106.73	125.64
1952	131.06	109.10	132.07
1953	124.49	110.10	137.06
1954	128.02	111.72	143.02
1955	131.65	113.34	149.21
1956	135.38	117.21	158.67
1957	139.22	119.08	165.78
1958	143.17	124.68	178.50
1959	147.22	126.80	186.77
1960	151.40	128.80	195.00
1961	155.69	130.42	203.05
1962	160.10	133.16	213.19
1963	164.64	133.66	220.06
1964	169.31	135.78	229.89
1965	174.11	138.27	240.74
1966	179.04	142.14	254.49
1967	184.12	146.63	269.98
1968	189.34	152.49	288.72
1969	194.70	159.72	310.97
1970	200.22	168.07	336.51
1971	205.90	176.70	363.82
1972	211.73	183.15	384.14
1973	217.73	193.15	446.45
1974	223.91	213.95	478.98
1975	230.26	233.17	536.89

Source: See Text.

In the second stage, per capita GNP for 1950 is again calculated by 1968 prices using the same method. The same calculation is made for 1975 per capita GNP. Then the yearly rate of growth between 1950 and 1975 is calculated to be 2.834 percent. It is supposed that the growth of per capita GNP has been uniform during this period. The same operation is repeated for every succeeding year. Then in order to find the current dollar figures these figures are multiplied by the U.S. national income deflators (see Table I-6).

The analysis of this conclusion would suggest that however small the difference between the annual actual growth rate and the rate calculated by this method (3.9 versus 2.8 per year), the main cause of the high level of per capita GNP at present ($833 at current exchange rate in 1975) is the great difference between per capita incomes in agricultural and nonagricultural sectors.

A through study of the Turkish situation shows that the probable reason why per capita incomes calculated are higher than actual figures is the great difference between per labor input value added in agriculture and in nonagricultural sectors. Although the terms of trade between agricultural and nonagricultural sectors have been about the same during the whole period, the difference between the value added has been again the same at the end as the beginning of the period.

The cause of this great difference is the fixing of the prices of goods and services produced in nonagricultural sectors at a very high level from the early years on and the continuation of this practice. One can object to this statement by saying that it is possible to look at the situation from the opposite angle, and it can be said that if the prices of agricultural goods are fixed much lower than what they should be, an abnormal relationship between two sorts of value added will appear. But if the goods produced by the agricultural sector are valued at higher prices, the per capita GNP will be greater than the actual figures and then the differences between expected and actual values of structural characteristics will be much larger (see section 5). What is more important, if goods produced by the agricultural sector are valued at higher prices, it would not be possible to export them at all; actually, a great proportion of export goods are agricultural products. This objection should, therefore, be discarded.

The problems connected with maintaining this great difference between two sorts of value added will be dealt with in books to be published later. It will be shown in these books that several conditions have made the keeping of such a great difference possible, but the continuation of this difference seems to have come to an end. There is no possible way to employ the increasing population in agriculture. Although the population increased twofold between 1950 and 1975, the number of workers in agriculture remained almost the same. In fact, there is every reason to expect that the number of people working in agriculture should decrease. If more and more people are given employment in nonagricultural sectors, and if necessary imported input for the economy is not procured by the sales of goods produced by nonagricultural sectors, the expansion of the production of nonagricultural sectors is impossible. Turkey seems to have come to this point. To express it in another way, Turkey has lived beyond its means since the 1950's. The demand for all sorts of goods coming from the population in the nonagricultural sectors has been higher than the possibilities of the country. If the per capita level of income of a great section of the economy is much higher than the other section of the country, this situation cannot continue for a long time." (UATE, pp. 213-216)

I must underline two points. Firstly, I must explain why I conducted my analysis in terms of dollars, and secondly, the difference of my analysis from the traditional ones.

The reason why I calculated new income in terms of dollars was as follows. I did not know what I was doing but I had something in my mind. If I had calculated it in terms of constant lira prices, I would have kept relative prices constant, whereas the calculation in terms of dollars might reflect the changes in relative prices. As a result, I could see the effect of the shift (the reallocation of resources) better than what we have in the examples found in the literature. This leads us to the second reason. In the existing literature, the price of nonagricultural goods is taken as it was, whereas I downgraded them. And agricultural prices were taken as a point of reference; because those prices were in line with international ones at the current exchange rate. To compare nonagricultural prices with international prices at the current exchange rate was irrelevant according to my procedure. Actually, the relative level of nonagricultural and agricultural prices was related to the level of exchange rates.

According to my calculations in UATE, the reduction of earning differences multiplier from 5 to 2.5 would make the average yearly growth of per capita income 2.8 percent in 1950-1975 period. If the growth of population (2.5) in this period is added to the growth of per capita income it would be 5.3 percent. The impact of the high multiplier of earning differences and the shift of resources from agriculture to nonagricultural sector would reduce the growth from 6.4 percent (the actual calculation) to 5.3 percent. The impact of earning differences was some 17 percent increase of national income. This meant that a good percent of the growth could be explained by the earning differences in nonagricultural and agricultural sectors. Yet two internationally known economists took my suggestions as serious and made the same calculation. They came up with some 10 percent swelling in national income. Our difference was related to the fact that I conducted my calculation in terms of dollar prices, whereas they conducted their analysis by constant Turkish prices. When I made the same calculation in terms of TL I came up with 10 percent increase which was exactly the same as theirs.

The problem begins here. In the terminal period my estimate of per capita national income based on the reduction of earning differences was \$ 536. If income differences were normal, it would be 10 percent higher, i.e, \$ 600. But here was the problem. The actual calculation of per capita national income was \$ 833 in 1975, the terminal year. What was the reason of such a difference? In fact, the decrease caused by earning differences only were taken into consideration. Yet the difference between $ 833 and $ 600 was huge. Here was the big discovery. 10 percent was due to growh effect as I define it now. On the other hand, the difference between $ 833 and $600 was related to the level effect I define it now.

Adding those two effects I could calculate the yearly average growth rate in the economy as 4.1 percent. And this was a very important contribution to economic analysis.

I thought that national income calculated by dollars should tell us something about the impact of level effect. This was because of my conclusion that there was a relationship between labor prices and national income level. On the other hand, if the country was in a position to reduce labor prices in order to sell more, the level of dollar rate of exchange should change along with that. As a result, a relationship between national income expressed in dollars and the level effect could be established. Another reason for this belief was that we could not determine the change in national income due to the level effect when we look into figures expressed by a national currency. In fact, if calculations are carried out in terms of constant prices, this is not possible. If, on the other hand, a new series in constant prices in which the change of labor prices is considered, the figure based on this series could not be comparad to the figure found by the old series. Therefore the change of national income calculated by dollars could give us a clue about the level effect. And this is validated by observing the Turkish figures.

I tried very hard to show that the change in labor prices are not related to the change of productivity only, but they may change without any change in their productivity. When I dealt with PPP, this question was tackled effectively. (See Chapter VI.)

When the rest of this book is read it would be seen that in 2004 I calculated the impact of the growth effect smaller than what it was in UATE in the sense that the the impact of the growth effect should make the growth rate of national income as 5.7 rather than 5.3 percent.The reason is that the 2004 calculations were carried out in terms of constant Tl rather than in dollars.All those will be explained in again in chapter XII.

§ 6- RESPONSES TO AN UNCONVENTIONAL ANALYSIS OF THE TURKISH ECONOMY AND ITS NOVELTY

My book entitled AN UNCONVENTIONAL ANALYSIS OF THE TURKISH ECONOMY (1978) was reviewed in several journals (see References).

1- THE LEVEL OF INCOME IN TERMS OF DOLLARS

In reviews of UATE, it is asserted that the reason why per capita incomes expressed in official figures in terms of dollars were rather high was related to the fact that the Turkish currency was overvalued, and as a result, once real value of the currency was established, per capita income would be some 30-35 percent lower anyway. Therefore if that was known in the literature, what was the idea of recalculating national incomes by a method not known in the literature? But nobody thought that even if this was done, the rate of increase of income, i.e., 6.4 percent, wouldn't change. I tried to say that the per capita income in terms of foreign currency should be related to relative prices in the country rather than to the absolute rate for foreign exchange: you can increase the dollar rate; as a result, you would come up with a lower per capita income in terms of dollars. Yet if relative prices are the same, the implication of that adjustment would be different from that when relative prices were changed. (In that case the rate of growth would change.) I was not talking about the absolute level of the exchange rate only. Without a change in relative prices, the fixing of the rate at this or that level would not mean much. In fact, even if GNP in dollars would be calculated lower right after a devaluation, this would not solve the problem. If relative prices were changed, the devaluation would be more efficient. In fact, in UATE I sought the true (in a way a sustainable) national income by a hypothetical change of relative prices. The exchange rate should be determined on this basis.

2- THE SHIFT OF RESOURCES

In UATE, on the face, the rather high growth rates of the economy is attributed to the shift of resources from agricultural sectors, where productivity was low, to high productivity nonagricultural sectors. It is even calculated by well known economists that some 60 percent of the total productivity growth (2.2 point in 1950-1975) was related to it. If this was my method of analysis, it could be said that this was known in the literature, and as a result there was nothing original in my analysis. But it was forgotten that my intention was to show that this was a false perception, and the problem lied in artificial high prices in nonagricultural sectors. When they were brought back to normal, national income growth should be much less than what was revealed by figures.

3- THE CALCULATION OF GROWTH

Upon my suggestion, two well known economists calculated the impact of higher earnings in nonagricultural sectors on growth. They came up with the conclusion that this should have increased national income by 10 percent, whereas my estimate was some 30-35 percent. The calculation of those economists was more sophisticated than mine; yet, their conclusions were much different from mine. Why? My horizon was much wider. My procedure promised to separate growth and level effects. (See Chapter XII § 9.)

4- THE IMPACT OF IMPORT SUBSTITUTION

Another comment of UATE was about my writings on import substitution, the policy followed in Turkey. I tried to show that this policy was one of the factors making the growth rate of the economy rather high. But it could not be sustained. Commentators were of the opinion that this was well known in the literature and there was nothing original in my writings. Viewed superficially they were right; but I was contending something not known in the literature. My conclusion was that once the economy turned outward, the historical growth rate had to decrease; whereas according to all scholars defending outward orientation, the growth of the economy had to increase after the export orientation. Although I could not explain it as clearly as I do now, I tried to show that as a result of a lower relative labor prices after outward orientation both the level and growth rate of the economy had to decrease. That idea has been developed after the publication of UATE.

5- THE PREDICTION OF THE FUTURE GROWTH RATE

It was predicted in UATE that the future growth of the Turkish national income would be less than 5 percent. "It has been shown above that the average rate of growth of the last decade was high if the potentials of the economy are thought of. There is also every reason to expect that the rate of national income increase will be even less than 5 percent in future years." (UATE, p. 174.) But along with the official estimates, almost every economist was of the opinion that the growth of income in Turkey would be around 6-8 percent in the future. In UATE I supposed that the expected decrease was related to the slackening of the shift of resources. What I say now is different as will be explained below; yet my way of thinking was suggested in UATE.

6- THE DIFFERENCE OF THE PRESENT INTERPRETATION FROM THE OLD

The present theoretical framework is an outgrowth of UATE. In the original book, in order to adjust national income I made agricultural sector, the products of which could be exported, a reference point and recalculated national income. I came up with a 30-40 percent lower figure for the national income at the end of the period, i.e., 1975. This included both the growth and the level effects. The difference with the present analysis is summarized as follows: I decompose it as the level and growth effects, different from what we have in the literature. In addition, I take labor prices in the nonagricultural sectors as a reference point. In UATE the reference was the agricultural sector. In the original version, a part of the growth rate is explained by the shift of production factors from low priced agriculture to nonagricultural sectors and the speed of growth of each sector. In the present version this is called growth effect. The difference is that in order to calculate the growth effect the relative prices and the speed of growth of labor and nonlabor intensive goods in the nonagricultural sector are taken as a reference point now.

When the original version (UATE) was written exports were originating from agricultural sector and the exchange rate was kept low. As nonagricultural goods were not exported and as there was import substitution in the country, national income in terms of dollars was higher than what it should be. This high level should not be attributed to the overvalued national currency only. In the present case it is shown that in order to export nonagricultural goods labor prices in nonagricultural sectors should be reduced. As this was materialized by high real dollar prices, the level of national income in terms of dollars decreased but this was only an end result of a high real exchange rate. Two cofactors were present: (1) labor prices in nonagricultural sectors; (2) the value of the currency.

7- WHY WAS UATE A PIONEERING BOOK?

Above, UATE and my comments about the responses to it by various scholars are summarized. When I view it now, I feel that UATE was a pioneering book in the sense that it opened new vistas to understand the impact of relative prices on national income. Traditionally when national incomes of a country were compared over time relative prices were kept constant, whereas in UATE I introduced the idea that they should not be.

In traditional growth theories the use of inputs and the increase of their productivity were considered as the main factors determining growth, whereas in UATE I suggested that in addition to them, the change of relative prices (in UATE the change of the relative prices of goods produced in nonagricultural and agricultural sectors) should be considered as another factor determining national income growth. It is shown that if relative prices of labor and capital are not taken into consideration, they cannot be lumped together for calculating the contribation of input to growth.

That idea was developed greatly in years ensuing its publication. Although the aim in UATE was to understand the economic growth in Turkey, I theorized it in time, and came up with a theoretically coherent framework which could be used to understand the growth of any country, developed and developing (see also chapter II).

§ 7- THE PRESENT INTERPRETATION OF AN UNCONVENTIONAL ANALYSIS OF THE TURKISH ECONOMY (2009)

The vanguard of my unconventional and challenging ideas was launched in the book entitled as AN UNCONVENTIONAL ANALYSIS OF THE TURKISH ECONOMY published in 1978. It was written in order to criticize the import substitution policy which had been followed in Turkey since the 1930 s to the date of the publication of this book. It had created all sort of problems for the economy, and it should be replaced by an outward looking policy along with the liberalization of the economy. This idea was shared by a well informed majority of international and national economists . What was original in this book was the illusion given rise by this policy, i.e., the officially calculated level of the Turkish per capita income was $ 833 in 1975, and the annual rate of growth of the national income was 6. 4 percent in 1950-1975. 1 contended that they were $ 550 and 4-4. 5 percent, respectively. My contention was based on the new approach or the unconventional theory of growth launched in this book, which was a novelty or a very important contribution to growth theory. What was more important was the fact that the novelty was not restricted to the analysis of the Turkish economy but it should be relevant for any economy. And it also opened new avevues or vistas for the understanding of growth problems and all sorts of problems confronting any economy, especially developing ones.

It was tried to demonstrate that the accepted methodology of estimating national income and its growth should be changed or improved. The main observation was the fact that in Turkey the economy was a dual one consisting of a very poor agricultural and relatively rich nonagricultural sectors. Once it was shown that the level of income in nonagricultural sectors was overswollen in the sense of high prices in this sector, this also meant that its level(real) and growth would be measured higher than what they actually were. Several problems had to be tackled before coming to that conclusion. 1- Why were prices high in nongricultural sectors? 2- How could that be demonstrated? 3-Would high earnings given rise by high prices mean higher growth of national income? 4- If it was considered high, would that mean high national income in terms of dollars? 5- Would high national income in terms of dollars correspond to high national income in terms of national currency? Some of those questions were asked and answered;some of them were not asked and answered when this book was published.

Firstly, let me summarize the answers to those questions asked in this book.

1- Were prices high in nonagricultural sectors? My explanation was as follows. Import substitution policy had made the cost of industries established on this basis very high. As goods produced in these industries should be bought mostly by town dwellers, the price of any good produced in nonagricultural sectors should be high as well.

2- This was verified by high earning differences between nonagricultural and agricultural sectors. According to worldwide observations, per capita earnings of nonagricultural sectors should be 2-2.5 fold of those in agricultural sectors, whereas this multiplier was 4. 5 in Turkey. I assumed that this was an index of the high level of income in nonagricultural sectors; in other words, high prices should mean high income. This should be so if agricultural prices were taken as a standard or reference.

3- At the beginning of the period under consideration, i. e. , 1950, the share of agriculture and nonagriculture in national income were 45 and 55 percent, respectively. Yet, at the end of the period it was 25 and 75, respectively. Therefore the main reason of the high growth rate and the level of national income should be high earnings in nonagricultural sectors without any respect to the productivity of factors and the shift of growing resources to the nonagricultural sectors of the economy. It is apparent that if national incomes of 1950 and 1975 are deflated by price increase index calculated for this period, this should be the case.

4- The main export items originated from agriculture; as a result, exchange rates were fixed according to the saleability of agricultural commodities. As the exports from the nonagricultural sectors were very small, this low rate of exchange rate or overvalued national currency form the point of view of nonagricultural goods could be kept. As a result, the national income in terms of dollars would be calculated high.

5- Would a higher national income in terms of dollars correspond to a higher national income in terms of national currency? I didn't ask this question properly in that book and I didn't answer it satisfactorily. What I did was as follows. I took earnings in agricultural sectors as a reference and supposed that nonagricultural earnings were 2. 5 fold of those in agriculture at the beginning and also at the end of the period(rather than 4. 5 fold as was the actual case). After the national incomes in terms of the Turkish currency was found, it was converted into dollars and I came up with $ 533 for per capita income in 1975. As the calculated official figure of per capita income figure was $ 833, 1 considered that difference as a rent earned in the country given rise by huge earning differences. Those earnings should be normalized; the only way should be a decrease of income in monagriculture sectors; those rents along with the high income could not be sustained. Rents were measured by huge earning differences. That meant that the reason of high incomes was those earning differences and once they were normalized, the growth rate should be measured lower. My estimate was 4-4. 5 percent and and per capita income as $ 550.

Two internationally well known economists took my findings as serious and calculated the impact of high earning differences, normalized them and came up with the conclusion that the impact should make national income 10 percent higher (See Table II-18). My findings were about the same. If my figure was made 10 percent higher, $533 would be $ 600. Yet the calculated per capita income was $ 833. Why was there such a big difference between them? The conclusion should be that the growth of national income could not be explained by earning differences only. There was something else. What was that something else?I discovered after the elapse of some 30 years that this could be explained by differentiating growth and level effects affecting national income. This was not known in the literature. .

Many economists were of the opinion that $ 833 per capita national income was related to overvalued exchange rate. **But my investigations suggested that this was not the case and even if the currency was not overvalued, we had to calculate national income growth as 6. 4 percent and also as long as the earning differences stayed the same, the growth performance of the economy would not change.**

CHAPTER II

MORE ON THE BOOK ENTITLED 'AN UNCONVENTIONAL ANALYSIS OF THE TURKISH ECONOMY'

§ I- INTRODUCTION

This chapter could be considered appendice to chapter I. Important ideas put forward in the historical book entitled AN UNCONVENTIONAL ANALYSIS OF THE TURKISH ECONOMY are summarized in that chapter. But there are less important ones.

In Chapter I, I used the formula developed by H. Chenery in order to test if my findings in the Turkish case were parallel to them. The ones I tested in Chapter I suggested that per capita income in Turkey should be less than what is officially calculated. In this chapter, the same is attempted but it is observed that except for one or two exceptions the expectation of Chenery would be proved right.

In chapter I the responses to UATE were summarized. In this one they are more extensively reproduced and commented on.

§ 2- THE TEST OF CHENERY CHARACTERISTICS IN TURKEY

Two different sorts of capital inflow figures are shown in Table II-1. Estimates made by SPO according to international conventions are shown in the first column of Table II-1.

TABLE II-1
CAPITAL INFLOW/GDP

Year	External Deficit (Conventional) I	External Deficit Millions of $ (Calculated by the author) II	GDP Millions of $ III	External Deficit (Calculated by the author) IV	Expected External Deficit V
1950		25.1	3,121.3	0.008	0.0127
1951		78.4	3,755.8	0.020	0.0121
1952		182.1	4,243.5	0.043	0.0115
1953		125.1	4,782.8	0.026	0.0109
1954		141.2	4,696.8	0.030	0.0111
1955		113.0	5,175.0	0.021	0.0107
1956		4.5	5,487.2	0.000	0.0105
1957		1.8	6,174.1	0.000	0.0100
1958		35.9	6,750.4	0.005	0.0098
1959		94.3	7,047.3	0.013	0.0097
1960		99.0	7,738.4	0.013	0.0096
1961		84	7,799.0	0.010	0.0094
1962	0.042	195	8,387.7	0.023	0.0092
1963	0.048	220	9,270.3	0.023	0.0089
1964	0.015	63	9,802.0	0.006	0.0087
1965	0.010	56	10,033.0	0.005	0.0086
1966	0.017	176	11,850.0	0.015	0.0083
1967	0.011	121	12,654.6	0.009	0.0092
1968	0.019	251	14,149.4	0.017	0.0080
1969	0.017	234	15,677.9	0.015	0.0078
1970	0.015	381	17,494.5	0.021	0.0077
1971	0.009	465	20,330.8	0.029	0.0074
1972	0.000	591	22,254.2	0.026	0.0073
1973	-0.023	616	26,651.5	0.023	0.0073
1974	0.026	1,954	33,940.5	0.057	0.0077
1975	0.057	3,017	39,228.6	0.077	0.0070

Source : See text.

The second estimates have been made by the author (Column IV) as the conventional estimates are thought to be meaningless in the interpretation of the Turkish situation (Column II/Column III.) The difference between conventional estimates and those called resource inflow is the inclusion of workers' remittances, factor payments and transfers to and from. Capital inflow figures show the difference between payments causing transactions and revenues creating transactions of the economy. Although workers' remittances create a sort of revenue for the economy, this revenue is a kind of revenue in the sense that it is not the result of the sales of goods and services produced by the economy.

There is no difference between foreign borrowing, foreign investments and workers' remittances in the sense that both are a surplus of goods and services over that the economy produces. Moreover, the surplus has the same characteristics, i.e., it consists of imported goods which have strategic importance for the economy and the lack of which exerts a very detrimental influence on the economy.

The level of workers' remittances reached a very high magnitude in the last decade. The economy could never have reached such high import levels in this period if it had not been for this huge volume of workers' remittances together with other items of capital inflow. The same is true of interest payments and profits paid abroad; they are in a sense components of the capital inflow. There is no difference, in this context, between them and payments for imports. Trade deficits (or resource inflow) are divided by $ GNP figures calculated by the author. Per capita $ GNP in 1950 is increased by real per capita GNP growths in subsequent years and then is multiplied by the mid-yearly population figures. This series show $ GNP (Column III). The reason why dollar figures are used instead of TL figures is the distortion caused by devaluations. It is evident that if TL figures were used, resource inflow ratios would be much higher than their actual values in years following devaluation and less in pre-devaluation years. (Note in 2009: in my calculations, trade deficits are considered as external deficits; this is not one hundred percent right; yet it gives an idea where I was going in 1978.)

Capital inflow figures seem to be much higher than expected, but it is quite evident that there is no reason why capital inflow figures should not be quite different from expected figures. Although their values decrease as countries develop, capital inflows are not structural characteristics closely connected with development like other ratios. If other characteristics of the Turkish economy did not suggest that the level of per capita GNP is smaller than what figures show, it could only be said that Turkey is a high capital inflow country, and nothing more. But with other characteristics, high capital inflow means much more than that. There are several connections between these two findings and computed per capita income levels, which are thought to be higher than real ones. The first reason is that if income figures were in line with expected figures, the actual ratio of exports to GDP would be nearer the expected figures. Let us give our own example. If, for example, Turkish per capita GDP was $ 600 instead of $ 883 in the terminal year, the actual ratio would be closer to the expected ratio.

There is always an excess import demand in the country; there is no surprise in that. In fact, the case is the same in almost every developing country. The excess is curbed by several import controls. What is important in Turkey is the fact that capital inflow (resource inflow) is very high if compared with expected values for the whole period and for the later years, it is even higher than exports. This observation shows the fact that imports were much higher than exports, yet import demand has not been fully satisfied, and there has always been an excess import demand.

This excess is, of course, highly connected with undervalued foreign currencies, but on the other hand, a low price does not create a high demand if there is not enough purchasing power. The purchasing power in this case comes from swollen incomes outside the agricultural sector of the economy. This problem will be fully discussed in the rest of the book; what is advanced here is the fact that high imports demanding purchasing power in Turkey is connected with the nonagricultural sectors of the economy. The income level of the nonagricultural sector of the country is swollen to such an extent that the purchasing power of the whole country in international markets is not commensurate with the level of income of the country in the sense that import demand is much higher than exports earnings. This does not mean that every country having higher imports than exports and compensation for this excess by capital inflow shows the characteristics of Turkey in this respect, i.e., per capita national income being less than what figures show. Greece, for example, has much higher imports than exports, and the excess is compensated for by capital inflow. But in Greece such discrepancies in the actual and expected primary production share do not exist. And the discrepancy between expected exports and actual exports is not as great as in the Turkish case (Chenery - Syrquin, 1975, p. 193).

Another reason to believe that the actual Turkish per capita GNP and the growth rate are below what figures show is the difference of values added per labor input in agricultural and nonagricultural sectors. The world standard in cases such as Turkey for the ratio of labor earnings between agricultural and nonagricultural sectors is 1.60-2.40, whereas the Turkish ratio was around 4 - 5. If this difference is added to the reasons adduced above, it can be seen that by inflating the prices of the nonagricultural sectors, income levels and growth rate have been artificially pushed up.

TABLE II-2

THE RATIO OF EXPECTED AND ACTUAL PRIMARY, MANUFACTURED AND SERVICE EXPORTS TO GDP (%)

	Primary Exports		Manufactured Exports		Service Exports	
Year	Expected	Actual	Expected	Actual	Expected	Actual
1950	10.99	8.21	4.72	0.21	2.78	0.35
1951	10.81	8.05	5.01	0.28	2.86	0.63
1952	10.64	8.24	5.24	0.20	2.92	0.57
1953	10.44	7.65	5.52	0.21	2.98	0.44
1954	10.43	6.33	5.28	0.22	2.89	0.36
1955	10.27	4.87	5.46	0.20	2.92	1.16
1956	10.19	4.05	5.68	0.20	2.90	1.89
1957	9.98	3.56	5.68	0.13	2.94	1.21
1958	9.86	2.07	5.72	0.09	2.93	0.90
1959	9.78	2.40	5.68	0.09	2.90	0.55
1960	9.67	3.96	5.66	0.32	2.88	0.50
1961	9.57	6.71	5.71	0.60	2.87	0.54
1962	9.45	6.11	5.78	0.39	2.87	0.47
1963	9.25	5.02	6.05	0.42	2.92	0.42
1964	9.14	5.75	6.08	1.65	2.91	0.40
1965	9.05	4.87	6.08	1.19	2.89	0.39
1966	8.80	4.40	6.42	0.97	2.95	0.37
1967	8.70	4.39	6.43	0.81	2.93	0.30
1968	8.52	3.79	6.60	0.63	2.95	0.32
1969	8.37	3.54	6.71	0.78	2.96	0.31
1970	8.21	4.05	6.82	0.87	2.96	0.23
1971	7.95	4.36	7.13	1.64	3.00	0.30
1972	7.78	4.59	7.36	2.11	3.00	0.30
1973	7.78	4.92	7.36	2.88	3.00	0.30
1974	7.42	3.94	7.56	3.61	3.01	0.30
1975	7.25	3.17	7.68	2.43	3.02	0.30

Source: See text; actual figures, Statistical Yearbook of Turkey, various issues; service exports 1950 - 1970, Ödemeler Dengesi, op. cit. and 1970 - 1975 personal Estimates. As figures are taken from different sources, there are insignificant discrepancies.

There is another point. Chenery's computations show that the decrease of the primary share from 0.454 to 0.266 of GDP would occur when per capita income would go up from $ 100 to $ 300. If per capita income had increased at a rate such as Turkey's (3.5 percent), the decrease would have taken place in 34 years, whereas in Turkey it has taken place in 25 years.

With a few exceptions, there are wide discrepancies between expected and actual values of other structural development characteristics, and all discrepancies are such as to suggest that per capita GNP in Turkey should be lower. Some comments will be made about them.

The actual distribution of total exports among primary, industrial and service exports is very different from expected distribution. At the beginning of the period expected industrial exports were around half of primary exports, and at the terminal years industrial exports caught up with primary exports. On the other hand, actual industrial exports were very small at the beginning period and in terminal years they expanded to some 60 percent of primary exports (See Table II-2).

At the beginning of the period there was a big difference between expected and actual values of ratios of investment to GDP (See Table II-3). Actual investment increased and at the end of the period it nearly caught up with the expected rate. But it can easily be seen that investment ratios of the first fifteen years correspond to income levels of per capita incomes $ 100 - $ 200, whereas in those years Turkish per capita GNP's were calculated to be between $ 280 - $ 380. Although in terminal years the actual level of investment ratios is higher than expect ones, this fact is solely caused by very high capital inflows (resource inflows) (See Table II-3).

Nothing much can be said about saving ratios as they are found by deducting capital inflow figures from investments; they are the differences between investments and capital inflows (See Table II-4).

TABLE II-3

EXPECTED AND ACTUAL INVESTMENT AS PERCENT OF GDP

Year	Expected Investment	Actual Investment(*)
1950	18.69	12.1
1951	19.09	11.8
1952	19.39	15.0
1953	19.73	14.4
1954	19.48	17.3
1955	19.71	17.6
1956	19.99	16.8
1958	20.05	15.3
1959	20.04	16.8
1960	20.08	17.6
1961	20.11	17.3
1962	20.21	15.8
1963	20.50	18.5
1964	20.56	18.2
1965	20.58	18.4
1966	20.92	20.7
1967	20.95	20.6
1968	21.13	22.1
1969	21.24	22.4
1970	21.36	21.9
1971	21.64	21.4
1972	21.17	21.7
1973	21.17	21.0
1974	22.04	22.8
1975	22.15	26.2

(*) 1950 - 1961, SIS estimates, fixed capital only; 1962-1975, SPO estimates.

Source : See text; actual figures, SIS and SPO.

The expected and actual ratios of government revenue seem to correspond to each other. In the last years actual government revenues reached higher levels than expected. Actual tax revenues were much less than expected at the beginning of the period, but at the end they nearly caught up with expectations. The time trend of these two ratios shows that the tax collection of the government seems to be satisfactory in Turkey (See Table II-5).

TABLE II - 4

SAVING AS A PERCENT OF GNP

Year	Expected Saving	Actual Saving(*)
1950	18.41	11.30
1955	19.73	15.50
1960	20.25	16.30
1965	20.89	17.90
1970	21.85	19.80
1975	22.79	18.50

(*) Slightly different from Chenery Calculation.

Source : Trade deficit Table ; Actual savings are calculated by deducting trade deficit ratios from investment ratios; expected saving, see text.

TABLE II - 5

GOVERNMENT REVENUE AND TAX REVENUE AS A PERCENT OF GDP

	Government Revenue		Tax Revenue	
Year	Expected	Actual	Expected	Actual
1950	16.28	19.07	15.98	14.18
1955	17.40	15.58	17.02	14.35
1960	17.84	14.75	17.44	12.91
1965	18.49	20.07	18.09	15.13
1970	19.62	25.24	19.23	17.48
1975	20.93	23.35	20.56	19.42

Source : Government and tax revenue FFYP and Basic Economic Data by SPO, Expected figures, see text.

The actual school enrollment ratio is below the expected ratio. But as the country develops the difference between expected and actual ratios decreases (See Table II - 6).

The difference between expected and actual shares of industry was very large at the beginning of the period (See Table II - 7) but the differences decrease as the country develops: at the beginning of the period the ratio of the actual to expected share was 66 percent, whereas at the terminal year it was 81 percent. These figures show that the industrialization pace in Turkey has been fast. But, as was shown earlier, there is a strong presumption that the narrowness of difference is caused by higher prices of industrial commodities rather than by a speedier industrial production.

TABLE II - 8

PRIMARY AND SECONDARY SCHOOL ENROLLMENT RATIO

Year	Expected	Actual (*)
1950	54.97	30.22
1955	60.45	36.30
1960	62.40	45.31
1965	65.04	51.50
1970	69.04	59.98
1975	73.63	-

(*) Slightly different from Chenery computation

Source : Actual figures, Statistical Yearbook of Turkey, SIS, various Issues; Expected figures, see text.

TABLE II - 9

INDUSTRIAL OUTPUT AS PERCENT OF GDP

Year	Expected	Actual
1950	19.76	13.04
1955	22.04	16.32
1960	22.95	17.84
1965	24.13	21.65
1970	25.93	23.97
1975	27.77	22.40

Source : See text; national income statistics.

The share of utilities seems to correspond to expected rates (See Table II - 10). Actual figures of service shares seem to stay around 36 which is some 4 points below the expected share and this, in its turn, stays stable (See Table II - 11).

The comparison of the expected values of other structural characteristics with actual ones is shown in Table II - 12, 13, 14 and 15. The discrepancies either show that per capita GNP should be lower or they are meaningless.

TABLE II - 10

UTILITIES OUTPUT AS PERCENT OF GDP

Year	Expected	Actual
1950	6.67	5.30
1955	7.00	6.40
1960	7.20	8.20
1965	7.39	9.30
1970	7.71	9.70
1975	8.06	10.80

Source: See text; the same as Table II – 15

TABLE II - 11

SERVICES OUTPUT AS PERCENT OF GDP

Year	Expected	Actual
1950	37.53	35.20
1955	38.69	33.10
1960	39.08	31.20
1965	39.59	33.30
1970	40.27	34.60
1975	40.79	36.30

Source : See text; The same as Table II - 15.

TABLE II - 12

EDUCATION EXPENDITURE AS PERCENT OF GDP

Year	Expected	Actual(*)
1962	2.59	2.54
1965	2.63	2.96
1970	2.75	2.95
1974	2.88	2.98

(*) Expenditures by the Ministry of National Education.

Source : See text; SPO.

TABLE II - 13

PRIVATE AND GOVERNMENT CONSUMPTION AS A PERCENT OF GDP

	Private Consumption		Government Consumption	
Year	Expected	Actual	Expected	Actual
1962	69.52	78.04	12.96	11.37
1965	69.19	72.21	12.98	12.06
1970	66.46	69.64	13.10	11.88
1975	70.82	70.28	13.28	11.93

Source : See text; and SPO

TABLE II - 14

IMPORTS (PERCENT OF GDP)

Year	Expected Imports	Actual Imports
1950	17.91	9.6
1951	17.91	11.1
1952	17.97	10.8
1953	17.99	9.7
1954	17.70	8.1
1955	17.65	6.2
1956	17.52	4.7
1957	17.48	6.5
1958	17.34	12.0
1959	17.17	10.8
1960	17.02	10.7
1961	16.89	11.7
1962	16.80	10.5
1963	16.82	8.3
1964	16.71	8.2
1965	16.57	8.5
1966	16.62	7.4
1967	16.49	7.7
1968	16.44	7.2
1969	16.36	9.3
1970	16.28	9.8
1971	16.29	10.5
1972	16.22	10.8
1973	16.22	14.2
1974	16.08	14.6
1975	16.00	13.8

Source : See text; actual imports, imports statistics.

TABLE II - 15

URBANIZATION

Year	Expected	Actual
1950	35.96	18.5
1955	40.69	21.1
1960	42.49	26.3
1965	44.92	29.9
1970	48.69	35.9
1975	52.55	-

Source: See text; population censuses

TABLE II - 16

INCOME DISTRIBUTION

	Highest 20 %		Lowest 40 %	
Year	Expected	Actual	Expected	Actual
1963	.558	.570	.112	.130
1968	.554	.600	.112	.100
1973	.540	.565	.113	.115

Source: Income Distribution; 1963, SPO Research; 1968, Bulutay T., Timur, S., Ersel, H., 1973, SPO Research.

§ 4 - MORE ON RESFONSES TO UATE

A- PROFESSOR M. BRONFENBRENNER AND EARNING DIFFERENCES

Professor M. Bronfenbrenner read my writings on earnings differences and commented on them. I think his comments give us a clue for measuring an alternative rent concept.

"The relationship between wages and employment can be shown by the so - called "vat-diagram" of the Japanese economists Mataji Umemura (see Figure II-1).

In the diagram, suppose a given labor force OO', be divided between employment sector I (urban) and employment sector 2 (rural). There is full employment; urban demand for labor as a function of urban workers' income Y is D_1, sloping to the right; rural demand as a function of Y is D_2, sloping to the left.

In a free market ON would be employed in the city and NO' in the country, with a common annual real income of Y. (Our analysis ignores both the special attractions of rural and urban life and the cost of movement between the two employment sectors).

However, labor organization or wage regulation may raise urban labor income to Y_1, at which only ON_1 are demanded. For full employment rural labor income must be Y_2 (below Y) with N_1O' workers in rural employment.

Four different kinds of rent can be distinguished in this diagram.

1 - Y_1Y_2 per urban labor

2 - YY_1, without subtracting any part of the negative rent YY_2 per workers assessable against rural labor.

3 - If some income level Y_2' is a customary or social rural wage, the diagram may be complex, but the full employment assumption can be dropped. Urban income and employment are as before. Rural employment is now N_2O' at labor income level Y_2'. Rent per urban worker may be now Y_1Y_2' or

4 - YY_2 per worker may be considered as rent. N_1N_2 workers are unemployed, presumably in the urban area."

The comments by Professo M. Bronfenbronner was a great honor for me. He sent his comments to me after he read my UATE.I imagined that he was impressed by my unconventional ideas about the economy. I used to measure, whereas he differentiated 4 kinds of rents alluded in UATE. His analysis was excellent; yet, my aim was to underline the swollen income level of nonagricultural sectors. We can consider any of his rents as genuine. But however we define or spot rents, it would support my belief that they were the measure of the swollen level of nonagricultural sectors. Their existence was approved by Professor Bronfenbrenner. The problem was to get rid of them, as a result of which both the growth rate and the level of national income had to decrease.

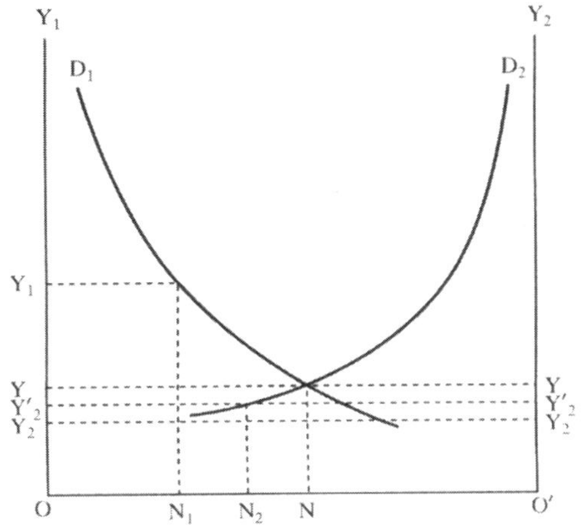

Figure II - 1

B - SKETCHY OPINIONS

The last sentence of the review in E.J. reads as follows: "We are presented... with Hatiboğlu's rather sketchy opinions on a wide range of topics" I think the commentator is right; I was aware of that fact and expressed it in the preface of my book as follows; "As almost every idea is new and original and, in most cases, contradictory to everything written about the growth of the economy, there may be mistakes and erroneous reasoning in this book. Yet I believe if a small proportion of what is said in this book is true, a great upheaval will have to take place in the analysis of the growth of developing countries in general" (Hatiboğlu 1978, p. VI).

Although the above quotation related especially to the main theme of the book, i.e., relationship between income growth and earning differences, I was also implying that some of my ideas were not fully developed and expounded. Some of the latter ones are listed below.

1) The unreliability of input-output calculations.

2) The irrelevance of the conventional measures of import substitution.

3) The irrelevance of calculations made to find out the comparative advantage of individual commodities.

4) The calculation of devaluation rates based on the level of income rather than elasticity arguments.

5) A new approach to the determination of interest rates.

6) The relationship between income distribution and earning differences.

7) The relationship between rents and unemployment.

8) A critique of the interpretation of capital intensity.

9) A critique of the conventional thought on the relationship between demand elasticity and industrialization.

10) Non-reliability of past relations in the predictions, etc.

I expected that all these sketchy ideas would have been criticized; nothing of that sort has been attempted. Were they true or was their examination and refusal not worthwhile? I am not in a position to answer this question. But if some of them are nearly true, it means that several holes in economic theory especially in development economics as we know them must have been filled.

I am sure that all those different and sometime contrary ideas to accepted ones are not totally worked out and expressed in my book. Moreover, they are not tested by a close observation of events and/or econometric studies. The latter is very much in vogue in Turkey and everybody, who happens to learn the very rudiments of econometrics, uses those methods. In some cases, the known propositions are tested by crude data taken from Turkey without making any necessary alterations relating to the Turkish economy. In others, which is the case for most studies, the use of that method is wrong. I have studied almost every econometric study concerning the economy of Turkey, but I have not been able to find any, which goes beyond an exercise in econometrics!

I wonder if the reviewer knows any scientific and true study which is more than a simple exercise in econometrics, and/or which is beyond a straightforward application of well known propositions of economics in Turkey. Original ideas may be expressed in sketchy from when they are put forward first and I have done the same!

The unifying aspect of all these sketchy ideas in the book was expressed in a sketchy form; by the unifying link I mean the rent concept.

If it was expressed in a sketchy from, the reasoning based on it would have to be in sketchy form. But that most important concept is clarified in this book and all those sketchy ideas may seem less sketchy after having read the book.

C - ARE MEASURES PRESCRIBED APPLICABLE?

My book suggested several measures to be taken if the economy of Turkey is to be saved from a complete destruction. Several commentators thought that such drastic measures would be difficult to implement in a democratic country such as Turkey. Measures prescribed in that book were almost similar to IMF's classical measures and in some cases they were even more stringent compared to them. It is well known that deflationary measures sponsored by IMF are ardently opposed in most developing countries, and it is much more so in this country. The public opinion, shaped mostly by university professors, opposes those policy measures on theoretical grounds as well as for the austerity probably to be imposed on the poorer section of the community.

It must be stressed here that there is no way out of the mess in which the economy of Turkey finds itself without applying such measures whether we like them or not.

D - THE BOOK BY ANNE KRUEGER AND THE UNCONVENTIONAL ANALYSIS

The concluding sentence of the review in JEL reads as follows:

"This book essentially covers the same ground as Anne Krueger's (1974), and the reader who has time to read only one book in this area would be better off reading Krueger. However, this assessment does not reduce the value of the various enlightening insights and generalizations one finds in this book coming from a first - hand observer of the Turkish Economy." (JEL)

I think that professor Krueger's book entitled **"Foreign Trade Regimes and Economic Development: Turkey"**, which is an excellent and well-documented work, is one of the rare scientific books on Turkey. Again, I concede that one of my books' main themes was similar to hers, i.e., the impact of the foreign trade regime on economic development. But I disagree with the value judgement of the reviewer on at least three issues. Firstly, my book contains a moderately detailed study of the recent economic history and the present structure of Turkey; whereas hers does not. Secondly, a most important section of my book was devoted to the analysis of past growth; whereas in her book the growth of the economy is analyzed superficially. Thirdly, and the most important of all, Professor Krueger's analysis is a straightforward application of conventional analysis to the economy of Turkey without questioning the validity of that analysis with reference to Turkey; whereas I showed in my book that if the economy is analyzed along these lines, the most important aspects of the economy cannot be perceived and several wrong conclusions will be reached.

But it is not difficult to agree with the reviewer: I tried to explain many different ideas in not very clear form. It is very difficult to appreciate fully ideas completely different from everything one has constantly heard and read about this country.

In order to substantiate the above contention, I have written comments on the Professor Krueger's book and included it in my books. Her books and articles are most widely referred to when the economy of Turkey is mentioned; rightly so; because they are among the few scientific books written about this country. Moreover, I must frankly concede that I have not been able to find many books or articles on the Turkish economy which are anyway comparable to Krueger's standards in scientific content and in description of that part the economy she deals with.

Everybody would obviously think that a book written by a famous American professor of economics, and sponsored and financed by the National Bureau of Economic Research and Agency for International Development would be superior to one written by an unknown Turkish economist working under conditions of scanty facilities, and I hope that a different verdict will be given after having read this book.

E - COMMENTS BY PROFESSOR M. FRY (1978)

Professor Maxwell Fry read my Unconventional Analysis after it was printed and made very interesting comments. His comments convinced me that some important issues raised in this book should be clarified in order to make them more understandable.

1 - I think that the meaning of the downgrading of per capita national income should be clarified. It is shown that the per capita income in 1976 is around $ 600 instead of $ 990. (The last figure is the conversion of per capita income to dollars by prevalent exchange rates.) Is this simply a measurement problem or has it welfare implications? In other words, it can be said that Turkey's high growth has been the result of overvaluing nonagricultural products; would the welfare of the country change if nonagricultural products are valued by world market prices? I think it would. The present level of per capita income has been sustained at the expense of a lower growth of the economy in the future and also by allowing for several distortions in the economy. If welfare is considered in a longer period of time, and if the connections between the per capita income level and distortions are seen, then it can be said that this is not a mere question of measurement. Downgrading the per capita income is not simply a question of measurement. A lower per capita income in dollars, which is not pulled up by domestic inflations after it has taken place, means a decrease in the demand of the nonagricultural population of the country. As was shown in Chapter VII of UATE the country can increase its export earnings meaningfully only by lowering the per capita income of the active population in nonagricultural sectors of the economy if several distortions do not occur. The same is true of lowering unemployment, inflation rates and inequality of income differences. All these changes imply changes in the welfare of the country.

2 - I have tried to show in several sections of the book that past relations are useless in the analysis of the economy when there are distortions existing in the economy. It can be said that if distortions continue, as they are likely to for a considerable time, past relations may help the analysis of the future development. That is true; present distortions may be helpful in the analysis of the future development; but this statement is true in the sense that they are important to indicate problems facing the country and their probable causes. But when it comes to infer from past relations as to the future of the economy, they are useless; in future, fundamental changes will have to occur which will make them unreliable in projecting the future. (The reader is referred to Chapter V, VI and VII. of UATE.)

3 - I have suggested that Turkey has lived beyond her means in several sections of the book. All I meant was that Turkey would have to decrease its growth rate in the future. It can also be said that acute problems facing the economy, i.e., inflation, large external deficits, unemployment, very bad income distribution are also signs of the fact that Turkey has lived beyond her means.

4 - I have tried to show that workers' remittances and capital inflows should not be considered on the same footing as export earnings. I think I am right. If the equilibrium exchange rate is to be determined instantaneously, they all are the same. But if the problem of determining the exchange rates is considered with reference to a longer period, they are not the same. It can be probable that workers' remittances might have created distortions in the economy, such is the case in Turkey. In that case they should be separately treated.

5 - One of the arguments showing that per capita GNP figures are lower than what figures show is based on the assertion that 1950, 1959 and 1971 are on the same footing as far as the equilibrium of the balance of payments is concerned. It may be objected that there is no objective support for this contention: I think that this point should have been explained at some length in the relevant part of the book. To put it in a nutshell, it can be said that these years exhibit the same characteristics. Firstly, import controls were less compared to other years and almost every commodity could be imported easily; trade was liberalized. Secondly price level deflated effective exchange rates were at their highest in each base period (1950, 1958 and 1971). And thirdly, it can be said that if price increases had not set in the periods following these years, large external deficits would not have occurred.

E - THE RESPONSES OF TURKISH ECONOMISTS

In his contribution in **Cumhuriyet Döneminde Türkiye Ekonomisi - The Turkish Economy in the Republic** (1979), Professor Sarç briefly refers to my UATE. He summarizes some findings existing in the book, such as the causes of the swelling of income by 30 percent (pp. 26-27). Sarç maintains that my method is based on the Cobb-Douglas function; yet this was not the only method I employed, and the source of growth was also calculated by means of hypothetical weights of capital and labor in their share in the national income. His attempts to criticize my book are also not well-founded for the following reasons.

1 - According to Sarç, the reason why the prices of industrial goods are high may be related to high input prices. But he failed to observe that I referred to the substantial value added and high factor earnings in nonagricultural sectors compared to agriculture. The relationship between industrial input prices and the enormous earnings differences in the two sectors of the economy is very difficult to perceive.

2 - Sarç believes that the prices of services in Turkey are low. Therefore, one cannot contemplate an approximate 30-35 percent swelling of the national income. But Sarç does not seem to be aware that there were factors which made service prices higher than what they should be. Several chapters of this book address this problem in detail.

Professor N. Kuyucaklı refers to my work in his **Türkiye Ekonomisi - The Economy of Turkey** (1985) (pp. 18-21). His comments appear to be based on an interview I gave for a daily newspaper although his criticisms are misplaced and seem to be founded on a misinterpretation of my work.

He has wrongly concluded that my rents are earned only in comparative cost industries such as textiles. But I attempted to show that rents are earned throughout the whole nonagricultural sector. Hence Kuyucaklı's attempts to demonstrate that the size of comparative cost industry in Turkey was not large enough to account for the high rents earned became irrelevant.

Secondly, Kuyucaklı has attempted to challenge my work by illustrating that the level of the national income in dollar terms depends on fixing the exchange rate. But he has failed to perceive that I refer to the sustainable and not the momentary value of national income. In fact, administrators can fix any exchange rate, and the level of the national income in terms of the new rate can be high or low for a short period. But the real problem which I addressed, and which Kuyucaklı did not perceive, is whether we could permanently fix the rate.

Comments made by Professor F. Şenses of the Middle East Technical University merit particular attention. His detailed review in the **Middle East Technical University Development Review** was in general favorable, although he makes some criticism which I shall now address.

His critical remarks concerning the formal deficiency of the book (although he reviews the Turkish version and not the improved text in English) are correct. Şenses' emphasis on my critical comments referring to the work of other economists (especially my Turkish colleagues) is also warranted. In self-defence I may immediately argue that my book was produced without the advice and support of others in the field. Indeed, apart from Professor Celasun, all my Turkish colleagues belittled, ignored or even attempted to prevent the propagation of my ideas. However, I must underline that in my opinion there has been no original and proper investigations of the Turkish economy.

One of his fundamental criticisms concerns my failure to explain fully the reasons for the adoption of an inward looking policy and its presentation in a historical perspective. Here Şenses' views are justified to an extent. In addition, he is correct to note that I failed to stress the difficulties of a transition from import substitution to export orientation. However, this criticism is valid for almost all economists who favor an export-led growth strategy (especially those connected with the IBRD and IMF). In this book (particularly in Chapter V) I have referred to the problems of this transition to which the literature in general has failed to address. But two points are in order here. Firstly, my explanation concerning the difficulty of transition is radically different from that argued by other economists (including Şenses). Also, my book was written to demonstrate that the policy of import substitution should be abandoned and an outward policy should be adopted at any cost. The only alternative was to seek to lessen the problems of the transition which is attempted in the present book.

The second basic comment made by Şenses involves my calculation of rents caused by an inward looking strategy of industrialization. This calculation is based on the income differences between the agricultural and nonagricultural sectors of the economy. In my work, the calculation of rents and the overswelling of the national income was based on four separate methods, in each of them different data are employed. There may be weaknesses in one or other of the methods, e.g., they may not be fully tested, but they all lead to the same conclusion, and the quantitative findings are almost identical. Moreover, the predictions based on investigations using these methods have been realized. This was in spite of the above criticisms made by various experts in the field.

Professor Şenses is correct to say that my recommendation was "impoverishment"; but does anybody know a better medication? The best that we can be done is to seek to lessen the problems caused by this impoverishment.

I must underline a false interpretation of Professor Şenses. I do so simply because this was the main idea of UATE. He writes that according to my view a good proportion of the growth of national income could not be explained by factors such as input increases, improvement in education, better allocation of resources, etc. The main factor was the shift of resources from agriculture to nonagricultural sectors. This is not true; I did not write so. I stressed the fact that the main factor was the overvaluation of goods and services in nonagricultural sectors. It is true that the shift must have given rise to an abnormal growth of national income. But, to repeat, the main factor was the overvaluation of goods and services produced in nonagricultural sectors.

TABLE III - 18 by B. Balassa

GROSS DOMESTIC PRODUCT, EMPLOYMENT, AND PRODUCTIVITY IN TURKEY, 1967 - 77

	(absolute figures)							(growth rates)			
	1967	1967C	1967D	1977A	1977B	1977C	1977D	1967 - 77A	1967 - 77B	1967 - 77C	1967 - 77D
Value Added (TL million 1968 prices)	**93737**	**93737**	**93737**	**183321**	**148491**	**169952**	**174984**	**6.9**	**4.7**	**6.1**	**6.4**
Agriculture	30506	46577	40107	42508	53471	64914	55893	3.4	5.8	3.4	3.4
Industry	24452	18613	14851	55314	42817	42102	33592	8.5	5.8	8.5	8.5
Services	38779	28547	38779	85499	52203	62936	85499	8.2	3.0	8.2	8.2
Employment (thousands)	**11621**	**11621**	**11621**	**14151**	**14151**	**14151**	**14151**	**2.0**	**2.0**	**2.0**	**2.0**
Agriculture	8160	8160	8160	7900	9937	1900	7900	–0.3	2.0	–0.3	–0.3
Industry	1545	1545	1545	2430	1881	2430	2430	4.6	2.0	4.6	4.6
Services	1916	1916	1916	3821	2333	3821	3821	7.1	2.0	7.1	7.1
Labor Productivity (TL)	**8066**	**8066**	**8066**	**12955**	**10494**	**12010**	**12365**	**4.9**	**2.7**	**4.1**	**4.4**
Agriculture	3738	5708	4915	5381	5381	8217	7075	3.7	3.7	3.7	3.7
Industry	15827	12047	9612	22763	22763	17326	13824	3.7	3.7	3.7	3.7
Services	20240	14899	20240	22376	22376	16471	22376	1.0	1.0	1.0	1.0

Source: Organization for Economic Cooperation and Development, **Turkey,** OECD Economic Surveys, November 1978. Some of the inconsistent productivity data have been corrected by accepting data on sectoral value added and employment as accurate.

Note: Variant A : Actual figures.

Variant B : Hypothetical figures calculated on the assumption of the unchanged sectoral composition of the labor force between 1967 and 1977.

Variant C : Sectoral productivity figures for 1967 calculated on the assumption that productivity ratios in industry-agriculture and services-agriculture comparisons in Turkey were the same in 1967 as in countries with per capita incomes of $ 200 to $ 574 in 1958 (Simon Kuznetz, **Modern Economic Growth - Rate Structure and Spread,** New Haven, Yale University Press, 1966, pp. 402-3) while taking overall productivity levels in 1967 in Turkey as given and calculating with observed sectoral employment and productivity growth rates.

Variant D : Sectoral output and productivity figures re-estimated in terms of world market prices by utilizing ratios between domestic and world market value added of 1.70 for agriculture and 3.68 for industry while taking overall productivity levels in 1977 as given and calculating with observed sectoral employment and productivity growth rates.

CHAPTER III

EARNING DIFFERENCES AND THE GROWTH OF NATIONAL INCOME

(The Original Work, 1978 and 1990)

§ 1 - INTRODUCTION

In the literature it is well known that in most developing countries per capita earnings in nonagricultural sectors of the economy are a multiple of per capita earnings in its agricultural sector. Yet this difference may be sustained as a consequence of the social conditions of the economy and/or its dual character.

This chapter aims to take an in depth look into this problem. It will be shown that the measure of the difference may lead to difficult problems, yet its existence is of crucial importance in an assessment of the factors leading to growth as well as to the actual increase of national income.

Although this problem has been studied to some extent in the literature, its contribution to growth is first analyzed in detail in my book named An Unconventional Analysis to the Turkish Economy (1978) (UATE).

Professors M. Bronfenbrenner from the U.S. and H. Myint from the London School of Economics have commented on my analysis, and Professors B. Balassa and M. Celasun of the World Bank have re-calculated the impact of earning differences on the growth of the Turkish economy after considering my work. (See Table II-18)

The aim of this chapter is to compare my calculations with others in order to demonstrate the strength of my approach to this question.

To put it in a nutshell, I will show that a calculation of the impact of earning differences in terms of the domestic currency would not be enough (this is the case with other academicians' work) to understand their effects.

Again, the literature and some observations in the world economy is summarized below.

§ 2 - THE TRANSFORMATION IN THE INDUSTRIAL STRUCTURE AND EARNING DIFFERENCES

Economic development occurs with several transformations in the economic and social life of countries. Among the most important of them is the transformation of the industrial structure, i.e., the change in the shares of various sectors in the national income and the shift of resources from one sector to another (See Kuznets 1966, pp. 86 - 159).

As it is well known, various economic sectors are broadly classified under three headings: primary sector, industrial sector (sometimes called secondary sector) and tertiary sector. The proportions are generally referred to as the industrial structure.

The primary sector includes agriculture as the most important component of this sector, with fisheries and forestry also included. Mining is classified under this sector by some authors and by others under industry. Industry includes manufacturing, construction, power, transportation and communications. The tertiary sector includes trade, finance, real estate, personal, business, domestic, professional and government service.

The relationship of these sectors as development proceeds was perceived some seventy years ago and its existence was verified later by most comprehensive empirical research of several economists. To put it in a nutshell, the theoretical and empirical research showed that as development proceeds the share of the primary sector in national income diminishes and that of industry increases; the share of the tertiary sector increases slightly. According to an earlier cross section study, the growth elasticity (i.e., the proportional change of value added in a sector divided by the proportional change in income) of various sectors was found to be as follows; primary production 0.494, industry 1.362, transportation, communication 1.288 and other services 1.066 (see, Chenery 1960).

In a most comprehensive piece of research by Chenery and Syrquin based on the experience of 101 countries and for a time period of 20 years (1950-1970) the tendency observed is exhibited in Table III- 1 (Chenery - Syrquin 1975, pp. 20-21).

TABLE III - 1

NORMAL VARIATION IN ECONOMIC STRUCTURE WITH THE LEVEL OF DEVELOPMENT
(For Countries Having more than 10 Million Population, 1964 Dollar)

	Primary		Industry		Services	
Per Capita Income	Share in GDP	Labor Allocation	Share in GDP	Labor Allocation	Share in GDP	Labor Allocation
100	.452	.658	.210	.091	.339	.251
200	.327	.557	.287	.164	.385	.279
300	.266	.489	.330	.206	.403	.304
500	.202	.395	.383	.258	.415	.347
1000	.138	.252	.449	.325	.413	.423
over 1000	.127	.159	.488	.368	.386	.473

Source: Chenery and Syrquin (1975), pp. 20-21.

In most analyses of industrial structure the change in the distribution of active population among different sectors is also analyzed and the tendency as to the distribution of the working population among sectors is also found. Along with sector shares, the share of labor exhibits a parallel tendency, i.e., the share of labor in the primary sector decreases and in other sectors increases (See Table III - 1). As industrial structure changes labor productivity in each sector changes differently, but this problem will not be taken up here.

Earning Differences

Tables III - 2, 3 and 4 show that there is earning difference between agricultural and nonagricultural sectors. The difference decreases as development proceeds. The factors determining earning differences are studied in the literature. The causes determining earning differences are classified into genuine and nongenuine, i.e., economic and non-economic, ones (see Myint 1971, pp. 331-340).

Geniune differences mean higher earnings caused by economic factors such as better technical knowledge, better education, higher capital intensity (Diaz-Alejandro 1965) in nonagricultural sectors (Myint 1971, pp. 315-347). Non-genuine differences are mostly connected with institutional arrangements such as the powerful trade unions, favorable attitude of the government toward the labor movement, the ability of foreign investors to pay high wages, etc.

TABLE III - 2

RELATIVE SECTORAL VALUE ADDED PER WORKER IN VARIOUS COUNTRIES

(The ratio of value added per worker in nonagricultural sectors to that in agricultural sector)

Per capita GDP, 1958	The Ratio
$ 575 or over	
(16 countries)	1.13
$ 200 - 574	
(5 countries)	2.37
$ 100 - 199	
(12 countries)	1.60

Source: Kuznets (1966), p. 402.

TABLE III - 3

RELATIVE SECTORAL VALUE ADDED PER WORKER

(The ratio of value added per worker in nonagricultural sectors to that of agricultural sector)

Per capita Income $ (1964)	Ratio
100	2.33
300	3.05
400	2.47
500	2.58
800	2.31
Over 1000	1.30

Source: Chenery and Syrquin (1975), pp. 21-22.

TABLE III - 4

RELATIVE SECTORAL VALUE ADDED PER WORKER
(The ratio of value added per worker in nonagricultural sectors to that of agricultural sector)

Per capita Income $ (1964)	Ratio
3000	1.36
1000	1.57
500	1.77
200	2.37
100	4.19

Source: Singh (1975), p. 109.

There are also factors, the classification of which under genuine or non-genuine differences is difficult. The first is the difference caused by higher living expenses in towns compared to rural areas and higher wages to attract workers to immigrate (Lewis 1966, pp. 77). The second cause difficult to classify is the high prices in nonagricultural sectors caused by protective policies or import substitution (Myint 1971, pp. 338-340). Thirdly, the relatively rapid increase of demand for the products of nonagricultural sectors can also cause earning differences (Hagen 1975, pp. 95-98).

The Relationship Between Earning Differences and the Transformation in Industrial Structure

It has been shown that as development proceeds labor shifts from the primary sector to non-primary sectors (from agriculture to nonagricultural sectors). It has also been shown that there is an earning difference between them. Therefore, the national income increases at the end of the shift of resources. On the other hand, if part of earning differences consists of non-genuine ones, it can be concluded that the income increase is caused by non-genuine factors to a certain extent. Then the nature of earnings differences becomes crucial if national income increases caused by non-genuine factors give rise to particular problems. In this case, both the degree of earnings differences and the problems caused by national income increases resulting from earnings differences must be studied carefully. This will be taken up in the next section.

Earning Differences and Growth of Income

It is well known that labor shifts from agriculture to nonagricultural sectors as development proceeds. As per capita earnings in nonagricultural sectors are a multiple of those in agriculture, the shift can cause national income growth. A method of measuring this has been developed by Denison (See, Denison 1974, pp. 284-290).

This fact can be illustrated by the following example. Let us suppose that the value added by a worker in the nonagricultural sector is five times that of a worker in agriculture. Let us suppose that 1000 persons are employed in a country. The workers are distributed evenly between agriculture and nonagricultural sectors. If the value added by a worker in agriculture is $ 100 and the value added by a worker in industry is $ 500, the national income of the country can be calculated as follows:

(500 X $ 100) + (500 X $ 500) = $ 50,000 + $ 250,000 = $ 300,000

It is clear that the national income of this country is $ 300.000. Now let us suppose that the distribution of population is changed, and that 300 are employed in agriculture and 700 workers in industry. As a result of this change, the income of the country goes up to 380,000 if other conditions remain the same.

(300 X $ 100) + (700 X $ 500) = $ 30,000 + $ 350,000 = $ 380,000

If the above argument is scrutinized it will be seen that there is circularity in it. It does not say anything as to the nature of income growth; the growth does not depend on the earnings of shifted labor. Shifted workers share a certain amount of income growth; in other words, growth is not caused by the shift of workers. Therefore, the growth of income caused by the shift of workers must possess particular characteristics.

§ 3 - EARNINGS DIFFERENCES

It is shown in previous papers that there is a close relationship between the earnings difference of two sectors of the economy and rents. If the earnings difference reflects real productivity difference between those two sectors, the growth in an economy can be analyzed in conventional terms. But if earning differences are caused by non-economic factors several problems arise, which have not attracted much attention in the literature.

In this section the nature of earning differences will be examined first and then it will be asked if earnings differences observed in Turkey and in some other developing countries in the world verify theoretical predictions put forward in this book.

Figures as to the earning differences are found in Table III - 2, 3 and 4.

In this section the literature concerning earning (or productivity) differences will be briefly surveyed. At the beginning of this discussion it must be made clear that earnings (or productivity) differences are divided into two groups, one being called genuine and the other non-genuine differences. By the genuine difference is meant higher earnings caused by economic factors such as better technical knowledge, better education, capital intensity, etc.

1 - When the earning differential of nonagricultural earnings over agricultural ones was first mentioned it was believed that they were mostly determined by two factors, i.e., firstly the difference between living expenses in towns and rural areas, and secondly the necessity of providing higher earnings in towns in order to induce more and more workers to immigrate to towns. A 50 percent difference was considered to be enough to serve this purpose. (Lewis 1966, p. 77). Apart from the observations which show that the actual difference was much higher than that, i.e., more than 200 percent, this observation concealed several important determinants of earnings differences. Firstly, the earnings difference of nonagricultural and agricultural sectors includes much more than the wage difference of nonagricultural and rural workers. The most important among these factors is the rents earned by non-manual workers. Moreover, it can be asserted, a priori at least, that the wages of the newly recruited workers are much less than those of workers already in the town, and the rural wages must be compared with those of new town settlers. Secondly, should the wage differential due to living expenses in towns and villages be considered as a genuine or non-genuine productivity difference? There are authors considering that it is a genuine difference. If the increase of productivity is somehow connected or correlated with the international saleability of goods and services and if, on the other hand, in different countries the difference of living between towns and rural areas is different, then it will be dubious to consider this difference as a genuine productivity difference.

2 - A certain portion of earnings difference is explained by factors affecting physical productivity. These are the quality and skill of workers, technical knowledge, education, capital intensity, etc. (Diaz-Alejandro 1965). It is not disputable that all these factors must have been influential in increasing wage differentials, and these factors must be included in the genuine group. But the share of these factors among others determining the earnings differential cannot be determined easily, quantitatively at least.

3 - The third factor which may be influential in creating earning differentials is connected with the shift of demand. (Hagen 1975, pp. 95-98). It is well known that the demand for goods and services produced by the nonagricultural sectors rises relatively more compared with those produced by agriculture as economic development proceeds. This relatively higher increase in demand bids up the price of those goods, which, in turn, gives rise to an increase in the value productivity of labor in nonagricultural sector. A classification of the earning difference as genuine and non-genuine is made quite arbitrarily if the difference is given rise by the shift of demand. It is evident that to include the earning difference caused by this factor in the genuine or non-genuine group is very difficult.

4 - The fourth factor which is included in the non-genuine group is connected with institutional arrangements. Nearly every economist writing about this subject has mentioned the fact that due to institutional arrangements such as the power of

trade unions, favorable attitude of the government toward the labor movement, ability of foreign investors to pay high wages, etc. the wages in nonagricultural sectors increase more than they should if they were determined by economic factors only (Myint 1971, pp. 331-340).

It seems that the increase of nonagricultural earnings due to these factors is somewhat exaggerated and the separation of wage increase caused by them from other genuine factors is to some extent difficult. The vague nature of productivity increase of what is called genuine factors and the difficulties created by them suggest that, in the Turkish case at least, these factors may be on the same footing as others which are called genuine productivity increase.

5 - The fifth factor which is classified under non-genuine wage differentials is the fact that in most densely populated developing countries labor is paid according to its average productivity rather than its marginal one, which is below zero. On the other hand, if workers are transferred from agriculture to nonagricultural sectors its wage is based on its average productivity in agriculture: "Thus the modern sector is being penalized by having to pay a wage rate high above the social opportunity cost of labor as measured by its marginal product in agriculture, and in order to correct this distortion the modern manufacturing industry should be given tariff protection." (Myint 1971, pp. 334).

6 - The sixth and probably most important factor making for wage differentials is the creation of higher margins by restricting the supply or production of several commodities in developing countries, especially imports. Restrictions are an important ingredient of intervention in the price mechanism in order to promote economic development when there are high margins; it is quite natural that workers try and succeed in getting part of the high margin. This point will constitute a very important ingredient of our reasoning.

TABLE II - 5

RELATIVE SECTORAL VALUE ADDED PER WORKER IN TURKEY

(The Ratio of value added per worker in nonagricultural sectors to that in agricultural sector)

Year	Ratio
1950	4.57
1960	4.16
1970	4.74
1978	4.37

Source: National Income Statistics of Turkey

§ 4 - EARNING DIFFERENCES IN TURKEY

It is shown in Table III - 5 that earning differences in Turkey are uncharacteristically high. Although the expected figure was 2.5 to 1, the actual figure has been over 4 in this country. (See Table III - 5). All theoretical and empirical consequences of this uncharacteristically high figure are drawn in various papers. In this section it will be shown that the earnings difference is not based on economic factors in this country. Some of the reasons leading to this conclusion are listed below.

1. Turkey is not rich in natural resources; in other words, value added in the country is caused mostly by labor. Turkey does not possess large mineral resources or fertile agricultural land. Therefore the nonagricultural sectors cannot exploit them to create large earning differences.

2. Capital used in the country as well as in the nonagricultural sector is limited; therefore it is not possible to adduce that the uncharacteristically high income difference is caused by capital intensity.

3. The proportion of exports to GNP in Turkey was some one third of what was expected according to the world experience until 1980. Moreover, the proportion of exports provided by nonagricultural sectors of economy was even less. All this means that Turkey draws very little from comparative advantages and specialization in the nonagricultural sectors. Therefore earnings in these sectors do not reflect real productivity differences in this meaning.

4. The earning difference may be caused by higher education and technical knowledge in nonagricultural sectors. Educational level of workers employed in commodity producing subsectors of the nonagricultural sector and those employed in agricultural sectors is not much different. There is no dispute that educational level of the labor force employed in some service subsectors of the nonagricultural sectors is much higher than those employed in the agricultural sector. But it does not mean much if the level of education is about the same in the commodity producing subsectors and agricultural sector. In other words, if the productivity in the commodity producing sector is low, there is a limit to the increase in value added in service sectors, however educated manpower may be employed in that sector (especially services are not exported, as the case is in Turkey). Neither is the effect of technical knowledge of a nature to create a large earning difference between these two sectors. There are several factors which support this conclusion. Firstly, the improvement of techniques used in agriculture was probably not less compared to that in nonagricultural sector in Turkey. Secondly, technical advance in Turkey has been in the form of a simple application of technical knowledge developed in western countries for their own needs and factor proportions. No technique is developed which could be used to draw on its comparative advantages.

5. It might be contended that by keeping agricultural earnings low, earnings in nonagricultural sectors could be raised; but it seems that this is not the case in Turkey.

In fact, if the level of and the difficulties in exporting agricultural products in Turkey are thought of, it can be concluded that agricultural earnings are not low in Turkey, especially if the viability of the economy and of the agricultural sector is taken into consideration. Moreover, the yearly rate of growth of the agricultural sector has been 3.3 percent over the last 30 (1945-1975) years, which is high in comparison to world standards. That means that agricultural incomes have increased at a rate which is satisfactory in world standards.

6. In centrally planned socialist countries a great difference can be created between earnings in nonagricultural and agricultural sectors. As Turkey is a country where the price mechanism is in operation, there is a limit in the ability to sustain a great earning difference between those two sectors. Therefore it is apparent that the earning difference observed in this country is produced within a framework of market mechanism.

7. It can be shown that the growth of the economy having large earning differences can be sustained if external funds flow in at a satisfactory level. The reason is simple: a large quantity of external funds can compensate for the deficiency of exports caused by the great earning difference and it can alleviate inflationary tendencies created by it; large external inflows can make larger investment possible, which may contribute to sustaining growth, and capital intensity may be encouraged by the great earning differences; it can create a large market in the nonagricultural sector of the economy; of course several more arguments can be added to this reasoning.

It is a fact that large foreign funds flowed in Turkey and this fact has made the growth sustainable until very recently.

8. Several factors, which are mentioned in the literature, creating great earning differences exist in Turkey. Turkey was an import substituting country; labor movement is favored by the politicians; unions in the nonagricultural sectors are very influential and the protection of industry is very strong, etc. All these factors are signs that the high earning difference is caused by noneconomic factors rather than economic ones.

§ 5 - EMPIRICAL EVIDENCE ON THE EFFECT OF EARNING DIFFERENCES

Very little has been written on earnings differences in the literature. Again there is no empirical work showing the impact of earnings differences on the economy. But another problem closely connected with earnings differences, i.e., the transformation of industrial structure, is used to sort out some observations in developing countries. One of the characteristics used by Chenery to define patterns of development is connected with the transformation of industrial structure. It is expressed by an index (production orientation index PO). This index is defined by the following equation :

$$PO = P - \hat{P} = (Vp - Vm) - (\hat{V}p - \hat{V}m)$$

where P is the actual value added in the economy, $\hat{P}$ is the expected figure, Vp is the actual value added of primary production, $\hat{V}p$ is the corresponding expected figure, Vm is actual value added in nonprimary sectors and $\hat{V}m$ is the corresponding expected figure. But it is doubted whether this index will be enough to define the pattern of the growth when earning differences are considered.

If what is written in this book is true, another characteristic to define the pattern of development can be added to Chenery's: it is the earnings differences. High earnings differences can be used to define import substituting countries. It is apparent theoretically that in import substituting countries earnings differences should be high. To verify this conclusion earning differences in countries classified as import substituting by Chenery are listed in Table III - 6.

The ratios relating to four of these ten countries (India, Brazil, Turkey and Mexico) fit perfectly well with the expected earning differences. In the case of four other countries (Bolivia, Ecuador, Chile, Uruguay) earnings ratios are normal. It is quite apparent that there is an important difference between two groups, i.e., the former countries have large populations, whereas the latter ones are small countries. It is therefore quite natural to expect great earning differences in the former countries but not in the latter. The reason is simple : in small countries there is not much room to increase earnings differences because of the lack of internal markets.

TABLE III - 6

EARNING DIFFERENCES IN IMPORT SUBSTITUTING COUNTRIES

	1965 Population (Mil.)	1965 Per Capita Income $	Share of Agriculture 1965	1965 Earnings Difference Ratio
India	481	84	0.489	2.88
Bolivia	4	124	0.375	1.90
Ecuador	5	195	0.360	2.25
Brazil	81	216	0.225	4.06
Columbia	18	228	0.338	1.87
Turkey	31	244	0.369	4.50
Chile	9	419	0.209	1.74
Mexico	43	434	0.513	5.27
Uruguay	3	497	0.146	1.28
Argentina	22	787	0.187	0.98

Source: Chenery and Syrquin (1975), p. 103.

There are two exceptions to this generalization : Argentina and Columbia. The case of Argentina can be explained easily. This country has much greater per capita income compared with the others; therefore it is expected that this country should have smaller differences. Again, the share of agriculture is much smaller compared with the other countries. Moreover, this country has very rich agricultural resources, a fact which may make high agricultural earnings possible. Lastly, partly due to the small earning difference the growth of this country has been much smaller than most developing countries. Columbia seems to be an exception to this generalization. I am not familiar enough with the characteristics of this country to find out the factors explaining this dissimilarity.

The explanatory power of earning differences may not be very high in defining pattern of development of the Chenery type; but it cannot be doubted that if it is brought together with the speed of transformation in industrial structure, it is very illustrative and it can be seen in the Turkish case. The theoretical reasons which create difficulties in countries having large earning differences are summarized in Hatiboğlu 1979 (See Chapter II). The same is done for the Turkish case in Chapter IV of Hatiboğlu 1979.

Does the evidence from other developing countries in the world support theoretical reasoning carried out in this chapter? The difficulty of finding data for the whole world in a country cut off from the world's academic circles such as Turkey, and the enormous work involved has prevented the author from launching a research work of this kind.

§ 6 - THE EFFECT OF IMPORT SUBSTITUTION ON NONTRADED GOODS

It is a well established fact that as countries develop the share of agriculture in GDP decreases and that of industry increases. Again, the increase of the share of industry is partly accounted for by means of import substitution. In one his pioneering studies published in 1960 (Chenery 1960) Chenery showed that the examination of a cross section of data taken from 51 countries indicated that 50 percent of industrialization was in the form of import substitution; import substitution is a phenomenon occurring along with development.

We know that with development the prices of non-traded goods increase relative to traded goods, and this does not create any special problem. But, on the other hand, a relatively high speed import substitution distorts the price structure. Again, it also causes a rapid change in the ratio of prices of traded goods to non-traded goods.

Now let us expand this point. If import substitution is pushed beyond the expected level, probably because of development, the prices of traded goods increase rapidly. In the case of imported goods, this is caused by tariffs and quantity restrictions and in the case of import substituting goods by the inefficiency of producing them in the developing country. As all these goods are traded goods and as the efficiency of producing them is relatively great in developed countries, their prices will be much higher in import substituting less developed countries. The price level of non-traded goods will not be affected directly by tariffs, quantity restrictions and the inefficiency of producing import substituted goods, and therefore a rise in their prices is not expected. But as a result of propagation of price increases, i.e., imitative price increases (especially due to factor price increases which were not relevant when traded goods were imported) in nontraded goods a certain amount of price increase can be expected. Even if there had not been price increases in non-traded goods (there is a clear statement that their prices will be pushed down, Kravis et al. 1978, pp. 221-222), the import substitution would create an upward bias in the national income by the upgrading of the prices of traded goods.

§ 7 - EARNING DIFFERENCES REVISITED (2008)

In my original writings on earning differences between agricultural and nonagricultural sectors the focus was its impact on the growth of national income. At face value, this was well known in the literature. What I did was a contribution to the literature or an enrichment in the sense that an additional factor giving rise to earning differences was found.. This was the impact of an import substitution policy, which pulled up labor prices in nonagricultural sectors. My main concern was to underline rents of a special nature given rise by this policy. Yet as a by-product, labor prices were pulled up as a result of these rents. This was one of the reasons giving rise to income differences.

It was shown in UATE that as the country develops the share of the agriculture in national income shrinks and increasing factors of production are used in nonagricultural sectors. The relatively higher earnings in nonagricultural sectors along with earning differences would make the growth rate of national income higher at the beginning of the development process. This had been so in Turkey, and a proportion of the Turkish economic growth could be explained by the high income differences between those two sectors. The difference between the literature and my analysis was to add another factor explaining earning differences between the two sectors. What was more was my assertion that as the shift of resources from agriculture to nonagriculture would become less in time and along with that if the growth rate caused by import substitution policy had to come to an end, eventually, earning differences would be less; and as a result, the contribution of the shift to growth would be less. Perhaps I did not stress the fact that part of the earning differences was related to higher wages due to the policy of import substitution. This was all I did in UATE.

But UATE was a springboard; the same was true of the analysis of earning differences. In posterior years to UATE this reasoning was transported to the analysis of nonagricultural sectors. The main actor, now, was the relative prices of labor intensive and nonlabor intensive commodities. In UATE it was shown that import substitution strategy should make labor prices higher than what they should be. If so, parallel to the reasoning in UATE, it was shown that the change of relative prices of labor and nonlabor intensive goods should affect the growth of nonagricultural sectors. I repeat the reasoning in UATE: if one of the sectors grows more speedily, the differences of earnings between agricultural and nonagricultural sectors would affect national income growth. Now, as in the period covered by UATE, the growth of nonlabor intensive sectors was speedier and if the prices of the nonlabor intensive commodities were higher, the growth of this sector would be higher. But when the relative prices of labor intensive goods decrease and their growth becomes speedier, this should give rise to a decrease in the growth of this sector. Is this not parallel to the reasoning in UATE? Yet there was more; I have also asserted that the relative fall of the prices of labor intensive goods should give rise to a decrease in the level of income, as well. Not only would the growth rate of national income be affected; its level should also be affected. This was my discovery after I wrote UATE. In fact, the shift of resources from agriculture to nonagricultural sectors would affect both the growth and the level of national income. But at that time I did not make this distinction and I had not brought them together. In UATE the relatively high incomes in nonagricultural sectors should make the growth of income higher than what it was. But was that caused by the high growth of national income or was it related to its level? This is shown 25 years later. Yet the springboard was UATE. In the following papers I shall try to explain how I have developed the new ideas.

One of the reasons of the high multiplier between the earnings in nongricultural and agricultural sectors was the overswelling of nonagricultural values.As this was not the case after the economy turned outward, the multiplier had to decrease. Actually it did;but not as much as it should.It went down from 4.5-5 to 3.7 by 2005.One of the reasons was the fast decrease of agriculture in national income:the present share is 11 percent only.In the recent future I expect that it will only be around 5-6 percent. In the end, the multiplier would come down to the expected level; but it needs years to come.

CHAPTER IV

THE EARLY UNCONVENTIONAL THEORETICAL WRITINGS: THE MAGNIFICATION OF THE LOSS DUE TO DETERIORATING TERMS OF TRADE (ORIGINAL VERSION)

§ 1 - INTRODUCTION

The birth of the unconventional economics dates back to the publication of my book entitled AN UNCONVENTIONAL ANALYSIS OF THE TURKISH ECONOMY, 1978 (it is noted as UATE). The aim of the book was to explain the rather high growth rate of the Turkish economy in the period of 1950-1975, and to predict that the growth had to slacken.

It was difficult to explain it by means of the tools of the existing literature on growth and development. The main idea was that the reason of high growth was the overvaluation of labor (or service) prices in nonagricultural sectors of the economy. But an adequate theory relating to the overvaluation of prices and its impact on the level and growth of national income was not found in economic literature. Yet in that book, without applying a formal analysis, the observed overvaluation of service prices was used to explain the growth performance of the Turkish economy.

My efforts in ensuing years after the publication of the Book were concentrated to formulate a general framework of analysis without referring to a particular country. I was not trying to formulate a completely new theory of growth and development. All I wanted to do was to underline a very important factor which had been neglected so far; yet its power of explanation of some of the abnormalities probably to be met in practical life was high.

My background in economic theory as well as my mathematical competence were not of the sort to formulate a well established theory all at once. All I have done in almost 30 years following the publication of the UATE was to work out and publish the building blocks of a theoretical framework which I was after. Although the essentials of a more cohesive and complete theory (or to put it better, a combination of several building blocks of a theory) is presented in Chapter VI and VIII of this book, a lot needs to be done (I don't think I can go any further) to call it a theory of growth and development by the standards of the present day economics.

The starting point of the unconventional analysis is the UATE. That book is summarized in Chapter I. I tried to show in that book that the national income of Turkey was overblown and as a result, the growth rate of the national income was shown to be higher than it should be. This was due to the high prices of nonagricultural goods relative to agricultural ones. The main items of exports in Turkey were agricultural goods: the exchange rate was fixed at a level which would guarantee the viability of nonagricultural sectors. If the prices in the nonagricultural sectors of the economy were determined in a way which reflected the world prices, an expected relationship between agricultural and nonagricultural earnings should have existed. Drawing on the world experience, I supposed that nonagricultural earnings per person should have been 2.5 folds higher than those of agricultural sectors, whereas they were 4-5 folds. Therefore, I tried to re-calculate the national income of Turkey in the UATE by supposing that the multiplier was 2.5 instead of 4-5. I came up with the following conclusion: the per capita income in 1975 should be $600 rather than $833 and the income growth in 1950-1975 should be 4-5 percent rather than 6.4 percent, which were the official figures. (At that time I couldn't distinguish growth and level effects as expounded in this book.)

My prediction as to the decrease in the growth rate after 1975 has come true. But how could I prove the decrease of its absolute level?

This book is, in a way, the story of the development of my ideas. The first stage of the development of my ideas after UATE is repeated above as in its original form along with a review of the original ideas. The latest developments are explained in the following chapters.

Here in this chapter I repeat firstly my early writings, dating back to 1989, which include my original thoughts about the theory I had in mind. That section is followed by comments by Professor Celasun. In the fourth section after spoting a flaw in the original writing, I end up with underlying the impact of the changes of relative prices.

The development of my thoughts can be summarized in 4 stages in chronological order.

1. It is known in the literature that a real devaluation would create a loss for the economy as a result of a deterioration of external terms of trade. (I ignore adverse effects of a devaluation, such as the loss of income due to the shrinkage of demand.) I tried to show in a book published in 1989 (TÜRKİYE İKTİSADININ GELECEĞİ - THE FUTURE OF THE TURKISH ECONOMY) that if relative prices of exported and nonexported goods remain constant, an additional loss to traditional external terms of trade loss is incurred due to the decrease of the prices in

nonexported goods with respect to a certain point of reference which I could not identify in those years; the loss was a result of the factor price equalization theorem. That means that the terms of trade loss would be magnified and the decrease in the national income should be higher than the terms of trade loss. However, how were we going to calculate it? Although there were some attempts in my 1989 book, I could not find a good term of reference to calculate it. My 1989 work is summarized in Section 2 below.

2. My posterior investigations lead me to the idea that the decrease in national income after a devaluation should be related to the decrease of the prices of nontraded goods (service prices) vis-à-vis exported goods. In other words, the change in relative prices might give rise to a change in the national income. I was trying to find the point of reference. In order to reach this conclusion, it is necessary that we should have at least two factors of production. This possibility was not considered in my 1989 work. My explanations, which were published in 1990 in a book entitled A THEORY OF GROWTH AND ITS VALIDATION BY THE TURKISH EXPERIENCE.

3. In the 1990 s my attention was focused on the factors determining the prices of nonexported goods (service prices or home goods prices) and I was caught up with the idea that the relationship between the return to capital and service prices, and the change in production of capital intensive and labor intensive goods would give us a clue about future growth rates. The observation of the existence of this relationship would direct us to observe the relationship between service prices and growth of national income. I showed that the relative decrease of service prices would give rise to a decrease in the growth of the national income. I came up with this idea in 1991, and it was first published in my book entitled AN UNCONVENTIONAL ANALYSIS OF THE TURKISH ECONOMY AND BEYOND, 1991.

4. Finally I investigated the problem of the determination of service prices, which was crucial in the whole explanation. It was first published in 1994 (TÜRKİYE EKONOMİSİNDE 1994 BUNALIMI-1994 ECONOMIC CRISIS IN THE TURKISH ECONOMY). My explanations relating to service prices are found in this book.

§ 2 - THE EXAMPLE: THE MAGNIFYING EFFECTS OF INCREASED EXPORTS ON THE IMPOVERISHMENT CAUSED BY A DETERIORATION OF TERMS OF TRADE (1989)

This section is the first stage of the development of my thoughts after UATE. The main assumptions are as follows: the relative prices among produced goods are the same; there are constant returns to scale; there is one factor of production (if so, relative prices should stay the same all the time); and there is perfect competition. I tried to show that in order to increase exports, an additional loss to the loss in the volume of goods at the disposal of the nation due to the deteriorating terms of trade should be incurred. While showing it we observe that traditional measures of income are not relevant, and we face the necessity of finding another point of reference.

In order to illustrate the effects of attempts to increase exports I shall take a simple example. Let us suppose that there is a single factor of production, D, and there are only two goods, A and B. This distinction is based on the following definition: A goods are exportable and B goods are nonexportable in view of the existing exchange rate which is fixed by the government.

Let us also suppose that techniques are constant and the level of production depends only on the volume of factors of production used in production. There are constant returns to factors of production and perfect competition prevails in the country. Therefore the price of each good depends on its cost of production.

There is only one factor of production (D) and by using one D, 12 A goods or 10 B goods can be produced. In that case 1.2 A is exchanged for 1 B. In other words, if the price of A goods is 10 Liras (taking Lira as the domestic currency) the price of B should be 12 Liras. We know that in the production of 1 A, 1/12 D is used and in the production of 1 B, 1/10 D is used. We suppose that there are 2 D's in the country. As a result of the preferences of the country population, 12 A's and 10 B's are produced. This can be shown schematically as follows;

Production Factors Used	Commodity	Production Volume	Price (Lira)	Total (Lira)
2 D	A	12	10	120
	B	10	12	120
		National income, total		240 L

Now let us suppose that the country has transactions with the outside world and the exchange rate is fixed at 1 lira = \$ 1. At this rate we suppose that the country exports 2.4 A goods. Again, we suppose that the price of imported goods (C) as well as exported goods (A) are \$10. If there are not transportation costs, the price of A and C is exactly the same. The following table can be made here:

Production Factors Used	Commodity	Consumption Volume	Price (Lira)	Total (Lira)
	A	9.60	10.00	96.00
2 D	B	10.00	12.00	120.00
	C	2.40	10.00	24.00
		National income, total		240.00 L

We suppose that the country in question wishes to increase its imports from 2.4 C to 3.6 C. Although a small country is assumed, on account of world market conditions it is imagined that the country will have to decrease the price of A goods by 25 percent in order to increase its imports by 50 percent (from 2.4 to 3.6).

In other words, the country is in a position to give 4.5 A goods in order to import 3.6 C goods. Since the price of C goods is $10, thus $36 is required. In order to earn $36 the country has to sell 4.5 A goods. This can be achieved by devaluing the currency by 20 or 25 percent: $0.80=1 Lira or $1= 1.25 Lira. (It must be noted that although a small country is assumed, a lowering of the price of export goods is required in order to increase exports. In practice this is quite common because of the nature of goods exported by the country in question. We suppose that nonhomogeneous goods are exported. In this case, as a result of differentiation, a lowering of export prices would be necessary.)

Attempts to increase exports would lead to a deterioration in the terms of trade and a change in the national income of the country. What would then happen to the welfare of the country? The national income in terms of domestic currency remains exactly the same, i.e., 240 Liras, whereas in terms of dollars it is $192 (240x0.80). We suppose that the monetary policy keeps the prices the same. It seems as if nothing has altered with the country producing exactly the same amount of goods. But in terms of consumption there are changes. It is quite apparent that the decrease in consumption cannot be measured by the decrease in dollar value, i.e., 20 percent. One way to measure the loss in consumption (perhaps welfare) is to measure national income in terms of A or B goods.

The loss brought about by the deteriorating terms of trade is straightforward when the production of B goods remains exactly the same. On the other hand, if the loss in terms of trade did not occur, it would be necessary to surrender 3.6 A goods in order to acquire 3.6 C goods, imported ones. Here, the payment is 4.5 goods and the difference is 0.9 A goods. The price of A goods being 10 Liras, the loss is 9 Liras. As the national income is 240 Liras, the total loss is equal to 0.0375 of the national income (9/240). This is in line with the standard literature, but the approach to be presented here is quite different.

The first point to focus upon is the impact of the terms of trade deterioration on the $P_{B/A}$ ratio (i.e., the price ratio of B and A goods). At first impression little appears to have changed. The price of B is 12 Liras and that of A 10 Liras. Therefore $P_{B/A}$ is 1.2,i.e, exactly the same as before. But viewed from another angle all is not the same.

The country produces two kinds of goods. Let us suppose that the first kind is consumed in the domestic market only and the price of this good can be fixed anywhere according to the preferences and cost conditions prevailing in the country. On account of the economic policy followed in the country, the relative prices prevailing abroad do not constitute a constraint for relative prices in this country. The second category consists of goods, a part of which are actually exported abroad. In the present case we suppose that A goods only can be exported. The price ratio between B and A abroad is of little interest for the country concerned. We are interested in how $P_{B/A}$ changes in the country after imports increase from 2.4 to 3.6 C goods. In the period before the increase, the import bill of C goods (3.6 C goods are imported now; that was 2.4 C before) in terms of original prices was $36 or 36 Liras, (3.6x10). Now, as 4.5 A goods are exported their value should be $36. In other words, the value of 4.5 A goods is lowered to $36, which according to the old $/Lira parity was 45 Liras. The value of remaining A goods, i.e., 7.5 A's, is 75 Liras. Hence the total altogether amounts to 111 Liras, 10x(7.5+3.6). (Warning: in constant prices.) The country can fix the relative value of A and B goods, which are not exported anywhere; but the value of exported proportion of A goods should be in line with international prices. (Please note that the calculation is carried out in terms of old prices and this conclusion will be changed.)

In the production of A goods the use of factors of production is 1D with a value of 111 Liras. As the same amount of D is used in the production of B goods the value should again be 111 Liras. This means that total B production should cost 111 Liras. Before the increase in exports the cost was 120 Liras. The $P_{B/A}$ ratio appears to be the same 1.2 (111/10:111/12=1.2) but the total value of income in terms of constant Liras has declined from 240 to 222 Liras. Income has decreased by 7.5 percent.

Another method to calculate may also be employed. The total income may be calculated in terms of a hybrid good consisting of A and C. Following trade transactions the country possesses 7.5 A's plus 3.6 C's. Under these circumstances the international value of 3.6 C for the country in question is 3.6 A. This and 7.5 amounting to a total of 11.1 A is produced by 1D - the same factor of production used in the production of 10 B's. Therefore, the total value of B goods in terms of A should be 11.1 This leads to the sum 11.1 + 11.1 = 22.2 A's. Before the increase in exports the total was 24 A's. Hence again there is a 7.5 percent decrease in the national income.

It should be immediately noted that the loss caused by a deterioration of terms of trade is magnified by the new valuation of A and B goods.

Why national income is calculated in terms of the hybrid good rather than B needs explaining. This is based on the idea that the volume of production of the hybrid goods constitutes a constraint on the production of B goods. If the latter could be exported at the present rate of exchange, the calculation of national income in terms of A or B would be immaterial. But we suppose that the country can export A goods only. It is also supposed that for the country's stability and growth a certain amount of exports are required and this can be obtained by selling A goods. Therefore, a balanced production of A and B goods is necessary and the calculation of national income in terms of the hybrid good seems to be more rational.

A New Measurement of National Income

Evidently, a new measurement of national income is necessary. This is required as a result of a different valuation of goods produced in the country.

To a large extent, the country is free to value various goods but the need to import introduces a constraint. Without the need of imports the relative values of goods could be fixed anywhere. But the need to import and export lowers the value of nonexportable goods along with exportable goods.

In the example given above it was concluded that after switching to export orientation national income in terms of domestic currency remained the same, i.e., 240 Liras. In terms of dollars it was $192. According to new calculations it should be $222. Now, if the country does not devalue and maintains importing 2.4 C, it is supposed that the country overvalues its national income by 18 (240 - 222) units. This is the cost of not importing 3.6 C goods; 3.6 C import would make the economy of the country function efficiently. The difference, i.e., $18, can be labeled rents earned and enjoyed by the country in question. But there is another problem concerning the length of time these rents are earned. This would depend on the length of time during which the country could sustain its growth by importing 2.4 C goods.

It should be noted that the actual national income after the devaluation was $192. But the decrease (192/240, i.e., 20 percent) does not measure the overvaluation of income in the country. The decrease caused by the overvaluation of goods is only 7.5 percent. This provides one with an important starting point to demonstrate that the overvaluation of national income is based on the relative valuation of goods which in this particular case is not easily visible!

We observe that there is a swelling in the national income in terms of international values. The price of B goods abroad is not known, but since they are not exportable they can be expensive. In the standard literature a method is employed to determine the overvaluation (Little, Scitovsky and Scott, 1972). The value of A goods is clearly expressed in terms of international currency. Likewise the same is true for B goods, whose value is lowered to their international scale whatever that might be...

To repeat: I intend to refer to the difference between 240 and 222, i.e., 18 Liras or dollars, as rent, which is caused by the overvaluation of B goods. But this overvaluation is determined much differently from accepted international practice, which is based on the existing exchange rate, and the valuation is made by using this rate. Here the method suggested is based on the smooth functioning of the economy. The new exchange rate facilitates this smooth functioning by being fixed at such a level to enable sufficient exports.

Here, an illustration is necessary. According to our assumptions the new rate is $0.80=1 Lira or $1=1.25 Lira. This rate has led to a decrease in income from $240 to $192, a 20 percent decrease. By our method it is $222 or a 7.5 percent decrease. When the deterioration in the terms of trade is considered, the decrease is 3.75 percent; but in terms of Lira it is exactly the same. Which one is true?

How does one measure the change in national income after switching to export orientation?

Above, four different measurements were employed to determine the effect of export orientation on the national income. There is actually one more criterion. To repeat our conclusions:

1. In constant domestic currency: According to our example it is zero.

2. The deterioration of terms of trade: In our example there is a 3.75 percent decrease of national income.

3. Measurement by hybrid goods: In the example given there is a 7.5 percent decrease.

4. The change in dollar value: In our example there is a 20 percent decrease.

5. The purchasing power measurement of national income: This is the additional criterion. There is a theoretical argument supported by empirical findings that the prices of nontraded goods are lower than their equivalents in developed countries (Balassa 1964, Kravis et al. 1975, Kravis et al. 1978). There is a very important implication here. If per capita incomes in a developing and developed country, each expressed by a common standard determined by the prices of traded goods, are compared, a downward bias in per capita income of the developing country will be observed. Therefore, if the per capita incomes of two countries are compared an adjustment in terms of the purchasing power of each currency should be made.

§ 3 -COMMENTS BY PROFESSOR CELASUN ON THE SUGGESTION ABOUT MEASURING NATIONAL INCOME BY TRADABLE GOODS PRICES

In the previous section, an important block of the unconventional theory is expounded. After reading it in one of my recent book entitled ECONOMIC THEORY AND THE TURKISH EXPERIENCE (1995) Professor Celasun, who had also contributed to the writing of my UATE, wrote three comments.

Although his comments are very favorable, he stresses the point that the theory put forward should be validated by the observations of numerous cases relating to various countries.

Professor Celasun formalized my explanations by setting up necessary assumptions properly, and drew formal conclusions from the reasoning. It seems that after a rigid formalizing his conclusions are exactly the same..

NOTE NO.1

BY PROFESSOR CELASUN: HATİBOĞLU EXAMPLE AUGMENTED BY OPEN ECONOMY - EXPENDITURE BALANCE

The purpose of Note No.1 is to reinterpret Professor Hatiboğlu's rent within an internally consistent accounting framework. Note No.1 is simply a prelude to Note No.2 in which I modify the present exercise to measure the degree of undervaluation and overvaluation of income in exportables and nontradable sectors, respectively.

PART I: PRELIMINARIES

1) Professor Hatiboğlu's example (Chapter II, here III) is augmented by open economy budget constraint or income expenditure balance, where;

$$\text{Domestic income (output)} = \underbrace{\text{Domestic expenditure}}_{\text{absorption}} + \underbrace{\text{Exports - Imports}}_{\text{trade balance}}$$

$$\text{or Domestic income} + \underbrace{\text{Trade balance}}_{\text{Resource gap}} = \text{Domestic expenditure}$$

2) Although the trade balance is always zero in the example (and its extensions), it is explicitly treated to explore the issue of relative price changes in a consistent framework.

3) Domestic expenditure normally includes consumption and investment with different deflators. Following the terminology of Hatiboğlu, domestic expenditure is simply referred to as consumption.

4) The system features no import tariffs and no export subsidies. Domestic prices of A goods output, consumption and exports are the same. In semi-open economy, this assumption may not be valid.

5) Additional notation

a) t= 1,2; time superscripts, denoting Period 1 (predevaluation) and Period 2 (post - devaluation)

b) $Q \times P_Q = Q_A x P_A + Q_B \times P_B$. where Q_A, Q_B are outputs of A and B;Q is total domestic output; P_Q is the aggregate price index of Q (or output deflator)

c) E_A quantity of (A) exports

M_C = quantity of (C) imports

CN_A , CN_B , CN_C = quantity of consumption of A, B, C goods, respectively

ER= exchange rate (lira/$)

P_A, P_B, P_C domestic prices of A, B, C goods, respectively

PW_A, PW_C = World ($) prices of A and C goods.

P_H= Paasche price index of hybrid good (A, C)

Remark: In all cases, $Q_A=CN_A+E_A$; $Q_B=CN_B$; $CN_C=M_C$

$Q^1{}_A=Q^2{}_A$ AND $Q^1{}_B=Q^2{}_B$. Thus we refer them Q_A, Q_B and $CN^1{}_B=CN^2{}_B=Q_B$

PART II: TRADE AND EXCHANGE RATE ADJUSTMENT

II.I PRE-DEVALUATION CASE

$$Q_A P^1{}_A + Q_B P^1{}_B = CN^1{}_A P^1{}_A + CN^1{}_B P^1{}_B + CN^1{}_C P^1{}_C + E^1{}_A P^1{}_A - M_C P^1{}_C$$

$$P^1{}_C = ER^1 \times PW^1{}_C$$

$P^1{}_A = ER^1 \times PW^1{}_A$, where

prices are: $P^1{}_A = 10$, $PW^1{}_A = \$10$, $ER = 1$ lira/$, $P_Q = 1.0$

$P^1{}_B = 12$ $PW^1{}_C = \$10$ $P^1{}_C = 10$

And quantities: $Q_A = 12$ $CN^1{}_A = 9.6$ $E_A = 2.4$

$Q_B = 10$ $CN^1{}_B = 10$ $M_C = 2.4$

$QP_Q = 240$ $CN^1{}_C = 2.4$

II. 2 POST DEVALUATION CASE

New data: $M^2{}_C = CN^2{}_C = 3.6$ and $ER^2 = 1.25$ lira/$

Furthermore, Hatiboğlu's example involves other assumptions, which are made explicit as follows:

(i) P_Q is maintained constant, that is $P^2{}_Q / P^1{}_Q = 1$

(ii) P_A and P_B remain unchanged despite ER adjustment. That is

$P^2{}_A = P^1{}_A = 10$ and $P^2{}_B = P^1{}_B = 12$

(iii) PW_C remains constant.

(iv) No trade balance is allowed

then it follows that

$P^2_C = PW^2_C \times ER^2$ and $PW^2_C = \$10$ imply $P^2_C = 12.5$

$P^2_C M^2_C = P^2_A . E^2_A$ implies $E^2_A = 4.5$

$Q^2_A = CN^2_A + E^2_A$ implies $CN^2_A = 7.5$

This (the post - devaluation income) expenditure balance becomes

$$\underbrace{Q_A P^2_A + Q_B P^2_B}_{240} = \underbrace{\underbrace{CN^2_A\, P^2_A}_{7.5\ \ 10} + \underbrace{CN^2_B\, P^2_B}_{10\ \ 12} + \underbrace{CN^2_C\, P^2_C}_{3.6\ \ 12.5} + \underbrace{E^2_A P^2_A}_{45} - \underbrace{M_C P^2_C}_{45}}_{240}$$

I- 3 HOW TO MEASURE THE DECLINE IN REAL INCOME

In the post devaluation period, the value of total output (income) is the same as pre-devaluation value. i.e., 240, but its purchasing power has declined. How to measure the decline in real income?

This should be measured by the use of a properly constructed consumer price index (CPI). The key point is that the output and consumption deflators are not the same (P_Q and CPI). In actual practice, this should be done by constructing a composite price index for domestic expenditure, including consumption and investment with different bundles of goods. Here, it is assumed that domestic expenditure consists of consumption only.

As usual, we have an index number problem regarding the choice of weights, either for period 1 or period 2.

Let us choose period 2 for the mix of consumption, leading to Paasche price index. Then, CPI can be constructed as follows;

Define $CPI^1 = 1.0$

$$CPI^2 = \frac{CN^2_A\, P^2_A + CN^2_B\, P^2_B + CN^2_C\, P^2_C}{CN^2_A\, P^1_A + CN^2_B\, P^1_B + CN^2_C\, P^1_C} = \frac{240}{231} = 1.03896$$

Let us define real income

$Y^t = (Q^t P^t_q) / CPI^t$

Then, for period 1 $\quad Y^1 = 240/1 = 240$

for period 2 $\quad Y^2 = 240/1.03896 = (240)\ (0.9625) = 231$

The implication is that the community's real income has declined 3.75 percent after devaluation. This is the real income decline associated with terms of trade deterioration as also pointed out by Professor Hatiboğlu.

PART III: HATİBOĞLU'S RENT CONCEPT: A REINTERPRETATION

In the context of our notation and income-expenditure balance, it is possible to reconstruct part of the analysis in order to arrive at Hatiboğlu's concept of rent.

The community's consumption may be split into two parts.

$$\underbrace{CN_A\ ,\ CN_C}_{\text{Hybrid good}} \qquad \underbrace{CN_B}_{\text{Consumption of nontradables}}$$

Consumption of tradables

Define $P^1{}_H = 1.0$, the price of the hybrid good.

$$CPI_H = \frac{CN^2{}_A P^2{}_A + CN^2{}_C P^2{}_C}{CN^2{}_A P^1{}_A + CN^2{}_C P^1{}_C} = \frac{120}{111} = 1.081$$

In fact, what Professor Hatiboğlu proposes to do is to measure total income in terms of tradable goods prices, i.e.,P_H. Let us define the new real income measure (YR) as follows:

$$YR^t = O^t\, P^t{}_Q \,/\, P^t{}_H$$

for Period 1 : $YR^1 = 240/1$

Period 2 : $YR^2 = 240/1.081 = 222$

$\Delta YR = -18$

Professor Hatiboğlu refers to $\Delta YR = 18$ as his "new" measure of rent.

Although it is technically possible to measure national income in terms of hybrid good prices, there are two basic operational problems with this kind of income conceptualization:

i) The proposed approach does not yield a proper estimate of the de facto real income loss, because it takes into accounts only the basket of tradables in deflator calculations. In practice, all nations-even when they have free trade and equilibrium exchange rate-consume a substantial amount of nontradables. The calculation of changes in real national income must therefore take into account the entire basket of goods consumed by the community.

ii) More importantly, in Hatiboğlu's demonstration exercise, the relative prices of domestic goods (A, B) are not explicitly analyzed in the post devaluation period. In reality, the ratio of P_A/P_B is always altered in the aftermath of a real devaluation, causing shifts in sectoral real income. This issue needs to be examined within the context of a numeric price and budget constraint of the economy. Note No. 2 provides a modified analysis to explore the latter issue.

On the other hand, the proposed measurement of real income in terms of tradable goods prices seems to have important implications for future empirical research as pointed out in the end of Note No. 2.

NOTE NO.2

MODIFIED EXERCISE; DOMESTIC PRICE RELATIVES

PART 1: PRELIMINARIES

Note No.2 builds on the notation of Note No.1 and data base of Professor Hatiboğlu. It presents an explicit treatment of relative prices and income changes associated with exchange rate adjustment and trade expansion in the economy.

In order to provide a greater import availability of C goods, exports of A goods increase, but at a reduced dollar price. This is accomplished by devaluation, which also affects the ratio of prices of (A) goods to the prices of (B) goods. This process results, not only in the fall of total real income, but it also alters income proportions in the country.

At the outset, it is emphasized that the reconstructed exercise is not fully a general equilibrium analysis, which would take into account the price responsiveness of output, consumption and trade, and determine endogenously all quantities and prices. The modified exercise merely intends to crystallize the directions of real income changes in this naive economy.

PART II: TRADE, EXCHANGE RATE AND DOMESTIC PRICE ADJUSTMENT

II- PRE-DEVALUATION CASE: PERIOD I

See Note No.1 on period 1, which also applies here.

II-I Post -devaluation case: period 2

ASSUMPTIONS:

1- The exchange rate depreciates 25 percent with respect to the aggregate output price P_Q, yielding 25 percent rise in P_A/P_B ratio.

2- Monetary policy maintains constant P_Q: that is $P_Q=1$ serves as numeric price.

3- The price adjustments do not induce changes in (A) and (B) outputs, but reduce CN_A and increase E_A with no impact on CN_B, while producing no change in trade balance (=0).

4- Domestic price of (A) goods output, consumption and exports are equal to each other.

5- To finance 3.6 units of M_C, (A) exports increase to 4.05 units at the lowered price of \$ 8.888 per unit. (See below.)

Remark: A full equilibrium analysis would yield different magnitudes, but distortions of changes would be the same.

Analysis :

The internal consistency in the price system requires the following:

(i) $Q_AP^2_A + Q_BP^2_B = QP_Q$

(ii) $(P^2_A/P^2_B)/(P^1_A/P^1_B) = 1.25$ where $P_Q = P^1_Q = P^2_Q = 1$

with two unknowns, the system solves

$P^2_A = 11.111 \quad P^2_B = 10.666$

then

$PW^2_A = P^2_A/E^2_R$ implies $PW^2_A = \$\ 8.888$

and

$PW^2_A \times E^2_A = M^2_C \times PW^2_C$ implies $E^2_A = 4.05$

$CN^2_A = Q_A - E^2_A$ implies $CN^2_A = 7.95$

The post-devaluation income-expenditure balance becomes (where prices are normalized around the numeraire $P_Q=1$);

$$\underbrace{Q_AP^2_A}_{133.332} + \underbrace{Q_BP^2_B}_{106.666} = \underbrace{CN^2_AP^2_A}_{7.95\ 11.111} + \underbrace{CN_BP^2_B}_{10\ 10.666} + \underbrace{CN_CP^2_C}_{3.6\ 12.5} + \underbrace{E_AP^2_A}_{45} - \underbrace{M_CP^2_C}_{45}$$

240 240 0

II.3 Decline in Total Real Income

The Use of CPI

Following the procedure in Note No.1 (II.3)

$CPI^1 = 1$

$$CPI^2 = \frac{CN^2_A P^2_A + CN^2_B P^2_B + CN^2_C P^2_C}{CN^2_A P^1_A + CN^2_B P^1_B + CN^2_C P^1_C} = 1.02$$

Total real income for period 1 : $Y^1 = 240/CPI^1 = 240$

Total real income for period 2 : $Y^2 = 240/CPI^2 = 235.3$

Total income loss : 4.7 units in terms of domestic purchasing power measured by CPI or 2%

THE USE OF P_H

In the spirit of Hatiboğlu's rent concept:

Paasche price index for hybrid (tradables) good: $P^1_H = 1$

$P^2_H = 1.154$ (the price index of the hybrid good is found by taking out the volume and prices of B goods in CPI equation: $\frac{7.95x11.1+36x12.5}{7.95x10+3.6x10} = 1.154$)

C) and total real income : $YR^1 = 240/P_H$ and $YR^2=240/1.154=208$

Thus, total real decline is 13.3 %[(240-208)/240)] x100)] in terms of purchasing power measured by P_H. Therefore, the so called rent element in pre-devaluation income is 13.3 %.

REMARK: Under this approach, the decline in total real income was 7.5 % in the original exercise. Here, the income loss is larger due higher P_A/P_B ratio after devaluation: 13.3 %.

PART III. INTERSECTORAL SHIFTS IN REAL INCOMES

In the present analysis, Q_A and Q_B are constant, and their utilization of factor (D) remains the same: 1 D for $Q_A=12$ and 1 D for $Q_B = 10$. In period 1, the factor earnings are equal to 120 in both sectors.

Let μ^t_A and μ^t_B to be income shares. Before devaluation $\mu^1_A = \mu^1_B = 0.5$

Let us presume that the institutional conditions allow sectoral differentiation of factor rentals after the exchange rate shock. Furthermore, let us also suppose that there are no tax transfer mechanisms to sustain the original income distribution. Let Y^t_A and Y^t_B denote real factor incomes in sector A and B in terms of domestic

purchasing power measured by CPI.

Then $Y^t_A = Q_A P^t_A / CPI^t$ and $Y^t_B = Q_B P^t_B / CPI^t$

On the basis of the findings of previous sections in this note, the real incomes are as follows:

$Y^1_A = 120$ $Y^2_A = 130.7$ Change in period 2 (+) 8.9 %

$Y^1_B = 120$ $Y^2_B = 104.6$ Change in period 2 (-) 12.9 %

$Y^1 = 240$ $Y^2 = 235.3$ Change in period 2 (-) 2 %

The consistency check is the following:

μ_A X 8.9 + μ_A X (-) 12.9 = - 2%, the decline in total income.

§ 4 - COMMENTS ON THE 1989 EXAMPLE LEADING TO A NEW CONCEPT OF NATIONAL INCOME (2008)

The main contention of the example was to measure the loss caused by deteriorating terms of trade on national income, and to show that it should not be just a volume loss as supposed in the literature; it was asserted that a value loss should accompany it ,which would magnify the loss previewed in the literature. In order to reach that conclusion I deflated the national income ($240 all the time) after deteriorated terms of trade by a price index based on the price change of A and C goods and also new shares of those goods in the total volume were taken as weight. In other words this was a Paasche index. As the price and the share of C goods was higher than those of A goods compared to what was in the base period, and again as the price of B goods was supposed to stay the same, the deflator should be higher than what it would be if the prices of all goods (including those of B goods) were taken into consideration.

Was I justified to do so? In other words why was I excluding B good prices in the calculation of the deflator? This is the crux of the problem. When I wrote the original example what I had in mind was the sustainability of national income (the level and growth): without importing more C goods the growth of national income could not be sustained. In addition, I was of the opinion that two conditions had to be satisfied. The first was the equalization of factor prices, and secondly, internal equilibrium. As was shown above, C good prices were higher and the quantity of A goods to be given for buying the same amount of C goods were more. As a result, the total volume of A + C goods, which I called hybrid goods, was less but the value of the same amount of A+C goods was more. Therefore the deflation of the national income (always 240 lira) by the hybrid goods price index would amount to a lower national income calculated by the constant prices. I believed that by doing so I was inserting a value dimension in the calculation of national income.

Under equilibrium conditions assumed in the example, two constraints should be satisfied. The first was the necessity of the price of the (sole) factor of production should be the same in the production of both A and B goods. This was a must for the factor price equalization theorem. The second constraint was that for the consistency necessitated by the internal equilibrium (based on the idea that prices should be equal to cost of production) in the economy: the price of B goods had to decrease. The total value of B goods should be equal to the total value of the now available A and C goods(111 L). I should make it clear that if national income in the second period (240 lira) is deflated by the price rise index of A and C goods, it would be 222 lira. (If A and B goods are produced by the same amount of factors of production ,the total value of B and A+C goods should be 222 lira in terms of their deflated prices.This could be made clear as follows.We know that 7.5 units of A goods remained after the devaluation. The price of each unit is 10 lira. In addition, there are 3.6 units of C goods .Although the current price of each unit of C good is 12.5 lira, when it is deflated by its price increase it is 10 lira. If that is the case the total value of the hybrid good is 111 lira (7.5x 10+3.6x 10).As the same amount of factors are used in the production of B goods its total value should be 111 lira.) Both conditions required that B good prices should decrease. As we supposed that the production of B goods were the same (10), their prices should be 11.1 liras (they were 12 Liras); whereas I supposed that B prices would have to stay the same. Therefore there was a slip in the soning. Let us remember that A good prices are kept as they were. This meant that the relative price of B goods had to decrease.

It is known in literature that if the currency is devalued,we should expect a price rise in imported(C) goods; as a result ,if the price of A good is the same (it is supposed that in order to sell more A goods, A good prices are left the same but they are made cheaper for the outside world at the end of the devaluation),and if B goods prices stay the same, we should expect an increase in general prices. Didn't I say the same? No! I assumed that the price index or the deflator should not include B goods. Would not the increase in C good prices compensate for the decrease in those of A goods? No! I keep A good prices the same; but B prices had to fall, as shown above. This was a very important discovery.

If the new national income was not deflated by the Paasche price index of the hybrid good, the internal equilibrium in national income would not be fulfilled. The deflation of the national income including all goods by the hybrid goods price index is necessary to find out the necessary price fall in B goods, which is a condition of internal equilibrium. The price change in B goods should be determined by the change in the total value of the hybrid good. But on the other hand, the change in the value of B good should be equal to A good prices (in fact there is no change in them). Let us remember that we supposed one factor of production. Again if there is no change in B good prices (that was the assumption), this is again inconsistent with the logic of the reasoning. In fact,in the original essay it was shown that national income had to decrease. But it is apparent that there was an inconsistency in the argumentation.

But that reasoning opened new avenues to show that the change in relative prices had to affect the value of national income in constant national currency, even if it was supposed to be the same when calculated by constant prices. Yet the mentioned inconsistency would have to be corrected. I did so by assuming the existence of more than one factor of production. Very shortly, if there are two factors of production, labor and capital and again if some of the goods are labor intensive and the others are nonlabor intensive good, those two requirement could be satisfied. In that case factor price equalization theorem could be satisfied; yet, a price difference between labor and nonlabor intensive goods could be sustained.

Let us summarize by stating that if the relative prices of domestic goods (B) decreases relatively to (A) , and if the production of the domestic goods is the same, this implies a decrease of national income which is more than the traditionally expected decrease due to the volume loss caused by the deteriorating terms of trade. I wanted to argue that if the country in question would be in a position to buy the less amount of domestic goods in terms of its value, this is a decrease in national income.

After I noticed the slip, I changed the nature of A and B goods. I supposed that A goods are labor intensive and B goods are nonlabor intensive ones. I supposed again that A goods are exported.If A goods prices are the same after the devaluation,it could be shown that the relative prices of B goods would have to increase with respect to A.The reason is that they contain more imported goods and less labor.I should warn that in the initial example B good prices decreased relatively to A ones, whereas in the second example the relative prices of B goods would increase with respect to A goods. The change was related to the relative decrease of labor prices. If the price of capital stays as it was, this amounted to a relative decrease of labor prices. Let us also remember that in the initial example only one factor of production existed. Yet in both cases national income had to decrease. Moreover, in the second case if the national income was measured by labor it could be considered lower in the sense that labor would buy lower income.

In the next stage I followed up the consequences of the impact of exporting goods which were not previously exported. The assumption was that goods having higher comparative advantages were exported firstly but when there was a necessity, goods having lower comparative advantages could be exported. In that case the same consequence would emerge in the sense that relative prices would change. Would that change be reflected on national income? It should for the reasons previously mentioned. Yet I showed by an example that if measured by a foreign currency national income would decrease but if measured by Purchasing Power Parity index, it should decrease less. Then I asked: if the country shifts its resources to the production of less comparative goods why would the lower efficiency not reflect on its national income? Then measurement in foreign currency should cover a certain truth and measurements in PPP should not be conclusive.

§ 5- COMMENTS ON PROFESSOR CELASUN'S COMMENTS

Above, 2 notes by Professor Celasun are reproduced.Their reading should make my ideas about magnification of the loss of deteriorating external terms of trade more comprehensible. He validates my suggestion by simple mathematics. As I corrected my slip in the first version, it would be useful to list my comments about his comments on my ideas expressed in 1990.

1-His comment about my assertion about the neglect the B good prices in the deflation of national income is irrelevant. I definitely include B goods in the calculation of national income after the devaluation. All I do is to include a value dimension in the calculation of national income, if there is a change in relative prices.

2-It is quite clear that in his deflation of national incomes of various periods he keeps relative prices the same all the times.But my main difference with traditional analyses is that if that is done, the value dimension in comparing national incomes over time would be lost.

3-In my present comments I tried to show that 2 conditions, i.e., factor price equalization and internal equilibrium, should be fulfilled.That required that B good prices had to change, whereas he did not notice that requirement.

4-In his Note 2 he changes relative prices of A and B goods and also he deflates the new national income figure by the hybrid goods prices index.That is inconsistent.The deflation by the hybrid goods price index would give rise to a change in relative prices.That was a double counting.

5-He increases A good prices from $ 10 to $ 11.1 and he decreases that of B goods from $ 12 to $10.666. My reasoning requires also a change in relative prices. But the factor I draw upon is different from his.

CHAPTER V

THE DEVELOPMENT OF UATE

§ 1- INTRODUCTION

UATE was published in 1978.Following its publication two steps were taken in the late 1980s.One was the explanation of the loss caused by the deterioration of the external terms of trade on national income(Chapter IV), and the other was the questioning of PPP approach (§ 2, 3,4 in this chapter).The next step was the publication of the book entitled COMMENTS ON CONVENTIONAL ECONOMICS IN THE LIGHT OF THE TURKISH EXPERIENCE which appeared in 1990.lt was a book of 312 pages.Along with a summary of UATE,and a reproduction of the above mentioned two steps , improved versions of almost every subject dealt with in UATE were included in this book.

In 1980, Turkey switched to an export orientation policy .UATE was the description of an economy adopting an import substitution policy and its consequences.In 1990, I could observe what was happening in the economy and also I could see if my predictions came true or not.This would make it possible to judge if the theory launched in UATE was right.The most original aspects of this book could be very shortly summarized under 7 headings.

1-The theory of growth relating to the impact of the shift of resources from agricultural to nonagricultural sectors was transported to nonagricultural sectors in the sense that this time the consequences of the relative prices of labor and nonlabor intensive goods in nonagricultural sectors are sought by the method suggested in UATE.I started to talk about labor and nonlabor intensive goods instead of tradable and nontradable goods.

2-Rents underwritten in UATE are related to earning differences;they are explained more in-depth by a devoting a chapter to the understanding of the nature of earning differences between nonagricultural and agricultural sectors.In fact,this chapter is reproduced above (Chapter III in this book).

3- The next important idea was expressed about the meaning of the purchasing power parity index in measuring national income. I tried to show that there was something wrong in the traditional approach based on this method. I showed under simplifying assumptions that if that procedure is used as it was, the change in labor prices would not give rise to any change in national incomes expressed in terms of purchasing parity power of the currency of the country, whereas my main discovery was that this was not true and the change in labor prices should affect national income. (§ 2 bellow)

4-But that analysis was based on the assumption that there was only one factor of production; I changed it and I assumed that there were two factors of production, labor and capital. After that is done, I tried to show that if labor prices were expensive for exporting labor intensive goods, they should be made cheaper, and as a result they could be exported. In that case my contention expressed above could be made more practical and meaningful. What is more important is that I started to introduce the differentiation of labor and nonlabor intensive goods. (§ 4 bellow)

5-The existence of rents caused protection was discussed extensively by Professor Krueger under the title of rent seeking activities. She tried to show that rents created by an import subsitution policy would be shared by rent seeking activities. The main idea was that rents were inconsistent with the operation of market mechanism; yet, I tried to contend that although rents were created as a result of the policy of import subsitution (like Professor Krueger), they would be annihilated by the lower growth and decrease of the level of national income rather than by rent seeking activities (§ 5-6-7 bellow)

6-One of the most important renovation of this book was perhaps my attact to the methodolgy suggested by Little, Scitovsky and Scott in the book entitled INDUSTRY AND TRADE IN SOME DEVELOPING COUNTRIES. The example to validate my views was not properly stated; yet it was of a character to imply what I used to mean in those years,or to say differently,it forestalled my present version of the unconventional theory.The authors were trying to measure the impact of protection on the magnification of national income practicing it,and they were puting forward a methodolgy based on the increase of value added of industrial goods (and partly agricultural ones) as a result of production under protection. They measure it by using world prices and they decrease it by a multiplier based on changes in world prices multiplied by an adjustment of balance of payments, whereas I tried to show that this was not the case and a dimension of value should be included in calculations. In other words, the change of net foreign exchange reciepts should not be enough to judge the impact of protection on national income. (see § 8 bellow)

7-One of the innovation was to show the necessity of measuring of factor shares in national income hypothetically,and I tried to devise a diagram to show it.

I should also mention the book entitled ECONOMIC THEORY AND THE TURKISH EXPERIENCE which appeared in 1995. Explanations in this book were somewhat improved versions of the previous book.The most salient feature of this book was perhaps the explanation of service or labor prices in depth. What was more important was that the explanations in this book forestalled the present interpretation of the impact of relative prices on national income. I include a long passage from that book to show what I meant.Below is the extract from this book,pp. 88-92.

The explanations there were crude and equivocal, yet they indicated or suggested the most important ingredient of the present version of my views about the impact of relative prices on national income.I think they forestalled my main discovery ,the level effect.Hints are apparent about the impact of changing costs on the level of national income.It is shown that if there is a change in costs in terms of volume, this change of costs would be captured in traditional analyses.Yet, if the price of one factor of production changes with respect to the other, it should affect national income.In my recent work, I tried to show that if labor prices become lower relatively to other factors of production, this amounts to a decrease of national income. (see the extract. § 9 bellow)

The next stage is the publication of the book entitled AN ABSTACT OF CONVENTIONAL AND UNCONVETIONAL ECONOMIC ANALYSES

In my 1999 writings the differentiation of growth and level effects appeared first time. I separated them by one example and also by one diagram. The example related to growth and level effects. Here is the example.

We suppose that national income is $ 1OO. The value of labor intensive goods is $ 70 and that of nonlabor intensive ones is $ 30. Again, suppose that next year the production of each category of goods increases by 5 percent. This means that the national income of the country increases by 5 percent. Now let us change one of our assumptions . We suppose that the production of goods in terms of quantity was as before but as a result of the decrease in prices of labor intensive goods, the market value of them is $ 50 now. In that case the growth of the national income would be 4 percent:

($50x 0. 05) +($30x0. 05)= 0. 04.

It is clear that the growth rate went down from 5 percent to 4 percent. I called this the growth effect given rise by the change of relative prices.

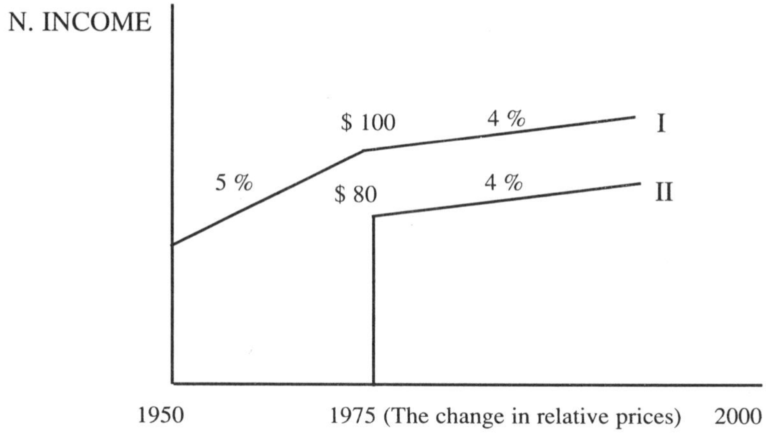

I showed the growth effect by means of a diagram. The change of the growth rate of the national income was depicted by decreasing the slope of the line showing the behavior of national income. Suppose the grand period was between 1950 -2000. And suppose that the relative prices of labor decreased in 1975. From that date on we could see the decrease of national income growth. Yet, at this date a second line parallel to the previous one is drawn, but its level was much lower. lt corresponded to a lower national income. Both the growth and level of national income was lower now. Why was the level lower? This was what I called the level effect. In 1999 I could not identify properly why. All I used to say was that after 1975 its level (national income) should be lower because lower imports and higher exports were compatible with this lower level of national income. And also as underlined in Section 5 below exports were considered vital for sustaining income and if they were taken as reference or a standard of measurement, the national income level should be low, yet sustainable.

A proportion of the fall of national income in 1975 should be related to growth effect and the other proportion level effect. In order to see the total fall in the grand period (1950-2000) we had to bring them together. I did not do so in my 1999 writings. Yet, I could separate two different factors impacting the growth and level of national income.

In 1999 essay I also stressed the fact that this analysis was important for the projection of national income. In order to explain it, I gave an example. I supposed that the growth rate was 5 percent in the first subperiod , 1970-1980, and it went down to 4 percent in the second subperiod, 1980-1990. When future growth is projected , one is tempted to say that it should be 4.5 percent, (5+4/2=4.5), whereas the expectation according to the theory it should be even less than 4.5 percent, and this is due to the impact of both level and growth effects.

N.B. In 2008 I perceive that the above statement was not as strong as I intended to say. It was right as far as growth effect was concerned. But as 1980 national income should be made lower as a result of the level effect, the welfare loss was much more than the reduction of the growth rate from 7 to 5 percent in future. This was my important discovery, which I was not aware of in 1999.

In order to validate my expectations I looked into the Turkish example. As a result of a real devaluation of 50 percent in the 1980 s the national income should be 40 percent less according to the new theory. If it increased by 3. 8 percent annually (the actual figure) from 1979 to 1996, it should be $ 92,406 million. It was astonishing that the actual figure was $91, 805 million. All that meant that if we verify the theory by means of the behavior of prices in terms of dollars, the expectation of the theory would be verified by facts. In fact, it was shown that national income of Turkey in 1975 which was officialy estimated as 183(billion Tl) was reduced to 103, which was 40 percent less than what it was in 1975 (see § 10 bellow).

§ 2 - THE IMPACT OF AN INCREASE IN EXPORTS OF COMPARATIVE AND NONCOMPARATIVE ADVANTAGE GOODS ON THE ECONOMY (1991)

In this section the determination of relative prices of A, B and D (services) goods along with the case of exporting previously noncompetitive goods will be studied. The effects of exporting A and/or B goods on relative prices will be investigated. The impact of changes of relative prices on the national income will be discussed later.

Firstly, an example will be given in order to show the determination of relative prices of A, B and D goods. Let us remember that D goods are labor and A and B goods are produced by D goods only. There is perfect competition and the price of each good is equal to its cost of production.

We suppose that for the production of 1 A, 2 D's and for the production of 1 B, 1 D is required. If there are 6 D's and if 1 A and 2 B are produced, the rest, i.e., 2 D's are used as services. (This is a developing country.)

We suppose that the exchange rate is fixed as 1 L = $1 (L is the currency unit of the country in question and $ is the international currency unit). A is exportable. If we ignore transportation costs, custom duties, etc., and if the price of A goods in foreign countries is $1, it should be 1 L in our country. (The prices of tradable or exportable goods should be the same in both countries.) As a result of the factor price equalization theorem, the price of B should be 0.50 L and that of D, 0.50 L. Altogether the income of the country should be 3 L or $3.

Now suppose that the cost of production in the trade partner is as follows:

2 D's produce 1 A,

1 D produces 2 B's

In that case the relative prices in the trade partner is as follows (the price of D is considered to be $ 0.50; this is because of the fact that international price of A goods is $ 1).

A = $1, B = $0.25, and D = $0.50

If that country has 6 D's, this suggests that the national income of the second country (the developed one) is $3.00 (it is supposed that 1 A, 4 B's are produced and 2 D's are used as services). If the national income of the country in question (the first country) is evaluated in those prices, the purchasing power of the income of the country in terms of dollars should be $2.50, calculated as follows:

1 A =	$1.00
2 B =	$0.50
2 D =	$1.00
	$2.50

It was discovered that if the national income of the developing country (3L) was converted by means of the official rate ($1 = 1L), it was $3, whereas if the international purchasing power of the national income (PPP) was calculated, the total would be $2.5 (see below).

This seems quite contrary to the expectations in the literature. It is shown that there is a downward bias in the national income of developing countries if it is expressed by means of an international standard using the official exchange rate as the conversion unit. In a richer country, the average wage can buy more goods and services relative to wages in a less developed country. On the other hand, wages tend to be equal both for traded and nontraded goods industries. Labor is more efficient in developed countries relative to developing countries. (In our case B goods are produced more efficiently; that is why this abnormal conclusion arises.) However, it is relatively more so in traded goods industries in developed countries. There is a very important implication in the above observation. If per capita incomes in a developed and developing country are compared, each expressed by a common standard, which is determined by the prices of traded goods, there would be a downward bias in per capita income of a developing country. The downward bias is caused, to repeat, by the close relationship between traded goods prices and those of international goods on the one hand and relatively lower prices of nontraded goods, on the other.

The conclusion above shows that it is just the contrary. The country in question is definitely less developed compared to its trade partner in the sense that the cost of production of B is less in the trade partner.

It will be shown that the difference of income in purchasing power or the bias depends on the kinds of goods which are exported, i.e., whether comparative or noncomparative advantage goods are exported. A good example for the developing country in question is the one which has huge petroleum reserves.

Now let us suppose that the country in question (the first country) turns outward and a substantial devaluation is made. The dollar is made 2 L; let us remember that it was 1 L before.

As a result, B goods could be sold in foreign countries. We suppose that there are as many D's as before, and A and B are produced at the same quantity, i.e., 1 A, 2 B and 2 D. In terms of official exchange rate the national income of the country is:

1 A = $1.00

2 B = $0.50

2 D = $0.25

$1.75

An explanation is needed. As B is exported, its price should be the same as it is in foreign countries. It is $0.25. Therefore its price is $0.25. In this case the price of D should be $0.125. As 2 D's are required to produce 1 B and as the price of 1 B is equal to $0.25, the factor price equalization theorem would make it equal to $0.25. Altogether 2 D's should be equal to $0.25. The international price of A goods is $1. (There is not a terms of trade loss.) As a result, its price in the country should be $1 or 2 L. Here we have an inconsistency with factor price equalization theorem. Although both 1 A and 2 B goods are produced by means of 2 D's, the price of A goods is twice as much compared to B goods. This means that the producers of A goods earn rents and this is not compatible with equilibrium conditions. Would producers not increase their production in order to earn more rents? Let us suppose, at the cost of altering our assumptions, that it is not possible due to the lack of specialized factors for its production such as natural resources or if they are produced, their cost would increase or there would not be enough time for switching factors from B to A. In other words, this annihilates our assumption that other factors are not used in conjunction with D or in order to produce A, different D's are used, i.e., their quality is different. (Later another more satisfactory solution will be presented.)

In terms of lira national income of the country would be 3.50 liras:

1 A = $1.00 = 2 L

2 B = $0.50 = 1 L

2 D = $0.25 = 0.50 L(*)

3.50 L

(*) 1 D is $0.125

If this is converted into dollars ($1=2L), the national income would be $1.75. Here is a summary: (The increase in imported goods prices is not considered.)

	$1=1L	$1=2L
National income in official $ rates	$3	$1.75
National income in L	3 L	3.50 L
National income in purchasing power parity	$2.5	$2.5
National income in constant L	3 L	3 L

The upshot of the above analysis is that the devaluation and the export of goods which have less competitive advantage would give rise to changes in the national income measured in terms of dollars. On the surface, this seems to be evident, and it does not mean much. In simple terms, if the dollar rate increases by 100 percent while domestic prices remain the same, national income in dollars decreases by 50 percent.

Based on the above conclusion many economists conclude that the change in the level of national income in terms of dollars is not relevant from the point of view of the welfare of the country: because the change of national income in terms of dollars does not show the change of the national income with the exception of the welfare loss caused by the deteriorating terms of trade. But on the other hand, the above conclusion suggests that the level of the national income in terms of its international purchasing power (PPP) does not mean much either. Simply because the calculations based on this method do not reveal the difference in welfare whether the country exports goods having comparative advantages or noncomparative advantages. According to the example above, the national income was $2.5 both at the beginning and the terminal years in terms of the purchasing power parity, whereas it was $3 and $1.75 in terms of official dollar.

The gist of the analysis lies in the following fact: the level of the national income in terms of dollar reflects the fact whether exports are based on goods having comparative or noncomparative advantages. In other words, if goods having comparative advantage are exported, the national income in terms of dollars will be more ($ 3) compared to the case when goods having no comparative advantages are exported. ($ 1.75)

Now, is the conventional belief as to the downward bias of national income calculated in terms of official exchange rates in developing countries wrong? Or are not services cheap in developing countries?

Here (by changing the foreign exchange rate) a discrepancy is created with respect to the changes in the national income in terms of dollars and L. They were the same in terms of dollar and L before the devaluation. Now they became different. And this is the result of different service prices in different countries. Before, service prices were $ 0.50 in both countries. Now while they are the same in the second country, they are 1/4 of the previous prices, i.e., $ 0.125, in the first country. As a result, national income in terms of dollar is lower than what it should be. This is due to the response of service prices to the devaluation.

N.B. (2009) When I read the above pages I noticed that this section could not be appreciated properly if the following additional explanations were not made. It is supposed at the beginning that the disadvategeous bias previewed in traditional literature is related to the measurement of national income of the developing country, whereas it shown that before the devaluation the national income of the developing country was calculated higher than it was. What was the reason of this contradiction? When the example in the original text is read it will be perceived that the developing country used to sell the commodity in which it had comparative advantages. (I called it A good). As a result, the exchange rate had to be determined according that transaction. Yet, after the devaluation the developing country could sell the goods in which its productivity (B goods) was less compared to the developed country. As a result, the exchange rate should depend on that relationship. In fact, in actual cases the B goods were labor intensive ones. Then, if the productivity advantage of the developed country in A good is more compared to labor intensive ones (B goods), the previewed bias is expected. Yet, eveything would depend on whether the developing country is selling A or B goods.

What I meant in this essay was that if the relative advantage of A good is more compared to B goods and if the developing country used to sell A goods, this bias should not exist.

§ 3 -THE VALIDITY OF PURCHASING POWER PARITY (PPP) METHOD IN MEASURING NATIONAL INCOME (1991)

In the original example in the previous section, it was supposed that there was only one factor of production and relative prices of A and B goods were the same, and only A goods could be exported in the first case. I changed that assumption and supposed that the existence of several factors of production could be possible; relative prices of A and B goods could change and B goods could also be exported. I tried to measure the loss in national income if B goods were exported.

I showed it by means of an example. According to the example if B goods were sold abroad by reducing their relative prices vis-a-vis A goods after a devaluation, the loss in national income should not be measured by means of PPP. Actually it is a well accepted practice that as the prices of various goods measured by means of official exchange rates are different in different countries, the relative welfare of each country should not be compared by per capita incomes calculated by a common currency, let us say dollars. This is especially true when it is remembered that as labor prices are lower in less developed countries compared to developed ones, per capita income of a less developed country should buy more goods compared to what it should if calculated by official rates of dollars.

It is supposed that if the country devalues its money and if as a result, it sells B goods, which are supposed to be labor intensive goods, its national income calculated by means of PPP would stay the same. Then I questioned the validity of PPP method. My example showed that the multiplier between national income calculated by PPP and official dollar prices would increase and yet we would say that national income in PPP was the same if labor prices were much lower in the second case, whereas we know that the multiplier in question is higher in less developed countries: the fact that the multiplier is higher means that the country is poorer. That example was important simply because it showed the deficiency of PPP method; its importance related to the impact of relative prices on the level of national income: it would open new horizons for future research.

Actually when I developed that line of thought what I had in my mind was to show that the export of less competitive goods should affect the level of national income, whereas PPP was not indicating it. Exporting less competitive goods could be possible by means of reducing their prices vis-a-vis external prices. But this should not mean that labor prices would be lower in the country.

§ 4 - THE FACTOR INTENSITY AND GROWTH (1991)

In the previous case, it was assumed that there was one factor of production. In this section, we assume that there are two factors of production, i.e., labor and capital. The other assumptions are the same except that there are two B goods rather than one.

We suppose that the country has a dual economy: a poor agricultural sector (A) along with a relatively richer nonagricultural sector (B). Let us assume that in the agricultural sector one commodity only is produced: cotton, which is partly exported, partly used for home consumption. In the nonagricultural sector two commodities are produced: refrigerators and textile goods.

Until 1980, we suppose that the country used to export cotton (an agricultural product) in order to import one import good: petroleum products. The main reason why cotton could be exported was the very low earnings in the agricultural sector of the country compared to the nonagricultural sectors.

But when it was found out that exporting cotton was not enough for importing the necessary quantity of petroleum products for the smooth running of the economy, the country decided to export one or both of the commodities produced in the nonagricultural sectors of the economy. As goods produced in that sector of the economy were expensive (at the then existing exchange rate) in foreign markets, a high rate devaluation of currency was made, and $/Lira parity increased by 100 percent. This made textile products competitive on the world markets, and enough of them were sold to finance the necessary imports.

If the relative price of refrigerators and textile products ($P_{R/T}$) were the same before and after the devaluation, the export of textile products should be attributed to two facts.

1. The techniques of producing textile products were more in line with foreign countries compared to refrigerators.

2. Textile products were more labor intensive compared to refrigerators and labor, which was relatively more abundant to capital compared to its trade partners, was made cheaper after the devaluation.

According to the expectation of the Heckscher-Ohlin theory textile products should be exported and refrigerators should be imported. Actually, this was not the case; and the country had to continue its refrigerator production and also had increase its textile products exports in order to import more petroleum products, which were imported previously by exporting agricultural products, cotton.

The country had to produce a great proportion of the previously produced goods in import substituting industries (refrigerators) simply because the need for imports of petroleum products was too great in the sense that a good proportion of the revenue received from the sale of textile goods should be used for it and no allocation could be made to import refrigerators. On the other hand, exporting possibilities of textile goods was limited because of certain constraints. First of all, textile goods were not homogeneous commodities such as petroleum goods which could be exported at any quantity without reducing prices too much. As a result of all sorts of differentiation and trade restrictions against increasing textile exports, high reductions in prices were needed and there were two alternatives to achieve that gool. The first is an increase of the devaluation rate and the second was a relative decrease of textile goods prices vis-à-vis other goods, in our example cotton and refrigerators. Now let us take the first alternative, i.e., devaluation. It is known that there is a limit to devaluation simply because it has all sorts of undesired consequences. One is deteriorating terms of trade and the second is inflationary pressures. Both are known in literature. There is another factor worth mentioning, i.e., its impact on the viability of previously import substituted industry. Although there are contrary arguments, it is quite certain that high devaluations would make competing goods for import substituting industries expensive and those industries would be able to price those goods high, and as a result, there will be a misallocation of resources. There is one more factor here making textile goods expensive: the rapid and great increase of textile production would increase its cost of production.

All those factors would make devaluations more and more detrimental to the economy. In other words, to rely on textile goods for the satisfaction of additional import needs would necessitate very high devaluations, and this would be very detrimental to the economy. The other alternative to devaluations is to decrease the price of textile goods vis-à-vis cotton and refrigerators, If so, this would require less devaluation. Is that alternative feasible? It is. Let us see how this could be achieved.

We know that textile products are more labor intensive. If we want to reduce textile prices with respect to refrigerators, labor prices should be reduced. As the production of refrigerators absorbs less labor, the decrease in labor prices would make $P_{R/T}$ higher ($P_{R/T}$ is the relative price of refrigerators to textile products). This could be achieved by the following mechanism.

We assume that textile products are more labor intensive. As was mentioned at the beginning, monetary policy keeps the domestic price index lower than the rate of increase in cotton prices which is supposed to be equal to the devaluation rate. In this case, the price of B goods, i.e., textile goods and refrigerator prices, decreases. But since textile goods are more labor intensive, and if the price of capital is more in line with international prices, service prices should decrease more compared to refrigerators prices.

It is quite evident that this expectation is contrary to the prediction of the Heckscher-Ohlin theory, according to which as more labor intensive goods were sold, the price of labor with respect to capital would have to increase. But under the circumstances described above this would not occur in the country. It is shown that capital intensive refrigerators had to be produced in the home country. Yet the price of textile products should be lower vis-à-vis that of refrigerators. The only way to achieve that is a decrease in the price of labor. This a sort of Ricardo effect. Ricardo had based it on the stability of general prices. I base it on the lower textile goods prices which were necessary for the smooth functioning of the operation of the economy. What a contrary expectation to the Heckscher-Ohlin theorem! In this book it is shown that the relative decrease in labor prices will give rise to a decrease in national income level and its growth. If this is so, it is demonstrated that there is a relationship between the growth rate of national income in constant national currency and its level in terms of dollars, i.e., when national income in dollars decreases its rate of growth in terms of constant domestic currency should also decrease. (More labor intensive goods are sold after the devaluation, a present note.)

§ 5- COMMENTS ON RENT (2009)

After having explained the alternative rent concepts and the difference of my rents with them I would like to add a few words in order to underline what I wanted to mean by rents.

Rent in microeconomics is the difference between offer and actual prices. According to the expectation of market mechanism as a result of the response of new production they (rents) are not sustainable in most cases(if the response is not expected or possible rents would remain.).Rents I am talking about are earned in the whole economy.They are not sustainable like others.Yet,equilibrium in this case is established not by increasing the production of rent earning commodities but by decreasing national income.This is because of the impossibilities of increasing the production of every commodities.The existing resources(inputs),the productivity and organization standards would not allow communitywide increase of all commodities.Therefore, I tried to show that rents earned in nonagricultural sectors of the economy should shrink as a result of a decrease of the national income of this sector.

§ 6- Krueger Rents and Beyond (Extracts from 1990 Book)

I have improved my concept of rent in post-1980 years in view of export orientation experience of the Turkish economy, and now it is based on a more solid foundation. In order to show it, it would be useful to review shortly the well known Krueger analysis relating to rents and their distribution by rent seeking activities.

Professor Krueger in her article (1974) discusses the resource allocational effects of rent creating activities, especially import licenses. She mentions several costs of import licenses: paperwork, the time spent by entrepreneurs in obtaining their licenses, the cost of the administrative apparatus necessary to issue licenses, the creation of higher capacities in order to obtain greater allocation of licenses in the case of investment and intermediate goods, the greater number of firms trying to obtain licenses for consumer goods, trips to the capital city, locating the firm in the Capitol, bribery, hiring relatives of officials, etc.

Professor Krueger tries to measure the resource cost of all these activities under very simplified conditions and relate it to the south-west shift of the community's indifference curve, which shows decrease in community's welfare.

Essentially the reasoning by Krueger leads to the main conclusion of Chapter III of this book: the earnings difference between nonagricultural and agricultural sectors is a source as well as a measure of rents earned in a country. She arrives at this conclusion under most simplified conditions. Her reasoning can be shown by quoting a passage from her article.

"Two commodities are consumed by the country under investigation: food and consumption goods. Food is produced domestically and exported. Consumption goods are imported. Distribution is a productive activity whereby a good is purchased from the agricultural sector, exported, and the proceeds are used to import consumption goods which are sold in the domestic market. Labor is assumed to be the only domestic factor of production. It is assumed that the country under consideration is small and cannot affect its international terms of trade. Physical units are selected so that the fixed international prices of both goods are unity" (Krueger 1974 p. 295).

Under free trade there is a free entry into both agriculture and distribution and competition equates the wage in the two activities.

If trade is restricted by import restrictions, the labor used in distribution will be reduced due to less imports (less distribution service is needed), and more labor will be used in agriculture causing a decrease in agricultural wages because of diminishing returns in agriculture. On the other hand, prices of imported commodities increase because of their restricted quantity. Labor being less after the imposition of trade restrictions in the distributive sector, a greater margin will be distributed among fewer laborers.

All this means that there will be an earning difference between the two sectors: this difference is called rent by Krueger. But competition requires that rents earned in the distributive sector should be shared by agricultural laborers as a result of their performing the rent seeking activities described above. In other words, competition does not exist vis - à - vis foreign goods but it exists within the country. It tends to equalize earnings between the two sectors of the economy by creating rents first and then attracting agricultural labor to the nonagricultural sector (here distributive sector) to share them.

Professor Krueger's aim is not to study further this aspect of rent creation but she is interested in its resource cost. Apart from the dissimilar aims in studying rents, earning diferences studied in this book are investigated within a diferent framework from hers. Actually, in our framework the competition between two sectors is not assumed due to the assumption of duality. This assumption prevents the exhaustion of rents. This does not mean that rent sharing activities (resource cost) could not take place in the nonagricultural sectors. But they will take place at the cost of either decreasing agricultural earnings or swelling the income level of the nonagricultural sector. In her analysis rent is a temporary phenomenon giving rise to disequilibrium; in our model rents may exist in equilibrium conditions.

Her analysis is very important and illustrative. Moreover, she shows that rents are reflected by the earning differences between two sectors. However, it does not give any clue to the actual amounts of rents that can be earned in a country. One of the most important problems here is the relationship between the resource costs caused by rents and their amount. More important than that is the amount of rents that can be earned in a country. Could rents be increased by an unlimited amount? If not, what is the limit to them? A clue is suggested in UATE as to their actual magnitude and their actual measure.

Now let us suppose that at the end of import restriction rents increase. But what is the highest limit of rents created in this way? It is the consequence of this analysis that by just contemplating the community's transformation curve and elasticities nothing much can be learned about the magnitude of rents, especially when the community transformation curve shifts to the right at the end of protection. Moreover, it is very dubious that under actual circumstances all rents would be exhausted by higher resource costs.

In my opinion the cost of rent seeking activities and the high cost of import substituting activities appear identical. In Krueger's version, the supply of imports is restricted, and, therefore, the services making them saleable on the domestic market are also restricted. As the price of imports in import originating countries were the same as previous, the price increase of restricted imports would be reflected in domestic services which would rise its price.

According to my version, the increase of the prices of goods as a result of using resources in fields having low comparative advantages is considered rent. If this is examined further from the national point of view, little difference between the cost increase caused by rent seeking activities and the high cost of import substituting activities is observed. Demand for goods produced by import substituting activities and demand for rent seeking activities is the determining factor for both rent seeking and import substituting industries.

The difference with Krueger

Going one step further, I have attempted to demonstrate that a proportion of rents, whether of the Krueger type, or resulting from an overvaluation of goods cannot be sustained. If so, national income based on them is could not to be sustained. I am tempted to call this proportion of national income as rent, and tried to measure it by a new method I have developed.

Before 1980, in my writings this measure was based on a difference of agriculture and nonagricultural earnings. But after that time my definitions have to an extent altered.

In Krueger, per capita earnings in agriculture was used as the point of reference to measure rents. Before 1980 I also followed this method. Now I believe that if the difference between nonagricultural and agricultural earnings can be sustained, they should not be considered as rent. Only that part of income which is unable to be sustained should be called as rent.

According to Krueger, rent is a result of the high prices of imported goods caused by their shortage. In my version, part of the price increase due to high production costs was also called rent. But 1 also questioned the nature of the community demand and factors determining it. The establishment of import substituting industries would enhance community demand which, in turn, would create rents. But the community would have difficulties in sustaining this high income. In order to appreciate this more fully a review of the definition of the national income is required. I tried to show that the these rents could not be annihiliated by rent seeking activities, but this would be possible by a lower national income.

§ 7- Towards a New Definition of Notional Income (Extract from 1990 Book)

The national income is probably the most practicable measure of index of the material welfare. As material welfare is the goal of all economic activities it should be properly measured. The standard approach is to measure material welfare in terms of domestic currency. As a result, the increase of the national income should be equal to the difference of national income in constant domestic currency between the first and base period. But this method fails when the incomes as well as their rates of increase in two different countries need to be compared. The national income of both countries should be measured by the same standard (let us say dollars) in order to compare them. There is literature which deals with the problems which arise from expressing the national income by the same standard, e.e., dollars (Kravis et al. 1975; see Chapter V above).

Let us suppose that the problem of comparing the national incomes of different countries is somehow solved. Would the yardstick to measure the change of national income by means of a constant currency be an appropriate one and would the same measure be used to compare it with foreign incomes?

The method developed by Kravis is very appealing and it is employed widely (for its application in Turkey see, Özcumur 1987). It is used to compare the incomes of countries with different levels of development, and findings based on this method may be used to measure the change of the income of a country between two periods. Actually, this method might be assistance if there is a significant difference between the figures in terms of national currency and in dollars. For example in 1950-1988 the annual average rate of increase of Turkish national income was 5.7 percent in constant national currency but 4.1 percent in constant dollars. Between 1980 and 1988 the yearly rate of increase was 5.6 in constant national currency but minus in constant dollars. Which was true? Could the nethod employed by Kravis give an answer?

In my opinion the method employed by Kravis is very limited. Consumption levels of various countries (especially at different stages of development) can be compared and conclusions drawn with regard to their relative welfare, but that is as far as the application of his method extends. The point is that when measuring national income it must be borne in mind that national income is a dynamic and not static concept. National income should be a point of reference for the future development of the country in the sense that future levels of national income should be compared with previous ones to observe that country's development. Here, the Kravis measurement based on the purchasing power parity method fails. To give another example; according to conventional measurements in terms of dollars the per capita income in Turkey was approximately $1200 in 1986, whereas by the method employed by Kravis the figure amounted to $4000 (see Özcumur 1986). Now suppose that the annual growth potential of the country (per capita income) is four percent. Does this mean that the per capita income will increase by $ 160 each year? And would this tendency continue? Of course, it is unacceptable to think in these terms. The growth should be based on the previous figure -$1200- and the cathing up of the high income countries should be based again on the latter figures. In other words, a country's growth is related to its national income based on the conventional method and not by the calculations employed by Kravis. Moreover, another dimension of the measurement of growth is the discrepancy between figures in terms of local currency and dollars. The Kravis method does not cover this.

§ 8- The Method Developed by Little, Scitovsky and Scott (1970) (Extracts from 1990 Book)

In order to compare the national income expressed by domestic currency with the incomes of other countries, and to compare the change of national incomes in different periods, the value added of each industry can be expressed by world prices.

There are several complications in this procedure. The method used by Little, Scitovsky and Scott (LSS) in their well known book (1970) is described in brief below.

The value added of industry is expressed by world prices first and then adjusted according to the expenditure patterns of income earned in other fields of economic activity. Half of agricultural income is taken as its is and the other half expressed in world prices and adjusted like industry value added. The income of the service sector is expressed in domestic currency.

National income may be expressed either in terms of national currency or in an international standard such as dollars. Prices are adjusted according to world prices and the particular conditions of the country are also taken into consideration. In both cases -whether national income is expressed in terms of domestic currency or dollars- the calculation is to some extent based on the official exchange rate. For example, when new value added is calculated in terms of domestic currency it is converted to dollars by means of the official rate.

The idea behind expressing industrial and some agricultural goods in terms of world prices is as follows. Tradable goods may be exported and imported and their prices are higher as a result of protection. On the other hand, if the price of services is maintained at the level that they should be, the higher prices of those goods would create an overvaluation of the national income. Yet if the income based on overpriced goods is spent on goods and services which, in turn, are overvalued, the adjustment of industrial goods according to world prices is unjustified. Therefore, the valuation of goods and services, on which income earned in tradable goods is spent, should also be taken into consideration.

The idea of adjustment with respect to income by world price is based on the effect of overpricing on the balance of payments. This is expressed by the authors as follows : "For the other half of agriculture and for the whole of manufacturing we have estimated value added at world prices, and then multiplied this by what can most simply be described as a rough measure of the overvaluation of the currency. The idea behind this is that value added by world prices gives a measure of marginal impact of tradeable output on the balance of payments, while to show the worth of this from the country's own point of view and in terms of its own currency, it must be corrected by the multiplicative factor, ϕ which is the ratio between internal and external values of a unit change in the balance of payments" (P. 73).

§ 9- Relative Prices and National Income (Extracts from 1995 book)

In this section, the effect of the changes of relative prices on the growth of the national income will be shown.

An understanding of the past growth of the Turkish economy and the projection of its future require a study of relative prices. To show it, let us take an example. Let us suppose that there are two commodities in the country: apples and pears. Two changes occur in the economy. Firstly, the production of both apples and pears increases by 20 percent. Secondly, the price of apples increases by 20 percent relatively to pears. According to the well known quantity indices, i.e., equations showing the increases of national income, the national income increase should be 20 percent. Both Laspeyres and Paasche indices would give the same figure.

$$\frac{\sum P_1Q_2}{\sum P_1Q_1} \times 100 \qquad\qquad \frac{\sum P_2Q_2}{\sum P_2Q_1} \times 100$$

Laspeyres Paasche

Prices are shown by P's, quantities by Q's and lower indices are related to periods. If the above figures are applied to those formulas, this is verified.

	The first period		The second	period
	P	Q	P	Q
Apples	10	100	12	120
Pears	10	100	10	120

If the national income during the first period was considered 100 the national income during the second period would be 120.

$$\text{Laspeyres } \frac{10x120+10x120}{10x100+10x100} \text{x}100=120$$

$$\text{Paasche } \frac{12x120+10x120}{12x100+10x100} \text{x } 100 =120$$

It is quite clear that although the price of apples has increased by 20 percent, relative to pears, we don't observe it in quantity indices used to calculate national income increases. Only quantity increases determine the increase in national income. Yet as the community values apples more highly compared to the first situation, something should have happened to the national income.

In that example the growth of production in each commodity is exactly the same. Under those circumstances we observe that the increase in the relative price of apples does not affect the national income. If, on the other hand, the growth rate of apples and pears were different two methods of measuring national income would have given slightly different results but the effect of price changes would not be visible. To see that situation let us give an example.

	Period 1		Period 2	
	P_0	Q_0	P_1	Q_1
Apples	100	100	120	140
Pears	100	100	100	120

$$\text{Laspeyres} \quad \frac{100x140+100x120}{100x100+100x100} = 30\%$$

$$\text{Paasche} \quad \frac{120x140+100x120}{120x100+100x100} = 31\%$$

It should not be lost from sight that an assumption is made above. There is an increase in the resources of the country and/or resources are more productively used, and as a result of which more apples and pears are being produced. There is a shift to right in production possibility curve. Again, as the prices of apples increase relatively to pears this would also mean a change in the indifference curve drawn between apples an pears. It is also evident that the relative increase of apple prices does not give rise to a change in the relative production of those two goods. Now, in order to analyze the situation better, let us assume that there is a budget constraint.

By a budget constraint we mean that the resources of the country to produce apples and pears are limited. They may diminish, stay constant or increase. In order to facilitate it let us suppose that labor is the only resource to be used for production.

A better assumption would be to add capital to labor and also to take productivity changes into consideration. Altogether we could talk of a productivity unit. But to make things easier let us talk of a labor unit.

In the example above we did not take into consideration the changes in the labor or productivity units which were concomitant with the increase of apples and pears production. As a result, we concluded that changes in relative prices would not affect the level of national income.

The example will be reconsidered under the budget constraint. It will be observed that relative prices would have an impact on national income. (N.B. I should underline that the example given below is only a beginning of my conception of the impact of relative prices on income) 2008

1. Let us assume that prices are equal to cost and there are constant returns, i.e., the increase in production would not give rise to costs. In that alternative the increase in production would be equal to increase in labor or productivity units. In

that case relative prices are irrelevant.

2. Suppose that the cost of apples increases relative to that of pears. When the national income is calculated it would be observed that the increase in national income would be less than that of resources. In other words, changes in relative prices would reflect on national income. Let us give an example. Suppose that total labor units at the beginning of the period was 20. It goes up to 22 units in the second period. The production of apples and pears in the second period is shown below.

	The first	period	The second	period
	P_0	Q_0	P_1	Q_1
Apples	5	10	5.45	11
Pears	5	10	5	10

Now let us show how the increase in national income is calculated. We assumed that labor units increased by 2. Suppose that the additional 2 units increase apple production by 1 unit. There are increasing costs. In that case, the average price of apples is $5.45. It is calculated as follows. The total spending of the community goes up from $100 to $110. (The actual number is not important; all we mean is that there is some 10 percent increase in spending.) As the price of pears is the same, $50 is spent on its production. The remaining 60 is spent on 11 apples making its price $5.45. The previous relative price between apples and pears was 5/5, i.e., 1, it went up to 5.45/5 or 1.09. If the known formulas are used to calculate the income increase we shall come up with 5 percent. (There is a slight difference between the P and the L.)

This example shows us that under certain circumstances relative prices would have an impact on the behavior of the national income. But this would not mean much in the sense that if the price change is parallel to costs, the growth of income would be caught by the increase of production rather than by changes in relative prices; relative prices were just balancing items. The effect of relative prices are, of course, important. But nothing we don't already know is shown,

3. Now, let us consider a different case. We suppose that the prices of apples and pears are not equal to the amount of labor units needed for their respective production. We suppose that both of them are produced by the same number of production unit. The price of pears is 4 times higher compared to that of apples This is what we observe in a dual economy. Now suppose that labor units are increasing by 5 percent. One labor unit produces either 1 apple or 1 pear. At the beginning period the country had 20 labor units, now it has 21 labor units.

	The second period		The first period		The second period	
	P	Q	P	Q	P	Q
Apples	5	10	5	10	5	11
Pears	20	11	20	10	20	10

By using those figures we shall calculate that if increased labor units were used in pear production, national income would increase by 8 percent; whereas if they were used in apple production the increase would be 2 percent. Let us remember that the increase in labor units was 5 percent.

This example shows us that relative prices would have an impact on the behavior of the national income.

4. It is shown above that the relationship between relative prices and the growth rate is quite visible when there is duality in the economy. Again, it can be shown that even if there is not duality, we may see that there is that relationship. In order to show it let us use the example given previously. In the country cloth and refrigerator are produced outside the agricultural sector of the economy. Relative Prices $P_{R/C}$ is 1. Suppose after outward orientation this ratio goes up to 2. We know that the relative cheapening of cloth is related to its labor intensive character of its production. If service prices decrease the relative price of cloth would be lower compared to refrigerators.

Now suppose labor is increasing in the country. An example will show us that as a result of 5% increase of labor the increase in the national income will be different when relative price of refrigerator and cloth was 1 or 2.

The first period ($P_{R/C}$ is 1)

	P_0	Q_0
Refrigerator	2	100
Cloth	2	100

In the second period $P_{r/c}$ is 2.

	When cloth production increases		When refrigerators production increases	
	P_1	Q_1	P_1	Q_1
Refrigerator	2	100	2	110
Cloth	1	110	1	100

According to the example above, if increasing labor is used in producing refrigerators and if we use Paasche index the growth in production is 6.66 percent, whereas if it is used in the production of cloth it will be 3.33 percent. If we use Laspeyres index the growth is always 5 percent.

Here there is a difficult question. Why would the economy prefer to produce cloth rather than refrigerators when refrigerator production would give rise to a higher rate of economic growth. In my previous writings I contended that this should be the case simply for the smooth functioning of the economy. But to prove the present conclusion it should be shown that it must be compatible with the profit maximization principle. But now I show that individuals are earning the same profit by using their resources (both labor and capital) in using them in the production of cloth and refrigerators. That means that the factor equalization theorem is valid and individuals are indifferent in producing cloth or refrigerator. In that case the production of cloth rather than refrigerators would give rise to a decrease in the growth of the economy.

§ 10 – THE 1999 VERSION OF THE UNCONVENTIONAL ANALYSIS (Original Text)(*)

1- The Extension of The Unconventional Analysis

The UATE was a preliminary and crude version of the unconventional analysis. In the following years it was refined and extended theoretically in such a way to cover events in the Turkish economy and what is more important, the foundation of a better theory of growth was laid.

In the first period, i.e., 1950-1977, the growth rate of the national income in Turkey was 6.4 percent. If it was analyzed by the source of growth approach, it would be found out that 3.93 percent of the growth of the national income should be attributed to input increases and the rest, i.e., 2.47 percent, to total productivity (TFP). When the same analysis was used for the nonagricultural sectors of the economy, where the growth rate was 8.18 percent, 4.80 percent of the growth could be attributed to the input increase and the rest, i.e., 3.78 percent to total factor productivity.

5.1 percent growth in 1980-1993 period should be decomposed as follows; 3.71 percent increase consisted of input increase and 1.39 percent total factor productivity. The growth of the nonagricultural sectors, which was 6.2 percent,

(*) *An Abstract of the Book Entitled Conventional and Unconventional Economic Analyses (1999), pp 28-41.*

could be disaggregated as follows: 5.2 percent input increases, and 1.0 percent total productivity growth.

Could the whole decrease in the growth rate be attributed to the diminishing impact of the ever decreasing shift of resources from agricultural to nonagricultural sectors. This could be effective to a certain extent but the whole decrease should not be explained by this factor only. As at the beginning of the second period the share of nonagricultural sectors was some 75 percent, the decrease should be sought in the dynamics of this sector. Moreover, when the growth of the nonagricultural sectors in two periods are compared, we could not take the impact of the shift into consideration, anyway. Although the growth of the whole economy should be under the influence of the shift of resources, this should not affect the behavior of nonagricultural sectors. Yet an important decrease in the TFP in the second period was much too visible.

Actually everything suggested that income should increase in the second period.

All changes after 1980 suggested an improvement in the performance of the economy: there were no more stops of the economy, no more scarcity of goods; the beneficial effects of rising exports, which increased from 4 percent of GNP to 14 percent, must have reflected on the economy, price mechanism operated much better, the foreign capital inflow quadripulated, the share of a more efficient private sector increased, what not...

As will be underlined below, the explanation of all economists didn't amount to anything reasonable.

The only factor which could affect the rate of growth negatively could be the impact of demand repressing measures taken after the economy shifted to the outward. But, on the one hand, this should lessen its intensity as time passed, and on the other hand, as a result of the ever existing inflation prevailing in the second period, it would be very difficult of talking of recessionary factors. Actually, figures show that the speed of increase of both investment and consumption was more after the turning point of the economy. Again, huge trade deficits and unbelievingly high foreign money inflows into the economy should annihilate those recessing impacts, if there were any.

The only visible factor which could be effective in accounting for the decrease of the growth of national income growth should be related to the change in calculating national income. As a result of the great fall of labor intensive goods vis-a-vis nonlabor intensive goods the weights to be given to several goods in measuring national income were altered after 1980.

In order to show the impact of the changes of relative prices on the growth rate of national income let us give an example.

We suppose that total national income is \$ 100. The value of labor intensive goods is \$ 70 and that of nonlabor intensive goods is \$ 30. Again, suppose that the production of each kind of goods increases by 5 percent.This means that national income of the country would increase by 5 percent. Now let us change one of our assumptions. We suppose that the production of goods in terms of quantity is the same but as a result of the decrease of the prices of labor intensive goods, the market value of labor intensive goods becomes \$ 50. If the increase of production of goods is the same as what it was in the previous example, i.e., 5 percent, the increase of national income would be 4 percent in terms of current prices:

$(50 \times 0.05) + (30 \times 0.05) = 0.04$

It must be noticed that in order that the growth rate should go down from 5 to 4 percent the absolute level of the national income after relative price changes should be \$ 80 rather than \$ 100, as was the case before. This important change will be taken up below.

Here the problem is to compare the new national income with the previous national income when the prices of labor intensive goods were not changed. Traditionally when two national income figures are compared it is supposed that absolute and relative prices were the same. In the above example whatever the price index which is used, either Laspeyres or Paasche, the growth of national income would be 5 percent, whereas in our unconventional calculation it is 4 percent. This is the difference of unconventional analysis.

If the relative prices change permanently and significantly, the constancy of relative prices should not be not assumed anymore. Again, in the unconventional approach I suggest a point of reference for the absolute level of national income in the sense that national income is measured in terms of one kind of the goods. Here in the Turkish case before 1980, as the bulk of exports were agricultural goods, the standard of measurement was agricultural goods, whereas after 1980 as the bulk of exports consisted of labor intensive goods, they are considered a point of reference or a standard of value. The reason for this practice is that exports are considered vital for the country. As stated at the beginning, international prices should be a constraint for exported goods while nonexported goods prices could be anywhere.

Here attention should be drawn on the practice in the first and the second period in Turkey. In the first period agricultural prices were taken as a point of reference and the relative price of the nonagricultural goods should be made lower hypothetically. As a result, national income calculations should be made on this basis. In the second period, the prices of nonlabor intensive goods should be left where they were, but those of labor intensive ones should be made lower parallel to the depreciation of the currency.

This is a very important change with respect to the point of reference. In the first case, (i.e., when natural resources intensive goods were exported) the point of reference was the prices of exported goods; but in the second case, i.e., when labor intensive goods are exported, we switch to a different point of reference. In that case the absolute level of the national income is made lower: the reference for the national income is the prices of labor intensive goods.

To repeat the main argument: when the relative prices change and when national income is calculated in terms of new prices and if the rod of measurement of national income is changed, the rate of growth can change without any quantity change in production. What is more important is the change in the absolute level of national income. According to the example given here both the rate of growth and the absolute level of national income must have decreased.

The change caused in the absolute volume of national income as a result of a change in relative prices should be looked into very carefully.

The main contention of the unconventional analysis is the impact of relative prices on the absolute level of the national income. It is asserted that when the relative prices of exported goods (in the present case the prices of labor intensive goods) decrease vis-a-vis the nonexported goods (here nonlabor intensive goods), the absolute level of national income must also decrease. This is because firstly, for the efficiency of the economic system and the sustainability of the national income growth, the amount of exports are very important, secondly, exportable goods can be transformed into nonexportable goods without any loss in their value, whereas nonexportable ones can be transformed to exportable goods only if their value decreases with respect to exportable goods. Those imply that exportable goods should be taken as a standard of value. On the other hand, if their price diminishes with respect to nonexported goods, the absolute level of national income decreases.

The measurement of national income should not be carried out in a vacuum. In the traditional analysis relative prices are taken the same all the time, the beginning or the end of the period prices, whereas according to the unconventional analysis when they change national income should be recalculated without any relation to past relative prices, and the level of the previous national income should be kept as it was, i.e., the change of relative prices should not affect its absolute level. This implies the use of inconsistent national income deflators and also when relative prices of exportable goods decrease, the absolute level of national income decreases.

There is more; there is a corelation between the absolute level of national income and several macro-magnitudes such as investments, savings, the share of various sectors in national income, government expenditure, etc., as demonstrated by empirical research by Chenery and his associates. As a result, the absolute level of national income should be adjusted when relative prices change. If it is thought as it was the same after relative price changes, an appropriate economic policy cannot be followed.

Here we need a clarification. It is shown that when the exports of previously exported goods are promoted by making their prices lower vis-a-vis the outside world, the loss of national income would be equal to the decrease in the volume to be consumed (and invested) in the country (which is equal to the traditional loss due to the terms of trade deterioration) plus an equal amount due to the impact of factor equalization theorem. (I called it as a magnifiying loss inflicted by the terms of trade deterioration loss.) When this loss was calculated it was supposed that the relative prices of exported and nonexported goods stayed the same, whereas in the present case the relative price of exported goods decreased with respect to nonexported goods. As a result, in addition to a loss caused by the terms of trade deterioration, there is another kind of loss due to the loss of value of exported goods vis-a-vis nonexported goods. If it is so this can, be shown in the diagram below. (Diagram V-1)

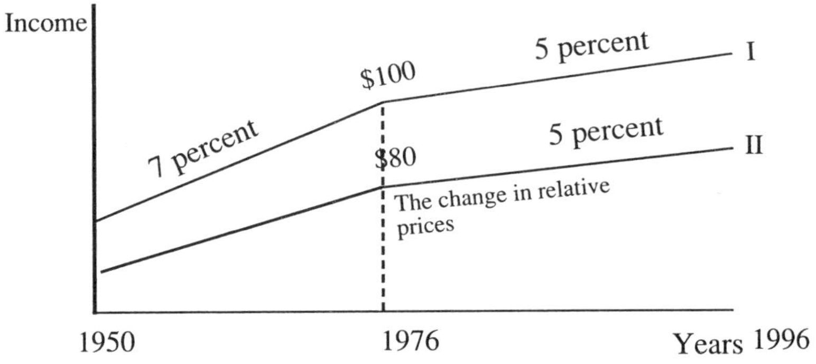

Diagram V-1

National Income After The Change of Relative Prices

The distance between line I and II would depend on the calculation of the national income in terms of new relative prices along with the fall of the prices of exported goods.

A very important consequece of the decrease of the growth and the absolute level of the national income is relevant in the projection of the future national income.

Let us give an example. We suppose that in 1970-1980 the growth rate was 7 percent. And in 1980-1990 it went down to 5 percent. When the future growth is projected, one is tempted to calculate it as 6 percent (7+5/2=6), whereas the expectation based on the unconventional analysis should make it (less than 5 percent, 2009) 5 percent. This is due to the relative decrease in the prices of the measuring rod of national income, here the prices of labor intensive goods. This must have very important implications in determining economic policy of the country.

This analysis is verified by the Turkish case. Let us look at it now.

2- The Theory And The Turkish Case

The observations after 1978 validated my expectations based on the above elaborated theoretical framework. The trend rate of growth has been somewhere around 4-5 percent after 1980. If we can discover the factors leading to the fall in the trend rate, we can refute the conventional theory easily. Before doing it, let us show that the fall in the trend rate was not temporary.

Many economists alleged that firstly, the fall of the growth rate of the economy was related to the quadripuling of the petroleum prices in the 70s and the depression in the world following it. As Turkey did not take necessary measures, the high external terms of trade loss would have to slow the economy. Secondly, the high devaluation rate of the currency and demand depressing measures would have to cause a decrease in the growth rate of the economy. Thirdly, the left wing economists asserted that the use of the price mechanism should slow down the economy.

If the naive arguments put forward by the left wing economists are ignored, the others, which seem to have substance, indicate that the causes of the slow down were temporary factors; the impact of which should not continue for such a long time. Moreover, as mentioned above, several factors should more than compensate them. Then, the conventional explanations are not worth anything.

Before answering this question more in depth, let us look at the diagram with figures relating to national income in Turkey. (Diagram V-2)

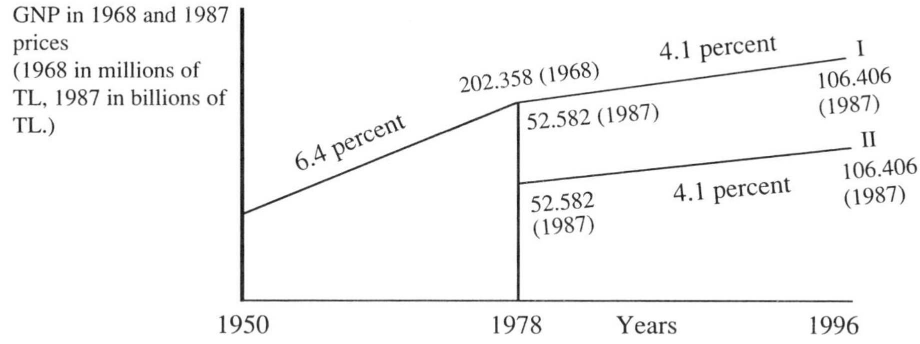

Diagram V-2
The Growth of the Turkish National Income.

In order to understand this diagram let us give a few explanations about the figures relating to national income. The first point to notice is the change of the base price in 1978. The base prices until 1978 are those of 1968 prices. After 1978, the base prices are those of 1987. Therefore the absolute income figures relating to pre-1978 should not be compared with those of the post-1978 ones. But one may presume that figures relating to income growth can be compared with each other. Here on the diagram, we have two lines, one starting after 1950 (line I) and the other below that line (line II). Again, it may be presumed that although the absolute figures cannot be comparable, both calculations would be exactly the same from the point of view of comparing growth rates. Let us try to explain the fall in the rate.

It will be shown right below that as the base prices were changed, a decrease in the growth rates had to occur under these circumstances. Let us remember that this is the most crucial point of the whole book. Starting from mid-1970s, the prices of labor decreased by 50 percent. As the share of wages was 44.7 percent of the national income in 1977, it became 20.2 percent in 1984. Again, although a bit equivocal, the real wages index, which was 212.9 in 1977, it became 110.6 in 1984 (the figures are all approximate). The low rate of wages must have been reflected on the prices differences of labor intensive and nonlabor intensive goods.

The most crucial contention of this book is that this widening of price ratios must push down the growth rate of the economy under certain conditions. But before looking into it, let us mention a most illustrative figure.

We have two calculations of the growth rate of the economy in 1968-1978 period: the one in terms of 1968 prices is 6.4 percent but the other in terms of 1987 prices is 5.2 percent. There is nothing more convincing than that: the relative lowering of the labor intensive good prices must have given rise to a decrease in the growth rate. Now its reason will be understood when we explain the fall of the growth rate after 1978.

Although there are other factors affecting the growth of national income, such as the diminishing impact of the shift of resources from agricultural to nonagricultural sectors and the impact of now more expensive and ever increasing volume of imported inputs, etc, the main reason of the decrease of national income is the change of relative prices of labor intensive goods, which should be considered as a point of reference.

Now the problem is to guess the distance between line I and II on the diagram, i.e., the decrease of the absolute level of national income. The unconventional analysis presumes that the decrease related to lower labor prices should make national income in terms of dollars lower after the full effect of the devaluation works itself out, which in this case is 30 percent as figures reveals.

Another point demonstrated by this analysis is that the decrease in the growth of national income should coincide with the fall of the absolute level of national income. The impact of this conclusion is immense for the theory as well as for the search of economic policy. All those problems are taken up in this book.

This conclusion would illuminate a very important discussion; should we measure national income in terms of constant national prices or in terms of foreign currency prices? If the belief as to the coincidence of the decrease of the national income and the decrease in the growth rate is true, the expression of national income in terms of a foreign currency is the true measure of national income. (in the long run). As shown above, otherwise we cannot understand the causes of the decline in the growth rate of the economy.

The decrease in national income after the devaluation is not only necessary for a comparison with the outside world, it also reflects the impact of relative prices on national income.

3- A Point of Reference for the Absolute Level of National Income in Terms of Dollars

The explanations in the previous section show that if the price of one good diminishes relatively, this would give rise to a decrease in the growth of national income even if national income calculations are made traditionally. Let me show this diagramatically with the figures of the example to be given below.

We suppose that as a result of the change of the relative prices the growth rate of the national income, which was 7 percent before, went down to 5.4 percent. This is shown in Diagram V-4.

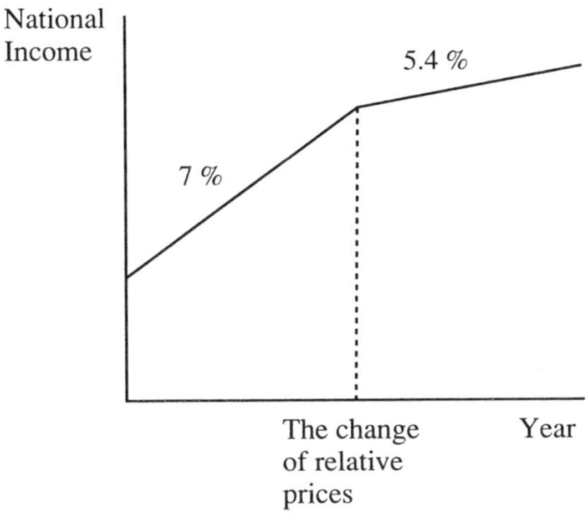

Diagram V-4
The Change of the Growth Rates

In the previous section it was shown that 1) if the relative prices of labor intensive goods decreases relatively to nonlabor intensive goods; and 2) if the proportion of labor intensive goods is higher compared to nonlabor intensive ones; and 3) if the price weights in the re-calculation of national income is changed, the growth of the national income would decrease.

Now let us give an example. We suppose that national income is $ 100, % 30 of which consist of labor intensive and and $ 70 are nonlabor intensive goods. When the price ratio of labor and nonlabor intensive goods was 1, the national income was $ 100 and 100 L ($1=1L). Now, suppose that the country was confronted with a necessity to increase its exports. But, on the other hand, the production of nonlabor intensive goods (they were the main items of exports previously) could not be increased. As a result, labor intensive goods had to be exported. It was found out that in order to export labor intensive goods at a desired quantity, the exchange rate, which was $1 = 1L, should be made $1 = 2 L. As the national income of the country was $ 100 before any price increase after devaluation took place, the national income in dollars would be $50.

The problem here is to determine the new value of the national income after the impacts of the devaluation on prices becomes effective. We supposed that in order to export labor intensive goods their prices should be half of their previous level in dollars. This translates to the following internal prices: nonlabor intensive good prices increase twofolds, making their value 60 L. As the prices of the exported portion of nonlabor goods is twice as much now, the prices of those goods which are not exported should be the same. This means that the value of the nonlabor intensive goods is 60 L. As the prices of labor intensive goods should stay where they were, this means, again, that their value should stay at 70 L as before. Altogether the national income is 130 L. It was $50 right after the devaluation but after price increases work themself out, it should be $65, 130/2. Let us notice again that this will take place in time. It could be one year or 3 years. It may be more. It depends on the adjustment time of prices.

Let us show it by meansof a diagram. (Diagram V-5)

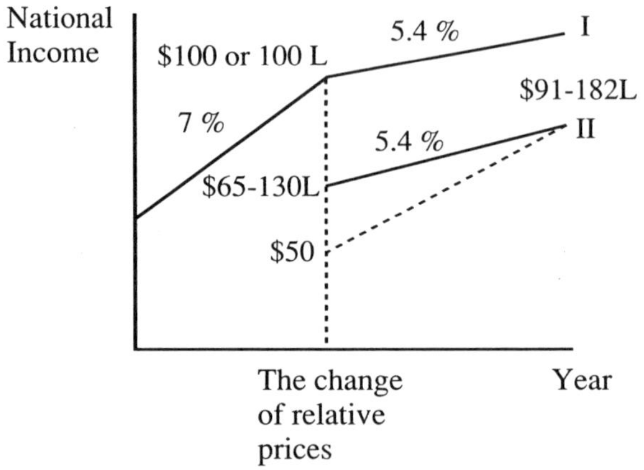

Diagram V-5

The Decrease of the Absolute Income

Let us see the level of national income after 10 years. It is suggested that the rate of growth goes down to 5.4 percent. If the price adjustments took place immediately, national income would be $65 rather than $50. If its yearly growth is 5.4 percent it means that at the end of 10 years it would be $91. This would be the case when price adjustments were in the intervening period. The important point to be stressed here is that when there is a relative price change, the initial value of the national income would have to change. In the example it is calculated to be 65 L, which is the value in terms of dollars after the price adjustments. This means that a 100 percent devaluation would give rise to a loss of 35 percent in the adjustment value of the national income.

The path of the dollar value of the national income is shown by the broken line.

The meaning of the above reasoning and also the diagram depicting it should be stressed. If there are no price changes and if the growth rate of the economy is 5.4 percent, the external equilibrium of the economy requires that the dollar value of the national income should be the same as depicted in the diagram. This means that the growth rate should be 5.4 percent in domestic constant prices but 6.2 percent (from $50 is $91 in 10 years require 6.2 percent yearly growth) in dollar. (Let us point out again that right after the devaluation the national income became $50.) If the growth rate is different, the economy will have to be confronted with all sorts of problems.

It is asserted that there is a relationship between the absolute level of the national income and its smooth operation. If the national income were higher than $65, imports and exports would not be compatible with a smooth operation, and the growth rate would not be 5.4 percent of 65 L. All that amounts to the original thesis of this book: we need a reference point and relative prices must be taken into consideration when it is determined.

The above contention can be illustrated and validated by the Turkish experience. National income in 1968 prices was 202,535 (millions of TL) in 1978, whereas if measured in 1987 prices it is 52,582 (billions of TL), again in 1978. If what is written above is true, 202,358 should be 40 percent less than this figure, 40 percent is calculated on the basis that the prices of labor intensive goods decreased by 50 percent (we know that the decrease in real wages is around that figure) and the proportion of nonlabor and labor intensive goods is 30 and 70 percent, respectively. Those figures suggest that the national income should be 40 percent less, relatively, when it is measured by the new relative prices. We know that the growth of the national income, if measured in constant domestic prices is 4.1 percent from 1978 to 1996; therefore 52,585 is supposed to be 60 percent of 202,358.

Now let us look into the growth of income in terms of dollars. We should expect that the growth of national income in dollars after a series of devaluation from 1980 to 1985 should be higher than the growth in domestic money in 1985 to 1996. This is due to a slack in the adjustments process of domestic prices.

Actually, the figures validate this expectations. For the smooth operation of the economy a 5 percent growth (this is the case in 1985-1996) seems to be compatible with the actual exchange rates and the domestic prices (actually Turkey was not confronted with an external payments crisis except for 1994 which was solved after the correction of the exchange rate in accordance with the expectations put forward in this book) The reasoning of this book suggests that the economy should grow by 8.7 percent in dollar terms from 1985 to 1996.

Now let us look at factual figures (Table V-1), original. As asserted above, as a result of a 50 percent real devaluation and a decrease of the prices of labor intensive goods, the national income of 1979 (the year before the devaluation) could be estimated to be 30-40 percent less, if calculated by the new weights. As the national income in 1979 was calculated as $ 81.696 billion, 40 percent less than this figure is $49.017 million. As it ($49.017) increased 3.8 percent from 1979 to 1996 (in terms of TL), it amounts to $92.406 million. It is shown in Table 1 that this has been a little higher than the expected. Those figures validate the theory.

Table V-1
Turkish National Income
in Current and Constant Dollars
($ Millions)

Year	Current National Income	Deflator For $	Turkish National Income in 1979$
1979	81,696	100.00	81,696
1980	68,391	108.96	63,079
1981	71,391	119.42	59,782
1982	64,209	127.06	50,558
1983	60,492	131.89	45,862
1984	59,098	136.77	43,209
1985	66,891	141.14	47,393
1986	75,173	144.81	51,915
1987	85,979	151.04	56,939
1988	90,460	156.93	57,654
1989	107,544	163.68	65,615
1990	150,758	170.55	88,681
1991	150,168	176.69	84,840
1992	158,122	181.82	86,880
1993	178,717	186.55	95,826
1994	132,307	192.14	68,909
1995	170,081	197.91	85,899
1996	183,611	200.00	91,805

All this means that in the period from 1985 to 1996 a 3.8 percent growth in national income has been compatible with the external equilibrium in view of domestic prices and the actual exchange rates.

It must be stressed again that the the fall of the growth rate to 3.8 percent is related to a growth and level effects. The level of national economy which is 40 percent less than of its pre-devaluation level. This means that the absolute level of the national income must have been affected by its level in terms of dollars.

The surge of inflation in this period may suggest that a lower growth rate should have occurred if inflation had been avoided. At this stage, I am not addressing this problem.

HIGHLIGHT

One of the most important discovery of my efforts is to underline the relationship among costs, value of inputs and that of output. It is shown that the change in the value of output given rise by relative prices of labor and capital would reflect on costs of inputs When constant price series are adjusted after the changes of relative prices 2 problems arise. One is the comparaison of national income calculated by new constant prices and that calculated with the previous constant prices. The second problem is that once an adjustment is made in output prices, input prices are left as they were before and as a result coefficients (alfa and beta in source of growth calculations) given to capital and labor when the contribution of inputs are calculated for the growth of national income are left as they were before. The second problem could make the calculation of TFP in Turkey lower, which is related to this false calculation. The origin of the problem is related to the fact that costs might be determined by the value of output rather than vice versa. This is called LEVEL EFECT. A discrepancy may exist between value and volume. This is the main actor.

The most important conclusion I should underline was that although I could see several important ingredients of inconventional analysis during the voyage in 1978-1999, the main discovery was in the air: I spotted it in 2004. When relative prices of nonlabor intesive goods were higher, an increase in their production might not be expected in some cases. This was why the level of national income would be considered as decreased.

CHAPTER VI

A CONTRIBUTION TO THE THEORY OF GROWTH AND ITS IMPLICATIONS FOR ECONOMIC ANALYSIS

§ 1 - INTRODUCTION

Factors determining growth are the subject of well known theories. Yet, I have a very important addition to them. If this is neglected, they cannot be studied properly. In this paper well known factors determining growth will not be taken up.

Although growth is the change in the level of national income, it will be shown that if the unknown factor to be introduced here is included, a differentiation between the growth and level of income would be in question.

The greatest inadequacy of the existing literature was the neglect in integrating the changes of relative prices into national income calculations when they were measured over time.

A relative price refers to the price ratio between two goods or services; for example, between apples and pears. There are, of course, thousands of goods and millions of relative prices in any country. It is evident that the change in relative prices must affect national income growth and economic analysis. It will be shown in this chapter that a change of relative prices is quite important in the analysis of growth and development, i.e., the change of national income between two different periods. I mean both the growth rate and absolute level of national income. Many of those relative prices are called macroeconomic relative prices. Some of them are: relative prices of agricultural and nonagricultural goods, relative prices of foreign and domestic goods, i.e., foreign terms of trade, the relative prices of capital, i.e., interest rate and other commodities, relative prices between tradable and nontradable goods, etc. The impact of the change of any of those relative prices on economic growth and other economic problems is studied in depth in economic literature. Yet, if the literature on the traditional calculation of national income and its growth is examined, it will become evident that there is not a uniform or unified analysis of the change of macroeconomic relative prices.

The theory expounded in this essay, which is universal, can be used in the analysis of the growth and development of any country. However, it has been suggested or inspired by the Turkish experience. Furthermore, it will be tested by the Turkish experience in the chapter entitled as The Validation of the Unconventional Approach by the Turkish Experience.

In practical life the decomposition of factory affecting growth and its prediction is probably the most important goal of economic analyses. Generally, the decomposition of the past growth rates of countries is conducted by means of the source of growth analysis, firstly quantified by Solow (1957).

It is evident that income changes or its growth are related to the changes of inputs and their productivity. This is the first disaggregation. Then inputs are disaggregated as labor and capital inputs. Productivity being the same, if inputs grow over time, national income must also grow. The problem here is to bring together the impact of the growth of labor and capital inputs. This is solved by taking a weighted average of the growth of different inputs. The weights are based on the income shares of labor and capital. For example, if the share of labor earnings in the national income is 40 percent and that of capital is 60 percent, the actual growth rate of each input is multiplied by those figures and then summed up.

It is shown by several economists that if the shares of each input are based on their marginal productivity, and if they stay constant over time, the factors determining the growth can be lumped together in the following equation:

$$G = \alpha L + \beta K + A$$

Here G is the growth rate of national income, L and K are the growth rates of labor and capital, respectively, A is the growth rate caused by the productivity increase of inputs, which can be referred to as a noninput factor or total factor productivity growth (TFP) or technical progress, $\propto$ is the share of labor income in national income and ß is that of capital ($\alpha+\beta=1$).

Noninput factors are brought together in A. They are disaggregated as the scale of operations, advances in education, technical advance, a better allocation of resources, shifts of resources from one sector to another, etc. The last one can be very important in the development of developing countries.

Although the above summarized analysis is criticized by several economists, it has a wide application in the analysis of growth.

This original analysis has been continuously developed and refined. But the main idea is there. The development has been in the direction of a decomposition of capital as physical and human capital, the quantification of the impact of externalities and policy variables, and making some variables, which were considered exogenous before, endogenous, etc. In the context of this essay I leave recent advances aside and try to spot very important weaknesses of the original version and to correct them.

Theories of growth and development are based on the assumption that national income consists of a single good. The idea behind it is that even if there are several thousand goods, they can be considered as one good in growth context simply because of the fact that the price of each good is commensurate with inputs used in their production and the prevailing technical knowledge under certain assumptions. As a result, their relative prices are also commensurate with the relative use of inputs. This means that once the growth of inputs and the state of technical knowledge are taken as the main determining factors of growth, there is no need to talk of relative prices as one of the factors determining it. But it is forgotten that relative prices may change as a result of changes of relative input prices, which could be meaningful in some cases. (Although the measurement of capital had given a lot of trouble to economists, this did not detract them from lumping together all goods as one good and to proceed with it.)

The assumption as to the irrelevance of relative prices is not taken away even when more disaggragative growth theories are put forward. It is there when theories based on various goods are formulated or in those explanations based on structural factors. For example, in the Chenery sponsored analyses (Chenery 1978) based on structural transformations, although there are various goods produced in various sectors, the dynamics of growth is attributed to a nonproportional growth of various sectors (both the inner dynamics of the sectors and the dynamics of the whole economy). Yet the assumption as to the equality of cost and prices is kept. As the productivity of inputs in different sectors is different, a transfer of inputs from one sector to a different one would give rise to growth. Yet, the possibility of the change of input prices within each sector, which might have different factor proportions, is not considered; this would give rise to a different incomes in each sector. Relative intersectoral prices would be different in this case.

It will be shown that when input prices are allowed to change within one sector, the traditional approaches should be modified and in that case relative prices become relevant.

Before explaining the importance of the modification, let me make it clear that I did not have this idea when I tried to explain why traditional theories had failed and how I remedied it. I was pragmatic in asserting that national income of Turkey should not be measured by all goods but one group among them should be given a priority.

In the traditional analyses once relative prices are taken as they are in each constant series, they are kept the same all the time when the national income of the same country is compared over time. (Even if different constant price series are used.) They can be the initial relative prices or the end ones. I try to show that if this practice is stuck to, the comparison of incomes over time does not indicate the change of national income when relative input prices change. This I am going to explain in a moment.

In traditional analyses, goods are collected under two groups: tradable and nontradable. The idea behind it is that traded goods prices are the same throughout the whole world (under their free exchange and when there are no transport costs) but those of nontradable ones are not. As the prices of nontradable goods are different in different countries, in international comparisons of per capita incomes in different countries, the same prices should be attributed to all goods. This leads to the purchasing power parity method, PPP. Actually it is evident that under this method a reference point for measuring income is sought. If the same reasoning is transferred to the comparison of the national income in a country over time, the reference point should be one of the groups of goods when input prices change. The whole idea is that a value dimension must be given to national income in overtime comparisons. This value dimension is given to it when it is calculated at one point in time in traditional analyses. National income is calculated by summing up the production of various goods. As their production volume is multiplied by their respective prices, this attributes a value dimension to it. But when we come to over time comparisons, and if in the case when relative prices change, and again if we stick to the same relative prices, part of the value dimension would be lost. At the beginning my contribution was to remedy it by measuring national income by one group of goods. This group was chosen by considering the kind of goods as a numeraire which were important in making the level and growth of national income sustainable. Otherwise, the comparison of national incomes would not show the exact situation. This is proved below.

In the traditional treatment, the grouping is based on tradable and nontradable goods, as mentioned before. But for the purpose of choosing the good to be the reference point, this distinction is not adequate. That was because of the fact that a change in the exchange rate or relative prices would make previously tradable goods into nontradable and previously nontradable into tradable. This is shown below. Instead, I switched to two groups: labor intensive and nonlabor intensive goods.

Now suppose we separated goods as labor and nonlabor intensive goods. If the prices of labor intensive goods decrease relatively to nonlabor intensive goods as a result of relative decrease of labor prices, it can be shown that both the growth rate and the level of the national income would decrease overtime. It is easy to see that nonlabor intensive goods are taken to be more important. This is because of the fact that they are movable around the world by the same prices. As labor prices are different in various countries, the move of labor intensive goods requires a change, as will be shown below, a decrease in their prices.

§ 2 - THE IMPACT OF CHANGES IN RELATIVE PRICES ON THE GROWTH OF NATIONAL INCOME: THE LEVEL EFFECT

National income consists of goods and services produced in a certain period, generally a year. In order to bring together various goods and services constituting it, it should be expressed by a common value standard. But the continuous changes in relative prices can make the meaning of national income rather vague. Suppose national income consists of apples and pears. If the relative price of apples with respect to pears increases and if the production of apples and pears are exactly the same, how are we going to measure national income? The evaluation of national income becomes more difficult when the absolute and relative amounts of apples and pears change from one period to another: economic growth.

In the literature, the method to solve this problem is to consider relative prices constant. Actually either the beginning (Laspeyres) or the end (Paasche) relative prices are considered constant. Would that lead to a correct interpretation of the change in national income? Before answering that question let us examine the traditional solution by means of an example.

	Apples	**Pears**
P0	$100	$100
Q0	100 Tons	100 Tons
P1	$140	$100
Q1	100 Tons	100 Tons

Here P shows prices, Q quantities, and 0-1 times. It is apparent that from the base period to the first period everything stays the same except for the price of apples. Now let us calculate national income after the increase of apple prices.

National income in the base period is: (Let me warn you that this is simplified.)

100 X \$100 + 100 X \$100 = \$20,000

In order to calculate it in the second period, we must calculate the price increase first. As quantities of apples and pears are the same in the second period, both Laspeyres and Paasche price indexes would be:

$$\frac{100 \text{ X } \$140 + 100 \text{ X } \$100}{100 \text{ X } \$100 + 100 \text{ x } \$100} = 1.2\text{, i.e., 20 percent increase}$$

The national income in the second period is:

100 X \$140 + 100 X \$100 = \$24,000

When national income is calculated by means of constant prices, it should be divided (or deflated) by the price increase. This would be \$20,000, (24,000/1.2=20,000).

We see that the change in relative prices does not affect national income if there is not a change in the production. This is what I am going to question. It will be shown that even if there is not any change in production volume,a change in labor prices would give rise to changes in national income.I call this level effect.If there are changes in production volume (for example, economic growth),the impact of the changes of labor prices would be more complicated.In addition to the level effect another factor would affect national income which I call growth effect.That will be expounded upon in the next section.

Firstly I take up the question from the point of view of an individual consumer. It is well established that the increase of his or her welfare could be shown by a quantity index, let us suppose the Paasche one. It could be written as follows.

$$I_q = \frac{P_1^t x_1^t + P_2^t x_2^t}{P_1^t x_1^b + P_2^t x_2^b}$$

P's are prices and x's are different goods. Upper indices are time (b is the base and t is the present one) and under indices are the first and the second good. I is the quantity index.

It is evident that if that index is over 1 there is an increase of the welfare of the individual. But when the same question is tackled for the whole community this is not true when a price dimension is included in the reasoning, as will be explained below. Shortly, it could be shown that in some cases the relative decrease of the price of a certain good or a change in tastes would not give rise to a change in its consumption. In that case another reason for the price dimension stands up.

Until 2004 my doubts about the traditional methodology in measuring national income were based on the fact that if that methodology were used, problems would arise with respect to the sustainability of national income and the consistency of internal equilibrium, which were ignored in traditional analysis. Jumping from that belief, I used to calculate national income by means of a good called the hybrid one, the price of which would change as a result of a necessity of exporting more. In that case the level of national income would change.

In years ensuing 2004 I tried to show that instead of relying on the deflator based on the hybrid good for measuring national income change, it would be more meaningful to see if labor would buy more or less goods after a change in relative prices.This was because of the fact that the level of labor prices could be different without any respect to their productivity. This was,in fact,the main factor making my analysis different from others. Along with that I have shown that when the relative price of a certain good decreases due to changes in tastes or to another reason such as securing the sustainability of income (our case), and if the community was not in a position to produce a lower quantity of that good (the cheap one) compared to the previous period, that could be considered as a decrease in national income.

In order to validate that assumption (i.e.,after the relative price fall there would not be a fall in the production of that good)I assumed that two goods are produced in the country: apples and pears. Again, I assumed that there are two factors of production, labor and capital. Apples are labor intensive and pears are nonlabor intensive commodities. I supposed that as a result of structural factors and / or when a necessity to increase exports occurs, labor prices are made lower. The domestic price of apples decrease and they become less expensive for the outside world and their exports increase. Meanwhile if the imported goods and capital content of pears are more, their relative prices increase vis-a-vis apple prices. Now, there is a second scenario: instead of the fall of domestic prices we can suppose that a devaluation is incurred and as a result, as domestic prices remain the same, they become less expensive in terms of the foreign currency. But pear prices should increase relatively to apple prices. As pears are more capital intensive goods, their prices must be higher than apples after the devaluation. It is evident that in this scenario relative prices of apples are less than pears prices again. In order to validate my contention I must show that the production of pears and apples should stay the same.We know that prices are determined by supply and demand.On the other hand, supply depends on cost.The change in cost would give rise to changes in the supply. Let us proceed. One of the reasons why pear prices are relatively higher is that they are less labor intensive and labor prices are lower now. On the other hand, when pear prices are higher and labor prices are lower, profits to be earned by producing each good would be the same and there would not be any incentive or disincentive to increase pear production or to decrease apple production. I should underline that even if the same amount of goods are consumed after the devaluation, their value is lower now.This is the supply side.

When it comes to the demand side we can show that there would not be a change in the production of both goods. The cost of production of pears is higher (relatively) and its price is relatively higher. Why would the community not demand cheaper apples more? Yet, if more apples are demanded, their prices would not be higher: because their cost is low now. Pears are expensive yet as the community is supposed to export more apples it must consume them less: there is a change in tastes. The higher preference for pears would be compensated for by the lower prices of apples.Both supply and demand conditions are making the production of the goods the same. What I contend is that national income is less now and I call that level effect.

§ 3 - THE GROWTH EFFECT

Now, I shall study the impact of changes in relative prices on growth. It may be thought that if two national incomes in different dates are compared, the deflation of the second one by means of a price index should take the change of relative prices into consideration. In fact, we know that when a price index is calculated, any price change is taken into consideration. But in the initial example we saw that the change of relative prices did not affect the level of national income. It must be noticed that in that example there is not any change in the volume of production, in traditional sense there is no growth. But I shall show that when there is a change in production, a change in relative prices should affect the growth rate. Now, I shall prove my contention by means of a example.

Suppose there are two commodities in the country. One is a labor intensive good (A good) and the other is a capital intensive one (B good). In 1980 the production of each commodity is 100 units and the price of each is $100. In that case national income is $ 20,000. Here is the calculation:

1980:

(100 x $ 100) + (100 x $ 100) = $ 20,000

Let us assume that in 1980 and 1990 the yearly production of A increased by 8 percent; whereas that of B by 5 percent. In addition, by 1990 the prices of both A and B become $ 200. In that case the national income in 1990 can be calculated as follows.

1990:

(216 x $ 200) + (163 x $ 200) = $ 75,800

In order to calculate the yearly income increase during the last 10 years the national income of 1990 in nominal terms should be expressed in terms of constant prices. Let us say in 1980 prices. In order to do it a price index showing the price increases in this period should be calculated and the national income of 1990 should be deflated by a price index prepared according to price increases in that period. Here is the price index:

$$\frac{(100 \times \$\,200) + (100 \times \$\,200)}{(100 \times \$\,100) + (100 \times \$\,100)} = 2 \text{ (Laspeyres method)}$$

If the national income of 1990 is deflated by the price increase in that period, we can find the national income in constant prices: $ 75,800 / 2 = $ 37,900. It means that national income increased from $ 20,000 to $ 37,900. This amounts to a 6.6 percent yearly increase. In other terms, the annual change of national income in constant prices is 6.6 percent.

Now, a very important fact will be underlined. If the change in relative prices gives rise to a change in nominal national income, the only determining factor would not be growth of the production of each good; the change in relative prices does cause a change in the growth of national income.

In order to show it let us look into the second period, i.e., from 1990 to 2000. We suppose that the growth rate of each good was the same as before but there was a change in their relative prices. The price of A good becomes $ 250 and that of B good $ 400 in 1990. By 2000 the production of A is 466 and that of B is 265 units. The national income in 2000 is $ 222,703.

2000:

(466 x $ 250) + (265 x $ 400) = $ 222,703

The price increase in that period is calculated as follows:

$$\frac{(216 \times \$\ 125) + (163 \times \$\ 200)}{(216 \times 100) + (163 \times 100)} = 1.57 \text{ (Laspeyres method)}$$

(Note: 125 is 25 percent higher than $200; this is because of the fact that the price of the good, which was $ 200 becames $ 250; the same mechanism is true for the other good.)

If that price increase is used to deflate the national income of 2000, i.e., 222,703/ 1.57, we shall see that the national income in constant prices is $ 141,849 and the annual growth is 6.4 percent. In the second period the growth rate of each good was the same. But the growth rate national income decreased from 6.6 percent to 6.4 percent. (If the price index is made by means of Paasche method, the growth would be calculated as 6.8 percent.) This means that the change in relative prices must give rise to a change in the growth rate of the national income. In addition, we must introduce another relationship. I shall give another example in order to show the impact of the other relationship, the speed of the increase of various goods when relative prices change.

Let us suppose that there are two commodities: A and B. The volume of production of each good is considered the same: 100 units. The price of both A and B goods is $10. In that case national income is $2000. We suppose that next year the production of A goods grows by 15 and that of B goods by 5 percent. In that case national income becomes $2200. That means a 10 percent growth rate. In the case when A grew 5 and B 15 percent, the growth rate of national income was the same: 10 percent. Now we suppose that as a result of the decrease of prices of inputs used in the production of A goods more intensively its price becomes $ 5, while that of B goods stays at $10. In that case the national income calculated with new weights is

$1500. Next year if the production of A goods increases by 5 percent and that of B goods 15 percent, national income grows by 11.6 percent, whereas if the production of A goods increases by 15 and that of B goods by 5 percent, the growth of national income becomes 8.3 percent. A change in the growth rate is apparent. That means that the relative prices are important in the growth of national income when the growth of the volume of each good is different... This is what I call growth effect. By doing so, I decompose the factors affecting growth. This mechanism is not apparent in the source of growth approach.

Now let us look into the consequences of this example. National income depends on the weights (the price of each good) given to various goods (here labor and nonlabor intensive goods) which are changed from time to time. If, for instance, the prices of labor intensive goods are made lower, and if the prices of nonlabor goods are kept the same, again if the growth of labor intensive sectors becomes speedier, then the growth of national income is calculated lower. Yet, the growth of inputs and the state of techniques are the same. This change is not detected by the traditional growth formula. It is doubtful to observe the decrease of the growth, even if the share of labor in national income is made lower.

The above explanation of the growth effect should be looked into very carefully. It is apparent that in order that the growth rate would be less in the second period, national income which was $ 2000 in the first period is reduced to $ 1500 in the second period; and again, weights to be given to various goods should be changed, and what is more important, is the fact that the relationship between the first and second national income levels are cut off in the sense that they are not comparable by traditional methods. In a way if two different constant prices are used in national incomes for two different periods, the alleged change in growth rates may emerge. Therefore all would depend on two constant prices. If the same constant prices are used, the so called growth effect would not arise.

That conclusion relating to growth effect would be important if we are confronted with national income calculations each made by different constant prices. The difference in growth rates might be related to that relationship underlined in this section.

It should be observed that if relative prices are constant, the change of the growth rates of each good does not make national income growth rate different. But if relative prices are different, the change of the growth rates of each good affects national income growth.

Now we have to solve a more important problem. It should be shown that the calculation of national income by constant prices would give the same figures. But they are not the same all the time. In fact, as shown in the above example when prices indices are prepared for deflating nominal national incomes, relative prices are the same. I underline this conclusion for the reason that in practice constant price series are changed from time to time. In new series relative prices could be changed. Therefore two national incomes calculated by two different constant price series, in which relative prices are different, cannot be compared properly. Let us look at some figures.

The first period national income: (1980-1990)

(100 x \$ 100) + (100 x \$ 100) = \$ 20,000	Growth rate
(216 x \$ 100) + (163 x \$ 100) = \$ 37,900	6.6 percent

The second period: (1990-2000)

(216 x \$ 250) + (163 x \$ 400) = \$ 119,200	Growth rate
(466 x \$ 250) + (265 x \$ 400) = \$ 222,500	6.4 percent

We see that the growth rates calculated by constant prices are exactly the same as those which we obtained by deflating nominal national incomes by the price index: 6.6 and 6.4. Let us repeat the crucial conclusion. The change in relative prices would give rise to a change in the price index, and in turn, when there is a change in the production volume, this would make growth rates different. The most important conclusion is this: as relative prices could be different in two constant prices series, the calculation of the growth rates in two periods would be different even if the rate of the volume of growth of national incomes is the same. But if, in the second period, growth is calculated by 1980 constant prices, the growth in that period would be 6.8 percent rather than 6.4 percent. This change is due to a change in relative prices. This is the most important conclusion. A part of the change should be attributed to the kind of constant price series we use.

(216 x \$ 100) + (163 x \$ 100) = 37,900	the growth rate is
(466 x \$ 100) + (265 x \$ 100) = 73,100	6.8 percent

This means that the change in relative prices should give rise to a change in the growth rate. But the impact of the changes could be more significant if the same constant price series is used.

Concluding Remarks

1- The conclusions reached by the method based on a calculation of national income by constant prices and also by the other method based on deflating nominal national incomes by price indices would produce the same results. In each of them relative prices are allowed to change. (This means that although relative prices are allowed to change, they are kept the same all the time in the period concerned.) As relative prices could be different in two series for two different periods, part of the change in growth rate in two periods would be related to the change in relative prices.

2- If constant prices of the first period are applied to the second period data, we observe a change in national income growth as a result of a change of relative prices, which are those of the first period. This means that when growth rates of various periods are compared the impact of relative prices should be more.

3- In all calculations we have studied the impact of a change of relative prices which is called the growth effect. On the other hand, the change of relative prices has another impact on national income which I call the level effect. This is taken up in the previous section. What I want to do is to attract the reader's attention to the fact that the impact of the level effect is not covered in the growth effect. In addition to a decrease of the growth rate due to the growth effect, there might be another factor which would affect the level, which in turn, would give rise to change in the growth of national income in the longer period, i.e., in our example in 1980 to 2000.

§ 4 - A HYPOTHETICAL EXAMPLE AND THE COMPARISON OF NATIONAL INCOMES OVER TIME

In order to summarize my contribution to the theory of growth, I shall give a hypothetical example. This example is prepared in order to show how the growth performance of that economy would be explained in the framework of the enriched theory of growth which is explained above. The goal is to show the deficiency of the traditional theory and the contribution of the enrichment suggested here to understand growth.

We set out to examine the performance of a hypothetical economy for a 20 year period, i.e., 1980 to 2000. We have two subperiods: one is 1980-1990 and the other 1990-2000. In the first subperiod the growth of the economy was 6 percent yearly, whereas in the second it was 4 percent only. The goal is to detect why they were so different.

In the whole period the contribution of the increase of inputs to growth was some 3 points in terms of quantity. Therefore TFP was 3 point in the first period; but it went down to 1 point in the second period. Why? What were the factors leading to that dramatic fall? Another observation about this economy was the great difference between growth rates in constant national money over the whole period and that in terms of dollars. While this difference is sought, the future of the national income growth is tried to be predicted.

In the framework of the existing theory, all sorts of factors could be drawn out: anybody familiar with the theory can list them. Therefore I ignore them.

I shall try to show that in addition to traditionally underlined factors, the change of relative prices of labor and nonlabor intensive goods should affect the level and growth of national income. When I investigate the impact of changing relative prices under the growth and level effects (not similar to what we have in growth theory) I shall show that the abnormal performance of the economy could be partly explained by them.

It is suggested that when relative prices of labor and nonlabor intensive commodities change, the level of national income changes. Again, it is also supposed in our example that in the first subperiod national income increase was 6 percent, whereas it went down to 4 percent in the second period. That was a very big change. The problem here is to find out the impact of relative price changes in the fall of national income growth. Again, it is evident that we talk about 2 factors affecting national income growth. It must be stressed at this stage that in each subperiod national income is measured by a different constant price series, in each preriod relative prices are different.

1- Factors not relating to relative prices. Among them are the growth of inputs and the change in productivity.

2- The change in relative prices. The impact of that factor could be decomposed into two subfactors: growth and level effects. Now, we shall try to find out the impact of each factor.

First, let us look into figures in our example. In the first period national income was supposed to have increased by 6 percent. It is assumed that national income consisted of two goods: one labor intensive and the other nonlabor intensive. In 1980, 50 units of each were produced. The price of each was $ 1. Therefore national income was $ 100. We supposed that labor intensive goods increased 7 percent and nonlabor intensive ones 5 percent, yearly. If so, national income in 1990 would be $ 179. In the second subperiod we observe two changes. Firstly, the price of labor intensive goods becomes $ 0.50 but that of nonlabor intensive ones stays the same. Secondly, the growth rate of labor intensive goods in terms of constant prices falls and it becomes 5 percent and that of nonlabor intensive ones becomes 3.3 percent. That fall may be related to a productivity change and/or to an input decrease (in our example it is related to a productivity fall). Both the first and second factors make the growth rate 4 percent in the second period. Our problem is to decompose the increase in the growth rate and to spot the contribution of each of those two factors.

Here I suggest an unconventional procedure to spot it. Before explaining it let me draw a diagram (Figure VI - 1).

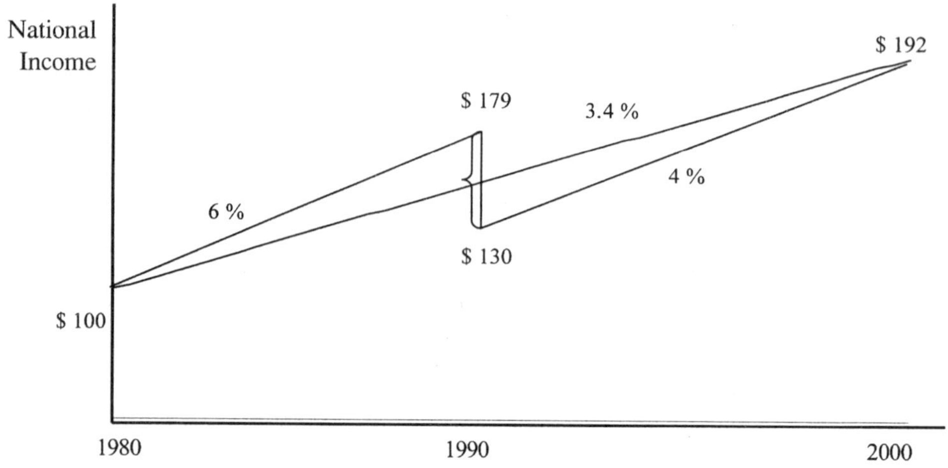

Figure VI- 1: The Growth of National Income in the Hypothetical Example

Firstly the fall of national income from $ 179 to $ 130 in 1990 should be explained. In 1990 we had 98 units of labor intensive and 81 units of nonlabor intensive goods (if we remember growth rates of each good). All together they were 179 units and $ 179. As the price of labor intensive goods is $ 0.50 now its total value is $ 49 and that of nonlabor intensive goods is $ 81; two together would make $ 130. (The reasons why in the calculation of the national income of 1990 the decrease of the prices of labor intensive goods is not considered, and why the 1990 figure is not deflated are explained above, and it will be taken up again below, see the last section. Yet let me remind that in the second subperiod we use a different constant price series; and as a result, we don't deflate $130.) We suppose that labor intensive goods grow 5 and nonlabor ones 3.3 percent in the second period, and their prices stay the same; that makes the value of labor intensive goods $ 80 and nonlabor ones would be $ 112: altogether $ 192, the growth rate is 4 percent. Let us remember that in 1980 national income was $ 100 and now it is $ 192. For the whole period the growth rate is 3.4 percent. We suppose that the price of nonlabor goods stayed the same and that of labor intensive ones are half of what they were, in the second our period.

Now the problem is to decompose the growth in the whole period. Here is my unconventional procedure. (I don't know if I am right.) If the absolute and relative prices were the same and if the national income grew 6 percent during the whole period, it would be $ 320 by 2000. Whereas it has been $ 192. The growth rate has been 3.4 percent rather than 6 percent; 2.6 percent difference is related to the above mentioned 3 factors: growth and level effects and the change of productivity. How are we going to decompose it? Before doing it let me draw a diagram (VI-2) (If the reader read the previous pages carefully, he or she could be sure that $192 should not be deflated by prices changes: in addition to the argument that we use constant price series, it is shown that when labor prices decrease without a change in quantities it is a decrease in national income.)

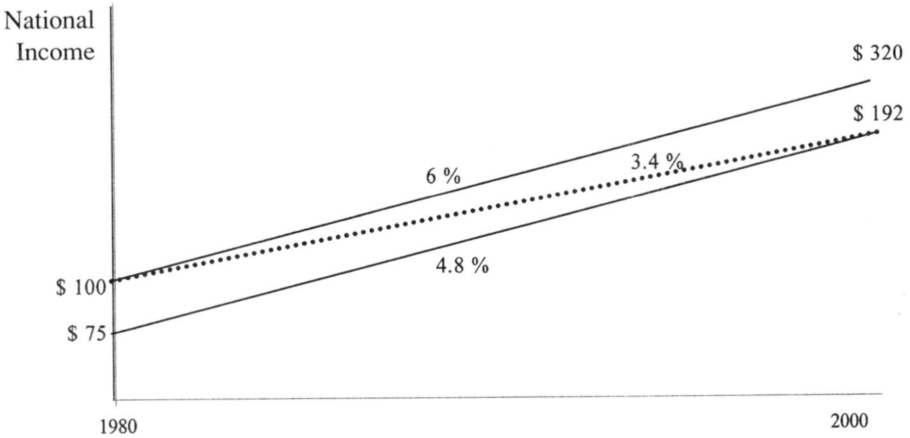

Figure VI- 2: The Decomposition of the Factors Determining Growth in the Example

Now let us ignore the impact of productivity. In that case I can say that the impact of the growth effect was 1.2 points in the whole period. We calculate it as follows. If the relative prices were the same as they were at the end of the period, national income would be $ 75 rather than $ 100 at the beginning. With the new relative prices it is $ 192 now. Therefore that factor is making growth rate 4.8 percent rather than 6 percent. That means that growth effect has reduced it by 1.2 percent.

Now let us turn to the level effect. If the level is included, we see that national income which would have grown 6 percent has grown 3.4 percent. This means that total reduction of national income is 2.6 percent yearly: the growth was reduced from 6 to 3.4 percent. As we assume that the impact of the growth effect was 1.2 percent: the rest, i.e., 1.4 percent, is due to the level effect.

It is apparent that productivity change in the second period should also be considered.. How shall we calculate it? This is influential in the second period.

Now let us look at the whole period. National income was $ 130 at the beginning of the second period. It went up to $ 192, whereas if the growth rates of factors of production were the same as they were in the first period, they would be 7 and 5 percent, respectively (as previously). That would make national income $ 228 at the end of the second period.

The fall from $ 228 to $ 192 in the second period means that the unfavorable impact of productivity change (inputs are considered the same) in the second period is 1.7 percent a year. As national income growth decreased 2 percent in the second period it can be decomposed as follows: 1.7 percent was due to productivity decrease 0.3 percent to growth effect. (Let me clarify that we are talking of the second period only.)

MACRO PRODUCTIVITY

The development of my analyses has lead me to a concept which I call macroeconomic productivity. In fact, this concept is known in the literature. In the literature it means a better allocation and administration of investments on an aggregate level, i.e., covering the whole economy. But I include another dimension into it: it is the labor prices.

I tried to show that the relationship between the value of labor (on an aggregate level or in the whole economy) and its micro-macro productivity could be loose in certain cases. If, for example, country exports are based on natural resources and if exports are high enough to satisfy import demand, labor prices in the country could be high irrespective of its productivity. In fact, if labor prices change, the value of national income would also change. But a parallel change in input prices might not be expected in that case. If so, that would result in a change in TFP. After having validated this assertion by the Turkish experience, I have shown that there is a relationship between this kind of the change in TFP and the measurement of national income by a foreign currency rather than by a constant price national currency. I have done that theoretically first and then validated it by theoretical reasoning by the Turkish experience.

I have ferreted out that reasoning and have come up with very important conclusions.

§ 5 - THE MEASUREMENT OF NATIONAL INCOME BY A NATIONAL CURRENCY OR AN INTERNATIONAL CURRENCY

The previous analysis suggests that a relationship between national incomes measured by a national currency (let us call it lira) and by an international currency (let us call it dollar) should be sought. That necessity increases especially when the long run trend growth of the national income is tried to be found. Should it be in terms of lira or dollar?

Let us start from the easy end..

1- If the national currency is devalued and if home prices stay the same, national income in dollars decreases at the same proportion of the devaluation rate. But the national income decrease in real terms (welfare) is definitely less than that.

2- If the prices of exported and imported goods would probably increase nearly at the proportion of the devaluation and those of home goods increase less than that, there is a decrease of national income in terms of dollars but it is less than the previous case. The same question now: is there a decrease in national income and would the decrease in terms of dollars indicate the level of decrease? That case fits better to what is said about the level effect above, and the figures in dollars should indicate better the level of national income decrease.

3- If the proportion of more labor intensive goods in exports increases, it can be suspected that the power of the dollar figures in measuring the new national income level is greater.

4- Why are figures in dollars better than figures in terms of L in measuring national income over time? Relative prices may be reflected on national incomes measured in dollars. If lower relative labor figures mean a lower national income, measurements in dollars are better.

5- If national incomes over time are in constant L and if relative prices are different those years, those national income figures cannot be compared, whereas those in terms of dollars they can be; this is true if relative prices are reflected on dollar prices.

Now let us give an example. We suppose that national income is $ 100, $ 30 of which consists of nonlabor intensive and $ 70 is labor intensive goods. When the price ratio of labor and nonlabor intensive goods was 1, the national income was $100 or 100 L. ($1=1L). Now, suppose that the country was confronted with a necessity to increase its exports. But suppose again that, on the other hand, the production of nonlabor intensive goods (they were the main items of exports previously) could not be increased. As a result, labor intensive goods had to be exported. It was found out that in order to export labor intensive goods at a desired quantity, the exchange rate, which was $1 = 1 L, should be made $1 = 2 L. As the national income of the country was $ 100 before any price increase after devaluation took place, the national income in dollar would be $ 50. We suppose that as a result of the mechanism explained above (growth effect) the growth rate of national income, which was 7 percent before, becomes 5.4 percent after the devaluation.

The problem here is to determine the new value of the national income after the impact of the devaluation on prices takes place. We supposed that in order to export labor intensive goods their prices should be half of their previous level in dollars. This translates to the following internal prices: nonlabor intensive good prices increase twofold, making their value 60 L. As the prices of the exportable portion of nonlabor goods is twice as much now, the prices of those goods which are not exported should be the same. This means that the value of the nonlabor intensive goods is 60 L. As the prices of labor intensive goods should stay where they were, this means that their value should stay at 70 L as before. Altogether the national income is 130 L. It was $ 50 right after the devaluation but after price increases work themselves out, it should be $65, 130/2. Let us notice again that this will take place in time. It could be one year or 3 years. It may be more. It depends on the adjustment time of prices.

It is asserted that there is a relationship between the absolute level of national income and the smooth operation of the economy.If the national income were higher than $ 65, imports and exports would not be compatible with a smooth operation, and the growth rate would not be 5.4 percent of 65L.All that amounts to the original thesis of this book: we need a reference point and relative prices must be taken into consideration when the national income is measured. Moreover, if the price adjustments are not quick, the growth rate in terms of dollars in years ensuing the devaluation should be higher than that in national currency.

§ 6- HIGHLIGHT

One of the most important discovery of my efforts is to underline the relationship among costs, value of inputs and that of output. It is shown that the change in the value of output given rise by relative prices of labor and capital would reflect on costs of inputs When constant price series are adjusted after the changes of relative prices 2 problems arise. One is the comparison of national income calculated by new constant prices and that calculated with the previous constant prices. The second problem is that once an adjustment is made in output prices, input prices are left as they were before and as a result coefficients (alfa and beta in source of growth calculations) given to capital and labor when the contribution of inputs are calculated for the growth of national income are left as they were. The second problem could make the calculation of TFP in Turkey lower, which is related to this false calculation. The origin of the problem is related to thr fact that costs might be determined by the value of output rather than vice versa. This is called LEVEL EFECT. A discrepancy may exist between value and volume. This is the main actor.

CHAPTER VII

A SHORT HISTORY AND STRUCTURE OF THE TURKISH ECONOMY

§ 1- INTRODUCTION

The aim of writings on the history, structure and operation of the Turkish economy is not to present information about this economy. Those chapters and sections are written in order to induce the curiosity of readers to think about the interesting events which have occurred in this economy. Along with that, theoretical writings are not left in a void.

I am of the opinion that if events are looked into, new ideas and illuminating analyses would emerge. Again, when challenging and unconventional ideas are suggested by the observation of this economy, they could be validated by what happened after they are put forward. Otherwise they would be left in a void.

The main event attracting the curiosity of economists should be the fall of the yearly trend rate of economic growth from 6.4 percent to 3.8 percent in the 1950-1977 and 1980-2007 periods, respectively. What is more interesting is the fact that in the first period an import substitution policy was followed but in the second period the economy was liberalized and the import substitution policy was replaced by an outward looking one. As expected, the share of exports in national income, i.e., 3.6 percent, went up to some 15 percent after the liberalization of the economy. Yet in fact, several macro magnitudes, such as inflation, balance of payment deficits, domestic and foreign debts of the country, etc. went astray beyond imagination. Was it a sign that a better operation of price mechanism was detrimental to the economy? Questions like these are asked and answered but answers are not satisfactory.

The reason why I devoted some pages (although very are short) to the description of events in this economy was to establish a sort of background for a better analysis of those problems.

§ 2 - A SHORT ECONOMIC HISTORY AND THE STRUCTURE OF THE TURKISH ECONOMY

Turkey is an oil importing middle income country. The Turkish economy has developed very rapidly since the establishment of the Republic in 1923. At that time the per capita income was around $ 500-600 (in terms of the present dollar). In 2000 the per capita income was approximately $3,000 and in 2007 it is around $ 5500 (according to new estimates it is $8500). In the same period(from 1923 to 2007) the population increased from 13 to 71.5 million. The present GNP of the country is about $ 700 billion (by new estimates $700 billion). Between 1950 and 2000 the annual rate of growth of national income in constant Turkish lira was 5.2 percent. (That can be disputed)

The period in question (1923-2008) is divided into 2 subperiods. Events which occurred in each are briefly summarized. The major turning-point was in 1980. Before then, an inward looking policy of industrialization and import substitution was pursued. In this pre-1980 period, Turkey encountered difficulties in exporting enough to sustain economic growth, and deficits in the balance of payments gave rise to many problems. The post-1980 period has become one of export-orientation. The share of exports in GNP rose from 3.4 (1979) to 16 percent (the mid-80s) and the balance of payments problem disappeared. Nevertheless, Turkey has experienced problems such as inflation, poor income distribution, unemployment, substantial external and internal debts, etc.

Turkey is situated in one of the most strategic geographical areas of the world. The area of the country is 779,442 km^2 of which 246,000 km^2 is used in agriculture; the area of land covered by forests is 201,000 km^2, the rest is not usable. The number of inhabitants per square km was around 77 in 2000.

When the Republic of Turkey was founded in 1923 the country offered all the typical characteristics of a developing country with the exception that it had never been a colony and the new republic was a hereditary of one of the largest empires of the previous years.

However natural resources are defined and however complex the separation of their contribution from other factors is, Turkey is not a country rich in natural resources, such as the oil-rich Middle Eastern countries or with great mineral resources or with ample fertile agricultural land. Therefore, it can be assumed that economic development is not initiated by the exploitation of rich natural resources.

Agriculture overshadowed the operation of the economy until the early 60s. In fact, in the 50s the share of agricultural production in GNP was nearly 50 percent. This has steadily decreased throughout the whole period, and it is around 11 percent now. But the proportion of the population living in rural areas is nearly 35 percent of the whole population. Again, nearly some 35 percent of total working population is employed in agriculture.

Practically no industry existed in the early days of the Republic. On the other hand, there has been a sustained effort on the part of the government to industrialize. This brought results, and the share of the manufacturing industry in GNP rose from 11 percent (1950) to over 26 percent in the 90s. In fact, development has meant industrialization in Turkey; active government intervention in the economy has been instrumental in achieving this result. By the early 70s, Turkey possessed a relatively advanced industry, producing consumer, intermediate and investment goods.

With a visible deceleration in economic activities in the Second World War (1940-1946) and a slight depression in 1958-1961, the performance of the economy, if measured by income increase, was satisfactory until 1976. Yearly income increase averaged around 5 percent in the 20's and 30's (according to some other calculations it was 7 percent); it was 6.4 percent between 1950-1976. Between 1977 and 1980 the economy plunged into a deep depression with yearly income increase averaging less than 2 percent. Along with that, seemingly insurmountable and unsolvable problems loomed ahead.

The overall growth rate, before 1977, should be considered as a remarkable achievement in the face of the characteristics of the country: Turkey does not have very rich natural resources (or if it has, they have not been discovered or exploited), the international trade carried on in this period was too limited to contribute to the fairly high rate of growth, no original technology was developed in the country and transferred technology was not of the kind conducive to a high rate of growth, and the high rate of population increase (2.5 percent yearly) created many problems. It must be noted that the investment / GNP ratio was around 11 percent in 1951; by 1975 it went up to 22-23, and in years following this period it fluctuated around this figure. It is definite that this must have influenced the growth rate.

Throughout the pre-1980 era (1930-1980) a strategy of import substitution was adopted in the country. Indicators such as the high level of effective customs duties, various import restrictions, foreign exchange regimes with all sorts of restrictions and the low and ever decreasing export volume (as a percent of GNP) bore testimony to the adoption of this strategy in Turkey. The last indicator is perhaps the most important for demonstrating the extent of import substitution. In fact, the export/GNP ratio at the beginning of the period was rather low: 7 percent. But it has continued to decrease and it was below 4 percent by the end of the period in question (1979).

The low export ratio to national income is more meaningful when it is taken into account that the official rate of the dollar (in real terms) was exactly the same at the beginning and the end of the period. The Turkish Lira (TL) was not overvalued in this period (in the sense of being the same at the beginning and the end of the period) yet the very low level of export was decreasing even further.

In the past, the low level of exports caused innumerable balance of payments problems and the economy came to a standstill several times (1958 and 1970); but in each case temporary remedial measures were taken which failed to provide a permanent solution to this acute problem.

Until the 1980's the financial markets were repressed: as a result of which banks, as monopolist institutions as a system, dominated the whole financial markets with a high spread between deposit and lending interest rates. The inexistence of capital markets along with the lack of other competitive instruments gave rise to an absolute dominance of banks in the Turkish financial markets.

There was a strong preference for a restrictive trade regime which sustained high cost import competing industries. During the pre-1980's inward oriented era, the dominance of public enterprises, a restrictive trade regime and financial repression gave rise to a compartmentalized mixed economy. That character of the Turkish economy became more salient after the onset of economic planning in the early 1960's.

The application of 5 year development plans began in 1963. The following appraisal of the Turkish development plans is a good summary of what was meant by economic development plans in Turkey: "In the formal sense, the planning techniques emphasized the consolidated treatment of government accounts, balanced macroeconomic projections, sector level consistency studies and improved methods of project selections. While providing compulsory guidelines for the public sector, the plans have been indicative for the private sector, relying on continually modified mixtures of specific incentive."

According to my own personal understanding, the most important impact of plans on the economy in the 1960's and 1970's was to prepare ground for a more penetrating import substitution strategy. This observation is strengthened especially when all sorts of incentives previewed for import substituting industry in plans are thought of.

One of the most important events of the pre-1980 period in the Turkish economy was the inflow of workers' remittances in huge amounts considering total foreign exchange earnings of Turkey. In the 1960's more than one million Turkish workers found employment in the western European countries, primarily in West

Germany. Foreign currency transferred to Turkey totaled over the half of the total export earnings.

In 1977-1980 the problems originating from low exports were so disturbing that the Turkish authorities decided to switch to an outward looking strategy. This new era commenced in 1980 and continues to the present day. As a result, exports increased immensely and reached approximately 16 percent of GNP in 1987 and 1988(they were 3.6 percent of the GNP). The long-standing balance of payments problem seemed to have disappeared and the Turkish economy appeared to have regained its historical momentum. Between 1980 and 1986 the average rate of increase in GNP amounted to 5 percent.

The rate of increase in export seems to be related to a very high real devaluation. The TL/$ parity (in real terms) in 1979 (one year prior to the devaluation) was almost the same as what it was in 1950. In the 8 years following 1979 the real exchange rate increased around 50 percent in terms of dollars. With some fluctuations the present real rate is the same as it was in 1988. The Turkish economy reacted vigorosly to this unbelievably high rate of devaluation. Economists of the World Bank had expected such developments and had also predicted that GNP would increase at a higher rate as a result of better resource allocation - the effect of a better ICOR was calculated.

The events in the period following 1988 gave rise to a new recession in the economy in 1994. In post-1988 years the growth of income fluctuated widely: 1989, 1.7 percent, 1990, 9.2 percent, 1991, 0.3 percent, 1992, 6.3 percent, 1993, 7.6 percent and 1994 minus 6 percent. The most noticeable policy change during that period was a revaluation of the Turkish currency (TL.) vis-à-vis the US$: in 1989 and 1990 revaluation was around 30 percent. This was a drastic policy change in view of the previously adopted continuous depreciations of the TL which had given rise to a fifty percent real increase in the dollar. Another policy change was approximately 50 percent increase of real wages in both public and private sectors.

So far attention has been focused on the successful nature of the export orientation strategy. But what of the reverse side of the coin? In 1979, Turkish national income totaled $81,696 million in contrast to $57,654 million in 1988 (in 1979 $). The level of Turkish GNP in dollars may be considered as a measurement problem and one may contend that the decreasing level may not show the decrease of welfare in the country. Moreover, the discrepancy between the average rate of increase of GNP between 1950-1988 in constant TL (5.6 percent) and in constant dollars (4.1 percent) may also be considered a problem of measurement. But it can be demonstrated that measurement in terms of dollars is of more significance than conventional reasoning would suppose.

Apart from the probable effects of the lower GNP in terms of dollars, Turkey has been confronted by several difficulties. The most important is the continuing and worsening inflation which rose over 50 percent, conditions for income distribution were not favorable in the pre-export orientation period and were worsening as a result of liberalization and the export orientation of the economy. Foreign debt reached almost $40 billion by 1988; in 1980 it was around $14 billion. The official unemployment figure totaled 15.2 percent in 1988, although the actual rate should be much higher. The country was shaken by a crisis in 1994; in that year national income decreased by 6.4 percent.

After the 1994 crisis the economy jumped upward in the years following it (1995-1997); the average growth rate of national income was around 8 percent. In 1998 the economy slacked off and the growth rate was calculated to be 3.6 percent. Actually as expounded in my different writings, the trend rate was around 4-5 percent. The following year was worse: it was first calculated to be minus 6.4 percent and revised as 6.1 percent, negative again. The deterioration of the economy is thought of as a consequence of the Asian crisis and that of Russian crisis following it. Meanwhile inflation continued to sustain its high level. But the real factor behind the low growth was pressure on the growth rate of the economy.

It should be underlined that the economy was confronted by acute crises: 1956-1958, 1968-1970, 1977-1980 and 1994 ones. Those of 1999 and 2000-2001 are the last ones.

The first three crises were given rise by a scarcity of foreign exchange; as the limited imports were not enough, the economy could not operate properly. The reason why they were rather cyclical was related to the following fact: they were remedied by measures recommended by IMF and other international institutions, and by foreign financial aids; but right after a little improvement in the economy, the government used to return to the same policy, i.e., import substitution, which created the same atmosphere giving rise to another similar crisis. The 1994 crisis was the end result of a lack of credibility on the part of international financial markets partly due to a reversal of the outward looking policy in the sense that the most important ingredients of that policy, i.e., lower real wages, low valued national currency and high interest rates, seemed to be abandoned by the government. The policy change had created a strain on the economy: import substitution was not the culprit; yet all those changes seemed to end up by a new stage of import substitution. The crisis was cured by turning again to the old policy, export orientation.

The crisis in 1999 was different. The Far East crisis as well as that in Russia might have a deepening effect, but the main culprit was the high rate of economic growth registered prior to that date.

The new coalition government which took power in 1999 made a stand-by agreement with the IMF at the end of 1999 and agreed to take the following steps or measures. The key elements of the government's economic program are:

1- A significant fiscal adjustment and tighter fiscal policy designed to put public finances on a sustainable path.

2- A nominal exchange rate anchor starting with an 18 month pre-announced crawling peg designed to lower expected inflation and interest rates.

3- A quasi-currency board arrangements where all base money is created through capital inflows without any room for sterilization.

4- A supportive, forward looking incomes policy in the public sector.

5- Structural reforms in the core sectors: social security, agriculture, infrastructure, and financial sectors.

6- Acceleration of the privatization program.

The government was determined to take such actions. Retrospectively, it can be concluded that except for structural reforms, the government stuck to the stand - by agreement with IMF. Although the goodwill of the government was quite visible in the case of structural reforms, the political and social atmosphere in the country gave the impression that this would be difficult to achieve. Again, there was pressure from international institutions such as the IMF, OECD, IBRD and EU for the completion of structural reforms.

As a result of the adoption of a great proportion of above mentioned measures, inflation, which stood at 65 percent in 1999 went down to 38 percent in 2000, and interest rates, which were around 100 percent in 1999, went down to 40 percent. Moreover, the economy seemed to be recovering, and the growth rate was estimated to be around 6 percent for 2000. This is a great achievement in view of stringent measures taken in 2000. What went astray was the deterioration of balance of payments: to be more exact, current account deficit, which was almost nonexistent in recent years, was 9 billion dollars.

Turkey was shaken by two crises: one in 2000 and another in 2001. The 2000 crisis set in in November 2000; while that of 2001 in February 2001. Actually those crises were the most destructive ones in the history of Turkey. And the depression in which Turkey found itself after those crises continued up to mid-2003. As the November crisis was at the end of 2000, its repercussions were not observed when the national income increase of 2000 was calculated. It was a 6 percent increase, whereas national income decreased by 9.4 percent in 2001.

A very short account of what occurred in Turkey in 2000 - 2005 will be reported here.

After an agreement with the IMF at the end of 1999 a 3- year stabilization program was adopted. It was shortly summarized above. If that program had been applied without the 2000 and 2001 crises, stability could have been established in the economy. Actually, the cooperation of the public on the economic policy was not obtained. One of the reasons was probably related to the perception of the general public as a result of a lack of proper communication with the government, which had goodwill. But this was not the main factor why the program had failed. The quasi-stability of the exchange rate due to the anchor along with a 6 percent increase in income in 2000 gave rise to a spurt in expenditure. As interest rates were high in Turkey and there was a guarantee that foreign exchange would not increase beyond a certain level, foreign currency flowed in and this raised the propensity to import and gave rise to an increase in open positions of banks and big companies. As a result, a huge foreign deficit occurred. Although there was no problem in financing the huge current account deficit, it was suspicious whether on not this could be sustained.

In November 2000 the crisis was triggered as a result of the search of necessary finance by some banks to pay their current debts. As a result of an increase of interest rates, the value of government bonds possessed by banks decreased; this contributed to the illiquidity as well. As a result, an upheaval occurred in financial markets. Although the Central Bank tried the provide necessary finances, interest rates increased and the huge amount of government bonds owned by banks lost value sharply. Open positions of banks made things worse. Money flowed out; yet it was compensated for by new facilities provided by the IMF.

In February 2001 an unexpected discussion on the top of the state triggered another crisis. It was much more destructive compared to the last one. By that time, it was clear that the existing financial status of the economy could not be sustained. There was huge foreign exchange demand from banks and foreign investors (stock market). Foreign exchange started to flow out in huge amounts. The exchange reserves of the Central Bank depleted rapidly. This could not be stopped by very high interest rates. The open positions and payment difficulties of banks exacerbated the difficulties. On 23rd February the foreign exchange policy shifted to a floating one. All of a sudden the rate of the dollar increased from 680,000 TI to 1,200,000 TL. and began to increase steadily. At the end of the year it was 1,400,000 TI. That was very destructive for banks and companies which had high amounts of debts in foreign exchange. All these gave rise to a loss of security on the part of consumers. According to an estimate of the Central Bank this gave rise to a decrease of some 30 percent of domestic demand.

It is believed that the lack of supervision and auditing of the economy properly by government authorities and faulty aspects of the stabilization program were the main factors giving rise to that crisis. Another factor exerting influence in the deepening of the crisis was the status of the financial sector weakened by duty losses of public banks. Those banks used to grant loans which had very low interest rates in order to subsidize agriculture and small producers; yet they were not compensated for by the government; as a result of those payments relating to subsidies, they were forced to enter the market and offer very high interest rates. In addition, several private banks were mismanaged especially by granting huge amounts of credit to their owners. In the end, the treasury assumed the responsibility by granting some $ 35 billion of public and private banks. It gave a special treasury bond to those banks. A good percentage of them were bought by the Central Bank. Several banks were transferred to the Saving Deposits Insurance Fund. As a result, liquidity increased greatly; that was necessary in order to avoid a complete collapse of financial markets. All these gave rise to an increase in government internal debt.

In May 2001 a new stand-by agreement was signed with the IMF and new financing was obtained. That was partly used for paying back government bonds. The main goal of the agreement was to revitalize the banking system and to make it operable. In order to stabilize the economy some 6.5 percent primary surplus in the consolidated budget was targeted (a difference between the government revenue and expenditure excluding interest payments).

The increase of exports after the devaluation and other foreign exchange inflows are supposed to cure the situation greatly.

The total external debt of the country in 2003 was around $ 145 (billion) which was some 61 percent of its national income. The domestic debt of the treasury in 2002 was estimated to be around a little over 100 percent of GNP; at the end of 2005 it went down to 63 percent of GNP. While the price index increase in 2000 was around 35 percent, it went up to around 80 percent in 2001. That of 2002 was around 35 percent. National income increase in 2002 was 7.8 percent.

In 2003 all macroeconomic aggregates indicated that the crisis was over, and the economy was recovering. The growth rates for 2002 and 2003 are estimated to be 7.8 and 5.8 percent, respectively. The proportion of the domestic debt to national income went down to a level which was not dangerous anymore for the solvability. The average inflation rate was around 15 percent; let us remember that it was over 80 percent 2 years ago. Nominal interests were around 25 percent and the real interest was 10 percent. It was 20-25 percent before. Exports are estimated to be $ 48 billion, 20 percent of GNP. Nobody would have imagined it 2 years ago. The financial discipline of the government has materialized and rules imposed by IMF have been strictly followed.

The macroeconomic data was even better in 2004: growth rate of national income was 9.5 percent; real interest rates around 9-10 percent; price increases around 10 percent; exports were some 22 percent of GNP; investments over 25 percent of GNP. The most alarming figure was related to current account deficit, which was some 5.5 percent of GNP.

The improvement continued in 2005, during which GNP growth was around 7.6 percent. (For other macroeconomic date see the next section.)

§ 3 - WHERE DOES THE ECONOMY GO IN 2005-2008

In the previous section a very short overview of the Turkish economy is found. In this section the present state of the economy (2007) will be summarized by shortly surveying optimist and pessimist views about it. Firstly, optimist ones are summarized.

1- After the 2001 economic crisis the growth of national income has been satisfactory. The average yearly growth for 2002-2007 period was around 7 percent, which when compared with the traditional trend (4 percent) it was quite promising.

2- Inflation, which was over 50 percent (annually) during the last 30 years, seems to have stabilized below 10 percent. In 2007 it was 8.6 percent.

3- The increase in exports is beyond imagination: in 2004, $ 63 billion and in 2005 $ 73 billion.That of 2007 is $ 107 billion. Let me remind that it was 3.6 percent of GNP in 1979 while at present it is over 22 percent.

4- It is observed that investments are high even when the real rate of interest is around 10 percent.

5- Deficits in the government budgets are decreasing continuously. Primary surplus is over 6 percent. That figure indicates that interest burden is getting lower every year.

6- In 2001 it was feared that the government could not pay its debts and interests. In recent years the rate of public debts to GNP is decreasing.

7- GNP of the country was around $ 400 billion by 2006; in the recent past it was below $ 200 billion. Again per capita income was a bit over $ 5000; whereas it was around $3000 in previous years. (According to new series much higher.)

8- New agreements were made with IMF, and a good proportion of IMF loans are paid off.

9- There is a noticeable increase in the import of investment goods. This suggests that an increase in the production capacity should take place in the coming years.

10- Employment seems to increase after 2004.

11- Foreign exchange reserves of the central bank are on a record level, around $ 75 billion at the end of 2007.

12- The government budget deficit was a bit lower than 3 percent of GNP by 2005. It was 13 percent in 2002.

PESSIMISTIC EXPECTATIONS

1- Current account deficits in recent years seem to be at an alarming level. In 2004 $ 15 billion and in 2005 it was 22.7 billion, some 6.5 percent of GNP. In 2006 it is 32 billion dollars, 8.5 percent of GNP. In 2007 it was 38 billion dollars. They are not sustainable. (This question will be taken up below.)

2- Real interest rates are still around 10 percent, which make productive investments very difficult; in addition they are socially harmful.

3- The increase in foreign debts is alarming. They were $ 101 billion in 1999; whereas in 2004 they climbed to $ 155 billion. What is worse while in 1999 the share of public debts to GNP was 52 percent, it went up to 65 percent by the end of 2004.Foreign debts in 2007 is around $ 240 billion, some 55 percent of GNP.

4- It is alleged that if hot money financing current accounts deficits outflows, this would give rise to acute crises in the economy.

5- Turkish currency is highly overvalued and this could not be sustained.

6- The increase of consumption goods in imports seems to be an unfavorable sign.

7- There are noticeable increases in unemployment in recent years, the present rate is 9 percent.

8- The value added in exporting goods is very low and the difference between imports and exports is getting bigger and bigger every year.

9- The making of market as dominant as it is nowadays should give rise to all sorts of socially difficult problems.

10- The preference for higher interest rates and keeping low foreign exchange prices should give rise to difficult problems in the near future. (This will be taken up below.)

WHAT HAPPENED IN 2008

The previous sections of this chapter are devoted to an overview of the recent history of the Turkish economy , and a short summary of pessimistic and optimistic expectations for the near future of the economy are shortly listed.Some figures relating to what happened in 2008 are found in the statistical abstract at the end of this chapter.Let me mention that the deterioration exibited by those figures are supposed to be related to 2008 and 2009 world economic crisis .Here is a short summary.

1-Price increase in 2008 were about the same as 2007.1n the first month of 2009 a decrease in prices increases is observed.

2-The decline of national income growth was rather dramatic.After some 7 years in which the average income growth was some 6.5-7 percent it was calculated as 1.1 percent for 2008. The first estimate of income growth for 2009 was - 3.6 percent;that of IMF was -5.5 percent

3-Unempoloyment figures were even worse.While they were around 10 percent of the national income;they climbed first to 13.5 percent, and at the beginning of 2009 the estimate was 15.5 percent.

4-The exchange rate for the US dollar went up from 1.2 to 1.6 Tl (mid-2009).In fact,in every recession which had occurred in previous years the first signal was the increase of exchange rates.

5-Current deficits,which were the main headakes of the economy, diminished unbelievably by the beginning of the first months of 2009.This was the same in almost every previous recessions.But this time the decrease in trade balance was related to a much higher decrease of imports compared to ones in exports.

6-Interest rates decreased from 16-17 perecent to 12 pecent (government bonds).

7-Investments for 2008 and 2009 are estimated and expected to be below 18 percent,which is much lower than the previous years.

8-Although a very short deficit in government budget was materialized in 2008,the figures of the first months of 2009 heralded a huge deficit for this year.

Now the problem is: who was right? Obtimists or pessimists? My answer is quite different from almost every economist.In fact,the impact of the world crisis was quite evident.lt is also a common belief that as a result of banking refoms following 2001, at the beginning of the economic crisis, banks were in a strong position and that sector was not affected by the worldwide crisis.

My strong belief suggested by the unconventional theory was that the deterioration in the economy had to occur anyway even without the occurrence of the crisis.I don't mean that what pessimists were expecting came true.The deterioration was partly related to the crisis..

The huge improvement of the economy after 2002 was related to the improvement of the financial structure,the huge increase of exports and the unbelievable high foreign money inflow due to the abondance of worldwide financial facilities, the stability of the economy and high interest rates offered .The outflow after the crisis was quite limited.

The decrease of national income growth and its level in terms of dollars had to occur.In this book it was contended that the trend growth of the Turkish economy could not be more than 4-4.5 percent.The necessity of employing 700000 people in nonagricultural sectors of the economy could be achieved by decreasing wages and, in turn, this should give rise to lower national income growth rate and a lower national income level.On the other hand,the rather high cost of living in towns should make the decrease of wages very difficult.Another factor was the difficulty of increasing investment level over 22-23 percent, which could facilitate technological advances.Another reason was high discrepancy between growth rates measured by dollars and domestic currency which had made growth rate in TL higher than what it should be.

§ 4- SALIENT FEATURES OF THE THREE EPISODES IN TURKISH ECONOMIC GROWTH: A SOFT LANDING TO UNDERSTAND THE PROBLEMS ENCOUNTERED BY THE ECONOMY

An overview of economic growth in Turkey is attempted in previous sections. The whole period is viewed coldly or softly in the sense that significant events affecting growth were underlined without any comment and interpretation. In this section the viewing is hotter or livelier, if the saying goes; yet it is soft again in a sense. Here the impact of ideology, underlying cultural factors, established institutions, beliefs, personal characteristics of administrators, and /or all those factors which are not quantified are coming into the picture.

Although the stages of growth were differentiated as inward looking (import substituting) and outward looking in the previous sections, in this section the first stage is divided into three substages, i.e., emerging economy,(1923-1950), the ruling of the democratic party (1950-1960) and strictly import substituting policy with socialistic traits (1960-1980).The next stage continuing to present is an outward looking-partly liberalized economy.

The first subperiod of the first stage is the emergence of the economy as mentioned above. The economy was established on the foundations laid by the Ottoman heritage, good or bad. The main driving force or the basic philosophy was the adage put forward by Atatürk: POLITICAL INDEPENDENCE ALONG WITH ECONOMIC INDEPENDENCE. It was simple at the face value.It reflected the reaction toward the conditions destroying Ottoman Turkey. What the founders of the republic found was the remnants of an economy put apart supposedly caused by the foreign dominance, especially by capitulations. It was quite natural that new rulers had to be against the foreign dominance in the economy. But when it came to detail the interpretation of economic independence was not so very easy. Was it a total repatriation or annihilation of foreign economic existence? Again, the meaning of international interdependence was rather cloudy. In fact, the impact of ideology appeared on this stage and its influence on the economic administration was quite strong. In other words, the driving force or the preponderance was ideology rather than economic facts or constraints. It is very interesting to observe its efficiency when economic achievements of this period are surveyed. Before doing it let me say that the impossible is reached by the ideology. In order to show it I would like to say a few words about the state of the economy in the emerging years.

When the Turkish republic was declared in 1923, not only did the country have a backward social structure, it was also devastated by continuous wars. The winner of the war of independence, the emerging nation was surrounded by a hostile international setting. As an open market of Western Powers, the Ottoman Empire was exploited by them for long years.

The administrators of the new republic began to work firstly by laying the legal foundations of a western oriented secularized State. The secularization of primary school education was perhaps the one of the first priorities.

Under the conditions described above it would be very difficult to assure an upswing especially when the financial resources possessed by the country were so poor. Yet the miracle materialized. The growth of national income in 1923-1938 is estimated up to 6-7 percent ,yearly. If only the great depression had not taken place, it would have been much higher. The ideology was supported by some other measures such as adherence to budgetary discipline, increasing numbers of state economic enterprises, keeping monetary circulation constant, which were all in the direction of the stability of the economy. Was economic stability so important?

In this period the discussion about the adherence of the government to a liberal economy or the dominance of a price-market economy on the mind of administrators and the merits of a centrally administered economy would be very instructive. Yet no concluding evidence existed there.

Another topic of discussion was the personal characteristics, especially loyalty and goodwill, of the new administrators. In fact, this has always been a point in discussion in the future years up to present. There is a belief that the Turkish economy would have grown at a higher rate if only it had better administrators in the sense of people better educated and also if they considered the benefits of the country rather than their own power and wealth. It is also believed that the establishment of democratic institutions and their proper working in the periods ensuing the emerging years were also important , to a certain extent.

In order to show it let us scrutinize episodes ensuing in the emerging years of the economy: the takeover of power by the democrat party in 1950,the preponderance of military power in the1960 s, the import substitution era after 1960 continuing to 1980,outward looking years from 1980 to the present. In all of them the same personal weakness persisted and it created difficulties in all those different episodes, and all those created economic crises and in the end, the average growth rate remained lower than the capacity of the economy would allow.

After taking power in 1950 the democrat party leaders had a good start. At that time the ideology changed in the sense that it tinted toward reaching the masses of people and to be beneficial to them, especially peasants, and to loosen the administrative chain rather than strengthening the power of the central government, and to open a wider room for a freer operation of price mechanism. But one interpretation is that the lack of proper knowledge of economics possessed by them and, along with that, their personal weaknesses created all sorts of problems. They all resulted in instability in the economy. What were they: deficit budgets, especially due to various subsidies to strengthen their power, especially the distribution of rents and enriching themselves, the increase in inflation as a result, trade deficits mostly due to constant foreign exchange rates on the face of ever growing inflations, deteriorating income distribution, the harmful effects of instability to the financial status of private companies etc; all inducing more intervention to price mechanism and detailed measures to the economy, while depleting foreign exchange reserves and increasing foreign indebtedness. In the end, an economic crisis would arise, which would make the overall growth rate lower.

While keeping the footprints of personal weaknesses of the old administrators, the new ones of the period ensuing the military coup were also more leftist minded. Old democrats were participating in the new government but there was a belief that the economic difficulties of the 50's were related to the operation of the price mechanism and the intervention of the central government should be strengthened; not only was the operation of a market economy detrimental to the growth of the economy, it also had antisocial consequences .To cure the situation the new driving force was the creation of a social state, whatever it was. The necessary apparatus was central planning. In fact, after establishing State Planning Department in 1961, 5-year economic plans came into existence. Was the government interested only in the overall state of the economy? Definitely not! In fact, the overall planning strategy degenerated into detailed interventions to the economy, i.e., prohibitions, incentives in all sectors; in the end nothing much remained from market economy. The behavior of administrators in the era covering 1960-1980,was perhaps a mixture of previous personal weaknesses with a love of socialistic applications. In the end, ever strengthening import substitution policies causing all sorts of troubles as described in the previous sections arose. Again 2 economic crises occurred: 1970 and the 1977-1980 one, the latter being the worst ever encountered up to that period. The diagnosis again was the ideology mixed with the personal weaknesses which was hindering the a higher growth rate.

The last stage, i.e., outward looking and more liberalized economy set in 1980. There was little import substitution and the operation of price mechanism was more in line with the fashionable practices on the world. Would previous economic difficulties disappear? At face value, in the beginning years they seemed to lose power. Yet others appeared :such as high inflations, the lack of budgetary discipline, the increasing foreign indebtedness, the huge increase of domestic debts as a result of replacing central bank loans of governments by domestic borrowings, very high nominal and real interest rates, deterioration of income distribution, very high trade deficits. Were all of them related to the shift to a more liberalized economic administration?

It was quite clear that the teachings of economics were learned better and several economists who could apply them were called to advise the governments, and again the public opinion was better enlightened by those people; yet the same problems persisted more intensely. Why? One explanation is the persistence of the personal weaknesses of administering people and conditions offered by the general environment for their prevalence.

On this point it is proper to repeat the questions asked by a prominent Turkish economist, Professor Oktay Yenal: would not the operation of the democracy a hindering force for the personal weaknesses mentioned above in the sense that if the administration failed, it would be replaced by a different one ,and old administrators would have to leave the stage? Would not the past experience be a lesson for them? He asks the questions but does not answer them.

In the years following the outward orientation, new tendencies were arising, which would give an impetus to the growth of the country. Wouldn't they overweight the previous weaknesses? They were the accumulation of technical knowledge which could be used by ever increasing educated people in the country, the strengthening of the spirit of entrepreneurship, innovative energy induced by a competitive environment. Wouldn't they overweigh static and conservative attitude persisting ever since the Ottoman era? Wouldn't they overweigh the ideology and the heritage of the past? The tendency of globalization, ever increasing outsourcing practices, a wider propagation of techniques and knowledge would perhaps give an impetus to the growth of the economy. Why wouldn't Turkey increase its growth rate?

There was more. The old complaint was against the detailed intervention of the government to markets. Now that the tendency weakened why wouldn't the growth rate increase?

What were the recommended measures to be taken to cure the situation after the 2001 economic crisis? Some of the measures, popular but perhaps scientifically oriented, could be summarized as follows: 1-A tax at the source for government bonds should be issued (it prevails now). 2-Big business should pay tax for their interest earnings. 3-Additional taxes on petroleum products should be received by the government (it prevails now). 4-The abolition of all subsidies (partially prevails now). 5-Savings in budgetary expenditures (it prevails now). 6-A limit to currency issue by the central bank (it prevails to a certain extent now). 7-The acceleration of privatization (it prevails now). 8-A new wage and employment policy (it prevails now). Almost all of those measures are taken; yet difficult problems loom ahead.

The so far achieved growth rate of national income is considered insufficient by the general public as well as by economists. There are all sorts of arguments to support that idea. I do not want to repeat them. I would like to underline some widely shared opinions of many economists. They take the present state of the economy as a data and they base their forecasts on it. The main problem was high inflation in the recent past .In order to cure, it was required to take an unpleasant medication, the adoption of which was very difficult politically. This was against the popularity of any government. Neither the political parties nor the general public was ready for it. Inflations and ever recurring economic crises were a result of high budgetary deficits, high interest payments, ever growing public debts, ever increasing currency volume. It is believed that governments are borrowing in order to pay high interests rather than for investments or paying for better education or health services. What is worse, a good proportion of the currency issues by the central bank is used to buy government bonds by banks. The increase of subsidies and an improvement of the status of wage and salary earners are the main issue in political party programs. Another practice was to borrow from the outside world to sustain economic growth. But this practice created all sorts of problems for the economy.

The end of the story is in the ensuing pages!

TABLE 1
FUNDAMENTAL ECONOMIC FIGURES

	2001	2002	2003	2004	2005
GNP (Trillion TL, Current prices)	176,484	275,032	356,681	424,129	485,058
GDP growth rate	-7.5	7.9	5.8	9.6	
GNP growth rate	-9.5	7.9	5.9	10.0	7.6
Population (Million people, mid year)	68.4	69.4	70.4	71.3	72.1
Employment (Million people)	21.5	21.4	21.1	21.7	22.0
Exports ($ Billion)	31.3	36.1	47.3	63.0	73.3
Imports ($ Billion)	41.2	51.6	69.3	97.3	116.4
Current accounts ($ Billion)	3.4	-1.5	-8.0	-15.5	-23.0
Current accounts / GNP	2.3	-0.8	-3.3	-5.2	-6.3
Foreign debt / GNP	79.1	71.4	61.0	53.9	47.9
Public borrowing requirement / GNP	16.4	12.7	9.4	5.0	0.9
Domestic debt / GNP	69.2	54.5	54.5	52.9	51.8
Total public debt / GNP	101.3	70.5	70.1	63.5	56.6
Primary Surplus / GNP	5.8	4.6	6.6	6.5	6.5
Tax revenue / GNP	22.5	21.8	23.6	23.5	26.2
Wholesale Prices index	88.6	30.8	13.9	13.8	2.9
Consumer prices index	68.5	29.7	18.4	9.3	7.7

Source: Central Bank Report (2005)

	2006	2007	2008
GNP (Billion, New TL, Current prices)	758.341	868.178	950.141
GNP (Billon, $, Current prices)	400	649	742

TABLE 2
THE GROWTH RATE OF NATIONAL INCOME

Year	%	Year	%	Year	%	New Series
1950	9.4	1968	6.7	1986	7.9	
1951	12.8	1969	5.4	1987	7.4	
1952	11.9	1970	5.6	1988	3.4	
1953	12.2	1971	10.1	1989	1.7	
1954	-3.1	1972	7.5	1990	9.9	
1955	7.9	1973	5.4	1991	0.3	
1956	3.2	1974	7.4	1992	6.3	
1957	7.8	1975	8.0	1993	7.6	
1958	4.5	1976	8.1	1994	-6.8	
1959	4.1	1977	4.0	1995	8.0	
1960	3.4	1978	3.0	1996	7.1	
1961	2.0	1979	-0.4	1997	8.3	
1962	6.2	1980	-1.1	1998	3.9	
1963	9.7	1981	4.1	1999	-6.1	-3.4
1964	4.1	1982	4.6	2000	6.2	6.8
1965	3.1	1983	3.2	2001	-9.2	-5.7
1966	12.0	1984	5.9	2002	7.9	6.2
1967	4.2	1985	4.9	2003	5.6	5.3
				2004	9.4	9.4
				2005	7.6	8.4
				2006	6.0	6.9
				2007	—	4.5
				2008	—	1.1

TABLE 2 A
Gross Domestic Products
in Current Prices, 2007
(Million TL)

		Share
Agriculture, Forestry	63,693	7.4
Fishing	2,212	0.3
Mining quarrying	10,536	1.2
Manufacturing	141,545	16.5
Electricity, gas, water	15,622	1.8
Construction	42,748	5.0
Trade	103,322	12.01
Hotel-Restaurants	19,323	2.3
Transport-Communication	117,307	13.9
Financial intermediation	27,234	3.2
Real estate ownership	90,964	10.6
Real estate renting	34,413	4.0
Public Ad., Defence, Social Sec.	33,093	3.9
Education	24,565	2.9
Health and social works	14,129	1.6
Other community services	14,533	1.7
Private houshold, employed	1,488	0.2
Sectoral total	756,729	88.4
Financial intermediation, indirect	12,929	1.5
Taxes-Subsidies	112,588	13.1
GNP (Purchaser's prices)	856,387	100.0

TABLE 2 B
Share of Expenditure on Gross Domestic Product, At Current Prices
2007

GNP		100
Final consumption Expen. of residents, non Res.		73.9
Final consumption of residents in the rest of the world		0.5
Government final consumption expenditure		12.2
Gross fixed capital formation		21.5
Public	3.4	-
Private	18.1	-
Change in stock		0.7
Exports of goods on services		21.9
Imports of goods and services		27.0

TABLE 3
PER CAPITA NATIONAL INCOME IN DOLLARS

Year	Per Capita Income ($)	Year	Per Capita Income ($)	New Series ($)	TL
1981	1573	1994	2200		
1982	1386	1995	2794		
1983	1280	1996	2945		
1984	1234	1997	3046		
1985	1353	1998	3171	4159	—
1986	1486	1999	2839	3733	—
1987	1670	2000	2987	3936	—
1988	1747	2001	2143	2878	—
1989	2005	2002	2563	3326	—
1990	2667	2003	3390	4341	6775
1993	2883	2004	4112	5478	8221
		2005	5100	6681	9923
		2006	5600	7933	10876
		2007	—	9333	11945
		2008	—	10.436	13101

TABLE 4
THE SHARE OF VARIOUS SECTORS IN GNP AND THEIR GROWTH (CURRENT PRICES)

Year	Agriculture (Share)	Growth Rate %	Industry (Share)	Growth Rate %	Services (Share)	Growth Rate %
1950	41.2		9.7		49.1	
1960	37.9	5.4	14.2	8.3	47.9	6.4
1970	25.9	1.8	16.9	9.2	57.2	6.8
1976	26.2	4.2	17.0	9.8	56.8	8.5
1985	19.5	2.2	21.5	6.8	59.0	-
1989	16.3	1.3	26.7	6.3	57.0	5.1
2002	12.0	1.7	25.6	4.1	62.4	2.1
2004	11.2	0.0	29.5	8.5	59.3	9.8

TABLE 5
FIXED CAPITAL INVESTMENT / GNP

Year	I / GNP	Year	I / GNP
1950	10.9	1995	25.3
1960	16.1	2000	22.8
1970	19.8	2001	19.0
1975	23.0	2002	17.3
1980	19.5	2003	16.1
1985	20.0	2004	18.4
1990	25.2	2005	20.4
		2006	—
		2007	21.4
		2008	18.1

TABLE 6
THE GENERAL EQUILIBRIUM OF THE ECONOMY
(Current prices, Billions of TL)

	2001	2002	2003	2004	2005
GNP	176 483 953	275 032 366	356 680 888	428 932 343	485 058 000
External resources	-2 360 709	6 639 998	14 920 066	26 530 062	34 573 935
Total resources	174 123 244	281 672 364	371 600 955	455 462 405	519 631 935
Total Investments	28 451 337	59 532 420	83 683 421	113 671 287	133 340 392
Public	9 835 398	17 222 805	16 714 837	17 941 050	25 983 014
Private	18 615 940	42 309 615	66 968 583	95 730 237	107 357 378
Fixed capital Invest.	33 470 391	47 482 293	57 423 184	78 781 779	98 653 353
Public	11 300 047	17 307 672	17 287 521	18 051 594	24 577 759
Private	22 170 344	30 174 621	40 135 663	60 730 185	74 075 594
Stock changes	-5 019 054	12 050 127	26 260 237	34 889 508	34 687 039
Public	-1 464 649	-84 866	-572 684	-110 544	1 405 255
Private	-3 554 404	12 134 994	26 832 921	35 000 052	33 281 784
Total consumption	145 671 907	222 139 943	287 917 534	341 791 119	386 291 543
Disposable public revenue	5 958 512	17 568 879	24 955 436	46 085 617	69 982 859
Public consumption	23 141 350	34 687 870	43 999 678	51 476 788	57 351 772
Public savings	-17 182 838	-17 118 991	-19 044 242	-5 391 171	12 631 087
Public investment	9 835 398	17 222 805	16 714 837	17 941 050	25 983 014
Public savings minus investment	-27 018 236	-34 341 796	-35 759 079	-23 332 221	-13 351 927
Private disposable income	170 525 441	257 463 487	331 725 452	382 846 726	415 075 141
Private consumption	122 530 557	187 452 073	243 917 856	290 314 331	328 939 771
Private savings	47 994 884	70 011 414	87 807 596	92 532 395	86 135 370
Private investment	18 615 940	42 309 615	66 968 583	95 730 237	107 357 378
Private savings menus investments	29 378 945	27 701 799	20 839 013	-3 197 842	-21 222 008
Private saving rate	28.1	27.2	26.5	24.2	20.8
Total domestic savings	30 812 046	52 892 423	68 763 354	87 141 224	98 766 457
Fix. capital Inv./GNP	19.0	17.3	16.1	18.4	20.3
Domestic saving /GNP	17.5	19.2	19.3	20.3	20.4

Source: Central Bank 2005 Report, p.193

	2006	2008
Domestic saving / GNP	**15.6**	**16.4**

TABLE 7
SOME INDICES FOR CONSOLIDATED BUDGET (%)

	2001	2002	2003	2005
REVENUE INDICES				
Total revenue / Total expenditure	63.2	64.4	71.4	93.3
Total revenue / Total non-interest budget expenditure	128.0	115.6	122.9	136.3
Tax revenue / Total revenue	77.4	79.0	84.3	79.3
Tax revenue / Total expenditure	49.0	50.9	60.2	74.0
Tax revenue / Non-interest budget expenditure	99.1	91.2	103.5	108.1
EXPEDITURE INDICES				
Interest expenditure / Tax revenue	103.3	87.0	69.5	42.7
Non-interest expenditure / Total expenditure	49.4	55.8	58.2	31.6
Personnel expenditure / Total expenditure	18.7	19.7	21.6	22.0
Investment expenditure / Total expenditure	5.9	7.2	5.1	7.8
Non-interest transfers / Total expenditure	18.4	22.5	25.6	24.3
FINANCING INDICES				
Domestic borrowing / GNP	43.9	35.0	41.7	-
Domestic principal payment / GNP	30.6	28.6	29.7	-
Domestic debt service / GNP	51.8	45.7	44.4	-

Source: Central Bank Report 2003, p.37 and Central Bank Report 2005, p. 33

TABLE 8
THE DISTRIBUTION OF DOMESTIC DEBT OF THE GOVERNMENT AMONG CREDITORS

	2002		2003		2004		2005	
	Trillion TL	%	Trillion TL	%	Trillion TL	%	Million YTL	%
1- Public sectors	79,107	52.8	92,626	47.7	83,3	37.1	75,5	30.8
a- Central Bank	28,112	18.8	26,900	13.8	22,1	9.3	18,4	7.5
b- Gov. Banks	24,278	16.2	27,239	14.0	27,4	12.2	25,0	10.2
c- Public Deposit Fund Insurance	11,029	7.4	15,056	7.7	8,3	3.7	4,5	1.8
d- Others	15,694	10.5	23,431	12.1	25,4	11.3	27,5	11.2
2- General Public	70,763	47.2	101,760	52.3	141,3	62.9	169,3	69.2
Total (1+2)	149,870	100.0	194,387	100.0	224,5	100.0	244,0	100.0

Source: Central Bank 2003 Report p.39 and 2004 p. 43, 2005, p. 39

TABLE 9
DOMESTIC DEBT OF GOVERNMENT
(SEVERAL RATIOS, %)

	2000	2001	2002	2003	2004	2005
Total Dom. debt / GNP	29.0	69.2	54.8	54.4	52.9	50.5
Cash Dom. debt / GNP	23.4	33.1	32.6	36.5	39.0	40.5
Total Dom. debt / M2	121.0	263.6	243.2	240.2	205.3	155.8
Cash Dom. debt / M2	97.8	125.9	144.9	161.2	151.4	123.6
Total Dom. debt / M3	67.0	117.6	111.5	129.7	121.1	104.9
Cash Dom. debt / M3-forex	54.1	56.2	64.1	87.1	89.3	83.2

Source: Central Bank Report 2003, p.43 and 2004, 2005, p. 44.

TABLE 9 A

	2004	2005	2006	2007	2008
Central Gov. Budget Balance (Bill.TL)	-29.2	-6.9	-4.6	-13.7	-17.1
as % of GDP	-5.2	-1.1	-0.6	-1.6	-1.8
Central Gov. Debt Stock (Bill. TL)	316.5	331.5	345.0	335.5	380.3
as % of GDP	56.6	51.1	45.5	39.6	40.0
Total Net Public Sector Debt (% of GDP)	49.0	41.6	34.0	29.5	28.6
Domestic	35.7	35.2	30.0	28.1	26.5
External	13.4	6.4	4.0	1.3	2.0

TABLE 10
AVERAGE INTEREST RATES OF GOVERNMENT DEBT

		Interest Rate	Maturity (Day)
1999		109.5	479
2000		38.1	411
2001		96.5	147
2002	January	74.5	292
	February	75.2	382
	March	71.6	345
	April	60.6	284
	May	56.5	277
	June	70.1	145
	July	72.1	156
	August	64.9	242
	September	63.3	207
	October	65.0	283
2003		44.0	297
2004		24.0	379
2005	December	14.2	-
2007	**October**	**16.0**	-
2009	**April**	**12.5**	

TABLE 11
PRODUCTION OF ELECTRIC POWER

		10^6 Kw/h	
	Total	Thermoelectric	Hydrolic
1950	789	759	30
1960	2,815	1,854	1,001
1970	8,623	5,587	3,036
1997	105,517	63,478	39,816
2004	150,689	106,606	44,083
2005	**161,956**	**122,396**	**39,560**
2006	**176,200**	**131,959**	**44,241**

APPENDICE CHAPTER VII

AGRICULTURE AND INDUSTRY IN TURKEY

§ 1- NATURAL RESOURCES AND AGRICULTURE: AN OVERVIEW

Natural resources include all sorts of resources provided by nature. Among these are arable land, mining and water resources, climate and natural transportation facilities. Accounting for the importance of natural resources in the economic development of Turkey is not easy. As is true everywhere, the difficulty arises partly from the definition of natural resources and partly from separation of their contribution from other factors. However natural resources are defined and however complex the separation of their contribution from other factors is, Turkey is not a country rich in natural resources such as the oil-rich Middle Eastern countries or with great mineral resources or with ample fertile agricultural land. Therefore, it can be assumed that economic development is not initiated by the exploitation of rich natural resources.

On the other hand, the volume of the natural resources of Turkey has not been a deterrent to economic development. The ratio of population to arable land and water resources seems to be more favorable than that in many countries. Moreover, a climate favorable to work and the geographical situation of the country offer possibilities for development.

The area of the country is 779,452 km^2 of which 246,000 km^2 is used in agriculture; the area of land covered by forests is 201,700 km^2; the rest of the area is not usable. The number of inhabitants per square km. was 80 in 1999.

The present use of rivers for navigation is very limited, and there is no prospect of expansion. But the use of water resources for energy production and irrigation purposes is huge. While the hydraulic energy produced in 1960 was one million kilowatt/hrs., it has reached about 40 million kw/hrs. by 1997, and it is estimated that the potential hydraulic energy production volume of the country is around 120 million kw/hrs. (Note: Maximum electricity production by lignite is estimated to be about the same as hydraulic one.)

Water resources providing drinking water may be more than sufficient for the foreseeable future. And the possibility of fishing in sea and inland waters is being exploited to some extent at present. The possibilities in these fields are huge.

The exact extent of mining reserves in Turkey is not known. Although the geological nature of the country suggests that there are rich mining reserves, the known deposits are limited, and the share of value added in the mining sector is very low.

The fertility of land in Turkey is not uniform; along with very fertile land there is arid land. The proportion of fertile land is limited; the fertile parcels of land are situated on the coastline where the rainfall is good; in great areas of the country rainfall is insufficient for good harvests, and the geological nature of a great portion of the land does not offer possibilities for good agriculture. Destruction of fertile land by erosion is very great. But. on the other hand, if the irrigation network were to be extended, the use of fertilizers increased and agricultural production techniques improved, the agricultural production would probably increase. This statement is not wishful thinking in view of the following facts.

1) Water resources available for irrigation are vast, and only a small proportion of them are being used.

2) The area which can be irrigated is vast, and only a small part of it is being irrigated at present.

3) Although production techniques have improved lately and the use of mechanical methods has increased, it can be said that agriculture is still in a primitive stage, and there is much to desire for education among peasant-farmers.

4) The land and climate offer possibilities for the production of almost all sorts of produce.

The growth of agricultural production has been satisfactory in the last 50 years. The annual rate of growth of agricultural value added (at compound rate) has been nearly around 2.5 percent between 1948-1950 and 1997-1999; it compares well with world performance. But, on the other hand, if the increase of population and per capita GDP is taken into consideration, the performance of agriculture should be placed somewhere in the middle.

The growth of agriculture can be analyzed in five periods, each offering characteristics of its own. They are: 1950-1960, 1960-1970, 1970-1980, 1980-1990 and 1990-2000. In the first period (1950 and 1960) the rate of annual growth of agricultural value added was 5.2 percent; in the second period (1960 and 1970) the rate was 1.8 percent, in the third period (1970 and 1980) it was 4.0 percent. in 1980-1990 it was 1.1 percent and 1990-2000 it was 1 percent. In the first period the growth was closely related to the extension of the crop area. The fluctuation of the agricultural production seems to have stayed almost the same; may be a bit less.

In the 1970-1990 period the effect of mechanization, the use of fertilizer, irrigation, new varieties of seeds and improvement of other agricultural techniques seem to have been very important in the increase of agricultural production. The same factors were also operational in the previous period, but the use of such inputs as farm machinery, fertilizers, irrigation, etc, have been much more extensive and, therefore, their full effects have been felt in the last period. The decrease of fluctuations in agricultural production, i.e., the effect of weather conditions, must have been caused by the improvement of agricultural techniques.

Agriculture is divided into three major sectors: agriculture, forestry and fisheries. The most important sector by far is agriculture proper; its value added constituted around 95 percent of the whole.

About two-thirds of the total agricultural production consists of crops and one-third of livestock. The rate of growth of crops is somewhat larger than that of livestock, and therefore the share of livestook decreases in the total. 40 percent of the whole crop production consists of cereals. Figures on production of various agricultural products and the yield per heetare of major commodities are shown in various tables in this seetion.

Although the share of agriculture has fallen to approximately to 8 percent of GNP, almost half of the total working population is still employed in agriculture. Moreover, a good percentage of exports consists either of agricultural goods themselves and/or goods whose raw materials are agricultural products.

It is quite evident that the growth rate of agricultural sector must have contributed to the general growth rate.

The increase in the first period is closely related to the cultivation of previously unused land. After 1960 the amount of land used in agriculture stayed almost the same. [in 1950-1957 the total crop area rose from 14,542 (1000 hectares) to 23,264, and has remained there since.]

Among other factors contributing to income growth, the most important one was the fluctuations in agricultural production. This, in turn, is closely connected with weather conditions. Especially in the early years of the Turkish economic development, the fluctuations in agricultural production seem to have influenced overall growth. But the effect of agriculture must have been less in recent years. Two factors can be mentioned here. One should be the expectation of a decrease in the width of fluctations in agricultural production due to methods to compensate the adverse effect of bad weather, such as irrigation, fertilizers, better seeds, ete. The second factor is connected with the decrease of the share of agricultural production in total income. in fact, the share of agriculture in GNP went down from around 45 percent in 1950 to 15 percent in the 90 s.

We must also stress that there is an indirect influence of agriculture on income. in fact, other sectors are influenced by its growth.

However, observations do not verify this expectation. We observed that during the whole period the growth rate for GDP and that of agricultural were parallel to each other.

STATISTICAL TABLES FOR AGRICULTURE

TABLE VII-A-1

AGRICULTURAL LAND AND FOREST AREA
(000 Hectares)

	1998	1999	2000	2001	2004	2007
Field area						
Area sown	18 751	18 450	18 207	18 087	18 107	17.131
Fallow	4 905	5 039	4 826	4 914	4 956	4.691
Vegetable gardens	783	790	793	799	805	853
Vineyards	541	535	535	525	520	513
Orchards	1 389	1 393	1 418	1 425	1 558	1.690
Olive groves	600	595	600	600	644	714
Forests	20 703	20 703	20 703	20 703	21 184	21.890

Source: Turkey's Statictical Yearbook 2003, 2007

TABLE VII-A-2
SELECTED FIELD CROP PRODUCTION
(Tons)

	1998	1999	2000	2001	2004	2006
Total production of field crops	68 284 658	59 346 066	63 433 032	54 192 949	59 794 857	58 275 647
Wheat	21 000 000	18 000 000	21 000 000	19 000 000	21 000 000	20 000 000
Barley	9 000 000	7 700 000	8 000 000	7 500 000	9 000 000	9 564 000
Maize	2 300 000	2 297 000	2 300 000	2 200 000	3 000 000	9 811 000
Lentils	540 000	380 000	353 000	520 000	540 000	623 624
Cotton (lint)	882 154	791 298	879 940	914 404	935 928	---
Cotton seed	1 334 778	1 157 583	1 295 066	1 353 888	1 425 850	2 550 000
Sugar beet	22 282 539	17 102 326	18 821 033	12 632 522	13 517 241	19 952 110
Tobacco	250 556	243 468	200 280	144 786	133 114	98 137
Sunflower	860 000	950 000	800 000	650 000	900 000	1 118 000
Potatoes	5 250 000	6 000 000	5 370 000	5 000 000	4 800 000	4 935 000

Source: The same as above

Tablo VII - A- 3

The Growth of Agricultural Sector in Various Periods

1950-60	5.2
1960-70	1.8
1970-80	4.0
1980-90	1.1
1990-2000	1.0

Tablo VII - A- 4

Year	**Area Sown (Hectore 1000)**	**Tractor Number**	**Artifical Fertilizer (1000 Tons)**	**Irrigation 1000 (Ha)**
1950	14.524	16.585	--	—
1960	23.264	42.136	295	1.115 (1962)
1970	24.296	105.867	2.217	—
1980	24.586	436.369	5.967	2403 (1976)
2006	22.131	1.037.373	10.455	—

Source: TSI

TABLE VII - A- 5

Productivity in Various Crops

	Wheat	**Cotton**	**Tabocco**	**Sugar Beets**
1963	1.273	410	510	—
1970	1.163	758	456	34.578
1971	1.559	758	518	—
1979	1.867	778	932	—
1980	1.893	744	1.018	38.928
1996	1.979	1.056	967	44.168
1998	2.234	1.357	912	44.168

Source: TSI

TABLE VII - A- 6

The Share of Various Products in Agriculture

	1968-72	1989
Total	100	100
1- Farm	63.3	61.2
A- General	27.7	19.7
B- Other	19.2	23.8
C- Fruit	13.3	13.9
D- Vegetables	3.1	3.8
2- Animals	33.1	35.5
3- Forests	3.0	2.3
4- Water Produce	0.6	1.0

TABLE VII - A- 6

Distribution of Agricultural Erea

	1963		1980	
Size of Farm (Ha)	**Share of Farm**	**Percent of Erea**	**Percent of Farm**	**Percent of Erea**
1-50	68.8	24.4	65.1	20.0
51-100	18.1	23.9	30.2	21.3
101-200	9.4	23.7	11.6	23.8
201-500	3.2	17.0	5.3	22.9
501 and more	0.5	11.0	0.8	12.8

Source: SIS

§ 2 - AN OVERVIEW OF THE TURKISH INDUSTRY

In all studies, the growth of the economy is first analyzed by breaking it down into the growth of agricultural, industrial and service sectors; then the growth of each sector is analyzed and special factors affecting the growth of each sector are separated. It is a well known fact that along with development, a systematical

TABLE VII - A- 7

GROSS NATIONAL PRODUCT, GROWTH RATE AND SECTORAL SHARES

	GNP					Sectoral shares in GNP (%)					
						At current prices			At constant prices		
	At current prices Billion TL	Growth rate %	At current prices Million $	At constant prices (1987) Billion TL	Growth rate %	Agriculture	Industry	Services	Agriculture	Industry	Services
1968...	164	-	18,050	31,635	-	39.8	16.7	43.6	33.0	17.1	49.8
1969...	183	11.9	20,193	33,003	4.3	38.8	17.0	44.1	31.2	18.4	50.4
1970...	208	13.3	19,031	34,469	4.4	36.7	16.6	46.7	30.7	17.5	51.7
1971...	261	25.6	17,244	36,897	7.0	34.5	16.9	48.6	30.2	17.8	52.0
1972...	314	20.3	21,968	40,279	9.2	31.3	17.5	51.1	27.9	18.1	54.0
1973...	399	27.0	27,947	42,255	4.9	30.7	17.3	52.0	24.5	19.3	56.2
1974...	538	34.7	38,242	43,633	3.3	33.0	16.6	50.5	25.2	20.0	54.8
1975...	691	28.5	47,452	46,275	6.1	32.7	16.7	50.6	24.5	20.6	55.0
1976...	868	25.6	53,684	50,438	9.0	30.6	18.1	51.3	24.0	20.5	55.5
1977...	1,108	27.7	61,264	51,944	3.0	29.5	17.4	53.0	22.8	21.3	56.0
1978...	1,646	48.5	66,828	52,582	1.2	30.2	17.3	52.5	23.1	21.7	55.2
1979...	2,877	74.8	81,696	52,324	-0.5	26.7	19.8	53.5	23.2	20.7	56.1
1980...	5,303	84.4	68,391	50,870	-2.8	25.5	18.3	56.2	24.2	20.5	55.4
1981...	8,023	51.3	71,504	53,317	4.8	23.5	20.9	55.6	22.6	21.5	55.9
1982...	10,612	32.3	64,209	54,963	3.1	21.9	22.1	56.0	22.7	21.9	55.4
1983...	13,933	31.3	60,492	57,279	4.2	20.7	21.3	58.0	21.6	22.4	56.0
1984...	22,168	59.1	59,098	61,350	7.1	21.0	20.8	58.1	20.3	23.1	56.6
1985...	35,350	59.5	66,891	63,989	4.3	19.7	21.9	58.4	19.4	23.6	57.0
1986...	51,185	44.8	75,173	68,315	6.8	19.2	25.0	55.8	18.8	25.0	56.2
1987...	75,019	46.6	85,979	75,019	9.8	17.2	24.9	57.9	17.2	24.9	57.9
1988...	129,175	72.2	90,460	76,108	1.5	16.7	26.3	57.0	18.3	25.1	56.7
1989...	230,370	78.3	107,544	77,347	1.6	16.2	26.5	57.4	16.6	25.9	57.5
1990...	397,178	72.4	150,758	84,592	9.4	16.8	24.8	58.4	16.3	25.9	57.9
1991...	634,393	59.7	150,168	84,887	0.3	14.5	25.1	60.5	16.1	26.5	57.4
1992...	1,103,605	74.0	158,122	90,323	6.4	14.1	24.8	61.1	15.8	26.5	57.8
1993...	1,997,323	81.0	178,715	97,677	8.1	14.7	23.7	61.6	14.5	26.5	59.0
1994...	3,887,903	94.7	132,302	91,733	-6.1	14.7	25.5	59.7	15.3	26.6	58.1
1995...	7,854,887	102.0	170,081	99,028	8.0	14.8	25.5	59.7	14.4	27.7	57.9
1996...	14,978,067	90.7	183,601	106,080	7.1	15.7	23.9	60.4	14.0	27.7	58.3
1997...	29,393,262	96.2	192,383	114,874	8.3	13.4	23.7	62.9	12.7	28.1	59.2

Source: SIS, Statistical yearbook 1998

Note: The growth rate of industry in terms of current prices are quite different from what was calculated in 1987 prices, especially when the economy turned outward after 1980. Again, the growth rate of GNP was around 6.3 percent in terms of 1968 prices in 1968-1978; it is 5.2percent in 1987 prices. This is a meaningful observation supporting my thesis.

change occurs in the shares of those three sectors: the share of agriculture decreases, the share of other sectors increases. As will be seen in Table VII-A-1, this has also happened in Turkey. The decrease of the share of agriculture in GDP has been very fast and it came down from 45.7 percent to 14 percent in 49 years. The increase of industry has not been very fast and it has proved to be in the expected direction. The increase of the service sector has been in the expected direction and at the expected speed.

In most analyses the rate of increase in each sector is first calculated and then is commented upon. A study of factors affecting the growth of each sector is a pet subject for ali scholars analyzing development.

Industrialization has always been the main goal of the Turkish Republic. At the foundation of the Republic (1923) there was a belief that modenization was industrialization; in order to reach that goal not only was industrialization induced, but the government assumed several industrial activities. What was the contribution of industrialization to growth? Again, what was the possibility of the growth of industry?

As was previously mentioned, the share of industry as a proportion of GDP has been steadily increasing since the beginning of the Republic. While its share was approximately 15 percent of GNP in 1950, it is now around 24 or 28 percent (Table VII-A-1) in 1997. Is this tendency going to continue? Another observation is the difference between the growth of the economy as a whole and that of industry; the growth of industry has been higher than that of other sectors.

The growth of industry has been different in different time periods.

TABLE VII - A- 8
THE YEARLY GROWTH OF INDUSTRY IN VARIOUS PERIODS (%)

1950-1960	8.4	1968 prices
1960-1970	9.7	
1970-1978	8.6	
1980-1990	7.1	1987 prices
1990-1999	3.8	
1993-1998	4.4	
1999-2002	2.4	
2002-2004	8.5	
1980-2004	5.5	

Source: SIS.

It must be mentioned that the importance of industry is also connected with its share in exports and in the share of industrial employment in total employment.

The speed of industrialization depends on the industrialization pattern, the productivity of inputs, economies of scale, industrial exports, demand from other sectors, and industrialization policy and strategy. Here are some clarifications for some of these factors.

Industrialization Patterns

Industrialization pattern concerns the relationship between growth of the economy and the relative growth of several industrial subsectors. Among them the relative growth of consumption, intermediate and investment (engineering) industries is important. It is known that (Celasun 1983) at the beginning of development, food and textile industries develop first and then chemical, petroleum refinery, metal and pulp industries follow suit. At a later stage machinery industries develop. One of the reason for this development is the pattern of increase in domestic demand. It is shown that the growth of industrialization in Turkey has followed this pattern.

There is no doubt that the prices for different industrial goods and the protectionary policy which was followed must have influenced this pattern.

It is expected that along with development the importance of consumption industries must have diminished, while others must have increased. The observation in Turkey supports this expectation. (Table VII-A9)

Some research works give the impression that the growth of internal demand was the main dynamic force influencing industrial growth (see Celasun 1980 and 1983, Korum 1977, Çiller 1976).

TABLE VII - A- 9

THE SHARE OF VARIOUS INDUSTRIES THE TOTAL

	1962	1989	1992
Consumption	62.3	36.1	36.2
Intermediate	27.8	47.8	42.3
Investment	9.9	16.1	21.6

TABLE VII - A- 10

INDUSTRIAL PRODUCTION INDEX
(Weighted by value added, annual averages, 1992=100, 1990-1999)

Sector	1990	1991	1992	1993	1994	1995	1996	1997	1998	1999
A. Index										
Food, beverages and tobacco	95.8	104.4	100.5	108.6	111.4	117.1	124.2	134.0	138.4	133.9
Textile, readywear and leather	104.9	95.9	100.0	99.5	95.4	110.7	119.7	127.8	120.2	112.3
Forestry and furniture	105.8	99.4	100.0	107.7	93.4	108.4	113.0	148.1	132.9	131.9
Paper, paper products and printing	96.7	91.1	99.9	119.2	105.0	116.7	112.0	110.3	103.9	105.3
Chem., oil, coal, rubber&plastic	97.3	96.9	100.0	107.4	102.7	119.3	122.8	136.3	137.2	134.3
Non-metallic mineral products	85.6	89.6	100.0	106.1	101.5	113.6	119.6	132.8	134.0	123.1
Basic Metals	101.9	94.0	100.0	113.7	108.9	113.7	123.2	134.8	134.0	126.5
Metal prod., machin., motor vech.	82.6	92.6	99.9	116.8	86.8	104.6	122.6	151.3	158.2	151.7
Others	97.7	72.8	100.0	101.9	68.3	97.6	111.1	124.7	139.1	144.6
Total Industry	92.9	95.4	100.8	108.2	101.5	114.3	122.9	137.0	139.4	132.2

Source: World Bank 2000

TABLE VII - A- 11

The Production of Some Industrial Goods

	1970	1996	2007
Paper (Ton)	18,406	376,447	622,780
Cement (1000 Ton)	6,373	35,213	49,552
Sugar (1000 Ton)	518	1,842	1,666
Crude Steel (1000 Ton)	1,156,380	5,863,094	25,760,889
Trucks (Number)	6,434	29,516	32,536
Automobile (Number-1971)	12,553	196,176	855,460
Bus (Number)	528	2,570	6,115
Refrigerator (Number)	126,508	1,655,956	6,161,317
Washing machine (Number)	60,009	1,051,499	5,409,789
TV receiver (Number)	4,687	2,509,716	12,591,569
Vacum Cleaner (Number)	23,247	1,055,344	1,575,817
Crude Iron (Ton)	—	—	6,225
Cotton Yarn (Ton)	—	440,000	542,000
Cotton Textile (Metr)	—	526,000	649,000

TABLE VII - A- 12

Workers in Manufacturing Industry (1997=100)

	2002(*)	2003	2004/1	2004/2	2004/3	2004(4)
Total	82.2	83.7	82.9	86.3	87.0	85.4
Public	71.1	66.3	54.7	58.9	63.1	58.9
Private	84.4	87.0	88.2	91.4	91.2	90.3

Source: Central Bank Annuel Report, 2004, P. 208

TABLE VII - A- 13

Real Per Hour Wage Index for Manufacturing Industry (1997=100)

	2002(*)	2003	2004/1	2004/2	2004/3	2004(4)
Total	90.0	88.3	89.6	89.2	91.9	90.2
Public	127.1	120.4	125.8	125.3	125.1	125.4
Private	85.4	85.8	89.1	88.6	91.3	89.7

Source: Central Bank Annual Report, 2004,

TABLE VII - A 14

The Share of Manufacturing Industry in Total Fixed Investment (%)

	Total	Public	Private
1973	34.0	23.8	40.8
1980	28.0	26.3	34.1
1990	17.5	4.5	27.5
1993	17.4	5.4	27.8

Source: SPO, Social Indexes (1950-1962)

The Share of Exports and Domestic Consumption of Manufacturing Industry

TABLE VII - A 15

The Distiribution of Manufacturing Industry between Exports and Domestic Consumption

Year	Export	Domestic Market
	%	%
1972	5	95
1983	11	89
1992	17	83

New Figurs (Exports)

	%
1997	15.5
2002	28.4
2005	34.5

Import Inputs in Manufacturing Industry

	%
1997	32.9
2002	37.6
2005	58.6

CHAPTER VIII

THE VALIDATION OF THE UNCONVENTIONAL APPROACH BY THE TURKISH EXPERIENCE

§ 1 - INTRODUCTION

My efforts to understand the growth of the Turkish economy extending over a period of 50 years have convinced me that the previous analyses of the growth of the national income of Turkey and the tools of the contemporary economics are not sufficient to understand and explain it.

Actually, the main analyses of the growth of the Turkish economy are summarily reported in my various books (see also Chapter XI below). But it does not seem that both the absolute level of income and the sharp decrease of its growth rate could be explained by them. Actually, nobody was able to predict the future growth rates: all analyses had failed. Once this is proven, another analysis, which I call unconventional, was offered to replace it, or to express it better, to fill the gap left by conventional analyses.

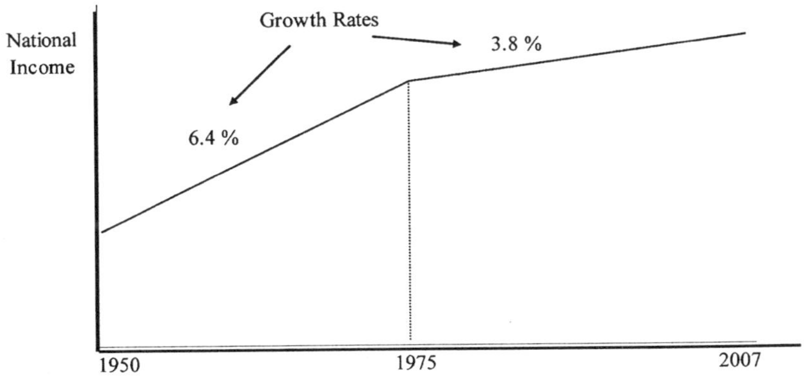

Diagram VIII - 1: The Growth of the Turkish National Income

Before embarking on the explanation of them (it is not easy to convince many people that everything so far put forward is not nearly enough to understand the growth in Turkey), let us examine a simple diagram showing the past growth (Diagram VIII-1).

It is easy to interpret this diagram. While the yearly growth rate in constant TL in 1950-1977 (1968 constant prices) was 6.4 percent, it decreased to 3.8 in 1978-2005 (1987 constant prices). A slowdown in the trend rate of growth is quite apparent.

It is evident that there are 3 problems here:

1- What are the factors determining the absolute level of national income? Although the question seems to be very innocent, it will be shown that the measurement of the absolute level of income is full of difficulties. As a result, the answer this question is very difficult.

2- What are the factors determining the trend growth rate of the economy in both subperiods? Couldn't we understand it by means of conventional analyses?

3- What are the factors giving rise to a sharp decrease in the growth rate of the economy? What are the relative shares of temporary and continuing forces?

The 6.4 percent growth in the economy (1950-1977) seemed very high and unsustainable to me in the 70s. This was high in view of the observed worldwide growth rates and the characteristics of the Turkish economy. Here are some factors which make me tend to think so.

1- The natural resources of the country were rather modest to initiate and sustain such relatively high rates. Turkey didn't have abundant natural resources and fertile land.

2- The level of trade conducted in this period was much lower than what stylized worldwide findings would suggest.

3- The macro-magnitudes such as investment and saving rates, foreign capital inflows, etc. were not high enough to suggest such relatively high growth rates.

4- Technical innovation or technical progress, it may be original or adopted, necessary for such high rates were not at the expected levels.

5- Turkey was confronted by acute economic problems which used to stop the economy almost cyclically. This suggested that something was wrong with the economy.

6- Nobody imagined that the measurement of the absolute level of the national income would be full of difficulties.

That list can be lengthened easily.

Starting from those observations I tried to find another approach to analyze the Turkish economy and used it in my book entitled AN UNCONVENTIONAL ANALYSIS OF THE TURKISH ECONOMY, published in 1978 (it is shortened as UATE).

Two observations in the economy suggested this approach:

1- In a dual Turkish economy, the per capita earning differences multiplier between agricultural and nonagricultural sectors was much greater than what was expected: 4-5 rather than 2.5, which was the expectation based on worldwide observations.

2- The shift of resources from agriculture to nonagricultural sectors was too fast: the share of the agriculture in national income, which was 45 percent in 1950, came down to almost 25 percent in 25 years.

As a result, the impact of this shift of resources should be very high on the national income and a very high percentage of the growth should be explained by the shift of resources from agriculture to nonagricultural sectors. Didn't the economists of the World Bank perceive this important fact? Actually, they did but their understanding and calculations were not one hundred percent correct, as will be shown below.

The source of growth analysis by some leading economists suggested that some two-thirds (4.2 points of the total growth amounting to 6.4 percent) of the growth rate could be explained by input increases, and the remaining 2.2 percent should be attributed to total factor productivity (TFP) (1950-1975), although a bit high, it was not too different from the world experience. Actually, 1.4 point in 2.2 point was supposed to be caused by the shift of resources from agriculture to nonagricultural sectors, and 0.8 point was related to productivity growth, wasn't it normal?

Then what was wrong with 6.4 growth rate of the economy? It could be easily explained. Moreover, this figure could easily be extrapolated ahead.

So far,so good. But if the same method was used for the 1978-2006 period, problems would arise.

The input increase in this period (1978-2007) was not much different (maybe a little less) from the previous period but the productivity growth was much less than 1. Let us not forget that in the previous period, it was calculated as to be over 2. What happened in Turkey to push down the TFP to such a low level?

All changes after 1980 indicated or suggested an improvement in the performance of the economy: the beneficial effects of rising exports, which increased from 4 percent of GNP to 14 percent (now 21 percent), must have impacted the economy; price mechanism operated much better; the foreign capital inflow increased and the share of a more efficient private sector in the economy increased, what not...

As will be underlined below, the explanation of all economists didn't amount to anything reasonable.

When I published UATE, I was trying to show that both the growth rate and the level of the Turkish national income calculated for 1950-1975 had to decelerate soon. Actually it did; but the factors underlined in that book were not enough to explain it. In fact, commentators agreed with me about my expectations and the factors leading to it; but they all insisted that my analysis was known in the literature. Although I tried to show that my explanations were different, and they were based on a different theoretical foundation, I was not able to convince anybody. From that time on, I have tried to develop a new theory or in other words I have made suggestions to improve the traditional analysis.

I am pretty sure that if this book is studied carefully, everbody would see the original aspects of the theory I expound.

This chapter is a highly developed and refined version of how I have demonstrated that the approach (see Chapter VI) I have developed is validated by the Turkish experience.

In my books, a fair idea is given about the history and growth of the Turkish economy. My theoretical suggestions are expounded in Chapter VI above. Does the Turkish experience validate the theoretical suggestions? Before answering this question let me stress again that all explanations based on traditional reasoning failed in predicting the future of the economy.

It will be shown in this chapter that there is a parallelism between theoretical expectations put forward in Chapter VI above and what is observed in the Turkish economy. The suggestions expounded there will be tested in two periods of the Turkish economy: 1950-1977 and 1980-2007 periods. It is found a perfect fit between the theory put forward and observations in both periods.

My innovative ideas were centered on two concepts: 1- The impact of changes of relative prices. By this it was meant that the change in relative prices should not be considered under the changes of TFP. 2- The change in the absolute level of national income caused by a relative decline in labor prices is not captured in traditional analyses. Those two hypotheses are tested in both periods separately. This was because of the fact that the first period consisted of the inward looking development phase of the economy, whereas in the second period the country had adopted an outward looking strategy. Moreover, in the first period the duality of the economy, i.e., income differences between agricultural and nonagricultural sectors, shaped the growth of the economy, whereas in the second period that faded away but instead, the relative prices in the nonagricultural sectors shaped or affected the growth of the economy. Yet the analysis was the same.

There is no doubt that the alleged factors in the literature determining growth should be influential in Turkey. But it will be shown that, as theoretically explained in Chapter VI above, the growth and level of national income in Turkey could not be explained without understanding the impact of relative prices. In this chapter factors determining the trend level of growth are spotted out. It is evident that the actual growth rate fluctuates around that level.

§ 2- GROWTH AND LEVEL EFFECTS IN TURKEY

There is no serious work to explain the drastic fall in the growth of the economy in the second period. Factors underlined in the literature are superficial. In fact, my writings about the growth effect seemed to be 100 percent verified by observations in Turkey. Growth rates calculated in the first sub-period are conducted by means of 1968 constant prices, whereas those of the second period are conducted by 1987 constant prices. The difference between the two is related to the fact that labor prices were some fifty percent less in the second period. As a result, the growth rate should be calculated lower when 1987 prices were used. Here are some figures justifying that conclusion.

It is apparent that real wages increased until 1976 during which national income increased faster. After the fall of wages following 1977 (some 50 percent) the fall of growth occurred. This should be explained: would the change of relative prices affect the growth rate; in other words, was the suggestion in Chapter VI validated by facts? We have a strong argument there. If the growth rate in the Turkish economy in the 1968-1978 period is measured in terms of 1968 prices, it is 6.4 percent. When the measurement is made in terms of 1987 prices it is 5.2 percent. There is even a better figure: the growth rate of nonagricultural sectors in 1968-1978 in terms of 1968 and 1987 prices are 8.2 and 6.2 percent, respectively. For a longer period we have similar figures. For 1970-87 the growth rate of the economy is 5.6 percent in 1968 prices, whereas it is 4.6 percent in 1987 prices. Could we find better figures to validate the argument? The problem is in the mechanism. (It must be warned that the impact of the growth effect was effective in the fall of the growth rate.)

Although those figures show the impact of relative prices in explaining the change in growth rates, that conclusion should be strengthened by additional arguments.

It is known that in post-1980 years relative prices of labor intensive goods were relatively lower compared to pre-1980 years. One of the reasons was the devaluation of the currency in post-1980 years. Most of the imported goods were nonlabor intensive goods; on the other hand, as labor intensive goods had to be exported, their price increase had to be lower than the devaluation rate. Otherwise they could not be exported. Actually, that prediction was verified by facts.

Moreover, in the second subperiod not only were the price differences of nonlabor and labor intensive goods widened, the speed of the growth of labor intensive goods became faster. Two together amounts to a lower growth rate in the second subperiod. According to an international scholar, while the speed of capital intensive and labor intensive goods were around 7.5 and 5 percent, respectively, in 1950-1970 period, they were 0.7 and 3.3 percent in 1979-85 period.

Those figures and observations are nearly enough to explain a very fast drop of the growth rate in the second period: from 6.4 percent to 4 percent.

In order to strengthen the argument again, let us look into the behavior of nonagricultural sectors. In pre-1980 years the growth rate of nonagricultural sectors was 8.3 percent. But it went down to 5 percent (1980-2005). It is shown that in the 1950-1975 period if 1987 constant prices were used rather than 1968 ones, the growth rate of nonagricultural sectors would be 2 percent less. Can we carry this argument to the post-1980 period? We should: as shown above both the price differentials between nonlabor and labor intensive goods were wider and the growth rate of labor intensive goods was faster; it was quite certain that even if the growth of inputs and that of productivity were about the same (which we shall consider in a moment) the growth rate in nonagricultural sectors would be lower by 2 points. My conjecture is around 2 or 2.5 points, due to faster growth of labor intensive goods whose prices were lower in the second period.

The easy explanation of the rather high growth rate in the first period is to think of the dualistic structure of this economy.In the agricultural sector the yearly average growth was 3.3 percent, whereas that of nonagricultural sector was 8.3 percent.At the beginning the share of agriculture and nongricultural sectors were about the same.As in 27 years ensuing 1950 the accumulation of resources took place in nonagricultural sectors,it was quite natural that the growth rate should be 6.4 percent in that period.But this is an easy explanation and it is known in the literature.The problem was to explain the high growth rate in nonagricultural sectors.My novelty was firstly to explain it differently.The main reason was related to an imitative price increase of all prices as a result of the high production cost of import sustituting industries.In order to sell their expensive products the prices of all subsectors in the nonagricultural sector should be high.And this could result in high factor prices, especially labor prices in this sector.This could not reflect on the agricultural sector as a result of the duality in the country. It is explained in the previous sections that if the relative price of the product of one subsector is higher and the speed of growth of that sector is higher, the growth rate of this sector would be higher. This was due to what I called growth effect.

In the first subperiod the calculation of national income was based on 1968 prices. When the income increase in the second period was calculated it was based on 1987 prices where labor prices of industrial goods were 50 percent lower compared to that of 1968 and that should also reflect, to a certain extent, on other subsectors.Again,as the growth of labor intensive goods was faster(one of the reasons being the huge increase of industrial exports), this should result in a slow growth in this period.But this is not enough to explain huge difference of growth between the two subperiods.The problem is the calculation the level and growth of national income in the first period.In fact,as will be shown below the growth rate in the first period would decrease by 1.5-2 percent as a result of switching from a 1968 to 1987 constant prices series.But the fall was more than this figure.

Before explaining it let us scrutinize some figures.I was contending that when new constant price series were applied to the same experience (rememeber the 2nd case above),where relative prices of labor were lower,the growth rate should be calculated lower.Astonishingly this was so in the Turkish case.The growth rate calculated by 1968 constant prices was 6.4 percent for the whole period (1950-1977), whereas if it were calculatad by 1978 prices in which labor prices were much lower,it would be 5.2 percent.Or more exactly,there was more convincing evidence.In the 1968-1978 period the growth rate of the nonagricultural sector in terms of 1968 was 8.3 percent, whereas in terms of 1987 constant prices it was 6.2 percent.

As a result, a good percentage of the decline of the growth rate from 6.4 to 3.8 percent in 1978-2007 could be explained by the fall in labor prices.In addition, the speed of the fall of the share of agriculture decreased and also the growth rate of agriculture decreased from 3.3 percent to 1.1 percent. Yet,this was not enough, again.

The decrease of national income in the grand period could not be explained by the decrease in the growth rate in the second period only.The impact of the level effect should be considered when the growth rate of the first period had to be re-estimated.That should be added to the impact of the growth effect. The average or trend growth rate could be calculated as follows.The growth rate in the second period is added to that in the first period and it should be divided to 2;if so, it would be 5.1 percent: (6.4+3.8)/2=5.1.Yet, I contend that the growth rate in the grand period should be 4-4.1 percent. This figure is found by adding the impact of level effect to that of growth effect in the first period which would bring it down from 6.4 to 4 or 4.1 percent. This is done by calculating the impact of the shift from 1968 to

1987 prices in which relative prices of labor are much lower and also by calculating the level effect.

It is shown above that when there is a fall in labor prices the absolute level of national income should decline in certain cases.And the Turkish case is a good example for that. The problem here is to compare 1977 national income calculated by 1968 with that calculated in 1987 prices;as relative labor prices were much lower the level of the national income would also be much lower.

Now let us explain the fall in the growth rate of national income in the grand period.. 1-The growth rate in 1950-1977 was 6.4 percent in terms of 1968 prices.2- If the relative earnings multiplier between nonagricultural and agricultural sectors in 1950 and 1977 was made 2.5 rather than 4.5(the actual case), the growth rate of the economy could be calculated as 5.7:this difference between 6.4 and 5.7 percent is considered the impact of growth effect:0.7. 3-According to the new definition, when the national income of 1950 was calculated as it was,i.e.,the multiplier between nonagricultural and agricultural earnings being as it was,4.5, that of 1977 was calculated as based on new earning differences (2.5 rather than 4.5), the growth rate would be calculated as 3.9-4.1 percent in the first period.Why?Here is the explanation: 0.7 was the growth effect ;the level effect should be added to it. The decrease of earning differences from 4.5 to 2.5 at the end of the period corresponds to the calculation of both the growth and level effects. lt is shown that if earning differences are kept as they are,the national income of Turkey in 1950 would be 38 (billion) Tl.If they are made to be 2.5,it would be 26 (billion)Tl.The calculated national income in 1977 was (in 1968 prices all the time) 183(billion)T1 ;but if earning diffrences are made to be 2.5 at the end period,this would be 105 (billion) Tl. That means that the growth rate in this period was 4 percent only,i.e. the growth rate between 38 and 105 is 4 percent,41 percent less.As 0.7 percent of 6.4 percent was due to the growth effect, the rest, 1.7 percent was related to the level effect. All this means that the loss of welfare given rise by the change of relative prices in 1950-1997 is 78 billion TL.

Here in this calculation the abnormality is apparent but it does not impede us to go on making that calculation. It is apparent that I started from the earning differences between agricultural and nonagricultural sectors;yet my reasoning is based on the decrease of relative prices of labor in nonagricultutal sectors. Are those not different events?In a way they are not. Simply because the decrease in the earning multiplier is due to the decrease of labor prices in nonagricultural sectors.

N.B. I should make it clear that I am calculating the relative impact of the growth and level efects in the first period. In the second period they do not exists.

There are at least 3 supporting arguments for this calculation.

1-THE DIFFERENCE IN THE CALCULATION OF TFP IN 2 SUBPERIODS.

In the first period it is calculated that employment in the nonagricultural sector increased by 3.9 percent, while the growth of capital was 5.6 percent in 1950-1977. (The growth of capital is calculated as follows. The capital/output ratio is assumed to be 2.5 in the nonagricultural sector; [we know that according to State Planning Organization for the whole economy in the first period c/o ratio was 3.5; if, so, it should be around 2.5 for the nonagricultural sectors; we know that a very high proportion of the growth in agricultural sectors is given rise by the increase of the erea of cultivation. As a result, ICOR in agriculture should be much higher and that in nonagricultural sectors, much lower than 3.5. Therefore, I assumed it as 2.5. Let us remember that the share of agriculture was nearly as much that nonagricultural sectors.] if net investments relative to the income of this sector is 14 percent, the growth of capital should be 5.6 percent, 14/2.5). Altogether if the share of capital and labor is considered to be the same, the contribution of inputs to growth should be 4.8 points. The remaining figure, i.e., 8.3-4.8, is 3.5; this is TFP. When we analyze the contribution of TFP to growth in nonagricultural sector in 1980-2005, we observe the following figures. The growth of labor is 4 percent. In the case of capital in the second period its growth (the percentage) should be lower. Although the net investments were higher, let us say 16 percent of income in this sector, the capital/output ratio should be much higher. We know that in that period the growth rate in this sector was around 4-5 percent. A simple calculation reveals that if capital investment is a bit higher yet the growth of national income is almost half of the first period, capital/output ratio should be measured much higher. I assumed that it was 4. If so, the growth of capital should be 16/4=4 percent. As the growth of employment was 4 percent the input growth would be 4 percent. If it is deducted from the growth of the sector, TFP should be 0.4 percent, 4.5-4 = 0.5. It is evident that this figure is much less than TFP calculated for the first period, (3.5). Was the productivity in the sector much less in the second period? It should not be. As a result, I turned to an unknown factor which would make traditional comparisons inadequate.

As stated above those comparisons are based on a traditional source of growth methodolgy. But we have problems there. We know that capital accumulation ratio calculations are based on capital/output ratio calculations. As the growth rate in nonagricultural sectors went down from 8.3 to 4.5 in the second period and as capital investments were higher in the second period, ICOR figures should be higher and this should make capital/output ratios higher. Although investment to income was a bit higher, the high capital/output ratio should make the growth of capital lower in the second period.

Let us remember that overblown prices in nonagricultural sectors and unsustainable rents were making growth rates of this sector 8.3 percent in the first period. The decrease of the growth rate from 8.3 to 4.5 percent in the second period should be explained by both growth and level effects affecting that in the first period. In fact, the observation of growth figures when they were calculated by 1987 prices rather than 1968 is related to the growth effect. In both at the beginning and end years relative prices are considered as they were like those in the end period: this was 2 point reduction according to observations mentioned above. Yet, in order to get rid of the impact of owerblowing prices we should consider the level effect. If the beginning relative prices are like the original ones, the decrease of the purchasing power should be taken into consideration. As a result, 8.3 percent growth should be perhaps 4.2 percent (see the next section), almost like that of the second period. I tried to show that the change in relative prices should make capital/output ratio almost twice of the actual figure. If so, capital output ratio would be 4 rather than 2.5 in that period. As a result, the growth of capital would be 3.5, 14/4=3.5. When the growth of labor was combined with that, input increase would be calculated as 3.7 (3.5+3.9=7.4/2=3.7). In that case TFP is 0.5 (4.2-3.7=0.5), almost the same of that in the second period. (I would like to warn that all those figures are approximations rather than exact ones; they show the direction.)

2-THE IMPACT OF DIFFERENT CONSTANT PRICE SERIES. As shown above, the shift from 1968 constant price series to that of 1987 one gave rise to a 1.2 decrease in the national income of the country, whereas that figure was 2.1 point for the nonagricultural sectors. That means that the decrease in income in nonagricultural sectors is more. This amounts to the conclusion that as the impact of lower labor prices was in the nonagricultural sectors, the level of income should be felt more in those sectors. It amounts to an expectation of lower nonagricultural income in the first period.

3-THE CHANGE OF NATIONAL INCOME IN TERMS OF DOLLARS. When national income is measured in terms of dollars, it should be some 40 percent less after 1979 and an increase by 3.8 percent (the same as the actual calculation in terms of Tl)after that period.Here two observations should be underlined. 1-This is the expectation of the unconventional theory. 2-The actual figures in terms of dollars are exactly the same.Could we expect a better validation of the unconventional theory?

Now let us include agricultural sectors in the calculation. The growth of agriculture was 3.3 percent in the first period; whereas it was 1.1 percent in the second period. The average share of the agriculture in the first period was 35 percent; in the second period it went down to 20 percent on the average. Then if the agricultural growth rates are added to that of nonagriculture, we come up with 6.5 for the first period (3.3x0.35+8.3x0.65:%1.1+5.4=6.5) and 3.8 percent for the second period (4.5x0.80+1.1x0.20=3.8). These figures are almost the same as the actual ones.

An alternative explanation or supporting arguments are presented below.

§ 3 - THE COMPARISON OF INCOME INCREASE OVER A LONGER PERIOD BY MEANS OF DIAGRAMS

It must be warned that what I did in the previous section was to show that the fall of the growth rate from 6.4 percent (1950-1977) to 3.8 percent (1978-2005) was related, to a great extent, to a switch from 1968 constant prices to 1987 ones. But for the whole period the impact of the fall of the national income level as a result of lower labor prices should also be taken into consideration. (I should stress here that growth effect is visible; yet, the level effect is my discovery.)

The method I have developed in order to decompose the level and growth effects is probably controversial. As I tried to develop the method, I used my findings in UATE, therefore it becomes more so. I should warn at the beginning that the original explanation of the level effect was based on the level of the relative prices of labor and nonlabor intensive commodities prices; whereas my present explanations suggested by UATE were closely connected with the earning differences between nonagricultural and agricultural sectors. What is the relationship between the two approaches? I shall explain it at the end of this section.

Let me briefly repeat the calculation in UATE. All I did was to consider per capita earnings of working people in nonagricultural sectors 2.5 fold of those in agriculture rather than 4.5 fold, which was the actual case. It must be underlined that all my calculations were carried out in terms of 1968 constant TL (Turkish currency unit) prices. (All figures are rounded.)

In 1950 the value added in agriculture was 15,868 (million) TL. (In 1968 prices.) At that time 8,834 (thousand) people were employed in that sector. That meant that per working person agricultural earnings were 1,796 TL. This figure was taken as a basis in calculating per working person earnings in nonagricultural sectors. It is supposed that nonagricultural earnings had to be multiplied by 2.5; this would give us (working person) per capita earnings. If it is multiplied by working people (2,260 thousand) in nonagricultural sectors, we would come up with total value added in nonagricultural sectors: 1,796x2,260,000x2.5=10,147 million TL. When the agricultural value added (15,868) is added to it, we would calculate total national income as 26 billion rather than 38 billion, which is the actual figure. If the same calculation were made for 1975, the value added in nonagricultural sectors would be 63,947 million TL: 4,457x5,739,000x2.5=63,947 million TL. If value added in agriculture (40,889) is added to it, it would be 104,836 million TL. The actual figure was 181 billion.

Now, after the adjustment, i.e., if national income is supposed to be 26 billion in 1950 and 105 billion TL in 1975, its growth rate would be 5.7 percent yearly, whereas in the actual case it was 6.4; the difference between those two figures (0.7) is the yearly growth effect calculated according to my unconventional approach.. This can be shown in Diagram VIII-2. (The growth effect.)

In my original writings in UATE it was asserted that as a result of the shift of resources to nonagricultural sectors, where productivity was much higher than in agricultural sectors, a 6.4 percent growth could materialize. It is shown now that if the productivity is reduced in nonagricultural sectors, growth rate would be lower: yet, 6.4 percent growth should include both growth and level effects.

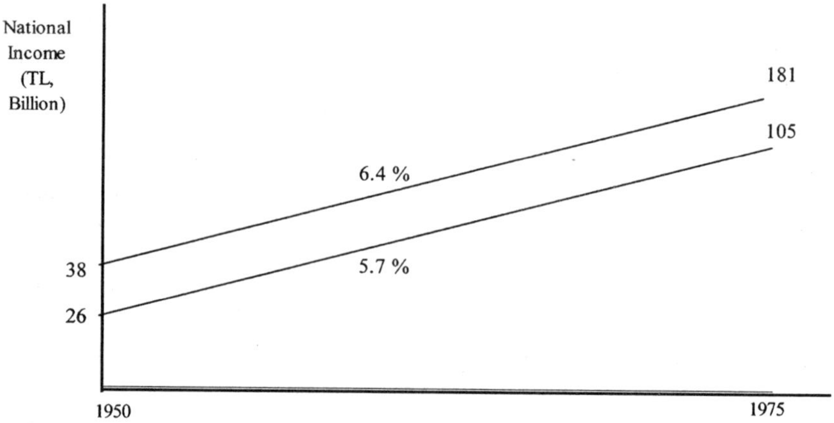

Diagram VIII-2: The Determination of Growth Effect

It must be stressed that if the growth of national income were 5.7 percent, TFP would be 1.5 percent rather than 2.2 percent. (It is calculated that TFP was 2.2 percent in 1950-1975 period.) Is not this what we have in the literature? Actually according to an international economist some 0.60 percent of TFP was due to the shift of resources from agriculture to nonagricultural sector. If the level effect explained above would not be in question, my approach would be parallel to the literature to some extent. But this is not the case. (In addition, there is another aspect of the problem which will be taken up below.)

The meaning of the level effect is explained above (Chapter VI). In the present case, national income, which was 38 billion in 1950 and 181 billion in 1975, was made 26 and 105 billion in 1975, respectively. That meant that national income, which was 38 billion TL in 1950 in terms of 1968 prices, went up to 105 billion in 1975, the decrease was related to both growth and level effects. This means 4 percent yearly increase in that period. This amounts to 2.4 percent lowering of the actual growth rate(6.4) in that period, out of which 0.7 percent is the growth effect and 1.7 percent level effect. What is more interesting, if the growth rate of the economy is 4 percent, the growth of the productivity is very small and almost the whole increase of national income is due to the increase of inputs. Actually if we think that the growth in agriculture was very much related to the increase in the use of land, and if the increase in nonagricultural sectors was closely correlated with the import substitution policy adopted in that period, this may not seem to be a wrong conclusion. (Note: There is also another fact which needs to be scrutinized. When level effect is taken into consideration the use of the source of growth methodology may become misleading. It could be shown that in that case if the level of national income is not reduced as a result of level effect, the calculation of the contribution of input growth might be smaller; therefore in the present case a higher productivity growth could be calculated. See the end of this chapter.)

In Diagram VIII-3 this could be shown.

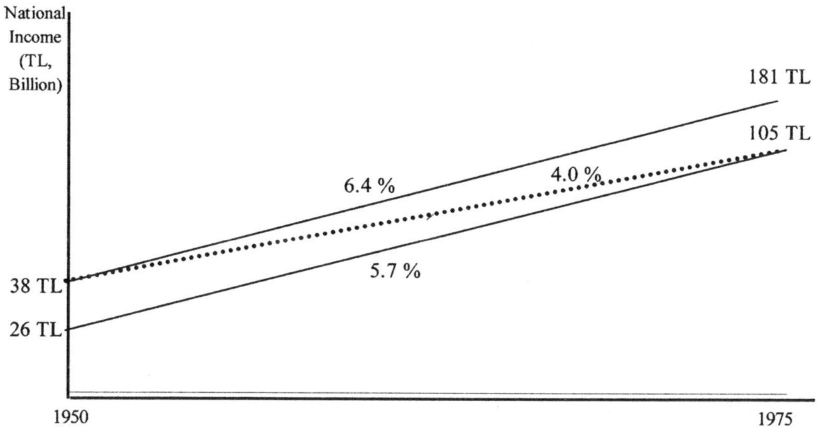

Diagram VIII-3: Determination of Level Effect

All those calculations were made in order to reduce the national income of 1975. It was found out that national income calculations in terms of 1987 prices should be 105 billion TL rather than 181 billion. In 1987 prices national income in 1975 was 46,275 billion TL. Firstly let us draw a diagram (Figure VIII- 4) in terms of original figures.

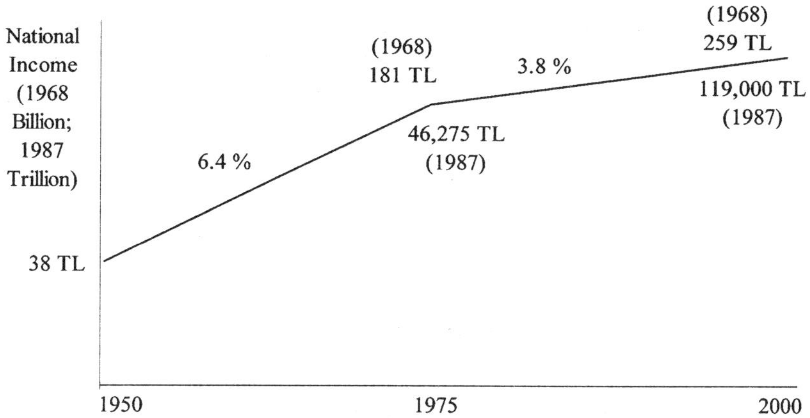

Figure VIII-4: The Growth of National Income in 1968 and 1987 Prices

After the new calculations 181 billion is made 105 billion TL. This is some 41 percent less than 181 billion. Therefore let us say that national income in 1975 was 105 billion.

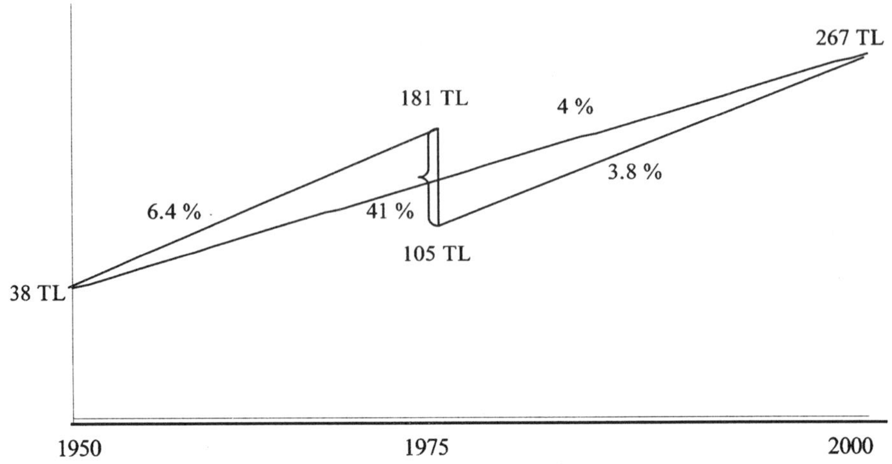

Figure VIII-5: The Determination of Growth Rate for the Whole Period

We know that national income increased around 3.8 percent annually in the 1975-2000 period. Therefore national income in 2000 would be 267 billion TL in terms of 1987 prices if an adjustment were made in 1975 by considering lower labor prices. As national income in 1950 was 38 billion TL the yearly increase between 1950 and 2000 would be 4 percent. This growth rate is an end result of taking out the impact of growth and level effects. In other terms, the impact of the change of relative prices is taken out, and that of traditional factors are determined. It is easy to see that Figures VIII-5 is based on Figure VIII-4.

All that means that the loss of welfare given rise by the change of relative prices in 1950-1975 is 76 billion TL, 181-105=76.

I suppose that after 1975 relative prices of labor and nonlabor intensive goods stayed at a level determined by 1987 constant prices. If the growth of inputs is considered as 3.5 percent for the whole period the yearly productivity increase (TFP) for the whole period should be around 0.5 percent a year.

What was the parallelism between the explanations based on the theoretical framework and explanations above? In theoretical explanations we talked about labor and nonlabor intensive goods prices; whereas we base our reasoning on the earning differences between nonagricultural and agricultural sectors. What is the relation?

Once the prices of nonagricultural sectors are reduced, it means that labor prices in nonagricultural sectors should be reduced more relatively to nonlabor prices in that sector. Here are the reasons: firstly, nonlabor prices should be more in line with world prices; secondly as the exchange rate increased in the second period, labor prices should be relatively lower now. All that means that the relative price between nonagricultural and agricultural goods reflects the relative prices of nonlabor and labor intensive goods prices in the nonagricultural sectors. This is a calculation based on the change of relative prices of nonlabor and labor intensive commodities.

An alternative analysis could be developed which would bring out the same conclusions. Actual figures reveal that if the growth rate was reduced as a result of growth effect the yearly average growth would be 5.7 percent rather than 6.4 percent. In that case national income in 1975 would be 152 TL. In addition, the impact of the level effect should be added to it. It is shown that it had to decrease 6.4 percent by 1.7 percent. As a result of both growth and level effect it was 105, therefore the decrease was about 30 percent. 105 is 60 percent of 181. An alternative explanation is that as a result of growth effect per capita national income was reduced to $600 (see the previouns chapters), whereas official estimate for that year (1975) is $ 833. $600 is about 30 percent lower than $833. According to the calculation above 181 (see Figure VIII-5) is reduced 41 percent. It is apparent that the dollar based calculation would be about the same.

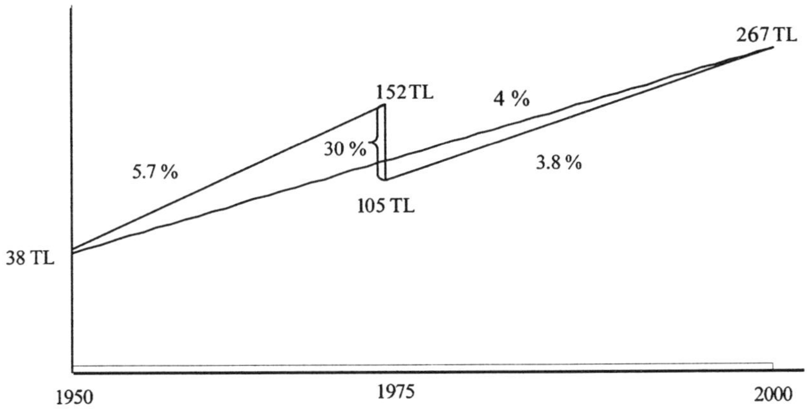

Diagram VIII-6: The Determination of Growth Rate for the Whole Period

Therefore, it can be concluded that about the same results would emerge by the argumentation based on the difference of agricultural and nonagricultural sectors. In the alternative explanation the observed decrease of the growth of national income calculations were made by 1987 prices rather than 1968 prices; this is growth effect. Let us remember that the figure we have for 1975 reflects the high national income due to high factor prices in 1975 also. In order to get rid of it I reduced national income for the second time. In the end, we obtained a figure which could be compared with the exact national income which could be compared with that of 1950.

In concluding it must be made clear that the growth rate in the 1950-1975 period was 6.4 percent if it is measured by 1968 prices. The decrease of the growth rate in the post-1978 period was related to the decrease of relative prices of labor intensive goods and their speed of growth. The calculated yearly 4.1 percent growth rate for the 1950-2000 period means that if 1987 constant prices were used for 1975, this would be the conclusion.The problem is if we are justified to do so should be discussed.

One of the most important messages of this chapter is to correct an inadequacy of the theory of the sources of growth. TFP in Turkey is calculated very low, (0.3-0.7 percent) for the whole period. This is related to the inadequacy of the logic of the source of growth methodology. Firsty, when input contribution to growth is calculated, as the relative prices of labor is lower now the share of inputs in growth would be calculated higher if the shares of labor and capital are left as they were before. Secondy the proportional growth of employment (labor) and capital is not considered. In Turkey the growth of employment (in nonagricultured sector) was around 4 percent; that of capital 5-6 percent. In that case the impact of using a better technology should be very low due to the nonproportional increase of inputs and we should not conclude that productivity growth in Turkey was low. The theory is OK for developed countries where the growth of capital is much higher than that of employment. This is a serious defect of that theory.

§ 4 - THE LEVEL AND GROWTH OF NATIONAL INCOME IN TERMS OF DOLLARS AND NATIONAL CURRENCY

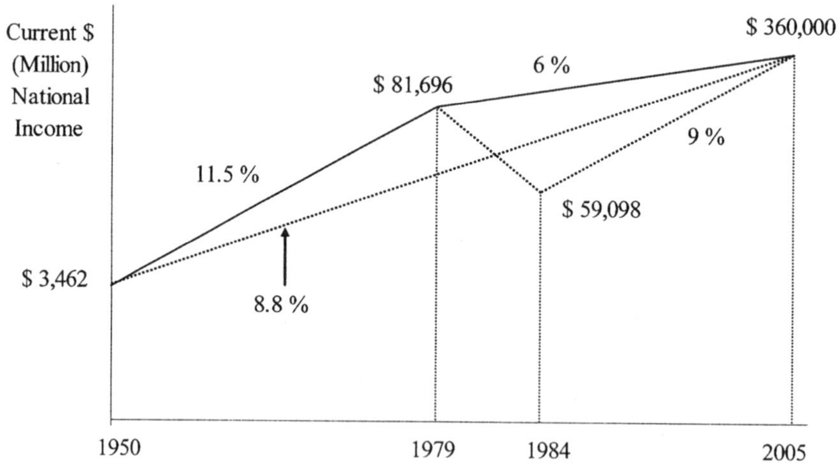

Diagram VIII- 7: National Income in Dollars

The growth rate of national income in Turkey for the period 1950-1979 was 11.5 percent in current dollars. While it was $ 3,462 (million) in 1950, it went up to $ 81,696 (million) in 1979. On the other hand, in 1979-2005 the annual growth rate was 6 percent. It went up from $ 81,696 to $ 360,000 (million). They are current dollars. If the increase of prices in dollars is deducted from these, we come up with 7.6 and 2.5 percent, respectively, for those two periods. The yearly price increases in the US were 3.9 and 3.5 percent, respectively.

These figures are plotted in Diagram VIII-7.

Before examining it thoroughly let us remember the findings of the World Bank for the period 1965-1997. According to it the growth rate of the Turkish economy for the whole period was 4.3 percent in constant dollars. In 1997 dollars it was $ 50 (billion-constant $ in 1997) in 1965; it went up to $ 192 (billion) in 1997.

Here there are two problems: one is the explanation of the fall in growth rate after 1979 in terms of dollars. The second problem is to have a deeper insight for the findings of the World Bank. The understanding of the second problem will throw light on the first problem. Diagram VIII-7 shows what happened in the period examined by the World Bank.

We notice several characteristics of the behavior of national income in this diagram. Firstly the growth rate of income in 1979-2005 is much lower than of what we observe for 1950-1979. Secondly, a sharp decrease in the national income in terms of dollars for the period of 1979-1984 is due to the sharp devaluation in the 1980s.. It must be remembered that the first increase in growth in terms of dollars (1984-2005) was predicted by the theory; it reflects the decrease due to the level effect. A conformity with the theory is astonishing.

A deeper investigation of the findings by the World Bank validates the theory expounded above. In order to understand the growth rate of the national income, the level effect should be distinguished from the growth effect. It is quite apparent here that the growth rate calculated for the whole period is affected by the sharp fall due to the devaluation. The average growth rate in terms of constant TL for the whole period is 5.1 percent both before and after the devaluation (1950-1979 and 1984-2005); it was much higher than the average rate. Then would the average rate (5.1, i.e., 6.4 and 3.8 percent) be taken as the trend rate of the economy? Definitely not!

It is apparent that there is a parallelism in the growth rates measured by labor intensive commodities and by dollars. Why? When Diagram VIII-7 is examined, it would be apparent that the fall of national income in terms of dollars after 1980 devaluation is about 25 percent. The same as what was estimated above by considering the fall of labor intensive commodities, which is equal to the level effect. This is because of the nature of goods which were exported more after the devaluation. In fact, the increase of exports was related to the fall of the relative prices of labor intensive goods. As a result, figures in dollars should reflect it.

According to figures above the growth rate in terms of constant dollars for the whole period the growth rate of the economy is some 5 percent, whereas in constant TL it is 4.3 percent; therefore I speculate that there is some 20-25 percent appreciation in TL.

Another interesting aspect of this analysis is the observation of the growth of national income in terms of dollars. After a series of devaluation at the beginning of 1980s, which ended up by 1984, the growth rate in terms of dollars after that date until 2005 was 9 percent (Diagram VIII-7). If the yearly inflation in the US, i.e., 2 percent, is deducted from that figure, it becomes 7 percent, whereas national income increase in terms of constant TL for this period is 3.8 percent. As price adjustments were not made immediately after the devaluations, and also there was an appreciation in Turkish currency, this was what we should expect, an unbelievably parallel rate to my theoretical expectations. The high figure in terms of dollars should not mean a faster national income increase. But it was also due to the price adjustment process.

HIGHLIGHT

The most important discovery of my efforts is to underline the relationship among costs, value of inputs and that of output. It is shown that the change in the value of output given rise by relative prices of labor and capital would reflect on costs of inputs When constant price series are adjusted after the changes of relative prices 2 problems arise. One is the comparison of national income calculated by new constant prices and that calculated with the previous constant prices. The second problem is that once an adjustment is made in output prices, input prices are left as they were before and as a result coefficients (alfa and beta in source of growth calculations) given to capital and labor when the contribution of inputs are calculated for the growth of national income are left as they were. The second problem could make the calculation of TFP in Turkey lower, which is related to this false calculation. The origin of the problem is related to the fact that costs might be determined by the value of output rather than vice versa. This is called LEVEL EFECT. A discrepancy may exist between value and volume. This is the main actor.

CHAPTER IX
FLUCTUATIONS OF NATIONAL INCOME AND MACROANALYSES

§ 1 - INTRODUCTION

A good proportion of discussions about current problems troubling economies revolves around economic fluctuations of national income, especially about factors that give rise to crises and recessions. A cure for crises and recessions is sought in two contradictory policies, one depressing (high interest rates, lower expenditure, financial dicipline, etc.) and the other, expanding (high demand, low interests, deficit financing, etc.).

While policies recommended (sometime imposed) by IMF-WB favor the first, several economists suggest rather an expantionary one (see, Krugman 2000 and Stiglitz 2002). I am suggesting a new and different dimension. In order to explain it I shall try to draw upon the Turkish experience.

Factors determining the trend level of the Turkish national income are discussed in previous chapters. But we know that national income fluctuates around the trend level. We also know that they are very wide in Turkey.

The most important observation about the fluctuations and/or the variability of national income is the fact that while it was not so variable during import substitution period of the Turkish economy (1950-1979), that increased incredibly in the export orientation period following import substitution. Again, in the second subperiods we also observe a great difference between 1980-1990 and 1990-2008, in volatility.

It is evident that the increase of variability has all sorts of disadvantages for the economy. Again, the most devastating crisis occurred in the end of the second subperiod, 2001-2002. If so, the expected question to be asked is whether the increase of the variability and the acute crisis is related to export orientation and liberalization of the economy along with steps to globalization.

In this chapter the explanations of various economists about the causes of the variability of income in Turkey will be expounded upon.

§ 2 - THE ANALYSIS OF 1970's by PROFESSORS CELASUN AND RODRIC

The analysis of the Turkish economy by Celasun and Rodric in their book entitled DEBT, ADJUSTMENT, AND GROWTH: TURKEY (NBER 1989) is very interesting. I agree with their analysis to a great extent. Therefore, I am going to summarize it in order to give an idea about how the up-to-date macroanalysis is aptly used.

Celasun and Rodric analyze 3 periods: 1) 1970-1977, 2) 1978-79, 3) post-1980. Here a short summary of their analysis for 1970-1979 period is found.

It should be stressed that the analysis by Celasun and Rodric is concerned with short run factors affecting national income.

The 1970-1977 Period

In 1970-1977 period three unfavorable events occurred in the economy: 1) Increasing petroleum prices, 2) an overvalued Turkish currency, and 3) public sector deficits. Those tree phenomena reversed the current account surplus, and it turned into a deficit. The deficit is financed by foreign borrowing. When in 1977 foreign lenders were alarmed by the huge amount of foreign debt, the debt crisis broke. Meanwhile accumulated foreign reserves, especially due to huge workers' remittances, depleted. The current account deficits were very large. As a result of the difficulty of obtaining foreign currency, current account deficits were tried to be solved by administrative measures.

As long as it is not shown that the stock of foreign debt was extremely high and policies were very wrong (both of them were not too bad) it is necessary to find an additional reason for the debt crisis. The authors show that this additional reason is convertible Turkish Lira Deposits (CTLD). CTLD protected borrowers from the foreign exchange risk, i.e., whatever rate is paid when the foreign currency is bought when borrowed, the same rate would be paid when the loan was paid back. Once ever increasing exchange rates were the expected prospect, then it would be easy to see how this would induce foreign borrowing even if very high interests were paid. Moreover, as will be explained below, this created an opportunity for public investments. This process could continue as long as foreign lenders continued to lend money. As soon as this slowed down the debt crisis broke.

The reason on the surface was the huge deficits in the current account. In fact, while the current account deficit of petroleum importing developing countries in 1977 was brought down to 2.1 percent of GDP in 1977, the same figure in the same year was 7.1 percent in Turkey. Other countries had taken necessary measures to ease their situation; in the case of Turkey problems worsened. Why was it so?

The most important reason was to use foreign deficits to finance public sector investments. Secondly, investment and saving decisions were mismanaged by incorrect pricing policies. However, those two reasons were not sufficient to explain the problem. The main reason was the dynamics of borrowing. While the government increased its expenditures, the crowding out effect was not created by granting security against foreign exchange risk for the private sector, and as a result, it was induced to borrow in foreign markets. But this was self destructive. While the real reason of the disequilibrium in the economy was the increase of investments in the public sector, the reason of the debt crisis was the behavior of the private sector.

From 1973 to 1977 the share of investments in national income increased from 18.1 to 25 percent. While private investments were 11.1 and 11.9 percent respectively in those years (1973 and 1977), the share of public investment were 7 percent and 13.1 percent, respectively. The foreign saving was 6.9 percent in 1977. A good proportion of investments was in roads and communication. The domestic savings in this period fell from 20.3 percent to 18 percent. This shows how the overvalued TL would induce consumption. The public borrowing requirement increased from 2 percent of national income to 10.6 percent. The foreign borrowing didn't cover public borrowing requirement directly. In fact the foreign borrowing consisted of only 1 percent of the national income, whereas the borrowing from the Central Bank amounted to some 6.6 percent of the national income. This might seem to be surprising if the relationship between the foreign debt and public deficits is thought of. To understand this contradiction we must look at the macroequilibrium of the economy rather than the micro relations. Although the public sector deficit is financed by foreign borrowing, this is materialized indirectly, i.e., via the banking system especially by the Central Bank. The intermediary was CTLD. This can be described as follows.

The foreign bank (or the foreign bank having money possessed by Turkish nationals) lends money to a Turkish company (generally there is a Turkish commercial bank as an intermediary). Foreign exchange obtained this way is sold to the Turkish Central Bank and TL is received. The money is used by the company in question. The foreign money accumulated at the Central Bank is sold to an importer since the demand of imports was much more than foreign money possessed by the Bank. The TL bought by the Central Bank is lent to the government. Everybody is happy. The borrower is happy because he or she doesn't have financing problems and can import as much as he or she wants. The government is happy because financing is no problem. The public in general is happy because the issue of new currency is limited and price increases are limited. The borrowers in CTLD are happy because if foreign exchange prices increase, they don't pay anything extra.

CTLD gave rise to an expansion of credits: both the private sector and the public sector were financed. As a result of the increase in investments, the growth of national income was enormous. This continued from May 1975 to July 1977.

Crisis without Adjustment: 1978-79

The government in 1977-1979 did not take necessary measures, because they would give rise to a decrease in public spending and to an increase in foreign exchange prices. In this case the macro equilibrium could be secured by an increase in prices. Inflation would have all sorts of undesired effects, especially politically. Since foreign banks knew what was going to happen, they refused to lend again and urged for the settlement of the existing debt. The decrease in the current deficit is secured by the limitation of imports, and that made things difficult. Investment decreased and no foreign exchange was available. Although public borrowing requirement and loans from the Central Bank to the public decreased, reserves depleted as well, and as a result currency issue increased. The inflation rate went up. The terms of trade between agriculture and nonagricultural sectors deteriorated, and real wages between 1977 and 1979 decreased by 43 percent. The public expenditure would have to diminish but as a result of inflation income distribution deteriorated. (See Tables IX-1-2 prepared by Celasun-Rodric 1989)

TABLE IX - 1
RELATIVE PRICE MOVEMENTS, 1978-80 (1978 = 100)[a]

	1978	1979	1980
A. Increases			
Real Exchange rate[b]	100	89	116
Real interest rate on 1-yr. deposits (%)	-25	-31	-38
Real sectoral net prices[c]			
Energy+mining	100	95	126
Manufacturing	100	111	120
Wholesale & retail trade	100	109	119
B. Decreases			
Terms of foreign trade ($)	100	100	77
Real product wage[d]	100	90	76
Real consumption wage[e]	100	86	66
Real sectoral net prices[c]			
Agriculture	100	88	84
Government services[f]	100	99	74
Memo item:			
Financial sector net price[c]	100	80	76

Source: Central Bank of Turkey for real interest rates (averages of quarterly highest returns); State Institute of Statistics for sectoral prices and terms of foreign trade, and SPO for nominal wage data ***(Türkiye Geneli İşçi Ücreti)*** *deflated as noted below.*

[a] *For all prices: 1978 = 100, except for the real interest rate (annual).*

[b] *Real effective exchange rate (TL / foreign currency; export weighted).*

[c] *Ratio of sectoral value added (factor cost) deflated by GDP deflator.*

[d] *Gross wages (labor cost) deflated by GNP deflator.*

[e] *Net wages (after tax and tax rebates) deflated by the implicit deflator for private consumption in the national accounts.*

[f] *Government services value added comprises gross employee salaries.*

TABLE IX-2

RELATIVE PRICE EFFECTS ON INVESTMENT-SAVING BALANCES, AND GROWTH OF REAL EXPENDITURE, 1976-1980

	1976-77 Average	1978-79 Average	1980
A. % GNP, current prices			
Investment	24.9	18.8	21.4
Private	12.5	8.9	9.9
Public	12.4	9.5	11.5
Domestic savings	19.1	16.0	15.9
Private	11.9	12.0	10.6
Public	7.2	4.0	5.3
Foreign savings[a]	5.8	2.4	5.5
Sectoral savings-investment balances			
Private	-0.6	3.1	0.7
Public	-5.2	-5.5	-6.2
Total (= -foreign savings)	-5.8	-2.4	-5.5
B. % GNP, constant 1983 prices			
Sectoral savings-investment balances[b]			
Private	-9.1	-1.1	-0.4
Public	-10.7	-7.7	-7.2
Total (= - foreign savings)	-19.8	-8.8	-7.6
C. *Growth of Real Expenditures (% per year)*[c]			
Private	8.2	-3.5	-6.3
Public	11.4	-0.5	2.0
Total	8.9	-2.9	-4.7
Memo item (% growth per year)			
Real GNP	5.9	1.2	-1.1

Source: SPO (1985) and the central bank's 1986 Annual Report for 1977-83 and 1984-86 data, respectively.

[a] *Current account deficit (after debt relief). The 1984-86 figures follow the revised presentation of the central bank for the balance of payments.*

[b] *See Table A.2 for other data in constant 1983 prices.*

[c] *Domestic final expenditure excluding inventory changes.*

[d] *Provisional estimates*

§ 3 - THE BASIC RELATIONSHIPS IN CONVENTIONAL MACROANALYSES AND SOME MACROANALYSES FOR 1973-1987 PERIOD TO EXPLAIN FLUCTUATIONS IN TURKEY

The fundamental equation in macroanalyses is Y=C+I+G+X-M, where Y is national income, C is consumption, I is investment, G is government expenditure, X is exports, and M is imports. Firstly, economists try to find out functional relationships and parameters determining each term and inter - relationships among several variables.

Recently several research works have been conducted on this line by using the Turkish data.

In most cases, findings validate the expectations of the traditional theory. Some of the expectations of the theory are mentioned below.

1 - There is a close relationship between I and Y.

2 - The behavior of Y is closely related to the trend rate of the growth of Y.

3 - There are close relationships between foreign inflow and the growth rate.

4 - I is closely related to its previous level, its trend level, interest rates, credit availability and inflation.

5 - There is a close relationship between fiscal deficits and current account deficits.

6 - The level of S (savings) is important in the determination of I, and its separation as government savings (Sg) and private savings (Sp), and transfers from one to the other have important economic implications.

7 - There is a close relationship between interest rate (r) and Sp.

8 - There is a relationship between public deficits and r.

9 - Current account deficits (CA) can be decreased by decreasing C, I, and G, and each has different implications.

10 - There is a relationship between public deficits and inflation.

There are many others; hundreds of them. But these are probably the most important ones. As mentioned above, they are all tested, and the conclusions which fit well with expectations make economists very happy. And when there is a discrepancy with the theory, they try to explain them conventionally. Below the findings of some of the macroanalyses conducted for the Turkish economy for the 1973-1987 period will be reported, and it is evident that a lot can be explained by them; and that they are superior to most economic analyses of the Turkish economy; but as the thoughts advanced in this book are not taken into consideration, satifactory conclusions connot be reached. Now a little detail.

1 - Empirical Relationship Between Investments and National Income

The most important and crucial macro relationship to be determined among several variables is that between investments and national income. Dozens of them are constructed by several economists. It is found that output is related to the share of capital formation in national income (investments) and capacity output. Statistical tests seem to be satisfactory to prove that relationship, in other words the theoretical expectations. For example in 1976-77 the share of investments to GDP was 25 percent and in those years income growth was very high. On the other hand, in 1978-79 that rate was around 18 percent and the economy plunged into a deep depression.

2 - The Growth of Permanent Income

The permanent income growth rate of the economy is found by bringing together past income figures by means of a regression equation. The time parameter in this equation is taken to be the permanent income growth rate. In order to enrich it, a dummy variable is added to the equation. As will be observed in one of the studies, the impact of the dummy was insignificant. According to one of those regression equations permanent growth of the Turkish economy is 5.8 for the 1970-1987 period.

The dummy is used to distinguish the period before and after 1978. It was 0 for 1978. The idea is to capture the severe downturn in 1978. It is found out that if the 1978-1980 period is taken out by means of the dummy the growth rate is 5.8 percent.

The determination of permanent income is very important. It has many implications in economic analysis. The first is the determination of a reference point for short term fluctuations of national income. If there is a deviation from the trend rate all sorts of policy measures are sought. Moreover, it is determined that several macromagnitudes, such as consumption, depends on permanent income rather than a factual one.

3 - Pivate Investment

It is found out that private investments are related to the following factors: a-Credit availability. b-The national income in the previous year. c-Expected real output for the next year. d-The lending rate. e-Capacity utilization. f-The share of infrastructure investments. g-The real exchange rate. h-Real interest rates earned in the economy. i-Inflation.

It is evident that those factors are exactly the same as theoretical expectations.

4 - Foreign Inflow and Growth

It is found that there is a close relationship between net foreign inflow and growth rate of the economy. The trade deficit can give an idea about the probable current inflow. There is no end to studies to show that relationship.

5 - Fiscal Deficits

In all macroanalyses fiscal deficits are emphasized. One of the reasons is that there is a relationship between the current account deficit and fiscal deficits. This is related, firstly, to the relationship between the current account and investment gap. If investments are more than domestic savings, this is compensated by current account deficits or vice versa. All those are written in texbooks. If, on the other hand, this is related to a relationship between private investments and fiscal deficits, i.e., for example if private savings are more than private investments, it must be compensated by fiscal deficits. Therefore, if private investments are equal to private savings, fiscal deficits should give rise to current account deficits. Why do I repeat all those textbook information? It is simply because of the fact that researchers are seeking those relationships in Turkey and when they see that that they are validated by the Turkish data, they believe that the traditional macroanalyses are in order in this country. In fact a good many economists are conducting this kind of research. When they observe that large financial deficits did not coincide with large current accounts, they say that that was related to high interests in the country.

6 - The Relationship Between Interest Rate, Savings and Investments

Several economists tried to establish a relationship between interests and savings, especially private ones. Many of them are of the opinion that high real interests induces high savings, whereas some of them, especially those on the left, tried to show that there is not such a relationship. According to one economist a 2.5 point percent rise in real interest rate would induce 1 point in private net savings.

It is believed that high interest rates would discourage investments and this would make national income lower. When it is observed that this was not the case, economists would find all sort of excuses. For example, it is asserted that investment incentives were increased, more credits were extended to private sector, governments shifted to complementary investments, etc.

7 - The Explanation of The Volatility in the WB 2000 Report

The reasons put forward by the WB in its year 2000 report about factors contributing to the volatility of the Turkish national income are summarized below.

After having shown the high volatility of national income in Turkey and its increase in 1990 s compared to 1980 s (the coefficient of variance, i.e. the relationship between the average growth rate and the standard deviation of growth, was 1.4 and 0.6, respectively), its causes are sought.

It is shown that although exports, agriculture, services and public consumption-investments were not closely correlated with that of the growth of national income, the volatility of the industry, private consumption, private investments and imports were quite correlated with growth.

In the report, the reasons of high volatility were expressed as follows: "Our hypothesis is that the economic environment is very uncertain, characterized the volatility of real interest rates, so that firms and housholds find the long run planning to be difficult" (WB 2000, p, 10). During crisis and uncertainty, consumer decisions are postponed. In addition to that, the policy response to shocks tends to magnify rather than dampen their cyclical effects.

Another factor underlined in the report is adoption of full convertibility in 1989. This exposed Turkey to additional external volatility.

§ 4 - THE VALIDATION OF MACROANALYSES BY THE TURKISH EXPERIENCE

In 1973-1977 (the first period) the growth rate was very high; in 1978-79 the economy (the second period) plunged into a deep depression; and as a result of turning outside, (the third period 1980-87) the economy seemed to regain its historical trend. Would all three of those phenomena be explained by the tools of the macroanalysis?

In the first phase of the period (1973 - 1977) all sorts of favorable conditions caused by the huge inflow of workers' remittances and the use of what is called Convertible Turkish Lira Deposits are probably the main causes of the high growth rate. In the following two years the economy plunged into a deep depression and the yearly growth rate decreased from some 7 percent to zero percent. This drastic change is easily explained by macroanalyses. Very simply, while investments were 24.9 of GNP in 1976-1977, they went down to 18.4 percent of GNP in 1978-79, Meanwhile, the deficit in current account in 1977-79 decreased from 3.8 percent of GNP to 2.4 percent. In the first period, the yearly increase in private consumption was 8.2 and in government consumption it was 10.4 percent. Whereas in the second period (1977-79) they were -3.5 and -0.5 percent, respectively.

Here is another observation which fits well with the expectations of macroanalyses. In 1973-77 government expenditures were very high; yet it was sterilized by the huge increase of external debt financed by Convertible Turkish Lira Deposits. As a result, the increase in prices was rather low considering the budget deficits.

The explanation of the third period (1980 - 1987) was also a pet subject in macroanalyses. It was easy to explain the growth of 1980-1985. Investments recovered from the low level they declined to in 1978-79. Foreign debt increased from $ 14 billion to $ 25 billion in 6 years, the current account deficits were around some 2 percent of GNP, and exports quadripuled, they went up from 4 percent of GDP to some 15 percent. All these should have given rise to high increase of national income. Actually, they did; the national income increase for this period was around 4.8 percent. So far, so good: macroanalyses fared well.

The good news about the efficiency of macroanalyses continued during the following years. In 1986-87 investment increased significantly; from 20 percent to 23.8 percent and the average growth rate was 8.3 percent along with a huge increase of foreign debt: it went up from $25 to S37.3 billion. Savings increased from 20.1 percent of GDP to 24.9 percent of GDP. As a result, huge increases in investments did not give rise to a larger current account deficit. The same was true of the increase in the public sector borrowing requirement in 1986 and 1987. All macroeconomic data was the same as before. All those figures validate macroanalyses. But in the next 2 years something went wrong. In 1988-89 investments were the same, even more, other macroeconomic data was about the same but the income increase was only 1.6 percent. If we look at figures for the following years we see that while the level of investments were some 15 percent (relatively to GNP) higher than those of 1980-85 period, the growth rate was about the same in the 1986-1997 period.

N.B.

For macroanalyses covering that period see, Odekon 1988, Conway 1988. Kumcu 1988, Rittenberg 1988, Rodric 1988, Nas 1988, Celasun and Rodric 1989, Baysan and Blitzer 1990. Conway 1990, Anand et al, 1990, Aricanli 1990, Taylor 1990, Celasun and Tansel 1993.

§ 5 - COMMENTS FOR MACROANALYSES

I have serious comments about macroanalyses. I am going to list them below.

1 - All those macroanalyses failed to predict 1994, 1999 and 2000-2001 economic crises. They definitely pointed out problems to arise as a result of some observed macro magnitudes but those should not be interepreted as a prediction of those crises.

2 - The econometric work to determine permanent income is completely misleading. A 5.8 percent increase in the national income was only a dream. It is a sort of a bringing together of the past data without any economic argumentation. That means that those economists were unaware of the fact of what I called growth

and level effects, which are explained in previous pages. They did not look into factors which made the growth rate of the pre-1978 years very high. All those show the inadequacy of macro analyses.

3 - Connected with the above, even if we forget about that they did not predict the trend fall of national income from 6.4 to 4 percent after 1980, they are not even able to explain the fall in the trend rate. All they do is that they bring together figures by means of sophisticated econometric analyses and believe in what the equations would tell them.

4 - I have not seen any macroanalysis which implied that exports could go up from 4 percent of national income to 14 percent in 4 years, and then to 22 percent in 23 years.

5 - All macroanalyses fail to explain very high interest rates in the last 20 years. When they do not find any economic explanation, they talk about expectations, which is a not a pure economic factor. Yet I think that there is an economic factor making interest rates so high. It is non-trasferability of several financial assets among them.

6 - The explanation of the variability of national income in the WB report does not consider the most important element giving rise to it. It is the impact of devergence from the trend national income.

7 - In macroanalyses there is a necessity that nominal figures are deflated. But the rate to be used for deflation is not a mere price index containing all goods.

8 - The impact of macromagnitudes expressed in foreign exchange prices is not considered seriously in any macroanalysis.

CHAPTER X
MACROMODELS

§ 1- INTRODUCTION

In this chapter. I criticize conventional macromodels and try to show the impact of my unconventional views on them. Did I do it as I imagined? No... But all I do is to indicate the starting point.

In this chapter two conventional macromodels are summarized in order to give an idea about the traditional approach.

There are no end to macroanalyses used to understand the Turkish economy and predicts future.

The first one, which is carried out by the Turkish planning department as background work for the 3 rd plan.

The macromodel in the Turkish economic plan, is a very simple one yet it fared much better than all those sophisticated macromodels, one of which is also summarized in this chapter: why was that so?

If this question is answered correctly, the problems given rise by the macroanalysis will be understood.

After a survey of two macromodels belonging to pre-1980, some macro-analyses for the post-1980 years will be summarized. Following them there is a criticism of macromodels as used in Turkey.

§ 2 - A TWO-GAP MODEL FOR THE THIRD TURKISH ECONOMIC PLAN

Planning in Turkey after 1960 was based on the two-gap theory. First a growth rate of the national income was chosen. This was, to a certain extent, a political-social wish; on the other hand, it was justified loosely by the resources and infrastructure of the country as well as by the past performance of the economy. The capital was necessitated by the desired income increase is calculated by means of input/output tables showing capital requirements of each production sector. Once they are determined the fixity of capital/output ratios is greatly adhered to. The first gap is related to the difference between capital requirements and the saving potential of the economy. The second gap was the foreign exchange gap resulting from the difference of exogenously estimated export earnings and imports requirements calculated by means of input-output tables.

Those two gaps, if they existed of course, were closed as follows. Foreign savings were taken exogenously and given to a certain extent. A certain trend figure for private saving was estimated and nothing much was done about it except for savings encouraging literature. The whole burden was laid on the public saving especially by means of increasing public revenue.

The foreign saving was taken as given; it should cover the difference between imports and exports. If not, this was closed by means of import substitution, i.e., part of import needs of the various sectors are supposed to be supplied by newly set up domestic production.

Economists and politicians of the country did not believe in export encouraging power of exchange rates until 1980, and therefore all sorts of imports restrictions are used to get rid of foreign exchange gap at the cost of a lower growth rate which would arise if enough import substituting industry could not be set up.

The Macro Plan of the Turkish Economy for 1973 - 1977

The basis of the third 5 year development plan of Turkey (1973-1977) is explained in a booklet entitled «The Model of Growth and its Solutions» published by the State Planning Organization (DPT, No: 58, 1971).

This is a consistency model based on a multi-sector input/output technique. There are 37 sectors. The input output table is prepared in 1970 according to data for 1967.

The model consists of 140 variables, 314 parameters, 64 base year values and 70 independent variables. 70 variables out of 140 are exogenous.

The findings of the model are exhibited in Tables X-1 and 2. In the sensitivity analysis 4 variables are changed. In each case the result of 11 alternatives are investigated. 4 variables are:

TABLE X-1

A SMULATION IN THE THIRD YEAR ECONOMIC PLAN

MACROECONOMIC MAGNITUDES IN 1977 (IN MILLONS OF TL) 1967 PRICES

		1977					
	Base Year (1972)	A_0 (g= 6.0%) (r=8.5%)	A_1 (g=6.5%) (r=10.0%)	A_2 (g=6.5%) (r=10.0%)	A_3 (g=7.0%) (r=10.0%)	A_4 (g=7.5%) (r=10.0%)	A_5 (g=7.5%) (r=10.0%)
		(1)	(2)	(3)	(4)	(5)	(6)
GNP	147,605	198,503	203,463	203,644	208,046	213,219	213,379
Per Capita GNP (TL)	(3,932)	(4,652)	(4,768)	(4,772)	(4,875)	(4,996)	(5,000)
External Deficit	1,700	-	0,400	0,720	0,720	0,720	1,000
Total Resources	149,305	198,503	203,860	204,364	208,776	213,939	214,379
Total Consumption	119,610	160,334	161,438	161,990	161,063	159,975	160,456
Consumption Per Capita (TL)	(3,186)	(3,575)	(3,783)	(3,796)	(3,774)	(3,749)	(3,760)
Total Investment	29,695	38,169	42,422	42,374	47,703	53,964	53,923
- Fixed C. Investment	28,332	35,813	39,870	39,834	44,877	50,803	50,772
- Stock Changes	1,363	2,356	2,552	2,540	2,826	3,161	3,151
Total Expenditure	149,305	198,503	203,860	204,364	208,766	213,939	214,379
Total Domestic Saving	27,995	38,169	42,022	41,654	46,983	53,244	52,923
Private Disposable Income	115,971	154,824	156,106	156,736	155,701	154,485	155,036
- Private Saving	15,956	22,249	22,429	22,509	22,395	22,262	22,333
- Private Consumption	100,015	132,575	133,677	134,227	133,306	132,223	132,703
Public Income	31,634	43,679	47,354	46,908	52,345	58,734	58,343
Public Saving	12,039	15,920	19,593	19,145	24,588	30,982	30,590
Public Consumption	19,595	27,759	27,761	27,763	27,757	27,752	27,553
Additional Public Finance		-2,134	0,209	-0,420	4,240	9,716	9,165

TABLE X-2

(CONTINUED)

	1977					
	A_6 (g=6.5%) (r=8.5%)	A_7 (g=6.5%) (r=8.5%)	A_8 (g=7.5%) (r=8.5%)	A_9 (g=7.5%) (r=8.5%)	A_{10} (g=7.5%) (r=8.5%)	A_{11} (g=8.0%) (r= 10.0%)
	(7)	(8)	(9)	(10)	(11)	(12)
GNP	203,125		207,721	212,894	213,054	218,112
Per Capita GNP (TL)	(4,760)	(4,764)	(4,868)	(4,989)	(4,992)	(5,111)
External Deficit	0,400	0,720	0,720	0,720	1,000	1,000
Total Resources	203,535	204,039	208,441	213,614	214,054	219,112
Total Consumption	160,096	160,647	159,721	158,633	159,115	159,462
Consumption Per Capita (TL)	(3,572)	(3,764)	(3,743)	(3,717)	(3,729)	(3,737)
Total Investment	43,439	43,392	48,720	54,981	54,939	59,650
- Fixed C. Investment	40,812	40,776	45,819	51,745	51,713	56,192
- Stock Changes	2,627	2,616	2,901	3,236	3,226	3,458
Total Expenditure	203,535	204,039	208,441	213,614	214,054	219,112
Total Domestic Saving	43,039	42,672	48,000	54,261	53,939	58,650
Private Disposable Income	154,576	155,206	154,171	152,955	153,505	153,924
- Private Saving	22,236	22,317	22,204	22,070	22,140	22,210
- Private Consumption	132,340	132,889	131,967	130,885	131,365	131,714
Public Income	48,559	48,113	53,550	59,939	59,549	64,188
Public Saving	20,803	20,355	25,960	32,191	31,799	36,440
Public Consumption	27,756	27,758	27,754	27,748	27,750	27,748
Additional Public Finance	1,738	1,109	5,770	11,245	10,694	14,175

1 - The growth rate of national income (g),

2 - The rate of increase of exports (r),

3 - Capital/output ratio,

4 - Marginal saving propensity.

For example in A0 alternative it is assumed that exports will increase by 8.5 percent, marginal saving propensity is 0.203 and capital/output ratio is supposed to be 3.46 (Table X-3). As a result national income will increase by 6 percent. The result of other simulations are seen in Table X-3.

It is evident that the model explained above is very simple. An explicit ingredient about the productivity parameter is not included in it. Everything is explained by means of mechanical relationships. Productivity is based on the past trends in input/output ratios of various sectors, whereas firstly it will be shown that a necessary change in price ratios to be probably to take place after the economy turns outward would have to change input output ratios and ICOR's of various sectors. Secondly, it is shown above that the measuring the performance of the economy by means of constant domestic prices only is inadequate. Thirdly, if the model is not enriched by several parameters relating to special conditions of the developing country such as Turkey (this is done in Dervis-Robinson model to be explained below), the model cannot be more than a classroom exercise.

TABLE X-3

SOLUTIONS IN THE THIRD YEAR ECONOMIC PLAN
SAVING PROPENSITIES AND CAPITAL OUTPUT RATIOS

	A_0	A_1	A_2	A_3	A_4	A_5	A_6	A_7	A_8	A_9	A_{10}	A_{11}
Marginal Saving Prepensity	0.203	0.255	0.247	0.318	0.389	0.383	0.275	0.267	0.337	0.407	0.401	0.440
Total Capital / Output Ratio	3.46	3.38	3.37	3.38	3.41	3.40	3.46	3.45	3.46	3.47	3.46	3.41
Fixed Capital / Output Ratio	3.27	3.20	3.19	3.20	3.22	3.31	3.27	3.26	3.27	3.28	3.27	3.23

§ 3 - THE SOPHISTICATED ANALYSIS OF THE TURKISH ECONOMY BY K. DERVIS AND S. ROBINSON

In the more sophisticated international literature economic development is analyzed by using more recent and advanced tools of economics. Firstly, a theoretical model is constructed. Then, national economic figures are calculated by econometric methods in order to determine the parameters of the theoretical functional relationship constituting the ingredients of the model. Thirdly, the future of the economy is projected by the model. Finally, policy alternatives are sought.

Many studies have adopted this approach. In this section the work of K. Derviş and S. Robinson on the Turkish economy is critically examined. Their work is typical of those models produced by more learned economists with reference to Turkey. Economists at the World Bank use this same approach in the study of the economies of almost all countries.

According to the estimates of IBRD 1975, made in the framework of a planning approach based on input-output and linear programming techniques (IBRD 1975), a 8 percent growth of income was feasible for the economy for 10 years following 1975.

In the planning approach of Derviş - Robinson a 5.5 percent growth of income could be expected if past policies were followed. It could be made 7.7 percent if money was devalued. A most sophisticated price sensitive planning model is used by them (Derviş - Robinson 1978).

The actual performance of the economy was as follows.

	Income Growth %
1977	4.0
1978	3.3
1979	-0.7
1980	-1.1

It cannot be asserted that the cause of this slowdown was the policy of governments adversely affecting the rate of growth and/or outside shock, such as high petroleum prices.

According to all those models the governments' economic policy should produce a much higher growth rate. In fact, if an exercise were made and if any feasible policy were plugged in the model without changing its parameters, the growth rate would be higher than actual figures. Because all those models are extensions of past relations (here, parameters) into the future. But as was shown above this cannot be done in the case of rent based growth in Turkey. Such parameters relating to factor substitution, ICOR's, productivity change, etc. cannot be taken as nearly stable if the model is projected into the future. Again, several meaningful variables, such as earning differences between sectors and rents existing in the economy are not included in the models. All those characteristics of models make them sensitive to exports and capital investments. On the other hand, policy variables affecting them are taken in consideration exogenously, without any respect to the level of rents.

It has not occurred to anybody that, in order to project the future, we need a different model, which should include additional variables and parameters.

Essentials of Derviş - Robinson Model

Now let us look more closely at the Derviş-Robinson model which constitutes the basis of 1980 IBRD report on the Turkish economy. This model is not only the best description of the Turkish economy, it also constitutes the basis of the policy adopted by the governments after 24th January 1980. Therefore, it is not wrong to say that the future of the country depends on it.

The Derviş-Robinson model is expounded in a World Bank Staff Working Paper (No 305) entitled "The Foreign Exchange Gap, Growth and Industrial Strategy" (1978). The main characteristics of the model are described by IBRD 1980 as follows.

"This model is in the family of multi-sector computable general equilibrium (CGE) models which have been developed in the past few years as instruments of planning and policy analysis for developing countries. It is a 19 sector model that endogenously determines product prices, factor prices and the exchange rate so as to clear the markets for commodities, labor, and foreign exchange. Market clearing is achieved by variation in prices, equating supply and demand in the various markets, with the behavior of the different «actors» in the economy - producers, consumers, government, and the rest of the world - being separately specified. Producers and consumers are assumed to be formal optimizers facing parametric prices. The distinctive feature of the present application is that the nominal exchange rate is fixed rather than flexible, reflecting the reality of the Turkish situation during the period analyzed. The adjustment mechanism to foreign payments imbalances is economy-wide import rationing leading to the emergence of an import premium rate that becomes the endogenous equilibrating variable. The model also specifies resource-absorbing rent seeking when import rationing is effective. For a detailed methodological discussion of the general class of models of which this model is an example, the reader is referred to Derviş, de Melo and Robinson, Planning Models and Development Policy, (forthcomings" (IBRD, 1980, p. 214) (See, Derviş, de Melo, Robinson 1982, Derviş et al).

Similar to any planning approach, the model consists of several equations and once their parameters are found all those equations are simultaneously solved.

A production function is written for each of 19 sectors of the economy. In line with the conventional analysis output depends on (1) labor and capital inputs (2) a productivity parameter (3) the utilization rate of the capacity.

Without explaining the intricacies of the model, its main characteristics and conclusions will be expounded below.

The fourth five year plan of Turkey is for the period covering 1979 to 1983. In The Derviş-Robinson model 1978 is taken as the base year and strategic macroeconomic magnitudes are projected by applying country data to equations constituting the model developed by them.

The determination of exports is one of the most important aspects of the model. The conventional treatment is again adhered to in the case of exports. As most export items of Turkey are only a small proportion of the world demand, the small-country assumption is kept and the country's export prices are accepted to be fixed in the world markets independently of the quantities exported. Yet «while faithful to the small-country assumption, this treatment of exports is quite inconsistent with the view of the world implicit in the specification of product differentiation and imperfect substitution on the import side.» (p. 25). Therefore, price elasticity of demand for exports is not taken as infinite. The price elasticity of demand for exports originating from 19 sectors is shown in Table X-4 «Exports are determined by the interaction of domestic supply and foreign demand with foreign demand elasticities and domestic supply elasticities jointly determining the sensitivity of exports to changes in the structure of relative prices» (p. 26).

The treatment of capital/output ratio by Derviş-Robinson is conventional. According to their findings ICOR's will decrease as a result of higher exports.

TABLE X - 4

EXPORT ELASTICITY

Sector	Export Elasticity
1 - Agriculture	F.W.P. (a)
2 - Mining	F.W.P
3 - Food	2.00
4 - Textiles	F.W.P.
5 - Clothing	2.00
6 - Wood and Wood prod.	2.00
7 - Paper and Printing	2.00
8 - Chemical	2.00
9 - Rubber and Plastics	2.00
10 - Petroleum and Pet. Prod	2.00
11 - Non-Met. Min. Prod.	2.00
12 - Basic Metals	2.00
13 -Metal Prod.	2.00
14 - Non-Elec. Machinery	2.00
15 - Elec. Machinery	2.00
16 - Transport Equipment	2.00
17 - Construction	2.00
18 - Infrastructure	1.25
19 - Services	1.25

(a) Fixed World Price.

The level of real exchange rate is taken as another strategic variable in the whole model. Its increase is supposed to give rise to more exports and to more imports and when it is high, ICOR's become smaller. The degree of increase of exports is found by means of elasticities of demand for commodities as shown in Table X - 4. Again, it is shown that industrial export commodities have smaller ICOR's compared to intermediate goods mostly constituting the subject of import substituting industrialization. The decrease of ICOR's will, of course, increase the growth of main sectors while giving rise to more investment which, in turn, will exert a positive influence on growth again.

The first exercise is made by assuming a fixed real exchange rate. The exchange rate to the dollar ($ 1 = 26 TL.) is supposed to remain stable in real terms. The new rate is determined by increasing it according to relative inflations in Turkey and abroad. The estimate as to the future yearly export increase seems to be 16 percent, yearly. When this increase is combined with other exogenous and endogenous variables the growth rate of the economy over the five years period becomes 5.5 percent on the average (see p. 79). To find behavioral equations, Turkish data are used (see Table X - 5).

The second exercise is made on the assumption that a real devaluation of about 30 percent is made in 1978 and 4.3 percent annually thereafter. Given a differential inflation rate that is projected to be only 5.5% after 1979, this implies a real devaluation of about 30% in 1979 and of 4.3% annually thereafter. As a result of this policy, exports are found to be increasing 25 percent which is much higher than previous export increases under conditions of stable exchange rates (16 percent). This export increase, along with smaller ICOR's gives rise to 7.7 percent increase in GDP, which is much higher than the previous one which was 5.5 percent (see Table X-6).

I think that the Derviş-Robinson model is superior to any study made on the economy of Turkey. But if the existence of rents and their relation to the change in the industrial transformation are not included in the analysis, its theoretical foundation lacks the most important ingredients.

Using a slightly modified Derviş-Robinson model IBRD 1980 projected the medium term growth prospects of the Turkish economy. Their base run showed that GDP for 1978-1985 would grow 6.2 precent annually. But after considering the petroleum price increases in 1979 and also increases in debt service they concluded

TABLE X-5

RESULTS OF A CONSTANT PLD-EXCHANGE RATE POLICY, MACROECONOMIC INDICATORS

	1978	1979	Experiment Base 1980	1981	1982	1983	FFYP Average Growth Rates 1979-1983
GDP Growth Rate***	2.5 %	2.6 %	6.1 %	6.4 %	6.2 %	6.2 %	5.5 %
Value Added Growth****							
Agriculture	5.6 %	2.3 %	4.2 %	4.3 %	4.3 %	4.3 %	3.9 %
Industry	3.1 %	4.2 %	7.0 %	7.8 %	7.4 %	7.4 %	6.7 %
Services	4.5 %	3.1 %	5.9 %	6.2 %	6.0 %	6.0 %	5.4 %
Growth of Consumption	0.9 %	0.3 %	5.9 %	6.1 %	5.8 %	5.9 %	4.8 %
Growth of Investment	-14.6 %	0.2 %	6.3 %	6.5 %	5.8 %	5.8 %	4.9 %
Total Urban Labor Force (1000)	7115	7435	7766	8093	8411	8724	-
Growth Rate	5.4 %	4.5 %	4.5 %	4.2 %	3.9 %	3.7 %	4.2 %
Employment in Industry (1000)	2319	2426	2512	2609	2691	2760	-
Growth Rate	0.2 %	4.5 %	3.5 %	3.0 %	3.1 %	2.9 %	3.6 %
Growth of Average Urban Wage, Real	- 6.3 %	- 1.3 %	1.7 %	2.0 %	2.1 %	2.4 %	1.4 %*
Average Economy-Wide Profit Rate	18.9 %	17.2 %	17.3 %	17.5 %	17.6 %	17.7 %	17.5 %*
Profit Rate in Manufacturing	32.2 %	33.3 %	34.3 %	35.3 %	36.0 %	36.6 %	35.1 % *
Investment Rate (of GDP)	21.3 %	22.6 %	22.9 %	23.1 %	23.1 %	23.2 %	23.0 % *
ICOR	9.1	7.2	3.0	2.9	3.0	3.0	3.8*
Exports (million $, current)	2310	2679	3113	3601	4181	4847	16.0 %
Imports (million $, current)	5064	5163	5958	6889	7916	9058	12.3 %
Import-Elas.	- 9.2	- 3.1	0.9	0.9	0.9	0.8	-
Net Invisibles ($)	407	628	755	907	1093	1322	26.6 %
Remittances ($)	1250	1400	1600	1800	2000	2200	12.0 %
Net Capital Inflow ($)	1200	550	600	650	700	750	650
Debt Service Ratio**	21.7 %	24.5 %	28.5 %	33.1 %	36.1 %	35.7 %	31.6 %*
Degree of Import Rationing	40.0 %	52.0 %	54.0 %	55.0 %	57.0 %	58.0 %	52.7 %*
Domestic Inflation	42.0 %	18.0 %	15.0 %	15.0 %	15.0 %	15.0 %	15.6 %*
Exchange Rate (to the dollar)	26.0	28.2	29.7	31.3	33.1	34.9	6.0 %
Devaluation (%)	42.9 %	8.3 %	5.5 %	5.5 %	5.5 %	5.5 %	6.0 %

* Average over FFYP period.

** Amortization + interest divided by exports + remittances + nfs.

*** Constant market prices, 1973 base.

**** Real value added, double deflated, 1973 base. Includes indirect taxes but excludes tariffs. GDP equals total value added plus tariffs.

TABLE X-6

RESULTS OF A HIGH EXCHANGE RATE POLICY, MACROECONOMIC INDICATORS

	Experiment B-1						FFYP Average Growth Rates
	1978	1979	1980	1981	1982	1983	1979-1983
GDP Growth Rate***	2.5 %	7.3 %	7.6 %	7.8 %	7.9 %	8.0 %	7.7 %
Value Added Growth****							
Agriculture	5.6 %	5.6 %	5.4 %	5.5 %	5.7 %	5.9 %	5.6 %
Industry	2.6 %	9.1 %	8.8 %	8.9 %	8.9 %	8.9 %	8.9 %
Services	4.5 %	7.1 %	7.2 %	7.6 %	7.5 %	7.7 %	7.4 %
Growth of Consumption	0.9 %	1.6 %	6.5 %	6.7 %	6.8 %	6.3 %	5.7 %
Growth of Investment	-14.6 %	9.2 %	8.6 %	8.6 %	8.6 %	8.4 %	8.7 %
Total Urban Labor Force (1000)	7115	7435	7744	8043	8334	8616	-
Growth Rate	5.0 %	4.5 %	4.2 %	3.9 %	3.6 %	3.4 %	3.9 %
Employment in Industry (1000)	2319	2400	2490	2569	2648	2716	-
Growth Rate	0.2 %	3.5 %	3.8 %	3.2 %	3.1 %	2.6 %	3.2 %
Growth of Average Urban Wage, Real	- 6.3 %	0.7 %	2.3 %	2.9 %	3.1 %	3.4 %	2.3 % *
Average Economy-Wide Profit Rate	18.9 %	17.8 %	18.0 %	18.1 %	18.3 %	18.3 %	18.1 %
Profit Rate in Manufacturing	32.2 %	30.5 %	30.8 %	30.6 %	30.2 %	29.4 %	30.3 %*
Investment Rate (of GDP)	21.3 %	22.9 %	23.2 %	23.3 %	23.5 %	23.6 %	23.3 %*
ICOR	9.1	2.6	2.5	2.5	2.5	2.5	2.5*
Exports (million $)	2310	3350	4076	4943	5986	7294	25.9 %
Imports (million $)	5064	5706	6736	7928	9315	10943	16.7 %
Import-Elas.	- 9.2	0.7	1.1	1.1	1.1	1.1	-
Net Invisibles ($)	407	496	563	640	123	805	14.6 %
Remittances ($)	1250	1400	1600	1800	2000	2200	12.0 %
Net Capital Inflow ($)	1200	550	600	650	700	750	650
Debt Service Ratio**	21.7 %	21.8 %	24.7 %	27.9 %	29.7 %	28.5 %	26.5 %*
Degree of Import Rationing	40.0 %	30.0 %	27.0 %	24.0 %	20.0 %	15.0 %	23.2 %
Domestic Inflation	42.0 %	18.0 %	15.0 %	15.0 %	15.0 %	15.0 %	15.6 %*
Exchange Rate (to the dollar)	26.0	36.0	39.6	48.6	47.9	52.7	15.2 %
Devaluation (%)	42.9 %	38.0 %	10.0 %	10.0 %	10.0 %	10.0 %	15.2 %

* Average over FFYP period.

** Amortization + interest divided by exports + remittances + mfs.

*** Constant market prices, 1973 base.

**** Real value added, double deflated, 1973 base. Include indirect taxes but excludes tariffs. GDP equals total value added plus tariffs.

that this would cause an important decrease in imports; therefore they reduce expected growth rate. In the original run it was estimated that total merchandise imports would increase at a rate of 5 percent a year. In the revised estimate it is brought down to 3.3 percent. It seems that this decrease in imports has brought GDP growth from 6.2 to 4.2 percent.

Comments on the Derviş-Robinson Analysis

One must first compare the D-R excpectations with the actual results observed in the post-1980 period (1980-1988). In fact, after 1980 governments have adopted the main proposals of D-R. Let us take 1980 as our starting point and examine the following eight years.

According to D-R, an annual 8.1 percent real devaluation would lead to a 25.9 percent increase in exports per annum, which, in turn, would give rise to an annual growth of national income by 7.7 percent. Between 1979-1988 the rate of yearly real devaluation was 8 percent (exactly the same as the D-R figure) and the yearly increase in exports was 20 percent. Although the export growth was a little less than D-R expectations, the difference was not that great. But in the case of the increase of national income there was a significant difference between the expectation and reality. In practice, instead of 7.7 percent, the actual national income increase was 5 percent (1980-1988). The difference was much more marked compared to the real devaluation case in D-R.

According to the D-R model, the economy is highly sensitive to the rate of export increase. In their two experiments, one maintaining a stable exchange rate throughout the whole period, i.e., 1979-1983, and the other an initial 30 percent devaluation (real) and 4.3 percent annually thereafter, the sensitivity is quite evident.In the first experiment, exports increase 16.0 percent (current dollars) annually, and in the second experiment they rise to 25.9 percent annually. As a result, average growth rates become 5.5 percent in the first case and 7.7 percent in the second case. There is little to dispute about the effect of exchange rate depreciation on the level of exports. The method is correct. World demand parameters may differ but adjustments in the method may then be made. In practice, there was an approximation between expectations and the actual result. It is quite possible that roughly 25 percent annual increase in exports would result in a 7.7 percent growth in national income. In the D-R model the relative prices of 19 sectors in the economy may change. As a consequence, figures in those sectors allow us to observe the price ratios of exportable and non exportable goods. But parameters in all 19 equations and their interrelationship are based on past economic figures. In the past, high protection rates and the scarcity of foreign exchange may have created such parameters in production functions and levels of income, which could not be adhered to during the outward orientation period. A crucial difference between D-R and my approach lies in the fact that the former leaves the determination of prices to the parameters of the 19 sectors and their interrelationship, whereas I demonstrate that there are constraints which if retained would create undesired effects, such as inflationary tendencies, poor income distribution, unemployment and foreign debt. The effects of the switch to export orientation on inflation, income distribution, employment and foreign debt are not possible to be observed in the D-R model.

There are also several other points to comment.

One point to comment on is the earning differences between nonagricultural and agricultural sectors of the economy between the base year (1978) and the terminal one (1983). In 1978 earning difference was 4.37; according to findings in this study it will be 4.04 in 1983. (Even if agriculture would grow by 4 percent.)

It is apparent that income differences will remain almost at the same level at the end of five years. It is shown that there is a close relationship between rents and large earning differences in the country. If such large earning differences are maintained, great amounts of rents will be earned. In an economy, essentially based on the working of the price mechanism, there is not any feasible index to measure rents; one of the possible exceptions is the decrease in the difference between the earnings of those two sectors. (All those are written in 1988.)

It is not possible to keep industrial wages at a level contemplated by the authors. They suppose that average urban wages (real) increase by 2.3 percent yearly. Actually during the period under consideration urban wages decreased. The average yearly decrease was more than 2-3 percent.

The export increase in the analysis is supposed to take place when high rents are earned in the country. If rents had been natural resource rents, then this would have been feasible; but Turkish nonagricultural export commodities, which are not natural resource based, cannot be sold in large quantities if their prices include high rents. If. on the other hand, they are subsidized to a great extent, high rates of inflations will set in and income distribution will worsen.

I do not agree with the fundamental structure of this model (like others). In the model most stratejic variables are determined exogenously. This may be true when the past growth of the economy is analyzed, whereas it is shown that they must be considered as endogenous variables when the model is projected into the future. One of them should be stressed here: exchange rates. On the other hand, return to capital is endogenously determined in the model, whereas it should be exogenously determined when the model is projected to the future.

The exchange rate is taken as an exogenous magnitude (policy variable) and its effects are determined firstly by means of the sensitivity of exports to price incentives and international demand, and secondly by means of capital intensity in various sectors of the economy. I totally disagree with that. They are all surface phenomena. The exchange rate is an endogenous variable and there is a close relationship between it and the level of income. This is not negated in the Derviş-Robinson model. In fact, a higher exchange rate will give rise to greater exports, and the increase of exports would cause an increase in growth rate. This should not be the case. The rate of exchange could not be determined without any respect to the level of national income. In other words, it is impossible to imagine a rate of exchange which is not one of the variables simultaneously determined with the level of income and its distribution between traded and nontraded goods.

The same is true of wages of organized labor. Derviş-Robinson take wages of organized labor as an exogenous variable. It can be shown that their level depends on rents earned in the country. If this is so, and if rents are part of the source of income growth, they cannot be considered as an exogenous variable when the past of the economy is analyzed. But they should be endogenous in the analysis of the future of the economy in the sense that they must be related to some characteristics of the economy rather than the power of unions, government action, etc.

There is more: the level of wages of organized labor is very important in determining the most crucial variables of the economy: exports, employment, income distribution and inflation. To take the level of wages of organized labor as exogenous is to take, to a certain extent, exports, employment, income distribution and inflation as exogenous as well.

Now let us see the treatment of the return on capital. It is taken as endogenous in the model; whereas it should be exogenous in an economy such as Turkey. In fact, by taking it endogenously, normal earnings are mixed together with rents. Let us look at the figure relating to overall return to capital in industry. It is around 35 percent. As we know that the industry owned by the public does not earn any profit, 35 percent would be over 60 percent return on capital in private industry. It is evident that this has no behavioral content. At a time when private business was ready to invest as much as they could at a rate, let us say of 25 percent, what is the meaning of offering 60 percent?

Rents are also included in this figure. The authors accept implicitly that an industry would be viable even if it earns continuously as much as 60 percent. More than that, they accept that an industry would be able to export even if it continually earns more than 60 percent on capital in a country having no ample natural resources.

The most important deficiency of this model is the fact that employment is taken endogenously, depending on the national income, investments, etc.

§ 4 - THE ANALYSIS OF PROFESSOR CELASUN

Professor M. Celasun of the Middle East Technical University had perceived the main point I was trying to contend since 1978 (See Hatiboglu 1978), i.e., the relationship between tradable and nontradable goods. He writes as follows: «In the future investigation of the Turkish economic transformation, a significant contribution would be to deflate the available 1-0 data into constant world market prices to remove the distorting effects of rents in national income formation, as aptly pointed out by Hatiboglu (1978).» (Celasun 1983, p. 135)

In one of his brilliant papers (Celasun 1986) Professor Celasun uses computable general equilibrium model developed by Dervis, de Melo and Robinson (1982) in order to compare the projections of the model with facts.

Here is his conclusion: «As the result of the present study Turkey's adjustment policy problems in the 1980 s cannot adequately be addressed by fixed price input-output models used in the official planning process and by macromonetary models which appropriately stress inflationary phenomena but eschew the structural interdependences of product, factor and foreign exchange markets... Hence our experience suggests a research focusing on relative price movements and their interactions with growth and structural change in Turkey» (Celasun 1986, p. 62).

§ 5 - THE DEFICIENCY OF MACRO-MODELS IN TURKEY AND THE UNCONVENTIONAL ANALYSES

Several macromodels are prepared in Turkey, some by the State Planning Organization, some by international and domestic institutions and some by individual economists. Some of those are simple and superficial while others are very sophisticated and up to the standards of the present day econometrics. Again, the methodology of various models differs. For example the selection procedure of exogenous variables are different and the determination of technical change also differs.

Although the analysis of the economy by means of macromodels constitutes the best approach to the understanding of the Turkish economy, it can be shown that in view of the theory presented in this book several deficiencies of those models would be evident. Those are listed below.

1-Firstly let us look at the changes of national income during the recent years.

Year	National Income Growth (%)	Year	National Income Growth (%)
1978	1.2	1988	1.5
1979	-0.5	1989	1.6
1980	-2.8	1990	9.4
1981	4.8	1991	0.3
1982	3.1	1992	6.4
1983	4.2	1993	8.1
1984	7.1	1994	-6.1
1985	4.3	1995	8.0
1986	6.8	1996	7.1
1987	9.8	1997	8.3
		1998	3.2
		1999	-6.1
		2000	6.3
		2001	-9.4
		2002	7.9
		2003	5.9
		2004	9.5

It is apparent that its fluctuation over the years has been very sharp. But on the other hand, let us examine the expectations and the methodology of macromodels we have. Apart from the inability of those macromodels to predict such wide fluctuations, it is apparent that right at the beginning many deviations are observed between the predictions and actual results. For example, according to a macromodel prepared in 1985, the growth rate in 1986 should be 4.8; whereas the actual growth was 7.9 percent, (Şenesen 1986). In another macromodel it was predicted as 5.4 percent, (Ozmucur 1986). Let us look into another macromodel prepared by two world famous economists (Derviş-Robinson 1978). Acording to that macromodel, after the export orientation of the economy its growth should be 7.7 percent, whereas the actual yearly average rate has been 4.2 percent after export orientation of the country. Several more deviations from expectations based on macromodels can be mentioned. Let me underline one of them. According to the best macromodel ever prepared, the trend growth due to the technical change was expected to be in the neighbourhood of 4 percent, i.e., on top of changes of factor increases; the income increase caused by the technical change should have materialized around 4 percent, whereas with the trend rate increase of factors, the total increase of national income during the last 16 years has been around that figure. Why? This shows how that model failed..

There is another deficiency of all macromodels which can be touched on briefly here. In all of them the growth trend of national income is taken as a base and it is supposed that the trend increase in factors could increase it. This assumption is quite opposite to the theory explained in this book. According to it, without taking service prices (labor) into consideration explicitly, nothing much should be expected from macromodels.

2- In a country like Turkey, where inflation is always very high, forced savings should be explicitly introduced into the macro models. As far as I know, apart from one of them, this is all neglected.

3- When exports are taken into models, total exports and/or a proportion of them are supposed to be equal to its trend amount or it is calculated by means of their demand elasticity in foreign countries. Again, in some of them the relative changes between domestic and external prices are taken as determining factors. But I tried to show that this is either wrong or partly true in view of the theory expounded above. A better assumption would be to establish a relationship between service prices and exports, and to include it in the macromodel somehow.

4- External deficits are taken as being endogenous in some macroanalyses but exogenous in other models. In fact neither is true. For example it was endogenous at the beginning of 1950 and between 1970 to 1977, but it was exogenous in other years. Again, it was endogenous in 1980-2004. Without understanding the dynamics of the Turkish economy nothing much could be achieved by this analysis.

5- The consideration of import coefficients as constant in calculating input-output tables could lead us to wrong conclusions. We know that there is a need for imported inputs, especially intermediate goods. As the petroleum production in Turkey is negligible there would be more need for petroleum imports when production increases. Yet some intermediate inputs can be produced domestically. Their quality may be low and/or their prices may be high. Yet, the experience in Turkey reveals that as importing gets more difficult and/or as a rasult of a political decision, domestic inputs may replace imported ones. The same can be said for imported consumption goods. All that means that imports may be endogenous or exogenous.

6- Government consumption and investment are taken exogenous in some models, whereas they are taken endogenous in others. In fact neither is true. The practice of one may be true in some conditions while the other one may be true in other conditions. Everything depends on the conditions and political decisions.

7- In most models profits are taken as endogenous; as a result, inquiries about income determination are affected by this practice. Yet, if we don't understand the relationship between service prices and profits, efforts in determining profits would not mean much. I feel that if we try to understand the long period growth capacity of the country, profits should be considered as exogenous variables.

8- The analysis of wages does not seem to be appropriate. For example, in some models wages of unionized workers are taken exogenous while those of non-unionized workers are taken as endogenous. But facts negate this practice. After 1977 the wages of unionized workers went down by 20 percent; again, another 35 percent decrease occurred in years following 1980. But on the other hand, there was some 40 percent increase in 1989-1993. Nobody familiar with the Turkish economy can think that they are exogenous. To a certain extent they are endogenous. Now, let us look at the wages of nonunionized workers. The seperation of agriculture from nonagricultural sectors should not allow us to consider all nonunionized workers in nonagricultural sectors as endogenous. In fact, to consider earning differences between those two sectors constant is not acceptable.

9- To include the relationships between money and prices in macromodels is very difficult. None of macromodels takes income velocity of money into consideration. Again, in some cases money can be made endogenous; we don't observe it in any models.

10- The determination of technical change is very difficult. In most models the historical trend is taken as a basis, which is wrong.

11- In macro models agricultural sectors and nonagricultural sectors are not separated, whereas it is shown that it is a must.

12- Some macro models are production flexible while others are price flexible. I tried to show that along with those, service prices flexible models should be prepared. They can give better results in the Turkish case.

13 - Every economist analyzing the economy of Turkey considers the level of investment as one of the main factors influencing growth over the period he or she is examining. For example investments increased fast from 1970 to 1977, and as a result the growth rate in this period reached the highest figure in the recent Turkish economic history. Again, in the 1980's investments once again started to grow and national income increased. It was necessary to finance the increasing investments either by increasing domestic savings or by accumulating larger foreign deficits. Over the 1970-1977 period increases were secured with foreign deficits, whereas during the 1980 s the contribution of domestic savings was more. My main contribution, which differentiates my analysis from those of all other economists, is that the growth rate would be higher if investments were financed with foreign deficits and/or the share of the non-merchandise foreign inflow increases. In fact, while the growth rate was some 6.4 percent during the first period, it was 3.8 percent in the post-1980. And what is more significant is that both the share of exports and imports in GNP were higher during the second period. This implies that the actual figures cannot be related to the efficiency increases due to higher trade volumes. I tried to show that this can be explained by the lower service prices prevailing over

the second period. This observation is not present in the existing literature on this topic.

14 - Economists carry out their macroanalyses in term of TL, and do not pay attention to the discrepancy between TL and dollar figures. I have tried to show that if, for example, money is devalued by 20 percent and if while relative prices and the general price level remains constant, national income in terms of dollars would decrease by 20 percent, but ignoring terms of trade effect there is not any welfare change in the country. However, if relative prices change, the national income in dollars would mean a lot.

If we carry macroanalyses in terms of both dollars and TL, the discrepancy between the two analyses will help us better understand the past, and the future would be predicted better. Although very difficult to explain, an example taken from the recent Turkish economic history might be useful to convey the main idea. The yearly growth rate of national income in Turkey in the period 1984-1993 in terms of constant dollar was around 11 percent, whereas in terms of a constant TL. it was around 5.3 percent. There is a visible discrepancy. Which figure reflects the true rate of growth? Would the divergence between the two figures be significant when a macroanalysis is conducted? On the surface, the divergence might be considered to be a result of the revaluation of the Turkish currency. In fact, the problem is more deeprooted.

Let us take a different example and suppose there was a devaluation in the country. If we accept one price rule (if there is not protection in the countries and transportation costs are zero) the prices of previously exported goods should increase by the same proportion as the devaluation. If monetary policy keeps general price increases below the devaluation rate, the prices of the previously non-exported goods (especially home goods) would increase by less than the devaluation rate. This implies a change in relative prices. If all prices remained constant or increased less but at the same rate, the decrease of national income in dollar terms would have no significance for the country's welfare apart from the loss experienced due to the deterioration of the terms of trade. In the case just described (i.e., the prices of previously exported goods increasing at the devaluation rate but the prices of other goods increasing less), there is a welfare loss. We know that a lower Ps/T (i.e., the relative prices of services in terms of previously exported goods) would give rise to a decrease in the welfare of the country.

If (as in 1984-1993 period in Turkey) there was a divergence between the growth rates in terms of the dollar and TL in favor of the former, this implies that service prices increased during that period. As long as a discrepancy existed between those two sets of prices this shows that the level of growth is related to a change in service prices and this provides us with a clue as to the reasons of past and future income growth. In other words, yearly national income increases were greater than what they should have been. Isn't this the main aim of macroanalyses? This means that the divergence between national income in dollar and TL prices must be identified.

15 - Several economists are perplexed by the relationship between devaluations and real wages: there appears to exist a dismal relationship, i.e., a trade-off between high devaluations and low wages. But they don't correctly identify the relationship. If, they show, the prices of tradable goods must decrease in order to increase exports, continuing devaluations would be required. (The same conclusion should follow if already exported goods are sold at lower prices.) If we want to increase exports, the goods with less comparative advantages on line are to be sold. This will lead to more devaluations. If we suppose that technological advances are slower in Turkey compared to other foreign countries, this is the expected conclusion.

Several economists underline the importance of real wages in the increase of exports after 1980; they also underline the undesired consequences of low wages on income distribution. The trade-off between exports and lower real wages rates is known by them. But there is another dimension to the problem which is underlined forcibly by the present author: if relative service prices decrease, i.e., real wages, the necessity of devaluations decreases. In other words: if real wages do go down, the same result can be obtained by a lower devaluation.

16 - The above criticism is also valid for those economists who claim that once the economy is oriented toward exports and if the free play of market forces is allowed, growth would have to increase. This is negated by the experience in last years. We are aware that the growth rate during the import substitution period, i.e.. 6.4 percent, decreased to 4 percent during the export orientation period. Why? Was the import substitution strategy better than the export orientation one? Definitely not! This is an example of post hoc fallacy. The growth during the import substitution period was a result of the overvaluation of nonagricultural goods. It could not be sustained. Once service prices were downgraded to a level compatible with the development level of the economy, the growth rate had to be reduced after the economy turned outward.

17 - The success of the third year plan (i.e., a very good prediction of the future) model and the failure of better quality macroanalyses in predicting the future of the economy are again related to the same fact. During the third five year plan period Turkey was still adopting import substituting strategy and as a result, parameters constituting the basis of the macroanalyses were relevant. After 1980, however, they become irrelevant. The mistake made by good economists was to utilize the same parameters and the neglect the relationship existing between service prices and export orientation.

18 - Based on their research by the macroanalyses several economists think that the decrease of the growth rate (for example as a result of a decrease in the rate of investment) is no cure for the problem of external deficits in the Turkish economy. On the other hand, I demonstrate that without reducing national income growth to around 4.5 percent per year Turkey's problems cannot be solved. Are not those two conclusions contradictory? Yes they are; however, there is the traditional error in the first point of view.

My expectation of the growth rate decline is based on the expected decrease of service prices. I do not predict a decrease in the rate of investment. As in the existing macromodels the level of service prices are not taken into consideration, this important dimension of growth is lost from sight.

When this important dimension is excluded from macromodels the only possibility for decreasing the growth appears to be the declining rates of investment. It is quite certain that without decreasing service prices the problem would not be solved.

19 - In all macromodels and macroanalyses, earning differences between nonagricultural and agricultural sectors are supposed to be endogenous variables. As a result, the high level at the beginning is kept constant when simulations are conducted to determine the possible changes in growth when several variables are given different values. In fact, it is shown in this book that a smooth functioning of the economy under high earning differences could not be expected. It should be considered as an exogenous variable to a certain extent.

20 - The wages in nonagricultural sectors are one of the most important variables determining employment and the growth of the economy. On the other hand, the treatment of wages is either very superficial or irrevelant in most macroanalyses. In some macromodels a certain increase in wages is assumed and then it is treated as a policy variable. In others, the level of wages is left to be determined like other endogenous variables. Both of these contradicting approaches are incorrect. Wages are service prices; if the determination of service prices is not given special attention, not much value is provided by those macromodel analyses.

21 - A theoretical criticism must be added to the above list. According to economists proponing Computable General Equilibirium models , the reason why the productivity growth decreased in import substituting countries was the decrease in investment rate (Chenery et al, 1983, p.330). This is a misconception, and also it is in contrast with the main point of view of my analysis. I try to show that the changes in relative prices disqualify the whole macroanalyses, especially those based on the impact of investment on national income, in the understanding of the economy. As was illustrated in the various chapters of this book, in all these models and analyses, the necessity of the change in the growth rate and the absolute changes

in the national income to be compared with the previous ones (and also with other countries) when relative prices change are not taken into consideration and/or they are not inserted in the analyses. As a result, it is probable that the predictions based on them should prove wrong when there are radical change in relative prices, as is the case of Turkey.

CHAPTER XI

A CRITICAL SURVEY OF CONVENTIONAL ANALYSES OF GROWTH AND DEVELOPMENT IN TURKEY

§ 1 - INTRODUCTION

In a rather long period covering 1950 - 2008, the average yearly growth rate of the Turkish economy in terms of constant prices was about 5.2 percent. In terms of dollars, per capita income was around $ 7500 (2006) and GNP was around $ 500 billion. As the level of income in terms of TL does not mean much for the non-Turkish readers, it is not mentioned here. Yet, all analyses are made by means of the constant Turkish Lira. The growth rate in the 1950 - 1978 period was around 6.4 percent but in the ensuing period it decreased sharply, and the average for the 1978 - 2008 period is 3.8 percent.

Several scholars studied factors determining both the level of national income and its growth. All sorts of modern tools of economics are used to achieve this by the best Turkish and world famous economists. This chapter is a very short summary of all those analyses, which are worth reporting.

Noticeable analyses are centered around three main lines: the source of growth, macroeconomic analyses and the impact of some transformations on growth along with patterns of development. There are, of course, other approaches, and they are also used to understand the Turkish situation. To mention a few: source of demand for the industry, political factors, the impact of the economic and social stability, inflation, the impact of external factors, ideological factors, the impact of the operation of the price mechanism, etc. Although a few words will be said about all factors, the main analysis is devoted to the first 3 approaches mentioned.

A few words will be said about the macroanalyses: the grossly aggregated macro-analysis based on the simple Harrod-Domar equation.

In this chapter factors determining long run growth (trend rate) of national income will be investigated. Actually, yearly growth rates fluctuate around the trend rate. The investigation of factors affecting fluctuations is found in the previous chapter.

§ 2 - THE EARLY ANALYSES BASED ON SOURCE OF GROWTH METHODOLOGY

According to an investigation carried out by (Krueger-Tuncer, 1980) the source of growth in Turkey in 1963-75 was as follows:

TABLE XI-1
THE SOURCE OF GROWTH IN TURKEY

Years	Growth of value added% (G_V)	TFP Growth rate% G_A	Share	Total factor input Growth rate% (G_F)	Share
1963-75	6.40	2.23	34.8	4.17	65.2

Growth of Capital Input (G_K) %	Growth of Labor Input (G_L) %	Capital Income Share (β_K) %	Labor Income Share (β_L) %
6.82	1.02	55.0	45.0

Source: Krueger - Tuncer (1980)

TABLE XI-2
THE SOURCE OF GROWTH IN TURKEY

Index (1958 = 100)	GNP at constant 1958 prices	Rate (%)	Capital Growth at constant 1958 prices	Rate (%)	Labor Force	Rate (%)	Land	Total Factor	%	Total Factor Productivity	Rate %
1958	100		100		100		100	100		100	
1975	277	6.2	421	8.8	133	1.7	200	228	4.9	121	1.3
Share of Factor Income			0.35		0.50		0.15				

Source: Calculations made by Leamer, Hansen 1991, p 356

Another study the growth reported by OECD is shown in Table XI-3 (OECD 1988)

TABLE XI-3
SOURCE OF GROWTH IN TURKEY (%)

	1973-76	1977-80	1981-84	1985-87	1973-87
Output	6.9	1.3	4.3	5.5	4.4
Factor input	5.1	3.1	1.7	2.1	3.1
Total factor productivity	1.8	-1.9	2.6	3.4	1.4
Labor productivity	1.2	-0.8	2.9	3.9	1.7
Capital productivity	2.4	-2.5	2.5	3.0	1.2

Source: OECD, 1988

After having examined those tables, Prof. Hansen (1991, p. 466-470) concludes that TFP was very low in those years. He thinks that the low figure should be related to very low productivity in agriculture. But as the share of agriculture should become less in posterior years, the low TFP should be explained somehow. He concludes that "it would be reasonable to expect a substantial residual... The explanation lies in the negative attitude of the government to foreigners and in the negative aspects of étatism." (1991: p. 467). "In Turkey étatism led to an increase in the accumulation of real capital (volume of gross investment) to what would have happened under private entrepreneurship. It is equally certain that productivity suffered under étatism." (1991: p. 467)

Another approach to growth by Hansen was to ferret out the impact of the absorption, i.e., consumption plus investment." In Turkey total domestic absorption declined from 106 percent of GDP to 102.5 percent of GDP with a decline in the trade deficit from 6 percent to 2.5 percent". p. 486.

§ 3 - THE IMPACT OF EARNING DIFFERENCES ON GROWTH

The calculation of total productivity growth should also be looked into. Syrquin (Syrquin 1987 p, 237) used the following formula:

$$G_V = \Sigma_i P_i G_{Vi}$$

$$G_y = \Sigma_i P_i G_{yi} + \Sigma_i P_i G_{ys}$$

Here, P is the share of the sector i in output, G_V is the growth of the value added. G_y is the growth of aggregate labor productivity. The formula is explained as follows: "The growth rate of total output, G_V, equals the sum of sectoral growth rates weighted by sectoral output shares. The growth rate of aggregate labor productivity, G_y, has two components. The first term G_{yi} averages the sectoral growth rates of output per worker. The second term (G_{ys}) measures the contribution to aggregate labor productivity growth of employment shifts among sectors with different labor productivities. I denoted this second term by A (y) and label it as the gross allocation effect. (Syrquin 1987, p.237)"

The total productivity growth is 2.23 in 6.40 percent yearly growth in Turkey. If the above formula is used to calculate the rate of reallocation effect, (the shift of resources from agriculture to nonagricultural sectors), it is found that it was 0.61 of the total productivity effect (Syrquin 1987, Table 8.9). This is the highest proportion calculated for 14 countries. What is more important is that the second highest is that of Mexico, which is 0.30 percent only. This meant that a very high proportion of the growth in Turkey is explained by the shift of resources from agriculture to nonagricultural sectors.

THE WRITINGS BY BALASSA AND CELASUN ON THE EFFECT OF A SHIFT FROM AGRICULTURAL TO NONAGRICULTURAL SECTORS IN TURKEY

Two economists tried to measure the impact of the switch from agricultural to nonagricultural sectors in Turkey (Balassa 1979, 1983 and 1985, Celasun 1983) by referring to my studies. (Tablo III-18)

Although they use the same methodology, Professor Celasun investigates the problem in depth.

When my analysis in UATE is compared with the approach offered by Balassa and Celasun a fundamental difference becomes apparent. I have reevaluated national income in terms of dollars (which includes both growth and level effect), whereas Balassa and Celasun use constant national currency. According to my calculations some 35 percent of national income should be attributed to earning differences and a rapid switch from agriculture to nonagriculture. Yet according to the calculations made by Balassa and Celasun the impact of earning differences and switch is around 7-10 percent (Celasun 1983, p.94). Why is there such a substantial difference in these calculations and which is accurate? That will be answered below (§9).

§ 4 - CAPITAL AND GROWTH

The simplest theories of growth are based on the relationship between capital investment and growth. This simple idea is used by several economists in Turkey to explain growth. It is known that the share of investment in national income went up form 12 percent in 1950 to over 25 percent in the mid-seventies. From then on it has fluctuated between 20 to 25 percent. If ICOR's are considered quasi-constant a connection can be established between the level of investment and growth. (See IBRD, 1974, 1980 and 1982.)

In several analyses of the Turkish economy an emphasis is laid upon this relationship. Again, several economists tried to discover the causes of changes in ICOR's. Factors such as planning efforts, an increase of imports and the allocation of investment between public and private sectors are singled out to explain it by several economists (Fry 1972).

A. Krueger, (Krueger 1974) by assuming the fixity of ICOR's in import substituting and export industries, tried to detect the consequences of a reallocation of investment between those two sectors.

The investigations about the factors determining investment rate would give rise to interesting questions. Although there is interesting research into a deeper insight on the respective contributions by domestic saving, external deficits and government budgets on the level of investment, they do not reveal unknown dimensions. (See, Celasun - Tansel 1993.)

§ 5 - THE ANALYSIS OF GROWTH BY THE WORLD BANK 2000

In the last quarter of 2000 a report entitled TURKEY: COUNTRY ECONOMIC MEMORANDUM, REFORMS FOR SUSTAINABLE GROWTH was published by IBRD. A good proportion of the structure and problems of the national income are analyzed in that report. Along with those, the source of growth of the national income during the last years is investigated. Our interest here is a summary and a critical appraisal of what is asserted in that report about factors determining growth. Actually it must be conceded that the best analyses of the Turkish economy originate from IBRD, and this report is no exception.

It is evident that the previous source of growth analyses sponsored by the IBRD (see the previous section) is a straightforward application of the growth analysis firstly formulated by Solow. Although the methodology of the present report is the same, advances since Solow's formulation are integrated into it; they are: an emphasis given to human capital, the quantification of the impacts of the adopted economic policy and a comparison of the Turkish parameters with the experience of other countries, especially by using up to date statistical methods. Moreover, instead of the growth of national income, the growth of output is sought.

What are the findings? The main findings in Pen Tables are embellished by recent research. Let us see first Pen findings: Output/Worker growth per year, which is 3.2 percent in 1960-1985, is decomposed as follows: the growth of physical capital, 1.3 point; human capital growth, 1.0 point and TFP growth, 0.9 point. Actually if the growth of working people is accepted to be 1.2 percent, the growth of national income can be considered as 4.4 percent for the whole period, whereas according to a calculation in terms of constant Tl it is around 5.2 percent. The difference is related to a sharp devaluation in 1980-1984. The problem is whether growth should be calculated in national money or in dollars.

The additional comments made in the report can be summarized as follows.

1- It is shown that secondary school enrollment in Turkey is a little less than the regression results based on countries of the same per capita income bracket. If it had been brought to that level, national income growth would have been some 0.4-0.6 point higher.

2- Some unfavorable policy parameters (budget deficits, inflation and the closed economy until 1990) are thought to have influenced the growth of the economy unfavorably. But after 1990 the openness adopted by the country seems to have increased the growth rate by 2.2 percent.

3- According to another study per capita output growth in Turkey would be 1-1.5 point higher in the 1990's if inflation had been in single digit.

4- The physical capital investment, especially in 1990s, in Turkey is a little above those in countries of similar per capita income level. Therefore there is no need to emphasize physical capital investment.

5- The main problem is a choice of a better policy and an emphasis on human capital development, which is of a nature to increase TFP. If it is made, national income increase by 2001 could be made to be 6 percent, which is almost 50 percent higher than previous growth rates in the last 20 years.

§ 6 - THE IMPLICATIONS OF THE EMPIRICAL RESEARCH

There are many forms of empirical research works to find out a parallelism with transformations in the economies and their growth. One of the pioneering works is that conducted by Kuznets to detect stylized facts occurring with development and also the kind of transformations given rise by it. The most important among them was the change in the industrial structure in the sense of the increase of the share in industry and a decrease that of agriculture in national income. Starting from Kuznet's findings, Chenery and his associates found several other typical changes by using cross country and time series data. The data revealed that there is a close relationship between some changes and the level of national income.

Those changes lead to, and also are caused by the income increase. Economists developing this method have tried to use it to explain growth rates by those transformations, and as a result, factors giving rise to those changes in economic structure.

The transformation is not uniform across countries and it is affected by the resource endowment, the initial structure of the economy and the choice of the development policy such as outward and inward orientation, etc.

The analysis is used to explain the historical growth as well as for the simulations for future growth. This is based on the comparison of the expected and actual figures relating to development characteristics.

TRANSFORMATION IN INDUSTRIAL STRUCTURE IN TURKEY AND THE IMPACT OF DEMAND

In all studies the growth of the economy is first analyzed by breaking it down into the growth of agricultural, industrial and service sectors; then the growth of each sector is analyzed and special factors affecting the growth of each sector are separated. It is a well known fact that along with development a systematic change occurs in the shares of those three sectors: the share of agriculture decreases, the share of other sectors increases. As will be seen in Table XI-4, this has also happened in Turkey.

The decrease of the share of agriculture in GDP has been very fast and it came down from 45.5 percent to 13.4 percent in 47 years. The increase of industry has not been very fast and it has proved to be in the expected direction. The increase of the service sector has been in the expected direction and at more than the expected speed.

In most analyses the rate of increase in each sector is first calculated and then is commented upon. A study of factors affecting the growth of each sector is a pet subject for all scholars analyzing development.

According to professors H. Chenery and O. Yenal, one of the reason why national income increased 6.4 percent annually, in 1950-1975, was related to high demand from agriculture (which increased 3.3 percent yearly) and elasticity of the industrial sector vis-a-vis demand originating from especially import substituting ones, and it could be said that although import substitution policy had several undesired consequences, it was also beneficial.

TABLE XI-4
THE TRANSFORMATION IN INDUSTRIAL STRUCTURE IN TURKEY (AT CURRENT PRICES)

Year	The Share of Agriculture in GDP %	The Share of Manufacturing Industry in GDP %	The Share of Services in GDP %
1950	45.5	10.7	43.8
1960	40.9	15.3	43.8
1970	36.7	16.6	46.7
1975	32.7	16.7	50.6
1980	25.5	18.3	56.2
1985	19.7	21.9	58.4
1990	16.8	24.8	58.4
1995	14.8	25.5	59.7
1997	13.4	23.7	62.9

PATTERNS OF GROWTH (Chenery)

The pattern of growth approach pioneered by Chenery (1975 and 1987) is used by many distinguished economists in analyzing the Turkish economy. According to their findings, almost all expected or predicted transformations necessitated by economic growth and development seems to have occurred in Turkey, and almost every observed and predicted change was at about the same magnitude. (See UATE.) In summary, Turkey had created most of the prerequisites for sustained development except a viable system of international trade. Exports were much less than the predicted figures; but the poor performance of this sector was largely offset by the sustained growth of agriculture, availability of foreign capital and workers' remittances. (Chenery, 1978) (See Table XI-5)

The explanation of the low level of exports is based on inward looking industrialization until 1980. Turkey fitted well with the large import substituting countries and its growth was related to that strategy first. At the beginning, the impetus of industrialization would give rise to a rapid growth but when the easy stage was accomplished, difficulties would arise. Actually they did after the mid-70 s. But they were delayed as a result of foreign capital inflows, workers' remittances, etc.

TABLE XI-5 (*)
STRUCTURAL CHANGE: A Comparison of Turkey to the Average Pattern
(Percent of GDP)

	Turkish Structure					
	Actual			Predicted		
	1953	1963	1973	1953	1963	1973
Per Capita Income	$370	$460	$670			
1. Investment						
a. Savings	11.5	12.0	14.8	16.3	18.0	19.8
b. Gross Investment	14.8	15.6	18.3	18.0	19.6	21.0
c. Capital Inflow	3.3	3.6	3.5	2.8	1.6	1.2
2. Government Revenue						
a. Govt. Revenue	16.0	16.6	21.1	15.6	16.8	18.7
b. Tax Revenue	12.6	13.9	18.5	15.0	15.8	17.8
3. Education						
a. Educational Expenditures	1.7	2.6	3.4	1.9	3.0	3.1
b. School Enrollment (%) :						
Primary & Secondary	33.3	43.4	56.1	46.4	57.0	65.4
4. Production						
(value added at factor cost)						
a. Primary	45.9	40.1	29.7	34.4	30.2	24.5
b. Industry	12.8	19.2	22.9	22.6	23.5	26.8
c. Utilities	5.7	8.8	10.7	6.2	7.1	7.5
d. Services	35.6	31.8	35.7	36.2	38.8	40.5
5. Trade						
a. Imports	11.3	9.6	11.4	17.0	16.2	15.6
b. Exports	8.0	6.0	7.9	17.3	15.2	14.8
c. Manufactures	0.6	1.0	1.8	4.4	4.8	6.0
6. Labor Allocation						
% Share of :						
a. Primary	79.2	77.6	64.8	56.9	53.8	47.2
b. Industry	7.4	10.1	13.6	15.8	17.9	21.7
c. Services	13.4	12.3	21.6	17.4	28.2	30.8
7. Income Distribution						
a. Share of Highest 20 %	-	57.0	56.5	56.1	56.1	55.7
b. Share of Lowest 40 %	-	13.0	11.5	11.7	11.5	11.2

(*) H. Chenery, 1978, p.14

§ 7 - VARIOUS CAUSES AFFECTING GROWTH

In addition to previously discussed factors, several of which are quantifiable, others will be discussed. Some will be listed below. (See especially several publications by TUSIAD, for example TUSIAD 1991.)

1- Political Stability

There is a widespread belief that political stability has been influential in the growth in Turkey. In fact, the development which started in the 1920 s and continued up to the Second World War, was closely related to the political stability in the country. However, Turkey couldn't escape from the unfavorable impact of the Great Depression of the 1930's. The depressing effect of the Second World War was also inevitable. The explosion of the economy and the fast growth following the switch of power to the Democratic Party after the first democratic elections in 1950 are ascribed to political stability. The military coup in 1960 is considered to be the main reason of the economic depression during the first years of the 1960 s. The political instability which occurred in the mid-1970 is again supposed to be one of the reason for the recession which took place during the last years of the 1970 s.

2- The Uncertainty in the Economy

The ever changing economic policy, as well as the lack of a clear or transparent economic policy, seems to have had unfavorable effects on growth. This argument was put forward with respect to the economic policy followed after 1980. There is also a widespread belief that the sluggishness in adopting rapid changes in techniques and demand conditions are other salient features of the recent economic policy.

3- Ideology

It is quite clear that the ideology has been very important in growth. There is no end to the discussion of this factor. A very short summary will be given here.

Let us look at the founding years of the Republic. The bias against modernization was dominant most of the time during the Ottoman Era. The successful struggle against world powers during the Independence War (1919-1922) was instrumental in the upsurge in the first years of the Republic.

Another factor, which can be classified under ideology, is the relationship between capitulations granted by the Ottoman sultans as favors (and exploited by Western Powers) and the downfall of the economy during the Ottoman Era. This is supposedly a characteristic of imperialism. That belief created a hostile environment towards acceptance of foreign capital and even created a bias against foreign trade itself. A strategy of self sufficiency which was the principal guide for years was probably the end result of that belief. There is no doubt that the Soviet propaganda supported and strengthened that belief. In other words, ideology was not only a reaction to the old, it was also a product of then fashionable ideas. Affected by this ideology, the administrators of the country closed the economy to the world and to global competition.

4- External Conditions

It is well known that external conditions affect the performance of any economy. It is probable that expansions and recessions in the world economy must have exerted an important impact on the Turkish economy. One typical example is the increase of raw material prices caused by the Korean war in 1950. External terms of trade for Turkey became favorable and this contributed to the upsurge in the 1950's. The second example is the petroleum price crisis in the 1970's. Actually, Turkey seemed to be unaffected at first, but its contribution to the downfall in the late 1970's was substantial.

5- Bottlenecks

The impact of some bottlenecks on the economy is well known. Some are perpetual while others appear from time to time and then vanish. These bottlenecks include: deficits both in private and public sectors, high interest rates, the lack of clear goals for the economy, the lack of competition, structural problems in agriculture, conflicts in value judgments, and high expectations about the future of the economy, etc.

6- Inflation

Except for short intervals, inflation has always been a burdening problem for Turkey. Although it is known that inflation has some beneficial effects on the growth in the short run, it is still detrimental to sustaining growth. A lot is written about it in Turkey. Particular problems include the creation of uncertainty and instability, the difficulty of economic calculations; and their undesired effects on income distribution are being discussed in Turkey.

7- Stabilization Policies

Turkey adopted the stabilization policies recommended by the IMF in the

1960's, the 1970's, the 1980's, and the 1990's. We know that in each of these periods there was slack in the economy (or a recession). Were they related to stabilization measures or was that belief a post hoc fallacy? The leftist economists along with some well respected experts on the Turkish economy tried to show that outward and market orientation led to high inflation and to a reduction of real wages without a noticeable increase in growth rates. There is no doubt that stabilization measures would lead to a decrease in the speed of demand expansion resulting in a shrinkage in the economy. But was there an alternative to them? They don't talk about any of them. The relationship between real wages and outward orientation is discussed in many parts of this book.

8- The Importance of Marketing in Foreign Countries and Competitive Power

If exports are considered to be an important factor contributing to growth, factors determining exports must be important in growth. This problem is dealt with in more detail in several books (for a detailed treatment of this problem see, TUSIAD 1991). Here, a few factors will be mentioned: the marketing of export goods and the competitive power of the country. The promotion of Turkish products in foreign markets is stressed especially in recent years. It is also shown that such factors as the design of export goods, their quality and differentiation are important factors. Again, the increase of the importance of marketing decreases the importance of cost. The determination of goods which are competitive in world markets and an emphasis of efforts for their sale are also important. Economists dwell on the fact that as a result of smallness of domestic markets in Turkey exports are crucial. There is a high correlation between the competitive power of the country and the volume of exports. Actually, Turkey follows Greece and Portugal with regard to the smallness of domestic markets in OECD countries. Again, recent trends in world markets exaggerate the importance of competitive power. Particularly a large mass of the population in the US and Europe have become rich consumers, and as their purchasing habits being the same, standardization of production, an ever increasing improvement in the East-West relationship, the high speed in the change of technology and fashion, sophistication in differentiation have all contributed to the increased importance of competition power.

Eight fundamental factors which determine the competitive power of Turkey are listed below, and the strength of Turkey based on then is shown by scoring each (the highest score being 5): 1- geographical location = 4; 2- natural location = 3; 3- the cost of labor = 3; 4- traditions = 3; 5- experience in industry = 2; 6- technical infrastructure = 2; 7- infrastructure = 2; 8- technology = 2. If those factors are taken into consideration, here is a list of sectors which have competitive power: tourism, food, tobacco, textile...

9- Other Factors

a- The long run impact of populism is accepted to be very detrimental for the long run growth of income.

b- Macroeconomic instability and uncertainty created as a result is considered to be one of the most important factors affecting growth.

c- The impact of stabilization policies on the economy is also shown as one of the factors affecting the economy. The fall of expenditure and undesired effects of high exchange rates are considered to be the main factors in the slackening of the economy after stabilization programs.

d- The impact of ethnic confrontations on the economy is considered one of the factors which have had a dampening effect on growth.

e- The high level of defense expenditure is a large burden on growth.

f- Domestic migration from rural areas to towns is taken to be one of the factors worsening the allocation of capital in the sense that more has been allocated to infrastructure investments whose contribution to short run productivity is low.

g- The inflow of direct foreign capital has been very low. Growth rates would be much higher if more foreign investment were attracted.

h- It is shown that macro productivity is very low due to special conditions in the country, such as the high share of investments in real estate, the rather long time to finish investments, etc.

i- Most of the economists think that long run growth trend is around 6-7 percent, and Turkey has the capacity to reach that figure.

§ 8 -COMMENTS BY TURKISH ECONOMISTS ON THE GROWTH OF THE TURKISH ECONOMY

Comments by the Turkish economists on the growth of the Turkish economy are grouped under 6 categories: A, B, C, D, E and F. They will be summarized below.

A - THE STRUCTURAL CHANGE OR RESTRUCTURING IN TURKEY (DISCUSSIONS IN THE 1980'S)

The debates on the economy in the 80's Turkey have centered around structural changes or restructuring of the economy. Many famous economists believe that the improvement in the Turkish economy after 1980 is due to its favorable response to real devaluation, and perhaps to the adoption of an economic policy based on signals coming from the market instead of the unbelievably aggravated intervention in it. Thus, decentralized decisions might secure a better allocation of resources. But these economists believe that the improvement would only be temporary and that later the economy would again deteriorate simply because the necessary structural change or restructuring of the economy has not taken place.

What are is structural changes and restructuring?

I have studied extensively works on structural changes. My findings are summarized below:

1. According to some economists structural change means the increase of production and the spread of modern services and consumer goods such as electricity, telecommunications, televisions, durable consumer goods, etc. If figures are scrutinized referring to the use of these commodities and services, it could be concluded that a structural change must have taken place in Turkey.

2. Other economic analysts have argued that structural change means rapid industrialization, high amounts of investment in industry, and an increase in industrial exports. In practice, these have all occurred in Turkey. The share of industry rose quite fast since 1980. Industrial production has very rapidly expanded. The share of industrial exports in total exports has increased fourfold, rising form 20 percent to 80 percent in seven years. But there is an objection to this interpretation of structural change.

Some economists have attempted to demonstrate that the increase in the share of industry is an expected change for any developing country. If this is observed in Turkey, it does not necessarily mean that the expected structural change is taking place. In practice, if the economy is to grow satisfactorily, the share of industry must rise. The growth in agriculture is limited (1-2 percent). Hence, satisfactory growth in the national income can be obtained by a rapidly expanding industrial sector which, in turn, will lead to the increase of the share of industry. Therefore, this can not be regarded as a structural charge. (Authors' note: according to the famous economist S. Kuznets, the increase in the share of industry is referred to as structural change.)

3.According to some economists the change of structure in the Turkish economy is the internationalization of the economy. By internationalization several changes are referred to. Here are some of them:

a) The increase in the share of exports from the low figure of 3-4 percent of GNP to 16 percent in 5 years.

b) The increasing impact of fluctuations in the world economy on the national economy.

c) The sensitivity of decision makers in investment and production to business conditions in the world economy.

d) The increasing effects of foreign exchange inflows and outflows on the economy. Since the government is unable to control foreign exchange and because various foreign currencies have their own relative prices, the controlling of the national economy becomes increasingly more difficult.

4. Some economists regard the change of relative prices as a structural change. They refer to the narrowing of the differences between relative prices in Turkey and abroad. According to this argument, as Turkey sells more goods abroad, the prices of goods having comparative advantages increase in Turkey vis-à-vis other countries and this leads to the diminishing comparative advantages of a country. As a result, relative prices at home and abroad narrow. Moreover, the rise in the price of exported goods may be regarded as a cost push inflationary factor. I think that argument does not show the Turkish case.

5. According to other economic analists, the change in structure means a change in people's mentality, cultural change, an alteration in institutional arrangements, the transition to democracy, improvements in worker's rights, more efficient functioning of the markets, a more stable parliamentary system, efficient budget control and less rent distribution activities undertaken by the government, etc.

6. One economist refers to structural change as the change of structural characteristics of the economy. Before 1980 the economy possessed five important characteristics.

a) The economy was unable to produce enough foreign exchange.

b) Insufficient savings were produced.

c) The economy could not generate enough public revenue.

d) Resources were not allocated satisfactorily.

e) Income distribution was steadily deteriorating.

This economist demonstrates that with the exception of the first and fourth characteristics the situation has not improved and may have even deteriorated further. Thus, no structural change has taken place in Turkey.

The same economist puts forward a number of arguments to defend this assertion. It is revealed that the growth dynamics of the economy depends on the internal market. Although the economy has turned outward, because of the stagnation of the existing capacity of the exporting industry, the dynamics of the economy lies in the internal markets. (Events in the post 2000 years negated that economist)

B - THE EXPECTATIONS OF SOME TURKISH ECONOMISTS ABOUT THE FUTURE OF ECONOMIC GROWTH IN TURKEY

A well known Turkish economist (Uygur 1991) asked some prominent Turkish economists (according to him) their expectations about the growth of the Turkish economy in future.

Before reporting their opinions, he listed the probable factors determining growth in Turkey. They are the use of more inputs, allocation of them to more productive fields and an increase of micro-productivity. Those are parallel to what we have in literature. Then he asks his question as to two alternative ways to induce growth in Turkey. a) Should the intervention to the economy be at a minimum level and would growth be left to its natural trend? Would a pressure on the economy not create a strain on it and give rise to inflation, and as a result, would not bottlenecks resulting from inflation decrease the trend rate of growth? b) Would a well conceived industrialization program induced by proper economic policies not raise growth rates as observed in several countries? In fact, the general belief is that unemployment and bad income distribution in Turkey should make a higher growth rate a necessity.

It was expected that economists believing in price mechanism would not like too much state intervention while the left wing economists (they are the majority) would prefer all sorts of state intervention. And parallel to that the latter group would expect a much higher growth rate as a result of the no operation of the price mechanism and more state intervention.

One economist (Professor Celasun) thought that the historical rate of growth, i.e., 5.5-6 percent, was high enough anyway and a pressure on it would not be proper. All of them thought that the historical trend could be raised, and some 6-7 percent growth could be considered feasible if proper economic policies were followed.

They all think that the most important impediment to growth was a lack of well qualified human resources and as a result, a better education system should be induced. Again, the impact of instability and uncertainty in the economy is another impediment to growth.

High interest rates are thought to be an handicap for the accumulation of capital. On the other hand, almost all of them expressed their view that as a result of turning to outside in 1980, the rise of interests did not induce higher savings. Again, some of them believe that the increase of savings by means of capital markets was not feasible. Meanwhile an economist insisted that an increase of investments and savings was not necessary but a better allocation of resources could be more effective in accelerating growth.

C - THE OPERATION OF THE MARKET ECONOMY, SOCIALISTIC OPINIONS AND GROWTH

Many economists writing about the economy of Turkey dwelt upon the consequences of the neglect of an efficient operation of markets. They tried to show that external deficits, ever diminishing exports until 1980 s, an inequal income distribution, the deficient absorption of labor force, high costs in the financial system are all caused by a lack of the operation of price mechanism (IBRD 1980 and 1982). Actually, the import substitution strategy adopted until 1980 could not be kept without an intensive intervention in the free operations of markets.

The birth and ever increasing domination of high costs industries were a symptom and the consequence of an intervention in markets. Another symptom and consequence of the intervention were problems created by state economic enterprises. They were quite efficient in the founding years of the Republic and they had contributed to the industrialization of the country. But the ever increasing intervention by politicians made them a burden rather than an asset for the economy (see, for example, Singer 1978).

There are also several economists (see, Avcıoglu 1973) who think that the rather modest growth rate in the Turkish economy (from 1950 to 1975, 6.4 percent) is related to the economic system adopted in this country, i.e., the operation of the price mechanism (just the contrary to the previous contention). He thinks that it could be made 10 to 15 percent (Avcıoglu, p. 594). He shows that in order to increase the growth rate the rate of savings should be made 25-30 percent of GNP; moreover, they should be used efficiently. Then he adds: this is not possible under the present economic regime-system. "In the face of the existence of to-days' dominating classes to incur an investment at a rate of 25 percent of national income is not possible (it has been around that figure in years ensuing his writings, author's note); again, investments could not be allocated efficiently" (p.594). According to Avcıoglu the problem is not a lack of capital; it is the use of surplus value efficiently. Some 32 percent of national income is earned by rich people. Their investment is rather low; moreover, they are not allocated properly. They use investible funds for luxurious consumption and real estate.

I don't think that Avcıoğlu's ideas about the future growth of national income are right.

D - THE IMPACT OF CAPITAL INFLOW

Professor Yeldan asserts that (2002, p.35) there is a parallelism between the appreciation of the Turkish currency and the growth of the economy, i.e., when the currency appreciates, national income growth increases and vice versa.

Another assertion is the parallelism between capital inflows and national income growth (see, for example, Kumcu 2002, p.33). This is not wrong; but it is a short run observation, and it is necessary to go behind that relationship. In fact, several economists dwell upon the impact of the convertibility of the currency on the volatility of national income making the flow of foreign capital free, which in turn, would make the growth rate rather low. (See Table XI-6)

The majority of economists were of the opinion that Turkey could not follow import substitution policy anymore and the outward looking policy should replace it.

E - CELASUN ON GROWTH

I think that the observations by Professor Celasun about the future growth should be looked into more carefully (see also, Doğu Batı 2001). His views are more balanced and they are more in line with the world literature. He firstly distinguishes the short, medium and long term analyses of growth. He shows that in the first one the demand, in the second one the interaction of demand and supply and in the third one the productivity should be underlined. Along with that he rightly mentions that in the third line of analysis the international cross section factual findings support his belief. Parallel to that he shows that newly developed growth theories inspire factual research.

According to empirical findings, the openness of the economy, educational level, equality in income distribution, the depth of financial superstructure, the unfavorable impact of inflation and stability are important.. He believes that the growth rate in the last half century is 4.5 percent. The contribution of capital is a little below 3 percent, that of the growth of labor inputs is 1 percent, whereas the contribution of the productivity growth is 0.5-0.8 percent. Are not those exactly parallel to my thoughts?

The question then was the low level of productivity growth. He mentions 4 factors making productivity growth low:

1- The quality of work force.

2- Investments are not allocated in a way to maximize value added.

3- The impossibility of full utilization of the existing capacity in the face of the instability in the economy.

4- R and D were very little.

Those factors are relevant in the whole economy. There are also specific factors relating to various sectors. For example, in the manufacturing industry the following factors are important: physical infrastructure, organizational problems, the regulation of competition, the quality of raw materials, etc. (Warning: in my analysis one of the factors moking productivety small was related to the measurement of inputs.)

F- SECTOR AND EXPENDITURE SHARES

One of the explanations of the increase in the Turkish national income is based on the analysis of the increases in the shares of various sectors along with the analysis of the pattern of expenditure, such as consumption, investments and exports (See Gökçe 2007).

The use of that methodology could be illustrated by comparing 2006 and 2007 growth rates.

THE CONTRIBUTION OF VARIOUS EXPENDITURE ITEMS TO THE GROWTH OF NATIONAL INCOME (%)

	2006	**2007**
PRIVATE CONSUMPTION	3.3	3.2
PUBLIC CONSUMPTION	0.8	0.3
INVESTMENTS	3.3	0.9
EXPORTS	1.6	1.6
IMPORTS	-1.9	-3.1
GNP	6.9	4.5

According to this analysis the reason why the growth rate decreased from 6.9 percent to 4.5 percent in 2007 is explained by the decrease of consumption and investment expenditures and the increase of imports.

TABLE XI-6
BALANCE OF PAYMENT DEFICITS AND GROWTH

Year	Income Growth (%)	Current Account ($ Million)	Trade Deficits ($ Million)
1989	1.6	938	-4,167
1990	9.4	-2,625	-9,343
1991	0.3	250	-7,454
1992	6.4	-974	-8,156
1993	9.1	-6,433	-14,083
1994	-6.1	2,631	-5,164
1995	8.6	-2,339	-14,072
1996	7.1	-2,437	-20,403
1997	8.3	-2,638	-22,298
1998	3.9	1,984	-18,947
1999	-6.1	-1,344	-14,084
2000	6.3	-9,819	-26,728
2001	-9.5	3,390	-10,065
2002	7.9	-1,522	-15,495
2003	5.9	-6,808	-21,856
2004	10.0	-15,000	-34,308
2005	7.6	-23,200	-53,000

§ 9 - COMMENTS ON VARIOUS INTERPRETATIONS ON GROWTH IN TURKEY

In the previous sections 8 main interpretations of factors affecting growth in Turkey are summarized. I think that all of them are relevant: some more so, others not so much. Each of them could be drawn upon in order to explain growth in this country. Yet, it is quite evident that they are all an application what we have in the literature. There is, of course, no harm to profit from well known literature in order to explain another actual case such as Turkey. But my belief is that the contemporary literature was not enough to explain the Turkish case. Moreover, specific unfavorable comments could be made for each of them. In this section each interpretation will be taken one by one and short comments about each will be made in line with the section number in this chapter.

1 - THE EARLY SOURCE OF GROWTH ANALYSIS

In that analysis the drastic trend fall of the growth rate from 6.4 to 3.8 is not predicted, whereas in my source of growth analysis, carried out even before that event, it was predicted. That means that something was wrong in that analysis belonging to the best known international economists. To put it in a nutshell, the growths of agricultural and nonagricultural sectors are not separated. Whereas it was shown that rents of a particular character earned in nonagricultural sectors should make that analysis irrelevant.

2 - THE IMPACT OF EARNING DIFFERENCES BETWEEN AGRICULTURAL AND NONAGRICULTURAL SECTORS

The impact of earning differences is calculated by two economists, Syrquin and Balassa-Celasun. Syrquin took the nonagricultural earnings as they were and came up with a very high contribution of the shift of resources from agriculture to nonagricultural sectors. It is shown that (Chapter I) nonagricultural sectors are swollen due to rents of a particular nature earned there, and as the high nonagricultural earnings could not be sustained, the very high percentage of TFP consisting of the shift could not be a part of productivity increase. In other words Balassa – Celasun made a much more detailed calculation of earning differences. Yet, their analyses could also be criticized.

When my analysis in UATE is compared with the approach offered by Balassa and Celasun a fundamental difference becomes apparent. I re-evaluated national income in terms of dollars (which includes both growth and level effects), whereas Balassa and Celasun used constant national currency. According to my calculations (see Chapter I) some 17 percent of national income should be attributed to eaning differences and a rapid switch from agriculture to nonagriculture.I call it growth effect now.Here was the calculation. (Chapter I Table-6) The annual growth of per capita income was calculated to be 2.82 percent on the average in 1950 and 1975. If the increase of population is added to it (2.5 percent), the growth rate of national income would be 5.3 percent.The actual figure was 6.4 percent. 5.3 is 17 percent less than 6.4 percent.There was not much difference between my figure and their figure (theirs was 10 percent). The reason of that difference was that my calculations were based on dollars.On the other hand, the growth rate in dollars in that period was 7.6 percent rather than 6.4 percent.That could explain the difference. Yet according to the calculations made by Balassa and Celasun the proportion is around 10 percent (Celasun 1983, p.94). Why is there such a substantial difference in these calculations and which is accurate?

The figures are as follows. In 1950 per capita income was $150 (current). If the swelling caused by high valuation is considered, it should be $114. The swelling was measured as 24 percent in 1950 and increased to 35 percent by 1975. The reason why I contended that the national income should be made 30-35 percent less was related to the impact of both growth and level effects.Here are the figures.According to my calculations per capita national income is $ 537in 1975, whereas the official figure is $833; the difference is 35 percent.

I attempted to calculate a new national income figure in order to observe its overvaluation. In contrast to other economists my measure of overvaluation was based on the sustainability of national income. According to my calculations there was a large difference in earnings between nonagricultural and agricultural sectors. If this was so, how could the effects of the earning differences be detected? In my opinion this could be done by means of income measured in terms of dollars. It is shown in posterior years to UATE that dollar figures would reflect the overvaluation of national income. A simple idea yet a very important one.

The crucial factor making the national income unsustainable is the difficulty of exporting at a level which is necessary for a smooth functioning of the economy. The reason why the economy does not reach a satisfactory export level is related to the prices of export goods which are very expensive in terms of dollars. If exports consisted of agricultural goods only, they would not be considered expensive in terms of dollars (in the sense that relative price changes would affect them).But on the other hand, if nonagricultural goods were to be exported, their prices should be in line with agricultural products. This is demonstrated in my UATE.

The analysis of the impact of earnings differences between nonagricultural and agricultural sectors and its calculation in Turkey by Balassa and Celasun as well as comments written before this book was published are summarized above. There was a fundamental difference between what I said and what was in the literature, I realize now (2008), and it also constitutes the main difference between my views and those of Balassa and Celasun.

Balassa and Celasun are trying to calculate the contribution of earning differences and the shift of resources from agriculture to nonagricultural sectors to the growth of national income by using traditional methods. Their aim is to separate the contribution of the shift and earning differences from other factors. It is found by Celasun that in the period under study this must have caused an increase of approximately 10 percent in the national income. Their analysis is basically correct although the main factor determining earnings differences is the overvaluation of the nonagricultural sector of the economy.

Here is a summary of the most important contribution of my work.

According to my calculations in UATE (see Chapter I) the reduction of earning differences from 5 to 2.5 would make the average growth rate of per capita income 2.82 percent in 1950-1975 period. If the yearly growth of population (2.5 percent) were added to it, the growth of national income would be 5.3 percent. The impact of the difference in growth rate (5.3 versus 6.4 percent) should reduce national income by 17 percent. But according to the same calculation the national income should be $ 533 (current, see Chapter I§5). That was 35 percent less than the offical figure. According to official calculations it was $ 833. How would that discrepancy be remedied; or was my calculation wrong? Moreover two internationaly (Balassa-Celasun) well known economists took my analysis seriously and calculated the impact of earning differences between nongricultural and agricultural sectors and came up with a reduction of national income as some 10 percent. The difference between my 17 percent and their 10 percent could easily be explained: this was due to the fact that I was calculating in terms or dollars, whereas they calculated it in terms of constant national currency. It was not surprising that when I made my calculation in terms of national currency my conclusion was exactly the same as theirs in the sense that according to my calculations the growth of national income in that period was around 10 percent. But the contradiction or inconsistency was there. If the growth rate of per capita income were reduced 10 percent as a result of growth effect, national income would be around $ 600. There was again some 25 percent difference between the official estimate and the actual figure. This was my important discovery but it was discovered after some 25 years of the writing of UATE.

My calculation and again the calculation of those well known economists related to growth effect, as I define it now. But the 25 percent differences ($ 833-600) should be related to the level effect. Those two important concepts are explained in the previous chapters; yet they were in the air when I wrote UATE. The impact of the level effect had to be added to the growth effect which was clearly apparent in my 1978 work and that of other two economists: as a result, the growth rate was calculated as 4.1 percent rather than 6.4 percent. The difference was huge but what was more important was the analysis.

3 - CAPITAL

Actually when scrutinized it becomes evident that ICOR's calculated on the basis of a 5-year moving average has been quite volatile. However, apart from the crisis years they were in the neighborhood of 3 prior to 1980, and after 1980 they seem to have gone up to 5. If we don't consider the crisis years, the main problem is to detect the causes of two absolute figures, i.e.,3 and 5; what is more important is the increase of the trend rate from 3 to 5. Actually nothing much is done in this respect.

In fact, ICOR's are ex-post or balancing figures and a mere contemplation of them does not show much. We need a theory behind it. The unconventional analysis advanced here may be helpful to answer questions asked above.

4 - THE ANALYSIS BY THE WORLD BANK

According to World Bank sponsored research in the early 1980's, the yearly productivity growth was 2.2 point in the pre-1980 period. On the other hand, according to another research work sponsored by the same institution, productivity growth rate including both the pre and post-1980 period was only 0.5 point. There is a contradiction. If the productivity growth rate was 2.2 point in the pre-1980 period, it could not be 0.5 percent for the whole period. In order to be so, and if pre-1980 TFP were 2.2 point, that in the post 1980 period should be much less than zero. This is impossible. That means that the traditional method used by WB economists was not leading to a correct conclusion. This was what I have been correcting for about 25 years.

5- THE CRITICISM OF THE CHENERY APPROACH

The problem with the Chenery approach is a lack of in depth analysis of observations in Turkey and the interconnections among growth characteristics found in this country.

1- The low level of exports is attributed to an inward looking policy adopted in the observed period, whereas as I go deeper into the problem, I explain it by more relevant factors, such as the overswollen earnings in nonagricultural sectors and the near sufficiency of exports originating from agricultural sectors at that time. Actually an inward looking policy is a factor on the surface. I underlined the relationship between sector shares and exports.

2- The main structural factor is not detected by the Chenery analysis. It is the higher labor prices which could not be sustained. Actually, this assertion has proved right and labor prices have decreased noticeably in the period following the Chenery analysis.

3- The calculation of the Turkish national income in dollars, which was crucial for the comparison of actual structural characteristics with the predicted ones, is based on wrong reasoning. In fact, it is shown that real national income for that period was some 30 percent lower than what the official figures reveal and as a result dollar figures would give rise to misleading calculations of structural characteristics.

4- The relationship among several structural characteristics found by his method is completely ignored by it.

6 - VARIOUS CAUSES AFFECTING GROWTH

They are all relevant. But they are factors affecting short time growth rate of national income. Fluctuations in the growth rates, which are quite wide, could be explained by them. But the trend rate is a different matter.

7 - INTERPRETATIONS BY TURKISH ECONOMISTS

A- Analyses relating to the change in the structure in the economy cover the case for post 1980 Turkey, whereas the forces affecting growth rate in the previous years are also effective in the understanding post – 1980 years. What is important than that is that there are all sorts of false assertions in those analyses.

B- Some of the ideas expressed by 10 economists in Uygur's interview are generally relevant. But if the whole is scrutinized closely, it will be concluded that the consensus of opinions as to the Turkish economic growth in the sense that its potential is around 7 percent is definitely wrong. None of them, expect Celasun, is aware of the factors determining growth in Turkey, especially when those explanations are contrasted with ideas expresses above.

C- The impact of the operation of price mechanism arguments are, of course, relevant; yet they are only commonsense and what is important is that they are not enough to explain the Turkish case. It is a fact on the surface only and one must go below the surface in order to explain the case, When it comes to the explanation of socialists, it is evident that it has no scientific content at all. It is all ideology. The idea that Turkey could grow by 10-15 percent annually is beyond imagination, to say the least.

D- The impact of balance of trade and current account deficits on growth is clearly visible if the Table 6 presented above is examined even cursorily. In fact every high growth rate coincides with a high balance of trade and current account deficits. On the other hand, whenever there is a decline in the growth rate those deficits are low. This is the cursory look. But that correlation reflects the impact of short term forces. That is commonsense and I agree with that. Yet when it comes to explain the trend rate, that is important and I am after it, things are different. A lot could be written about it. But just one remark here. In post 1980's both foreign money given rise by invisible transactions and the volume of foreign loans were much higher than the previous period; yet the growth rate is lower.

E-Ideas expressed by Professor Celasun are very much the same as mine. I think that they are best analyses I am aware of. Yet, as he did not distinguish the growth and level effects, his analysis should be supplemented by additional arguments, especially measurement of inputs.

F-The analysis in terms of the share of various sectors and also the pattern of expenditure is a short time approach of accounting type. A lot could be learned from it yet this is not of much use in the explanation the intermediate or long run trend in the growth of national income.

In addition to its being a short time analysis of growth, it is also inconsistent with long time growth. It is apparent that according to this analysis the increase of minus current accounts exerts a negative influence on growth. We see that export increase ratio in both years is exactly the same, i.e., 1.6; whereas that of imports in 2007 is higher than what it was in 2006. According to this analysis this contributes to the lower growth rate in 2007. But it is quite evident that the increase in current accounts deficits means an increase of investments and this, in turn, should give rise to a higher growth rate. Apart from the logical and technical inconsistency the deflation of various items of expenditure this should also contribute to the illogical character of this analysis.

CHAPTER XII
TWO PAPERS BY CHENERY AND YENAL

§ 1- INTRODUCTION

In 1979 Professors H. Chenery and O. Yenal presented papers to a seminar organized by the Conference Board in Istanbul.Not only were these economists internationally well known individuals, they were also quite familiar with the Turkish economy.Their central theme were problems given rise by import substitution policy followed in Turkey and the necessity of adopting an export orientation policy as soon as possible. I included the paper of Professor Chenery as it was and a summary of Yenal's paper. Moreover, in these years Professor Chenery was trying to discover the relationships between stuructural changes in less developed countries and their development. He presented a large amount illiuminating data he gathered in various developing countries and compared them with what was observed in Turkey.By doing that he tried to discover the factors which gave rise to growth in Turkey and also problems encountered in this country. I was of the opinion that Chenery's efforts were worth of being considered.Yet, they were not enough to explain the Turkish case.In fact, before his paper appeared I used his findings in UATE and drew very interesting and vital conclusions from them. He was the discoverer but he could not apply his discovery properly. As I did that before the conference, I tried to criticize him and expressed my findings in a long speech.There is a translation of this speech in this chapter. After listening to my speech he tried to answer.lt is also translated in this chapter. If they are examined carefully, it would be apparent that he didn't understand what I was trying to contend. He didn't prabably want to understand the criticism of a economist from Turkey whose scientific standards were supposedly very poor.

§ 2- A COMPARATIVE VIEW OF TURKISH DEVELOPMENT

Dr. Hollis E. CHENERY

Vice-President, Development Policy

The World Bank

Over the past quarter century Turkey has been among the most successful countries in achieving rapid growth within a democratic framework. Since it is a large country with diverse resources, Turkey has so far been able to industrialize on the basis of its growing domestic market with relatively little attention to exports. Now the limitations inherent in this strategy have become increasingly apparent, however, and it is widely agreed that Turkey must adopt a more outward - looking trade policy in order to sustain further growth of income and employment.

Turkey shares this need to shift strategies with other large semi-industrial countries, in which industrialization was at first based on import substitution but has increasingly shifted toward external markets. The purpose of this paper is to highlight some of the common elements of this problem that may be useful in the current effort to redesign Turkish policies.

I. A BASIS FOR COMPARISON

In formulating a development policy, economists must combine elements of economic theory and empirical observation. The postwar experience of countries at a similar stage of development serves both to put Turkish performance in perspective and to illustrate the results that can be expected from different types of policy. It may therefore provide a useful starting point for the more detailed examination of individual policies that is contained in other papers to this conference.

Methodology

To evaluate the Turkish experience, I will proceed in two steps. The first is based on a worldwide statistical analysis in which changes in the principal elements of a country's economic structure are associated with several independent variables : the level of income, the size of the country, and the pattern of its international trade(1). The resulting estimates describe average patterns of development in the postwar period, which are defined by the change in early structural indicator as the level of income increases.

Using these estimates, Table 1 compares the actual changes in the structure of the Turkish economy over the period 1953 to 1973 to the typical patterns for a country of Turkey's size and income level. Over this period Turkey's per capita income grew from \$ 320 to \$ 670 (in constant 1976 dollars) and population grew from 23 to 38 million. These comparisons are analyzed in the next section.

The second step will be to compare Turkey's development to that of other large countries. Table 2, below, gives selected indices of growth for virtually all of the large, middle - income countries, defined as those having a population of 20 million

---

(1) This approach is developed in Chenery and Syrquin, Patterns of Development, Oxford University Press for the World Bank, 1975.

or more and per capital income in 1976 of between \$380 and \$3000[(2)]. For purposes of comparison, the group also includes two large centrally planned economies (Poland, Romania) in this income range.

Characteristics of Large Countries

Despite their political and geographical differences, all large countries have several common features that distinguish them from smaller countries. Because of their large domestic markets and more diverse resources, large countries tend to produce more for their domestic markets and less for export. They can also take advantage of economies of scale and introduce some types of heavy industry at an earlier stage in their development.

These economic influences tend to be augmented by nationalistic tendencies that have led many large countries to prefer an autarchic pattern of development. Virtually all the countries in Table 2 started to industrialize by developing local production to replace imports and have maintained these inward - looking policies for a substantial period. The result has been to discriminate against production for export, particularly of manufactured goods.

Since about 1960 there has been growing recognition by many large countries of the advantages of greater international specialization. The first group to move in this direction - the Republic of Korea, Republic of China (Taiwan), Yugoslavia, Spain- did so by reducing or eliminating the discrimination against exports that is inherent in the protection of domestic industry through tariffs, quotas and exchange restrictions. As a result of those policy changes, these countries have now had ten years or more of rapid growth of manufactured exports which in turn has been an important factor in accelerating the overall growth of the economy. Manufactures now constitute the bulk of the total exports of these countries, and total exports have reached a relatively high level.

Most other large developing countries have also moved to reduce the discrimination against industrial exports and to develop manufactured products for international markets. This trend has also extended to the other centrally planned economies in the group, Poland and Romania.

Largely as a consequence of this change in strategy, the large semi - industrial countries have been quite successful in accelerating the growth of GNP and sustaining it during the past several years of worsening terms of trade and slower

(2) A full list of developing countries is given in the World Bank's World Development Report, 1978, Table 2 includes all large countries in the specified income range except the USSR, China, South Africa, and Nigeria, whose experience is of less relevance to Turkey. The Republic of China (Taiwan), with a population of 17 million, is included to provide an additional example of an outward-looking strategy.

growth of world markets. For the 14 large countries in Table 2, the median growth of GNP per capita was 4.8 % a year during 1960 - 1976, compared to 2.8 % a year for all 57 middle income countries(3).

II. TURKEYS DEVELOPMENT PERFORMANCE

The general features of Turkish development in the postwar period are described in Yenal's paper for this conference(4). Some of the principal structural changes that have taken place are shown in Table 1, which compares them to the values predicted by cross-country regressions.

In most respects the structure of the Turkish economy was less developed in the early 1950's than would be predicted for a country of its income level. It lagged especially in levels of saving, investment, education, industrial output, and exports. Over the next two decades, however, structural change was quite rapid in all of these dimensions except exports. The increase in the share of industry in the economy and the rise in school enrollment were particularly notable. As a result, the structure of the Turkish economy now approaches the norm for a country of its size and income level, with the main exception of the level and composition of international trade.

Although the 4.2 % per capita growth of the Turkish economy over the period 1960 - 1976 has been slightly below the large - country median, it was well above the average for all developing countries. Until recently the poor performance of the export sector was lagely offset by the sustained growth of agriculture, the availability of external capital and the growth of workers' remittances.

The trade policy followed by Turkey for the past thirty years has been characterized by overvalued exchange rates and chronic shortages of foreign exchange in all except a few years(5). As a result, Turkey now has one of the most closed economies in the world, with recorded exports of only 5 - 6 % of GNP in recent years and imports of 10-12 %. Even if there are substantial volumes of unrecorded trade, Turkey is still the most closed economy among the semi - industrialized countries in Table 2, which include Poland, Yugoslavia and Romania. Only Argentina has been comparable to Turkey in its continued neglect of exports and periodic exchange crises.

(3) See World Bank, World Development Report, 1978, page 76. (The median in Table 2 is not affected by the additions of Romania and Poland.)

(4) O. Yenal, "The Reasons Underlying the Inward-Looking Structure of the Turkish Economy".

(5) See A. Krueger (1974) and her contribution to this conference, "The Role of Exchange Rate Policy in Opening Up the Economy".

In summary, Turkey has created most of the prerequisites for sustained deevlopment except a viable system of international trade. Comparing Turkey's economic structure to that of other developing countries underlines the importance given by this conference to moving toward a more open economy. Some aspects of the policies used only semi - industrial countries in making this shift will be examined in the next section.

III TRANSFORMING THE EXTERNAL SECTOR

Apart from two exceptional mineral exporters (Iran and South Africa), all large, middle - income countries have shifted the composition of their exports from primary products to manufactures as they have increased their level to GNP. It is the fact that Turkey has delayed so long before undertaking this transformation that underlies the current balance of payments crisis. The extent of this basic sutructural problem was concealed in recent years by the rapid growth of workers' remittances, but this merely deferred the need to developed manufactured exports. Although the Turkish experience is extreme, most of the other countries that have followed inward - looking policies for long periods have abandoned them after persistent import shortages made it apparent that they were no longer sustainable.

Semi - industrial countries shifting from inward to outward - looking strategies face quite different problems from countries that adopted such polices at an earlier stage. This difference is brought out in Table 3, in which the principal exporters of manufactured goods are divided into three groups. Group I A consists of developing countries that have specialized in manufactured exports for a number of years, including some of the most successful smaller countries that have now attained high levels of manufactured exports. Group IB (apart from Korea) consists of the inward - looking semi - industrial countries, most of which have been shifting toward manufactured exports in recent years. Group II consists of countries that have developed significant manufactured exports although they still specialize in primary products.

In this classification Turkey stands out as an anomaly. The composition of exports is typical II. Although it is similar to those in this group, there is not enough agricultural products which could make its development sustainable as long as the present production structure lasts. The workers' remittances could not support sufficiently for a long time. As a result,Turkey should develop an export level consisting of industrial products like the group II countries. A good number of I B group countries began to establish an industrial superstructure before starting the export of industrial goods.As could be seen in Table 3 their specialization in textiles, clothing and skin industries was less compared to what we observe in the other group. As a result of their diversified industrial structure, they could obtain competitive advantages in various consumption and investment goods.The advantages of low wages are less in those industries.

SUMMARY

The aim of this paper is not to suggest some policy recommendations.Rather,it is tried to prepare a ground for discussion in future.Turkey has developed its industry for its domestic market and it is protected against foreign competition.This fact would make it difficult to predict the sectors which would have competitive advantages after Turkey would make export markets as advantageous as domestic markets.lt is shown in the paper by Krueger submitted to this seminar that as the determination or fixing of the exchange rate is much below the inflation in this country,this could not induce exports.

The experience of other populated semi-industrial countries shows that if enough incentives are offered, exports from various industries would be profitable. This is supported by a report prepared by Derviş-Robinson based on the inter-industry relations in Turkey.According to them, a sufficiently high exchange rate would be helpful to fulfill this aim.

Although the recession in OECD countries prepared ground for protection,its effect seems to be concentrated in only some industries.In Table 4 figures are found showing estimates of growth rates of important groups of exported goods.This is prepared by the World Bank after the impact of protection in these countries is felt.According to the writers of this report the exchange rate should be at the level of 1970.Although the probability of success for textile and clothing industries is less,it is expected that other sectors would grow at higher rates.According to this expectation, although Turkey had to diversify ,the main impediment is not foreign demand.

§ 3- COMMENTS BY PROFESSOR ZEYYAT HATIBOGLU

Mr.Chairman, I would like to begin by stating that it was a great opportunity for me to lissen to Professor Chenery. Not only is he one of the economists who has produced important research work on development problems in the world ,he has also had close interest and contact with the Turkish economy.As a result, he is perfectly aware of our economy and its problems.In addition,his views and comments have always proven to be right, and they are validated by facts.

As far as I understand, he discusses the Turkish economic problems under four headings.The first is the low level of exports. The second observation is the satisfactory growth-development performance. The third is two strong aspects of the economy (about which I am going to talk in a minute);the fourth is the necessity to switch to an export led economic policy.

I agree with him on his views of the first and the fourth ones.He is quite clear on these comments.But I disagree with the ones under the second and third headings.

The problem could not be solved if we talked about the development of Turkey in past years. The past annual 6.4 growth rate is satisfactory; but the main problem is the expectation of economic growth in future years, such as 1977-1985.Without thinking about the growth in the near future the past growth does not mean much. I am sure that in the coming years the growth rate will have to decrease. Let me remind you that the growth in 1976 was 7.5-8 percent;yet it went down to 4 percent in 1977.lt is expected that the rate would be 2.7 in 1978.1 am sure that a zero growth rate in future years would be a great achievement.All this suggests that when the development of this country is studied, we should not rely on 1950-1975 figures.The expectations for future years should also be considered.We know that the import substitution policy which has been so far adopted gave rise to four important problems. All those problems began to be noticeable after 1975. They are the balance of payments deficits, unemployment which will be more troublesome in future years,inflation and bad income distribution.All these problems will be worse in future years ,which,in turn,would make the growth rate lower.

It is not right to say that the per capita income in Turkey in 1976 is around $ 1000. According to my calculations it is around $600-650. The solving of the problems mentioned above could be achieved by decreasing per capita income of the country.Although this is the case, the Turkish State Department of Planning is preparing a development plan in which the growth for the next 5 years is expected to be 8 percent, annually. I had hoped Professor Chenery would comment about this view of mine.

Professor Chenery talked about two strong aspects of the Turkish economy.One of them is a very high growth rate in agriculture.lt was 3.3 percent which was above the world standards. But while noting it, we should also underline the great earning differences between nonagricultural and agricultural sectors.We know that the expected multiplier of earnings is 2-2.5; yet the Turkish figure is 4-5.1 am sure that in order to come to a compatible figure with world standards the growth rate in nonagricultural sectors had to decrease and this should make national income growth lower.My belief is that as long as there is such a discrepancy Turkey cannot solve the difficult problems confronting it.

The second strong aspect of the Turkish economy according to Professor Chenery was high foreign capital inflow to the country.I am not of this opinion.But before explaining it I must stress the fact that according to my calculation the foreign capital flow is much higher than the Chenery figure:it is 7 percent of national income.This is one of the most fragile aspects of the economy. I think that a very important factor giving rise to difficult economic problems in Turkey is high foreign capital inflows.We were all very happy when workers' remittances increased very much in the I960's.We thought that we could solve our problems.Nowadays, I think that this made them worse.Labor prices were made very high because of huge foreign inflows and this made exports difficult.

§ 4- CHENERY'S COMMENTS ON COMMENTS

I am going to answer to a proportion of comments about my presentation.I am not in a position to say much about policies to be adopted in Turkey. My aim is to offer data for the comparison of the Turkish performance with other countries.

Several commentators talked about the growth of the Turkish economy.They stated that if growth rates were calculated differently, the findings would be lower than what it was in official figures, and its main reason is the inward looking policy in Turkey.I agree with that. All sorts of discrepancies are observed in countries which adopts an import substitution policy .It is true that if high cost import substituting industries are established, an incorrect allocation of resources might be the case in those countries.The most important disadvantage of these policies is to allocate recources to capital intensive industries rather than labor intensive ones.This disadvantage does not exist in outward looking policies.lt can easily be observed that in Turkey, industrialization did not create employment as much as it should have.Then it can be said that as time passes income distribution will deteriorate and unemployment would increase.I know them well ;that is why I did not stress this point. Although we do not have good figures about income distribution in Turkey and those similar ones to it,we are confident that the inequal distribution must be the case as a result of the concentration to capital intensive industries. This might not give rise to problems in a short time but it gets more and more annoying in a long time perspective. Exports may be induced by decreasing the prices of exported goods,or subsidies could be given to exports.By these methods balance of payments problems could be solved.But this has all sorts of disadvantages. Now let me talk about the problem of appraising the Turkish national income by means of international prices. Yes, if it is done the growth rate would be lower.But the same is true of all countries compared with this country.I do not know if Turkey would be different from the present Turkey..The same bias does exist in all international statistics.In each country following import substitution policy, industrial income gets bigger but that of agriculture gets smaller.Measuring Turkish national income in terms of dollars is not important. Measuring it in national currency is important.

§ 5- A NOTE IN 2008

This chapter consists of a paper submitted to a conference by a famous, internationally known professor,my comments about that paper and his answers. They all are a product of 1979. During the years following the conference I have developed my views a lot. Yet, I see that even in 1979 my criticism to a world famous economist was pertinent.

In those years Professor Chenery used to talk about the aboption of domestic prices to international ones. As this problem existed in all developing countries there was no sense in my approach and it was not original.I was of the opinion that he did not understand what I was trying to say. My aim was not to establish a relationship between the nonagricultural and international prices. Rather ,my preoccupation was to discover the level of labor prices in nonagricultural sectors and I was contending the necessity that labor prices should be the basis for all other prices.There was not any reason why prices in Turkey should be like those in interenational markets.But all economists along with Chenery didn't pay any attention to this view.If this is not understood,nothing much could be said about the economy of Turkey.The best proof is what we observed after 1978.Everything I expected materialized,and all economists failed in their expectations.

A very important problem was related to the determination of the foreign exchange rate. The level of the rate determined the relationships observed by the Chenery methodology. Professor Chenery insists that growth should be calculated by the national money rather than in dollars.But as was stressed above, we could not see the impact of the level effect (my discovery) if national currency were taken as a measuring rod.Morever, I tried to show in the years following 1978 that if there are changes in relative prices, calculations based on national money would not correspond to the exact growth of the economy.

TABLE XII- 1
STRUCTURAL CHANGE: A Comparison of Turkey to the Average Pattern
(Percent of GDP)

	Turkish Structure					
	Actual			Predicted		
	1953	**1963**	**1973**	**1953**	**1963**	**1973**
Per Capita Income	$370	$460	$670			
1. Investment						
a. Savings	11.5	12.0	14.8	16.3	18.0	19.8
b. Gross Investment	14.8	15.6	18.3	18.0	19.6	21.0
c. Capital Inflow	3.3	3.6	3.5	2.8	1.6	1.2
2. Government Revenue						
a. Govt. Revenue	16.0	16.6	21.1	15.6	16.8	18.7
b. Tax Revenue	12.6	13.9	18.5	15.0	15.8	17.8
3. Education						
a. Educational Expenditures	1.7	2.6	3.4	1.9	3.0	3.1
b. School Enrollment (%) : Primary & Secondary	33.3	43.4	56.1	46.4	57.0	65.4
4. Production (value added at factor cost)						
a. Primary	45.9	40.1	29.7	34.4	30.2	24.5
b. Industry	12.8	19.2	22.9	22.6	23.5	26.8
c. Utilities	5.7	8.8	10.7	6.2	7.1	7.5
d. Services	35.6	31.8	35.7	36.2	38.8	40.5
5. Trade						
a. Imports	11.3	9.6	11.4	17.0	16.2	15.6
b. Exports	8.0	6.0	7.9	17.3	15.2	14.8
c. Manufactures	0.6	1.0	1.8	4.4	4.8	6.0
6. Labor Allocation % Share of :						
a. Primary	79.2	77.6	64.8	56.9	53.8	47.2
b. Industry	7.4	10.1	13.6	15.8	17.9	21.7
c. Services	13.4	12.3	21.6	17.4	28.2	30.8
7. Income Distribution						
a. Share of Highest 20 %	-	57.0	56.5	56.1	56.1	55.7
b. Share of Lowest 40 %	-	13.0	11.5	11.7	11.5	11.2

TABLE XII- 2

INDICES OF GROWTH, 1960 - 1976 : LARGE MIDDLE INCOME COUNTRIES

	LEVELS			AVERAGE ANNUAL GROWTH RATES (PERCENT) 1960 - 1976						
	Per Capita GNP 1976 (US $)	Population 1976 (mill.)	Total GNP 1976 (bill. US $)	Per Capita GNP	Population	Total GNP	Agriculture	Industry	Exports	Imports
Romania	1450	21.4	31	8.4	1.0	9.8	8.9[a]	12.3[a]	n/a	n/a
Iran	1930	34.3	66	8.2	2.9	10.1	7.0	13.5	7.4	19.8
Korea, Rep. of	670	36.0	24	7.3	2.3	9.4	4.7	17.2	33.7	16.1
China (Taiwan)	1070	16.3	17	6.3	2.8	8.5	2.5	15.3	20.0	15.3
Yugoslavia	1680	21.5	36	5.6	1.0	6.6	3.4	6.4	7.0	6.9
Spain	2920	35.7	104	5.5	1.1	6.4	2.6	7.9	10.6	11.4
Brazil	1140	110.0	125	4.8	2.9	9.3	3.7	10.7	7.5	8.8
Thailand	380	43.0	16	4.5	3.1	7.4	4.9	10.0	7.4	7.4
Turkey	990	41.2	41	4.2	2.5	6.6	3.9	8.7	3.7	7.6
Poland	2860	34.3	98	4.1	0.9	5.4	n/a	n/a	14.7[a]	19.4[a]
Mexico	1090	62.0	68	3.0	3.5	6.4	2.7	8.0	3.1	6.2
Colombia	630	24.2	15	2.8	2.9	5.8	4.0	6.4	1.4	– 0.7
Argentina	1550	25.7	40	2.8	1.4	3.7	2.4	4.7	2.5	– 0.4
Philippines	410	43.3	18	2.4	3.0	5.7	4.5	7.4	3.2	5.9
Median	1115	35.0	38	4.7	2.7	6.6	3.9	8.7	7.4	7.6

([a]) 1970 - 1976.

Source : **World Development Report**, 1978 and **World Bank Atlas**, 1978.

TABLE XII- 3

EXPORTS OF MANUFACTURES AND COUNTRY CHARACTERISTICS OF SELECTED COUNTRIES

	Total Exports 1976 US $ mill.	Manufactured Exports 1976 US $ mill.	Manufactures as % of Total Exports		Per Capita			Growth of Manufactured Exports 1965-75 (%)
			1960	1975	Manufactured Exports Per Capita 1976 (US $)	Clothing and Footwear 1976 (US $)	Other Manufactures 1976 (US $)	
I. Semi-Industrial Countries								
A. Small								
Greece	2543	1252	9	48	138	62	76	28.7
Portugal	1820	1198	55	71	124	55	69	7.8
China (Taiwan)	8156	6921	14	81	425	187	238	28.8
B. Large								
Korea, Rep. of	7716	6675	14	82	188	94	94	36.0
Spain	8727	6025	12	70	169	32	137	22.6
Yugoslavia	4878	3383	44	72	157	33	124	9.9
Argentina	3916	972	4	25	38	9	29	16.7
Brazil	10128	2332	3	27	21	6	15	25.4
Mexico	3298	2327	12	52	38	6	32	21.2
Turkey	1960	466	25	36	11	8	3	32.2
II. Emerging from Primary Specialization								
Venezuela	9149	115[a]	0	1	8[a]	0.2[a]	7.8[a]	20.1
Iran	23380	208[a]	3	1	6[a]	4[a]	2[a]	8.9
Chile	1684	109[b]	4	8	11[b]	0	11[b]	n/a
Malaysia	5707	667[a]	6	8	54[a]	8[a]	46[a]	18.2
Tunisia	789	203	10	20	36	18	18	15.0
Colombia	1694	306[a]	2	21	13[a]	5[a]	8[a]	17.3
Ivory Coast	1620	117	1	12	17	5	12	17.4
Morocco	1262	197[a]	8	13	12[a]	7[a]	5[a]	16.6
Philippines	2433	255[a]	7	17	6[a]	2[a]	4[a]	7.8
Thailand	2980	305[a]	2	23	7[a]	2[a]	5[a]	30.0

([a]) 1975.

([b]) 1974.

Source: Chenery and Keesing, «**The Changing Composition of Developing Country Exports**», World Bank Staff Working Paper No. 314, January 1979.

TABLE XII- 4

PROJECTED GROWTH OF LDC EXPORTS OF MANUFACTURES, 1975 - 1985*

Product Group	Average Growth Rates (% p.a. in 1975 prices) 1970–75	1975–85	Percent of Total 1975	1985
Clothing	20.3	8.3	13	9
Textiles	17.8	6.2	12	7
Chemicals	16.5	13.0	10	11
Iron and Steel	10.7	14.5	6	7
Machinery and Transport Equipment	20.3	17.3	23	36
Other	10.2	10.0	36	30
All Manufactures	14.9	12.2	100	100

(*) **Source:** World Bank, **World Development Report,** 1978, Table 27.

§ 6- INWARD LOOKING STRUCTURE OF THE TURKISH ECONOMY

Dr. Oktay YENAL'S PAPER

The World Bank

Resident Mission in India

It has been argued above that the inward looking policies of Turkey were basically the result of the activist inclinations of policy makers. Although the immediate stimulus for extensive trade and exchange controls came from balance of payments difficulties, these difficulties had their genesis in the same attitudes as well, that is, in the readiness of the policy makers to finance large expenditures by monetary expansion. But the association of the strategy with the fast industrial growth that occurred in Turkey must have contributed to the durability of these policies and their acceptance by the public. Indeed, given the internal buoyancy of demand that came especially from agriculture, the inward looking policies may have even contributed to the growth of the Turkish Industry in its early stages of development. Looking to the future, it is clear that Turkey cannot continue any longer to manage its economy in the same manner that it did over the past 28 years because the financial consequences of the inward looking strategy have become untenable. Any viable alternative will have to aim at raising the level of foreign exchange earnings. What this means in terms of specific policy changes and their timing will be discussed in the subsequent sessions of the seminar. My view is that the reoritentation of the strategy should include a more flexible and realistic exchange rate policy, a slower domestic inflation rate, and a nationwide export campaign including measures that will introduce an export bias in the incentive structure of the economy. Turkey's industrialization experience and the comparison of this experience with that of India highlights the crucial role of buoyant demand for industrial growth. Turkey was reasonably successful with inward looking policies in the past because it could sustain a demand dynamism thanks to the momentum provided by agriculture and investments. The outward looking policies in the future must also attach high priority to the demand factor - maintaining the domestic momentum and supplementing it with a vigorous export drive.

MORE ON PROFESSOR YENAL'S PAPER

In addition to the above summary in English of the proceedings of the conference, I want to translate some important passages.

Two factors played noticeable role in the industrialization of Turkey.One of them is the high demand elasticity for industrial goods.When Turkey started its development efforts in 1950, per capita income in this country was $ 250 (in terms of 1973 dollars). An income at this level should give rise to a high income elasticity for non-food consumption goods.

The second factor is continous and fast increase of agriculture in 27 years from 1950 to the present:the growth rate of this sector is 3.8 percent.

These factors were the main factors of the rather high growth of the economy :in 1950-1977 it was 6.8 percent. It could be concluded that import substitution startegy has been beneficial simply because an industry could not be created without this strategy.

CHAPTER XIII

A TEST OF THE METHOD OF THE PURCHASING POWER PARITY (PPP) IN MEASURING NATIONAL INCOME

§ 1 - A CRITICAL EXAMINATION OF PPP

My work on growth sugested that the measure of national income in terms of its purchasing power of currency should be viewed differently from what we have in the literature.The main goal of the analyses relating to PPP was to show that a difference between per capita incomes of a developed and a developing country, each calculated by the official exchange rate of dollar, does not reflect the real purchasing power of those incomes. The purchasing power of developing countries should be higher than what it was measured by the official price of dollars.The reason is that labor is cheaper in developing countries, if measured in dollar, as a result, it would buy more goods compared to what it would buy in the U.S. This theoretical conclusion is verified by several works of research covering almost every country in the world. Therefore the main problem was to understand why labor was cheaper in developing countries.

The explanation is based on the idea that the exchange rate is determined by the relative prices of tradable goods in each country. But on the other hand,the productivity of labor relating to tradable goods in developed countries is much higher compared to developing countries. As prices reflect productivity, or relative prices reflect productivity differences, labor prices must be higher in developed countries. On the other hand, labor prices must be the same both in tradable and nontradable goods production.Yet ,it is known that there is not much difference in the productivity between the production of nontraded goods,even if there is, it is smaller compared to that in tradable goods.As a result,the purchasing power of labor in developing countries should be higher than calculated in terms of dollars.All these are well known in economic literature;this is even a textbook material.

When this fact was understood,the multiplier between per capita incomes in terms of dollar and that in terms of PPP ,which varies around 1 to 3, should reveal the development level of the country,i.e.,it was calculated around 3 for the poorest country and it was about the same for countries having the same level of per capita income of the US.Numbers in between show the development level of any country.

Why do I repeat that textbook information? The reason is that this is not general and we should no rely on that or this generalization based on that;therefore the judgements based on these analyses should be used very carefully.I am going to show it theoretically first and my belief would be validated by the Turkish experience.I shall put forward 3 arguments: 1-The change in labor prices giving rise to a change in national income is ignored in this approach. 2-This argument depends on the intensity of labor in exported goods. 3-The adoption of an import sustitution policy and the shift to an outward orientation would bring out cases which are contrary to the expectations of this theory. All those contentions will be expounded below and they will be verified by the Turkish case.

1-We suppose that the national income of the country is \$ 100.Half of that consists of labor intensive goods and the other half is nonlabor intensive goods.Again, we suppose that \$ 1 = 1 L (the currency of the developing country).In that case national income of this country is 100 L .We suppose that a devaluation is made and the rate is \$ 1= 2L now.

Now, let us calculate the national income of this country by means of PPP.We suppose that the prices of labor intensive goods are 3 times higher in the US,a developed country, compared to our developing country. Then before the devaluation, national income in terms of PPP was 50+ (3x50)=200 dollars. After the devaluation we suppose that the prices of nonlabor intensive goods do not change in terms of dollar, but as the dollar price is 2 rather than 1 L, the total value of nonlabor intensive goods goes up from 50L to 100L. Yet, those of the labor intensive ones stay where they are.The prices of nonlabor intensive goods are made lower in terms of dollars in order to sell them abroad.In fact, this is the aim of a devaluation and this is well known in the literature.As the national income was 150 L now, it would be \$ 75(150/ 2). In order to calculate PPP,50 lira worth of labor intensive goods are multiplied by 6. The reason is simple. Therefore in order to calculate the national income, 50 should be multiplied by 6 rather than by 3 which was the case previously. Therefore it is: 100+ (6x50)=400L. If that is divided by 2 it is \$ 200,the same as before, whereas I advance that according to the new approach I have developed it should be less.From the beginning on I tried to contend that if labor prices get lower, national income of that country should be lower as well.Yet according to PPP methodology there would not be any difference.

2-As soon as I tried to develop the innovative theory of growth, I preceived that labor prices in terms of dollars should depend also on the kind of goods which are exported. If the export of a country consisted fully of natural resources such as petroleum products (as the case is for Saudi Arabia), the generalization by PPP would not be valid.In other words, if exports consisting of natural resources are enough to satisfy import needs, the relative productivity in producing tradable goods in two countries would not be relevant in determining the exchange rate.Wages would depend on the level of the national income which would require a level of imports equalling the level of exports.That national income would be shared by capital and labor.If the national income after the share of capital is divided among workers,this is the wage rate prevailing both in tradable and nontradable sectors.In that case wages in nontradable sectors are not determined by those in tradable sectors as the case was according to the traditional theory.It must be carefully underlined that wages are not related to productivity in this case.Again, the level of wages would make the national income higher than what it would be if exports were of labor intensive goods.

3-The impact of a import substitution policy would distort the information to be given by a comparasion of national incomes calculated by dollars and PPP.If an import substitution policy is adopted, import demand would be lower and as a result,exchange rates would be lower.In that case per capita income in terms of dollars would be calculated higher than what it were.On the other hand, the multiplier should be less than the case was when there was not import substitution.

§ 2-VALIDATION BY THE TURKISH CASE

All those three objections to PPP are validated by examining the Turkish case.

1-The impact of the lowering labor prices.As statistics reveal, if the annual per capita national income increase for 1977-1999 period is calculated in terms of dollars, it is 3.2 percent;whereas if they are calculated in terms of PPP it is 5.3 percent and yet in terms of constant currency it is 2.3 percent.It is apparent that the growth rate in terms of PPP is much higher than in terms of dollar or in terms of TL.The reason is the fall of national income due to lower labor prices; they are not indicated by PPP.In fact this was the intention of the first argument. (See Table XIII-1)

2-After 1980 Turkey started exporting labor intensive goods.Before that period a great percentage of its exports were nature intensive agricultural commodities.In addition, the labor prices in agricultural sectors were also very cheap compared to those in the nonagricultural sectors.We should expect that the multiplier had to increase after 1980.This has been the case:while the multiplier was 1.31 in 1979 ,it went up to 2.47 by 1985.

3-In fact when Turkey practiced imports substitution policy the multiplier between national income calculated by PPP and dollars was 1.31 in 1979, whereas after Turkey switched to an outward orientation policy, it went up to 2.40 by 1985.Didn't the theoretical reasoning suggest that increase in the multiplier?After 1980 labor prices declined and Turkey started to export labor intensive goods.According to may arguments the multiplier should behave as observed.

The validity of this classification showing the inadequacy of PPP could be straightened by looking into a resaerch by a Turkish scholar (Özmucur 1987). In this research it is asserted that in 1985 per capita income in PPP in Turkey was $ 3,972, whereas in terms of current dollars it was $ 1,041;the multiplier was around 4, whereas for a country like Turkey the expected multiplier should be around 2.5.If this figure about PPP is right, Turkey's per capita income in terms of PPP was some 25 percent of that of the US.But in terms of current dollars the US per capita income was around 15 times higher than that of Turkey.Could that be imagined? Could the multiplier in Turkey be much higher than those of the poorest countries in the world,i.e., 3. I do not mention other findings. Yet, all of them shows that there is something wrong with PPP methodology and it should be used very carefuly.

§ 3 - THE THEORY BEHIND PPP

When the national incomes of two countries (each being at different stage of development) are compared, several difficult problems appear.

Several research works suggest that price ratios exhibit an expected pattern as countries develop. I will begin expounding this important conclusion by a simple statement. If tariffs and quantity restrictions and transportation costs do not exist, the prices of imported goods are the same as international prices. (International prices are measured by an international standard such as dollars, and home prices are converted into the international standard at the official exchange rate.)

The exchange rate has a crucial importance in determining the prices of freely imported goods, but its role diminishes in the case of goods subject to quantity restrictions.

The impact of international prices and exchange rates is also very strong in the case of export goods; their prices must be equal to international prices if there are no export subsidies.

Import and export goods are called traded or international goods. They can be contrasted with nontraded goods. There is a theoretical argument, supported by empirical findings, that the prices of nontraded goods in a less developed country are lower than their equivalents in a developed country (Balassa 1964, Kravis et al. 1975, Kravis, Heston, Summers 1978). The reason is simple. In a richer country, the average wage can buy more goods and services relative to wages in a less developed country. On the other hand, wages tend to be the same both for traded and nontraded goods industries. Labor is more efficient in developed countries relative to developing countries. But it is relatively more so in traded goods industries in developed countries.

There is a very important implication of the above observation. If per capita incomes in a developing and a developed country are compared, each expressed by a common standard, which are determined by the prices of traded goods, there will be a downward bias in per capita income of the developing country. The downward bias is caused, to repeat, by the close relationship between traded goods and international prices on the one hand and the relatively lower prices of nontraded goods, compared to those in a developed country, on the other.

The above reasoning suggests that if all goods and services were priced at the same prices in both a developed and a developing country, the per capita income in the developing country would be relatively higher than the income measured by an international standard. This fact has been known ever since the beginning of the first scientific writings in economics.

In a most comprehensive study carried out by Kravis and associates in 1975 (Kravis et al. 1975) the authors used a direct approach to this problem and recalculated the national incomes of sixteen countries by measuring each item constituting the national income by the same prices. This study verified the theory mentioned above: per capita income in developing countries with reference to a developed country is a multiple of what is found by a conversion of currencies by exchange rates.

In a later study Kravis and his associates (Kravis et al. 1978) showed the downward bias for each country vis-à-vis the U.S.. As the countries studied included both developing and developed countries, the relationship between downward bias and degree of development is generalized to find the per capita income likely to be found if a detailed calculation had been made for 100 countries.

The following is a summary of the formal proof as given in a textbook (Sachs-Larain, 1993, pp.657-688).

Assume that the same two goods are produced in two countries, and that there is one factor of production, labor. One of the goods is tradable while the other is a nontradable one. Each is differentiated from the other by a subindice below the letter designating it. The indice for the tradable good is T while that for the nontradable one is N. The production functions of each good in the first country are as follows:

$$Q_T = a_T L_T$$

$$Q_N = a_N L_N$$

Q_T designates the volume of tradable goods. Q_N the volume of nontradable goods, L_T is labor used in tradable goods, and L_N is the labor used on nontradable goods. a_T and a_N are coefficients showing the marginal productivity of labor, i.e., the volume of goods produced by one labor unit in each field of production. There is a linear relation between labor and the amount of production, and competition in the countries is assumed to be perfect. Under those assumptions labor should earn the same income whether it is used in the production of this good or the other.

If entire labor force is employed, $L = L_T + L_N$. Combining this equation with above production function equations results in the following equation:

$$L = \frac{Q_T}{a_T} + \frac{Q_N}{a_N}$$

We can write Q_N as a function of Q_T :

$$Q_N = a_N L - \left(\frac{a_N}{a_T}\right) Q_T$$

That equation is a production possibility equation. If a certain amount Q_T is produced in the country, we can find the amount of Q_N which can be produced (when the amount of L is fixed).

According to our assumption, the cost of each good should be equal to the amount of labor used in its production. In order to produce one unit of tradable good, we need $1/a_T$ unit of labor. If wages are w, the labor cost of producing of a single unit of tradable good (Q_T) should be w/a_T. The price of a unit of the nontraded good should be w/a_N. Then:

$$P_T = \frac{W}{a_T} \qquad P_N = \frac{W}{a_N}$$

Here P_T is the price of tradable good and P_N is the price of the nontradable good.

The determination of prices of the nontraded goods in different countries is at the center of this paper. This problem can be now solved by means of the above explanation. We know that nontraded goods in rich countries are more expensive compared to the same goods in poor ones. Its cause becomes evident now.

The price of tradable goods should be the same in each country, rich or poor. (We assume that trade is free and that there are no transportation costs.) If so, there would be no price difference between countries, although actually there is. The difference should originate from the different prices of nontradable goods. This question can be tackled as follows. In rich countries, wages should be higher than those in poor countries. However, this answer is not satisfactory. Because as productivity is higher in that country, wages should be higher than those in poor countries. Therefore we must look for another answer.

In order to compare national incomes of two different countries, each should be measured by the same unit. P represents prices in the developed country and P^X is the prices in the developing country. As a result, in terms of prices in the first country, prices in the second country should be EP^x. Here, E is the rate of exchange, i.e., the amount of currency of the second country in terms of the first country's currency. All we must do then is to compare P with EP^x.

P and EP^x are equal to a weighted arithmetic mean of the prices of both tradable and nontradable goods. If we designate the weight of tradable goods by (α), 1- α is the weight of nontradable goods (α<1). Suppose that weights are the same in both countries.

Then

$$P = \alpha P_T + (1-\alpha)P_N$$

$$EP^x = \alpha P_T + (1-\alpha)P_N$$

Now suppose that the theory of purchasing power parity theory is true for tradable goods. In that case the prices of these goods are the same in both countries:

$$P_T = EP_T^x$$

If the prices of tradable goods are the same, P can be more than (EP^x) only if P_N is higher than $EP^x{}_N$.

Our problem now becomes this: what determines the prices of nontradable goods? The level of wages depends on the price of tradable goods ($P_T = w/a_T$ or $w = P_T\, a_T$). Yet, labor prices in nontradable sectors should be the same. This equation shows that the level of wages depends on the price of the tradable goods (P_T) and the productivity coefficient (a_T). On the other hand, the price of the nontraded goods depends on the labor used in their production, because one unit of nontradable good requires $1/a_N$ units of labor. The cost of labor becomes w/a_N.

The price of the nontraded good is $P_N = w/a_N$; since $w = P_T\, a_T$ and $P_N = w/a_N$; that means that wages are the same in two sectors. Then we can write the following equation.

$$P_N = P_T\left(\frac{a_T}{a_N}\right)$$

It is evident that the price of the traded good is equal to a multiple of the nontraded good. The equation for the second country to be compared with the first is:

(Note: For the derivation of that equation see Sachs-Larain, p.674.)

$$EP_N^x = P_T\left(\frac{a_T^x}{a_N^x}\right)$$

When we examine the equation determining the value of P_N, we see that if labor is more efficient in the production of tradable goods, the price of nontraded goods would be high. The reason is simple. If the productivity of labor is high, it earns high wages; if productivity is high in the production of traded goods, wages would be high if expressed in terms of traded goods. In that case, high wages would make the cost of nontraded goods high. That means that if a_T is high, P_T would also be high. If labor is very productive in the production of the traded goods, the prices of nontradable goods will be high. It is assumed that wages should be the same in each sector. The result is that a high value of a_T, i.e., productivity coefficient, means a high price of P_N. "At the same time, nontradable prices will be low if labor is highly productive in the nontradable sector, that is, when a_N is large. When labor productivity in nontradables is large, the amount of labor used in per unit of production in nontradable is small. Thus, a high value of a_N means a low price of P_N" (Sacks-Larain, p.674). As a result, the price of nontraded goods (P_N) depends on the relative productivity of labor in two sectors: a_T/a_N. If high productivity in the tradable sector is expressed in terms of tradable goods, it means high wages. But if high productivity in the nontradable sector is expressed in terms of nontradable goods, it means that labor input is less. Thus, the price of the nontraded goods (P_N) is related to a_T/a_N rather than to the productivity in each sector individually.

It is possible to compare the prices of nontraded goods in two countries. If $(a_T/a_N) > (a^X_T/a^X_N)$ the first country is more expensive. If $(a_T/a_N) < (a^X_T/a^X_N)$, the first one is less expensive. It means that if relative productivity is more in the first country compared to the second, prices in the first country would be more expensive.

The above explanations have an overwhelming importance. Productivity increase in developed countries are faster in traded goods compared to nontraded goods. This means that a_T/a_N is higher in developed countries compared to that in developing countries. Thus developed countries are more expensive compared to developing countries. This means that when national incomes of developing countries are compared to that of developed countries, the national income of the developing country as measured by the official exchange rate should be multiplied by a multiplier which would compensate the cheapness in the developing country.

§ 4 - CRITICISM OF THE TRADITIONAL APPROACH

It can be shown that the determination of the relative prices of domestic goods in Turkey, (as well as many other countries) could exhibit such a particular character that the expectations in literature would be irrelevant. As soon as we suspend the assumption of the nonexistence of any protection, we would see that the correlation between the level of development of the country in question and the level of prices of home goods would diminish.

My previous investigations left me with the impression that in the understanding of the mechanics of growth in Turkey relative prices along with their changes should be carefully studied. In my initial studies, which covered the 1950-1975 period, my attention was directed toward the relative prices of agricultural and nonagricultural goods, which could be represented by earnings differences between those two sectors, or in other words, its index was the level of earnings differences. It was shown that if earnings differences were higher, the growth rate would be higher as well. In post 1980 my attention turned to the relationship between traded and nontraded goods. But the definition of traded and nontraded goods was made differently from what it was in the literature. In the literature physical characteristics of both goods are important. In my definition the fixing and/or the determination of exchange rates is also as important as their physical characteristics in determining which good is a traded good and which is a nontraded good. If the determination of exchange rates is not left to the market, (I don't mean only the official fixing of the exchange rate; I also mean the imposition of trade restricting measures), any good can be made a nontraded good.

Based on this definition, the relative prices between tradable to nontradable goods can be crucial in determining national incomes of different countries to be compared with each other. In traditional literature, the relative prices between tradable and nontradable goods (especially service prices) are actually considered very important in comparing the national incomes of two countries, each calculated by means of official exchange rates. In my analysis I made two important changes: one is the impact of relative prices in determining the growth rate. The other is the relationship of service (labor) prices to the level of development in the two countries concerned.

It can be shown that the traditional theory cannot cover the Turkish case as well as that of other developing countries.

In order to show that the traditional theory expounded above is not general let us take a theoretical example. We assume that production is carried out under the assumptions made by Sacks-Larain as explained above (Section 3). There are two countries, one developed and the other developing. We suppose that parameters are as follows: $a_T=2a^X_T$ and $a_N=a^X_N$. (We know that a's show productivity parameters, T is traded goods, N is nontraded goods and x figures the developing countries.) Let us call the currency unit of the developed country $ and that of developing one L. As nontraded goods cannot be exported, the developing country has to export traded goods. Thus if the developing country desires to export, the exchange rate parity between $ and L in this example would be $1=2 L (transportation costs and custom duties are ignored). It was $1 = 1 L before.

Let us assume that $a_T=10$, $a_N=5$, and $a^x_T=5$, $a^x_N=5$. We assume again that wage rates are $50 and 50 L in developed and developing country, respectively. If there is only one traded good, we cannot go on with this example, i.e., the same good is sold and bought. Therefore in order to make the example realistic let us suppose that there are 3 tradable goods. T1, T2 and T3 and a's are different in each country and for each good. We suppose that $a = a^x$ and call T1 cotton, $a_{T2} = 2a^x_{T2}$, call it cloth and $a_{T3} = 4a^x_{T3}$ call it refrigerator. If the developing country is willing to export T1 goods only, the exchange rate would be the same, $1=1L, whatever other a's and other a^x's are. If wages in developed and developing country are $50 and 50 L, respectively, the prices of nontraded goods would be the same, i.e.,

$$P_{T1} = \frac{\$50}{10} = \$5 \quad P^x_{T1} = \frac{50L}{10} = 5\ L \quad \text{if} \qquad 1L = \$1,\ P^x_{T1} = \$5$$

T_1 could be exported.

$$P_{T2} = \frac{\$50}{10} = \$5 \quad P^x_{T2} = \frac{50L}{5} = 10\ L \quad \text{if} \qquad 2L = \$1,\ P^x_{T2} = \$5$$

T_2 could be exported.

$$P_{T3} = \frac{\$50}{10} = \$5 \quad P^x_{T3} = \frac{50L}{2.5} = 20\ L \quad \text{if} \qquad 4L = \$1,\ P_{T3} = \$5$$

T_3 could be exported. We suppose that all a's are 10 in the developed country.

If $P_N = P^x_N$, each being $50 or 50 L, in other words, if service prices are the same in both countries, only T_1 could be exported. But if the developing country starts exporting the commodity in which she is less efficient compared to the developed country, then service prices become less expensive.

Now let us suppose that the developing country decides to increase its exports but cotton production cannot be increased or if increased, cost of production will increase immensely or terms of trade will deteriorate. In order to sell the commodity next on line in terms of productivity, L is devalued. The price of cloth should be made \$5 in order to sell it in the developed country. In that case \$1=2L. But as a result of one price law, the price of T1 good, i.e., cotton, should be 10 L (10L is \$5 in terms of new \$/L parity). If so, wages in cotton industry should be 100 L (100/10 = 10). As this is not compatible with factor price equalization theorem, the same wage rate (50 L) should be prevalent in the cotton industry but the rest, i.e., 50 L, is the rent earned in this industry. (Let us remember that this problem is solved by drawing upon the distinction between labor and nonlabor goods and by changing labor prices. As a result, rents would not be created, see Chapter IV and V).

In this situation, service prices are \$50 and 50 L in developed and developing countries, respectively; but in terms of dollars they are \$50 and \$25, respectively. (Let us notice that this conclusion is reached as a result of a realistic change in our assumption.)

This argument suggests that the widely accepted calculation method by means of relative purchasing parity power is not general. Now let us expand this point by first writing the above formula about the prices of nontraded goods in a developing country.

$$EP_N^x = P_T\left(\frac{a_T^x}{a_N^x}\right)$$

In this formula it is supposed that E should stay the same all the time (this is because of the fact that the exchange rate is determined by the relative prices of traded goods in two countries), and the absolute magnitude of the difference between a_T^x and a_N^x does not affect E. But it can be shown that even if a_T^x/a_N^x stays the same and if the developing country starts practicing protection and import substitution, the value of domestic currency will have to increase in terms of foreign currency, i.e., E will have to decrease. In this case if P_T, a_T^x and a_N^x stay the same, P^X_N must increase. The problem here is to understand why E should decrease.

If the amount of tradable goods is rather high and the amount of goods having high comparative advantages are enough to provide necessary imports for the country and/or if the great difference between a_T^x and a_N^x induces import substitution, E would be determined at a low level. Let us look into the second case, i.e., after import substitution real exchange rate will increase.

Many goods were imported before an import substitution strategy was adopted. After the adoption of this strategy import demand would decrease, and as a result the need for foreign exchange will have to decrease (as a proportion of national income, of course). This would give rise to a decrease in the price of foreign exchange.

The explanations above are related to the effects of the adoption of an import substitution policy, whereas we supposed that there would be no restrictions in trade. Now, let us look into that case. We suppose that as a result of a reduction of labor prices some labor intensive goods become exportable. As the efficiency in more labor intensive goods were lower a^x_T / a^x_N should get lower now (a^x_T is lower now). P_T is the same as before. As a result, the left side of the formula should become lower. It was supposed that the export of more labor intensive goods should be possible if P^x_N gets lower. But we concluded that the left side of the formula had to become lower. If that is made possible by the lower P^x_N only, there is no need for E (unit of domestic currency for per unit of foreign currency) to become lower. To repeat, there is not any need for of P^x_N to become lower to compensate exactly the decrease in a^x_T / a^x_N. Therefore if P^x_N does not get low enough to keep E at the same low level (this is more probable), E will have to become lower. That means that there is a tradeoff between a depreciation of the currency and the prices of home goods (labor prices). All that means that the PPP method is not reliable. Everything would depend on the labor prices and the share of labor intensive goods which are exported.

CONCLUSION

The formula does not offer any hint about the tradeoff between labor prices and the exchange rate. As the PPP method is based on the levels of the exchange rate, and again as the change of labor prices are not considered as a factor determining income level, this method is not reliable.

Let us suppose there are three countries, each offering structural differences.

The first country is supposed to be the one having the characteristics of Saudi Arabia, which has ample petroleum reserves. This country is in a position to sell large quantities of crude oil at world market prices. If the cost of capital used in petroleum production, marketing costs and wages earned in that sector are deducted from the sale revenue, the rest is natural resources rents earned by this country. Let us assume that there are no protective measures and that almost all tradable goods in the traditional sense are imported, and nontradable goods and services are produced in the country. What would be their prices? It is evident that the most important determining basis is the sales revenue of the petroleum industry: we have to deduct four items. Firstly, wages of people working in that industry (there is a complication here; but let us ignore it for the moment), secondly, the cost of capital, thirdly, the accumulation of foreign assets by the allocation of petroleum income, and fourthly the import bill. A proportion of the petroleum sales revenue will be used to buy nontradable goods. This is a very important item in the determination of the prices of nontradable goods. It is evident that in this example the level of rent and the import bill would be very important in determining the price of home goods and labor prices. (There are obviously other factors determining home goods prices but let us ignore them.) Suppose that the import bill shrinks as a result of protection in that country, and a proportion of petroleum rents is used to buy the products of the inefficient import substituting industry. Since the same amount of commodities would cost more (because the new industry is less efficient), the same amount of money will buy less and the purchasing power of wages will tend to decrease. What is more important, labor prices will decrease as well.

Here in this case wages in the tradable goods sector (the exporting sector) are determined by wages paid in the nontradable goods sector, rather than vice-versa as predicted by the conventional theory.

That example leads us to the second country: this is pre-1980 Turkey. We know that the comparative advantages of the country lie in the agricultural sector. However, the capacity to produce in that sector is limited. If agricultural production increases more than what its traditional trend would allow, the cost of production would increase rapidly. Again, if more agricultural goods are sold abroad, the terms of trade would deteriorate a lot. In that case some of the previously nontradable goods in the nonagricultural sectors can be sold abroad but it may require a very high exchange rate, which might be politically and socially impossible. In that case (i.e., the impossibility to increase agricultural production in order to increase exports and by that way to import several industrial commodities) the feasible alternative is to establish an import substituting industry by means of all sorts of protective measures. If this is the case, the exchange rate can be kept at a very low level, low enough to prohibit exported agricultural goods from earning rents, which should otherwise be earned as a result of their comparative advantages. In that situation the wages of workers producing home goods at the nonagricultural sectors would be at the same level as wages of those workers producing goods having comparative advantages (there are always differences in wages earned in agricultural and nonagricultural goods due to productivity differences), and the downward bias in the national income of the developing country well known in the literature would not be created. In that case wages in non-exporting sectors determine those in exporting sectors.

Now let us look into the third case: Turkey after 1980. We know that goods produced in the agricultural sector were hardly enough for necessary exports. The sale of more nonagricultural goods could be achieved by a large devaluation. In that case, previously exported goods will earn rent but newly exported goods should not earn rents. This is exactly the same as in the second case, with the difference being that both the exported and non-exported goods are in the nonagricultural sector.

High rates of devaluation would be required for them to be sold. As a result, the prices of newly exported goods determine the prices of home goods. The previously exported goods are earning rents but newly exported ones don't earn rents. In fact, they are made exportable but their prices remain as they were before the devaluation. As a result, there is a difference in the price of the previously traded goods and nontraded goods although the difference is not as high as assumed by the traditional theory. In that case service prices are determined by newly exported goods. Thus a bias between the prices of the developed and developing countries would exist.

There is another factor to be taken into consideration here. Service prices depend on the foreign exchange inflow that comes from foreign exchange revenue earned by transactions such as foreign debt, tourism income, worker's remittances and illegal transactions revenue, etc. If the foreign exchange revenue of invisible transactions is high, there is no need for low service prices. As long as there would not be a need to increase the export of labor intensive goods, service prices may be high. This means that the elegant relationship between the level of development and the level of service prices does not hold.

If nontradable goods can be made tradable goods smoothly, the distinction between them and the measurement of national income in terms of purchasing power parity, which is based on this distinction, does not mean much. To replace this distinction I suggest a distinction between exportable and non-exportable goods. We shall use this distinction in understanding the impact of relative prices on income.

There is a more convincing argument showing that measurements based on PPP would lead to wrong conclusions. (I repeat the previous argument expounded in §1.)

We suppose that the national income of the country is $100. Half of it is labor intensive and the other half is nonlabor intensive one. Again, we suppose that $1 is equal to 10 L (The currency unit). In that case the national income is 1000 L. After the devaluation the exchange rate is $1=20 L.

Now let us calculate national income of the country by means of the purchasing power parity method. We suppose that labor intensive goods are 3 times higher in the US, a developed country, compared to the country in question. Then, before the devaluation, national income in PPP was 50+(3x50)=200 dollars. After the devaluation we suppose that as the prices nonlabor intensive goods tend to be the same as those in the US, they go up from 500 to 1000 L but those of labor intensive ones stay where they are, i.e., 500 L. The prices of nonlabor intensive/goods are made lower in terms of dollars so that they could be sold in foreign markets. As national income was 1500 L now, it would be $ 75 (1500/20). In order to calculate PPP, 500 L has to be multiplied by 6. The reason is simple: as the prices of labor intensive goods were 3 times higher before in the US, they must be 6 times higher now; this is because of the fact that while their prices in L is the same, the price of

$ is now 20 L rather than 10 L. Therefore national income is 1000+(6x500)=4000 L. In terms of PPP it is 4000/20, i.e., $200, the same as before. While the multiplier of PPP income to income in $ was 2(200/100) before, now it is 2.66 (200/75). It is known that a higher multiplier implies a lower national income.

There is more to suggest that national income of the country has decreased. In the new situation, i.e., when relative prices of labor intensive goods are lower, the country starts producing less competitive goods. Moreover, as labor prices become lower, the fourth sector of the economy expands. To give an example, more labor is used as servants, peddlers, etc. All this means is in that situation national income must have diminished.

APPENDIX TO CHAPTER XIII

A contemplation of figures of national incomes in Turkey calculated by current dollars, by PPP, by constant prices and by changes of per capita incomes in PPP/ in $ (multiplier) (see Table XIII-1) would validate the unfavorable comments about PPP expressed above.

TABLE XIII-1
PER CAPITA GNP IN TURKEY

Year	Population (1000)	GNP Billions of TL	Current Prices Per Capita GNP (TL)	Per Capita GNP ($)	Per Capita GNP by PPP	Per Capita PPP/$
1977	41.768	1.108	26.534	1.488	1.945	1.31
1978	42.640	1.646	38.602	1.604	2.081	1.30
1979	43.530	2.877	66.081	1.760	2.198	1.25
1980	44.438	5.303	119.335	1.570	2.299	1.46
1981	45.540	8.023	176.169	1.598	2.582	1.61
1982	46.688	10.612	227.293	1.412	2.768	1.96
1983	47.864	13.933	291.096	1.299	2.935	2.25
1984	49.070	22.168	451.757	1.238	3.179	2.56
1985	50.306	35.350	702.706	1.356	3.354	2.47
1986	51.433	51.185	995.174	1.487	3.598	2.49
1987	52.561	75.019	1.427.282	1.668	3.971	2.38
1988	53.175	129.175	2.404.824	1.693	4.119	2.43
1989	54.893	230.370	4.196.709	1.979	4.217	2.13
1990	56.204	397.178	7.066.713	2.710	4.699	1.73
1991	57.063	634.393	11.117.411	2.666	4.806	1.80
1992	57.992	1.103.605	19.053.294	2.766	5.143	1.86
1993	58.782	1.997.323	33.978.473	3.093	5.629	1.82
1994	59.641	3.887.903	65.188.426	2.195	5.362	2.44
1995	60.500	7.854.887	129.832.846	2.841	5.745	2.02
1996	61.425	14.978.067	243.843.179	3.005	6.123	2.03
1997	62.411	29.393.262	470.962.845	3.110	6.507	2.09
1998	63.391	53.518.332	844.257.576	3.247	6.706	2.06
1999	64.337	78.282.967	1.216.779.613	2.880	6.083	2.21
2000	65.293	124.405.569	1.905.343.130	3.060		

Now General Remarks : (Written in 1985)

Let us suppose that the level of the Turkish national income calculated by the purchasing power method is three or four times higher than what official figures in dollars indicate. Does this mean that the welfare of the country is three or four times greater? The majority of Turkish economists answer in the affirmative but I have serious doubts. If per capita income in Turkey is $5000 (in PPP) rather than $1300 (1985), does this mean that when the per capita income increases by 4 percent per annum, the welfare of an average Turkish citizen will increase by $200 yearly ($5000x0.04=$200) (an incredible figure) or $52 ($1300x0.04=$52)? Obviously, the increase of welfare is around $52 and not $200.

If the initial increase had been $200, in the next 25-30 years Turkish income levels would have matched developed countries in Western Europe, believe it or not! (We know that per capita income in Turkey is 1/10 of western countries.)

Moreover, when the per capita income of Turkey is compared with countries of a similar economic standing no adjustment is necessary.

The inadequate nature of figures based on the purchasing parity method may also be observed when the level of exports are compared with the income level calculated by it. In practice, if the level of the Turkish national income is four times greater than official statistics show, then it should be around $280 billion (70x4) in 1988. If so, the proportion of exports would be some 4 percent (exports in 1988 were around $12 billion). Thus, there is scope for a considerable increase of exports. In fact the level of exports in 1988,let alone a two or threefold increase, created difficulties for the economy in that year.

The purchasing parity method is of limited value when there is not a balance between tradable and nontradable goods. It is known that the price of nontradable goods is less in developing countries. There is a limit in the production of nontradable goods (including exportable goods). If the proportion of nontradable goods increases with respect to tradable products, the economy may experience problems. There is a relationship between the level of income and imports which are required to sustain it. If a country has an excess quantity of bread but not enough petroleum products, the production of bread may be increased if it is to be sold abroad. Thus, there is a limit to the cheapness of nontradable goods which affects the level of income.

It is shown that there is a much more meaningful criticism to the approach by economists, which is also true for the literature on which they base their analysis. I have shown quite clearly that the relative level of service prices depends on, in addition to relative level of development of the country, the kind of goods exported by this country. If so, the attempts to calculate national income on the basis of service prices are meaningless. The same is true of for the regularly published national income figures based on the calculation of the World Bank.

Another proof about the validity of my analysis is detected when the recent figures relating to Per capita income in PPP / Per capita income in $ are examined. Here are the figures.

2003	2004	2005	2006	2007	2008
8,878/4531	10,137/5779	10,852/7027	11,582/7609	13,203/9305	13,998/11,228
1.93	1.75	1.54	1.52	1.40	1.24

It is evident that there is a decrease in the multiplier. It went down form 1.93 to 1.24 in 6 years. The decrease is related to the undervaluation of dollars. My contention was that PPP was not a right indicator for measuring the level and growth of national income. In this period the annual growth of per capita national income is 16.4 percent in terms of dollars; whereas in terms of PPP it is 8.1 percent only. As a result, the multiplier went down form 1.93 to 1.24. Could we say that the welfare of the country increased so much in recent years?

CHAPTER XIV

EMPLOYMENT

§ 1 - INTRODUCTION

Employment was not a highly troubling problem until recently in Turkey. In rural regions of the country almost everybody was employed somehow. The unemployed people who migrated to towns did not have great problems for their daily living (until they found employment) because of family relations. In fact, the fourth sector, i.e., occupations with very low productivity such as peddling, household helping, etc., absorbed a good proportion of the new migrants. Again, as earnings, especially in the fourth sectors, were very low to support those people, densely populated shanty towns continued to increase around the towns. But this could not continue forever. Then the problem was to find out factors determinig employment which could procure decent earnings.

Statistical figures about population and employment are given at the end of this paper. In this paper like in others the theoretical aspects of employments and my unconventional ideas along with traditional ones will be dealt with.

§ 2 - THE ANALYSIS BY IBRD (1980)

The analysis of employment conducted in IBRD 1980 report is both representative of current thoughts on this pressing problem and one of the best analyses of employment in Turkey. Therefore, a summary of this analysis will be given here in order to offer a glimpse on the dimensions of this problem. Actually, according to 1980 IBRD report, unemployment is one of the three pressing problems facing Turkey and therefore a special emphasis is laid upon it.

As the supply of labor depends on population, trends relating to the population are first investigated. The historical growth of population (1950-1978) was in the neighborhood of 2.5 percent yearly and there are indications that it is decreasing. According to estimates of IBRD report the population in 2000 will be around 64 million, and its growth rate will be 1.5 percent per year. The problem is, therefore, to provide employment for an ever increasing population.

As was underlined by the report, in the intermediate run the supply of labor is more connected with the participation rate, i.e., the percentage of labor force to total population of working age, 15 + years. Several conclusions are drawn from data relating to the 1962-1977 period. The relevant paragraphs of the report are reproduced here: 6.9-6.10-6.12-6.13.

6.9. The past growth of the working age population, the labor force and employment are shown in Table XIV-1. The following trends, germane to the employment problem, are noteworthy. First, the total labor force has grown more slowly than the total population of working age, reflecting a decline in the labor force and of total employment but has not resulted in a rapid increase of unemployment because of the migration of workers abroad. Between 1967 and 1977, the total labor force increased by 2.3 million while total employment increased 1.5 million; over 0.5 million of the difference was accounted for by the increase in the stock of Turkish workers abroad. Finally, the total number of unemployed has increased both absolutely and relative to the size of the labor force. The numbers of unemployed (excluding surplus or underemployed labor in agriculture) have increased from 600,000 in 1967 to 1.5 million in 1977, or from 4 percent of the labor force to over 9 percent.

TABLE XIV - 1

POPULATION, MANPOWER, AND EMPLOYMENT LEVELS

					Growth Rates		
	1962	1967	1972	1977	1963-67	1968-72	1973-77
Total Population (millions)	28.9	32.7	37.1	42.0	2.5	2.5	2.5
Working Age Population (millions)	16.4	18.5	21.2	23.9	2.4	2.8	2.4
Labor Force (milions)	13.1	13.9	15.0	16.2	1.1	1.6	1.6
Participation Rate (%)(1)	80.1	75.0	70.6	67.7	-	-	-
Total Employment (millions)	12.6	13.2	13.9	14.7	0.9	1.0	1.1
Unemployed (millions)	1.4	1.7	2.0	2.2	4.0	3.3	1.9
of which: Agricultural Surplus Labor	1.0	1.1	0.9	0.7	-	-	-
Unemployment Rate (%)	11.0	12.1	13.3	13.1	-	-	-
Unemployment Rate (exclusive of Surplus Labor)	3.1	4.3	7.3	9.3	-	-	-
Labor Stock Abroad (000)	13	204	634	815	73.4	25.5	5.2

(1) Percentage of Labor Force to total population of working age, 15 + years.

Source: Statistical Annex Table 1.1, 1.2.

Labour Force Participation Rate (LFPR)

6.10 Declining LFPR's are characteristic of countries during the process of development. The reasons for such a decline are numerous: the transformation from agriculture to industry results in early retirement for the elderly and increased educational opportunities for the young. Occupational changes brought about by rural-urban migration and changes in definition of employment between urban and rural areas can cause an "artificial" decline in the LFPR. Also, there are fewer opportunities for marginal work which one would qualify as actively employed in the urban area. Lack of employment opportunities in general, and for females in particular, also causes a decline in the female LFPR. If extra earnings are available from urban employment, then the withdrawal of females from the labor force may be the result of choice. Factors which induce an increase in LFPR with development are few in the short run. In the long run, the LFPR is likely to swing upwards due to increases in employment opportunities in the organized sector, increases in education, changes in attitudes, etc. In conclusion, it appears that developing countries can undergo significant changes in LFPR simply because of the changing structure of production, i.e., the transformation from a rural, agriculture based economy to an urban, industrialized one.

6.12 Partial and direct evidence for the hypothesis that the decline in LFPR for Turkey reflects **both** structural changes (para 6.10) as well as the discouraged worker effect is provided in Table 34 (here Table XIV-2). Since the data relates to the prime age group (25-54 years) considerations about educational expansion and early retirement are irrelevant. The figures clearly indicate the following: (a) the largest drop in LFPR is observed for females-from 81.5 percent in 1950 to 46.6 percent in 1975 - and this possibly reflects stuctural change; (b) the male LFPR declines from 97.7 percent in 1950 to 92.0 percent in 1975. That the decline is observed in both the urban and rural areas is supportive of a discouraged worker hypothesis. (Note that a decline of one percent in the male 25-54 participation rate represents about 65,000 workers).

6.13 The growth and sectoral distribution of employment is shown in Table 35 (here Table XIV-3). Employment in agriculture has declined in absolute terms and its share in total employment has decreased by about 15 percentage points during the 15 year period of 1962 - 1977.

TABLE XIV - 2
HISTORICAL TREND IN LFPR FOR TURKEY: PRIME AGE GROUP
(25-54 Years) (Percent)

	Turkey		Urban (1)		Rural	
	1950*	1975	1955	1970	1955	1970
Total	89.5	69.4	60.8	53.6	93.6	85.4
Male	97.7	92.0	95.8	91.2	99.1	96.6
Female	81.5	46.6	19.1	11.6	86.3	75.8

(1) Urban areas with population of 10,000 or more.

Source: SPO **Trends and Prospects in Turkish Labor Force, 1962 - 1983,** August 1978.

During this period the bulk of the increase in employment outside agriculture occurred in services, whose share in total employment increased by over 10 percentage points. Industrial employment has increased at between 4 and 4.5 percent per year on the average during the three plans, but its share in total employment (around 13 percent in 1977) is still quite small.

TABLE XIV - 3
SECTORAL DISTRIBUTION AND GROWTH OF EMPLOYMENT

	Percent Shares				**Growth Rates**		
	1962	1967	1972	1977	1963-67	1968-72	1973-77
Agriculture	77.0	72.2	66.9	61.8	-0.4	-0.5	-0.4
Industry(1)	7.9	9.2	10.7	12.6	4.2	4.1	4.5
Manufacturing	7.2	8.2	9.7	11.0	3.5	4.4	3.8
Services	15.1	18.6	22.4	25.6	5.2	4.8	4.2
Total Civilian Employment	100.0	100.0	100.0	100.0	0.9	1.0	1.1

(1) Includes mining, manufacturing, electricity, gas and water. (Note: There is a problem in this Table)

Two additional aspects of the employment problem are emphasized in the report: one is the effect of external migration and the other is internal migration.

The Turkish planning strategy puts the growth of the nonagricultural sectors (especially industry) in the foreground, and the growth of employment is supposed to depend on it. As this has not occurred, several other factors are drawn upon to explain this unexpected development.

1- According to the IBRD 1980 report "the import substitution development strategy that was followed channelled a relatively large part of investment to sectors and sub-sectors with high incremental capital labor ratio. With the progress of import substitution into basic and intermediate goods industry in the 1970's, this trend became more pronounced." (IBRD 1980, 6.20). The experts then reproduce a table showing the allocation of investment within subsectors of manufacturing industry and employment creation. The findings seem exactly parallel to experts' expectations.

2- Another point over - emphasized in the IBRD 1980 report is the reorientation of development policies towards exports. According to experts if this is done, industries having relatively low capital - labor ratios would be developed, therefore more employment would be created.

3- Most research on development are conducted on a sectoral basis, and a sector's absorption of employment is sought. In other words, the employment absorption of various sectors is sought.

4- Although there is research emphasizing the labor absorption in agriculture, most experts are of the opinion that nothing much can be expected from agriculture.

There are several calculations showing that labor prices increased faster than machinery prices, therefore inducing capital replacement for labor.

§ 3- ECONOMISTS' ARGUMENTS ABOUT FACTORS DETERMINING EMPLOYMENT. A CRITICAL SUMMARY

Economists writing on Turkey, especially before 1980, draw upon some of the factors mentioned in the economic literature to explain employment (or unemployment), and try to support their theoretical arguments with factual informaton. Some of them are pertinent, but it is not possible to agree with a great proportion of them. (Miller 1971, Demirgil 1971, Öngüt 1971, Burk 1971, Celasun 1971, Hamurdan 1971, Işıklı 1998, Ekin 2000, SPO 2001, Sayan 2001.)

1- There is a consensus that in Turkey there is a correlation between the growth rate and employment. One of the official recent document is a typical example (SPO 2001). It is supposed that in coming years annual GNP growth would be around 6.8 percent and this would create a yearly 1.5 percent increase in employment. As a result, 22.8 million employed people would be 47.3 million by 2023. As population would be 86 million, the employment/population ratio in 2023 would be 54 percent. If this is compared with the present 32 percent employment/population ratio, this could be considered as a solution for employment problem. The estimates of SPO show that participation rate of the labor force could increase from the present 49 percent to 72 percent by 2023. This would be a 2.8 percent unemployment rate. (Sayan 2001, p.241).

(Note: It seems that there is a flaw in these calculations. 1.5 percent annual increase should be 32.1 million rather than 47.3)

2 - The cost of capital in Turkey has been kept low in the pre-export orientation (1980) era. The intervention to interest rates was in the form of keeping it low. Moreover, the selective credit and interest policy has fixed interest rates for some kind of loans extremely low. In addition to that, the overvaluation of currency has made the cost of imported capital goods much lower than they should be. The impact of inflation on real interest rates exerted the same influence. Again, the low cost of capital induced capital intensive techniques.

3 - The inequal income distribution in Turkey is also adduced to have caused capital intensive production techniques. It is advanced that the wealthy section of the population is in the habit of purchasing commodities which are produced by capital intensive techniques. This fact creates unemployment.

4 - One of the factors determining urban unemployment was the rapid growth of population (2.5 percent), and the migration of rural population to urban areas. Nothing much can be said about population increase; it should be absorbed somehow if an unemployment situation is not created. The emigration of rural people is the main factor determining urban unemployment. It is supposed that the possibilities of the agricultural sector to absorb ever increasing population is very limited. On the other hand, high wage differences between agricultural and nonagricultural workers and difficulties of finding employment in agriculture would attract the whole increase in population to nonagricultural sectors.

5 - One of the reasons of unemployment is supposed to be the shrinkage of the public sector after the 1990's where many enterprises used more than necessary workforce.

6 - The most important factor in the analysis of employment is probably employment absorption possibilities of various nonagricultural sectors.

Conventionally, employment absorption of every sector (subsectors also) is found by input-output tables. Employment projections are made by using this method in Turkey. But as was shown above several times, past relations in Turkey should not be relied upon much if future tendencies are sought. A comparison of international observations with the Turkish case shows that the employment absorption has been less than expected.

Economists have supposed that there is a relationship between national income increase and labor absorption, i.e., when national income increases faster, it absorbs more labor. The conclusion on this subject in a research made by an economist is shown in Table XIV-4. He calculates national income increases which are necessary to absorb a certain amount of population growth. The effect of the level of per capita income is also considered. The population increase was around 2.5 percent, and the fourth column is relevant here. Income level in this period was between $200 and $1000; therefore the third, fourth and fifth rows of the column four show income increases necessary to absorb the population increase in Turkey. The average figure is 6.5 percent. National income increase in Turkey was around this figure, and according to his estimate, the population increase in Turkey should have been absorbed. In fact, it has not been nearly absorbed. Some one million workers have found employment in Western Europe and yet the unemployment rate has increased.

TABLE XIV - 4
REQUIRED GROWTH RATES FOR LABOR-ABSORPTION AT DIFFERENT GROWTH RATES OF POPULATION(*)

(1)	(2)	(3)	(4)	(5)	(6)
50	3.5	7.1	8.8	10.6	12.4
100	3.1	6.3	7.9	9.5	11.1
200	2.8	5.7	7.2	8.6	10.1
500	2.6	5.2	6.5	7.8	9.1
1000	2.4	4.8	6.1	7.3	8.5
1400	2.3	4.7	5.9	7.1	8.3
2000	2.3	4.6	5.7	6.9	8.1
2400	2.2	4.5	5.7	6.8	7.9
3000	2.2	4.4	5.6	6.7	7.8

(*) Col. 1 Per capita income ($)
Col. 2 Required growth rate of GDP at 1 % rate of growth of population
Col. 3 Required growth rate of GDP at 2 % rate of growth population
Col. 4 Required growth rate of GDP at 2,5 % rate of growth of population
Col. 5 Required growth rate of GDP at 3 % rate of growth population
Col. 6 Required growth rate of GDP at 3,5 % rate of growth population
Singh (1975) P. 111

It seems quite clear that this conclusion and analysis do not apply in Turkey. The explanation is not difficult. It is perhaps wrong to think that national income had increased by 6.5 percent in this period; it might have been much less than this, somewhere between 4-5 percent.

7 - A closely connected fact is the role of agriculture in development in Turkey. In fact, in plan startegies employment possibilities are sought outside agriculture. Citations from the second and third plans give an idea on this subject. "Development in the agricultural sector depends on a better use of existing resources rather than an extension of arable land. Therefore, the possibility of agriculture to create employment is limited... Efforts to be made in the short run to increase employment will not be concentrated in areas preventing the development of an advanced and capital intensive technology which is required by the prospective planning period."

8- Employment in agriculture is decreasing, or at least as the work force is increasing steadily, it does not increase. The increase in employment occurs in service sectors rather than in industry. This means that labor is employed in low wage and low productivity sectors.

9- The productivity of non-wage family workers is very low; as a result, a great proportion of people employed in agriculture should be considered as unemployed.

10- The official employment and unemployment figures are based on subjectively determined workforce figures. The decrease of the ratio of the workforce to population is found to be very fast. If it is supposed that the decrease in workforce was not so fast, the unemployment figures would be much higher (see, Kepenek 2001).

11- The employment in the public sector is not genuine employment. That constitutes a burden on the economy.

12- The slowdown in the population increase and the increase of people coming to working age should increase the ratio of workforce to population. This is an advantage for the economy; but it also gives rise to an increase of the necessity of finding employment for people coming to the labor market every year (see, Sayan 2001).

13- Hansen claims that (1991, p. 539) "if market forces do not directly affect wages in public and private sectors in Turkey, wage developments do have an impact on the market and may help explain unemployment". In Turkey fluctuations around the trend are strong, reflecting changes in the political situation much more than changes in the labor market.

14 - Another assertion by Hansen is as follows. "In Turkey therefore during both the 1960's and 1970's the changes in competitiveness were more or less neutralized by changes in import controls"(Hansen 1991 p. 540) and the same was true for the impact of union militancy in those years. All this meant that to find a correlation between wages and employment could not be possible.

All these factors seem to be contributing to employment in Turkey. But there are additional factors not elaborated in the existing international literature. Yet, they seem to have noticeable impact on employment in Turkey. Before taking them up, let me underline a notable flaw in 2001 SPO analysis on employment. A 6.8 percent yearly growth performance for the Turkish economy for 2000-2023 period is unimaginable. What is more important is the impossibility of creating 1.5 percent employment increase. In the recent past, the growth of employment was 1.2 percent. According to my findings, the growth rate of national income in 1950-2006 was 4 percent. If past figures are taken as a reference, 4 percent growth should create 1.2 percent increase in employment. If so, the estimates of SPO are not reliable. As will be explained below, there is a relationship between employment and growth, which is just the contrary to expectations.

§ 4 - THE UNCONVENTIONAL ANALYSIS OF EMPLOYMENT

It is shown above that the conventional analyses of employment are carried out on the assumption that the driving force in the creation of employment is the growth of national income: the faster the growth rate, the faster the employment growth. Again, it was shown that according to the world experience, the 2.5 percent growth of population should be absorbed by 6.4 percent growth of the national income in the 1950-1980 period. It is again shown that it is not absorbed.

It is apparent that the proportion of employment to population decreased until 1985 but this has stopped after that (see the Statistical Tables). All that meant that 6.4 percent growth of national income could not absorb the increasing population. If what is written above is remembered, it would be easy to explain that situation: the growth of national income was less than 6.4 percent; because it was overswollen.

When we look at the figures after 1985 (1985-2007) we see that although the growth of national income was much less than 6.4, i.e, 3.8 percent, the difference between the growth of income and employment becomes smaller. Why? The explanation lies in what is asserted in this book again. The overswelling in the national income is taken out by lower labor prices after 1980.

A very important dimension of the analysis of employment in Turkey is the relationship among the growth rate, average wages and employment. Although this has not attracted the attention of anybody, it is, in my opinion, the most crucial factor.

The population of Turkey was 42 million at the beginning of 1970. The yearly population increase was around 1,000,000 people. Suppose that some 60 percent of this figure sought employment at the beginning of the 1990 s. The withdrawal of people from the work force due to aging can be calculated as follows. The calculations involves 60-65-year-old people. When they were born the yearly population increase was 300,000 people and the labor participation rate was 50 percent. This implies that each year 150,000 people would have to leave the work force. Thus in the 90 s, every year 450,000 new job opportunities would have to be created in order to absorb the increasing population. As there are no new job opportunities in agriculture all these people should be employed in nonagricultural sectors. In 2007 that figure went up to 650,000 - 700,000 as a result of the ever decreasing working people in agriculture.

Now let us calculate. Suppose that incomes in the agricultural sector will have to increase by 3 percent. The share of agricultural income was some 10 percent of

GDP. If this is multiplied by 3 percent, this indicates the contribution of agriculture to the total income increase. It is some 0.40 point. Let us accept the reasoning put forth in this book that the future income growth of Turkey would be around 4.5 percent per year. If we consider the growth rate in the agricultural sector, this implies that the nonagricultural sector will grow 4.6 percent per year. As 14 million people were employed in the nonagricultural sectors (1990) this implies that employment in those sectors should grow by 4.1 percent. If the income in the nonagricultural sectors increases by 4.6 percent and employment there grows by 4.1 percent, the per capita income of the working population in those sectors would stay about the same. If this is so, the relationship between employment and the level of wages cannot be negated. If the size distribution improves and also if the share of the capital income becomes less, there is room for an increase of wages in nonagricultural sectors. But that possibility seems to be remote. (I would like to note that there is a circular reasoning here. The reason why the yearly growth rate was calculated as 4-4.50 percent was the relatively diminishing wages.)

What is advanced here is validated by the recent experience in Turkey. In 1980 - 2007, as a result of a huge decrease in real wages the yearly absorption of employment in nonagriculturae sector has reached 3.9 percent in that sector. That means that there is a close relationship between wages and employment. Moreover, if the absorption continues at that figure, there is no room for the increase of wages. But this is not all.

Should we conclude that there is a relationship between wage rates and the growth rate of the economy? Actually the problem is much more complicated.

It can be said that the reason why the growth rate was 6.4 percent in 1950 - 1977 was related to higher wages, rather than vice versa. When wages are high and when national income is sustainable at that level, which was the case in Turkey, what I advance was plausible. Yet this growth rate cannot absorb the increasing population. In other words, if the rate of growth is related to wages, a high growth rate may not absorb the population increase.

Was this an example of the traditional belief that when productivity gets higher, a lower absorption of labor would materialize? Again, TFP was estimated lower in post- 1980 years but the absorption was a bit higher. It is asserted that in the pre-1980 years the high level of TFP was related to high wages; and as a result, a relationship could not be established between wages and the level of employment. Yet, in post- 1980 years as there was not that relationship between TFP and wages, we should expect a relationship between wages and employment.

To repeat, I have 3 unconventional ideas about employment.They are: 1-The level of income is related to prices of labor. If labor prices are high,the level of income would be high as well.As a result,to establish a relationship between wages and employment may be misleading.2-It is not wrong that when wages are lower employment would get higher;this is possible when rents explained in this book do not exist.3- The relationship between the labor force and total population is more complicated than what is thought.

When we look at the figures after 1985 we see that although the growth of national income was much less than 6.4, i.e, 3.8 percent, the growth of population has been absorbed. Why? The overswelling in the national income is taken out after 1980.

I try to contend that when labor prices are lower, employment increases; yet national increase becomes lower, or vice verse. Lower wages should induce income growth. All this should give an impression of the shift of employment from more productive sectors to less productive ones.

The yearly rate of increase in employment has been 1.2 percent (1955-1997). The rate of increase of agricultural employment has been almost zero percent, even negative. But the nonagricultural population increased 3.96 percent in that period. The increase (in the nonagricultural sectors) in the 1955-1985 and the 1985-2007 periods have been 3.2 and 5 percent, respectively.

TABLE 1

POPULATION - TOTAL, URBAN AND RURAL
(as of October of each year)

	Millions		Urban/ Total
Year	**Total**	**Urban**	**Population**
1927	13.6	3.30	24.2
1935	16.2	3.80	23.5
1940	17.8	4.35	24.4
1945	18.8	4.68	24.9
1950	20.9	5.24	25.0
1955	24.1	6.92	28.8
1960	27.8	8.86	31.9
1965	31.4	10.81	34.4
1970	35.7	13.69	38.5
1975	40.2	16.87	41.8
1980	44.7	19.64	43.9
1985	50.7	26.44	53.0
1990	56.5	33.44	59.2
2000	**66.2**	**38.9**	**58.7**
2002	**68.4**	**41.0**	**60.0**
2006	**72.6**	**45.4**	**62.5**

N.B. 2007 population shows that 2006 figure is wrong; it is found that population in 2007 was 71,5 million.
Source: Censuses of Population.

TABLE 2

AVERAGE ANNUAL RATES OF POPULATION INCREASE (%)

Year	Total	Urban	Rural
1927-1935	2.2	2.1	2.2
1935-1940	1.9	2.9	1.6
1940-1945	1.1	0.9	1.2
1945-1950	2.2	2.0	2.2
1950-1955	2.9	5.8	1.9
1955-1960	2.9	5.2	1.9
1960-1965	2.5	4.0	1.7
1965-1970	2.52	4.8	1.5
1970-1975	2.50	4.2	1.3
1975-1980	2.06	3.0	1.3
1980-1985	2.49	6.1	-1.1
1985-1990	2.17	4.8	-0.6
1990-1995	1.85	3.8	-0.1
1995-2002	1.62	1.7	0.0
2002-2006	**1.50**	**2.5**	**0.0**

Source: Censuses of Population.

TABLE 3

POPULATION AND EMPLOYMENT IN TURKEY (MILLION)
(OLD SERIES)

	1955	1977	1985	1997	2000	2004	2005
TOTAL POPULATION	24.9	42.0	50.7	62.8	67.8	70.7	71.6
LABOR FORCE	-	16.2	18.3	22.4	21.5	24.1	24.6
EMPLOYMENT	11.8	14.7	15.9	20.0	21.6	21.7	22.0
AGRICULTURE	9.5	9.1	9.4	11.3	9.7	10.0	9.2
NONAGRICULTURE	2.5	5.6	6.5	9.7	11.8	11.7	12.8
UNEMPLOYMENT (PERCENT)	-	9.2	8.7	6.4	6.5	10.3	10.3
EMPLOYMENT / POPULATION	0.50	0.35	0.31	0.33	0.31	0.32	0.31

TABLE 4

EMPLOYMENT FIGURES AFTER THE NEW POPULATION CENSUS

	December 2006	December 2007
Civil population	**68.490**	**69.246**
Population over 15 age	**48.812**	**49.575**
Labor force	**23.203**	**22.875**
-Employed	**20.758**	**20.443**
-Nonempeoyed	**2.445**	**2.432**
Proportion of labor force (%)	**47.75**	**46.2**
Employment ratio (%)	**42.5**	**41.2**
Unemployment ratio (%)	**10.5**	**10.6**

Source: Milliyet, March 18, 2008; and April 16, 2009, Sabah

CHAPTER XV

THE ANALYSIS OF INCOME DISTRIBUTION IN TURKEY LEADING TO UNCONVENTIONAL COMMENTS

§ 1 - A SURVEY OF FIGURES

Table XV-1 shows the findings of several research work on income distribution in Turkey. Although they are not fully reliable, the main tendency is quite visible: although there is not a noticeable improvement in income distribution throughout the whole period under study, it is very unequal. In fact, while Gini coefficient was 0.49 in 1994, it went down to 0.44 in 2003. This suggests that there is a slight improvement.

TABLE XV - 1
INCOME DISTRIBUTION IN TURKEY

Proportion of Families		SPO 1963	Bulutay 1988	SPO 1973	Celasun 1983	TUSİAD 1986	SPO 1988	Kongar 1988	SIS 1994	SIS 2003
The first	20%	4.5	3.0	3.5	2.6	3.9	4.0	3.1	4.9	6.0
	20%	8.5	7.0	8.0	6.9	8.4	7.0	9.0	8.6	10.3
	20%	11.5	10.0	12.5	12.6	12.6	13.0	12.2	12.6	14.5
	20%	18.5	20.0	19.5	21.4	19.2	21.0	16.6	19.0	20.9
The last	20%	57.0	60.0	58.5	55.9	55.9	55.0	59.1	54.9	48.3

More detailed information on size and functional distribution of income is found in my book entitled A Survey of the Turkish Economy, 1920-2004. Although there are some studies on functional income distribution, their reliability is very low. They may give an idea about it. The decrease of wage income in recent years is quite noticeable. Whether it is hundred percent true or not is quite suspicious. Yet there is no doubt that there has been a decrease in wage income in recent years. (Table XV-2)

TABLE XV - 2
(1) Real Wages in Turkey
(1965 = 100)

	Real Wages
1962	92.7
1965	100.0
1970	151.3
1977	212.9
1980	127.5
1984	100.6
(2)	
1988	100.0
1989 (*)	119.8
1990 (*)	126.6
1991 (*)	159.8
1992	135.9
(3) The Change of Real Wages in Manufacturing Industry %	
1992	4.4
1993	3.9
1994	- 19.2 (**)
1995	- 14.4 (**)
1996	- 0.8
1997	0.8

(*) Money was overvalued
(**) Depression years
(***) Source:Central Bank Annual Report 1997,p.30

(4)The change of real wages in manufacturing industry	
2000	-2.4
2001	-8.3
2002	- 1.0
2003	- 1.9
2004	2.5

Source: *The same as above 2002 ,p.31 and 2005, p.29*

§ 2 - THE CONVENTIONAL ANALYSES OF INCOME DISTRIBUTION

The aim of this chapter is to present a short summary of the conventional and unconventional analyses of income distribution in Turkey, and to show that, firstly, all analyses are straightforward applications of the well known traditional literature, and secondly, although several aspects of the distribution in this country are captured by them, many distributional issues are unanswered. Moreover, some of the conclusions reached by those analyses are not justified, and we need, in addition to conventional ones, a different approach, an unconventional one in order to reach more satifactory conclusions.

The causes of the inequalty are investigated by many economists, Turkish and foreign. Below, a systematic summary of a very good sample of books and articles written in this subject is presented. (Özbudun - Ulusoy 1980, Mardin 1980, Derviş-Robinson 1980, Özbudun 1980, Ergüder 1980, Berk 1980, Danielsen - Keleş 1980, Kuran 1980, Mumcuoğlu 1980, Aksoy 1980, Önder 1980, Aral 1980, Beyarslan 1982, Celasun 1986, Özmucur 1987, Törümer 1989, Oktan 1990, Boratav 1990 a and b, Ekinci 1990, Hansen 1991, Turel 1990, Oyan 1980, Ekin 1990, Kazgan - Önder - Kirmanoğlu 1991, Tuncer 1992, Özmucur 1992, Kepenek - Yentürk 2001.)

My first reaction after the scrutinization of the literature was that comments were a sort of repetition of writings in any textbook on income distribution with a minor change in the form that the name of Turkey and Turkish data were inserted to it.

All those surveys can be studied under 5 headings: A-Political factors determining income distribution. B-Factors giving rise to inequality in the size distribution of income within the two main sectors of the economy: agricultural and nonagricultural sectors. C- As average earnings in nonagricultural sectors of the economy are about 4-5 times higher than those in the agricultural sector in the highly dual Turkish economy, a lumping together of income distribution data for the whole economy should give a biased picture for the overall income distribution in this country; as a result, the impact of this fact on income distribution needs to be understood. D - Ideological aspects of income distribution. E - A glimpse of writings about functional income distribution in this country.

My criticism of the existing work and suggestions of an unconventional analysis are found in Section 3 of this paper.

The political and ideological dimensions of income distribution are mixed with economic ones; as a result, a neutral analysis of income distribution in a developing country such as Turkey is more difficult compared to those in a developed country. Moreover, as a great proportion of the Turkish scholars in economics are on left wing, many analyses by them are highly biased in the direction of blaming bad distribution as an expected end-result of the operation of the price mechanism.

It must be stressed again and again that a detailed survey of all analyses on income distribution is not reported in this book, which is an abstract. Although a fairly good idea about income distribution in Turkey is given, the main aim of this chapter, as the others, is to underline the main characteristics of the traditional analysis, but more important than that, its inadequacy. In addition, it has been attempted to remedy this explored deficiency, and the essentials of the unconventional analysis are presented.

THE CONVENTIONAL ANALYSES OF INCOME DISTRIBUTION

A - The Political Aspects of Income Distribution

The political and ideological aspects of income distribution are very extensive in developing countries. Turkey is no exception. Although income distribution is mainly an economic problem, a neutral look into it is very difficult. This has been very much so in a developing country like Turkey. Almost all practical interferences to it as well as writings about it are mixed with political and ideological considerations.

In Turkey, regional disparities are very sharp, uncertainty and insecurity of people are very high. A desire to integrate the territory and to assure the safety of the Republic have always been one of the driving forces of the administrators of the country. It was the same in the one party rule of the Republic (1923-1950) as well as the multi-party one (from 1950 to now). To achieve that goal an interference of distribution has always been required. Otherwise, social unrest as a result of distribution has always been a danger. What could have been done? Let us list them: the distribution of infrastructural investments, the distribution of government services, support prices and subsidies for agriculture (the poorest but the most populated sector of the economy), the encouragement of social security for town workers, unionization, the offering of several government services such as education and health with no cost, etc. All those measures must have affected income distribution. Yet, it seems to be very unequal.

B - The Conventional Analyses of Income Distribution within Agricultural and Nonagricultural Sectors

Turkey has a highly dual economy. Its two main sectors are separated by sharp lines. As a result, distribution in each sector must be investigated separately.

According to surveys, income distribution in agriculture seems to be worse compared to that in nonagricultural sectors. However disputable, Gini coefficient in agriculture was around 0.56, whereas that in the nonagricultural sectors it was 0.50.

DISTRIBUTION IN AGRICULTURE

Factors determining income distribution (size) in agriculture are listed below.

1- Distribution of land is unequal in agriculture. For example, according to a survey some 79 percent of all families receives 27 percent of the total agricultural income.

2- Productivity of land is very different in the various regions of the country. As the mobility of people among several regions is limited, earnings in different regions are quite different.

3-The educational, cultural and technical level of the population living in different regions is quite different. As a result, the skills of those people are varied. All those factors must have given rise to productivity differences. In turn, this gives rise to earning differences.

4- The distribution of all sorts of subsidies (in the form of support prices, input subsidization, teaching for technology, allocation of credits, distribution of the government owned irrigation, etc.) favors rich and big land owning peasants. This is documented in several studies. This gives rise to inequalitiy.

5- The distribution of infrastructure such as roads, schools, communication, and legal services among several regions of the country is very unequal.

6- A good proportion of agricultural production is consumed by city dwellers. In order to subsidize them the prices of many products are repressed. Although before 1980 exchange rates were kept rather low, the earnings of export goods such as tobacco, hazelnuts and cotton producers were still higher than those producers producing domestically consumed products.

DISTRIBUTION IN NONAGRICULTURAL SECTORS

Factors affecting distribution in nonagricultural sectors are listed below.

1 - The allocation of several public resources is in favor of the richer section of town dwellers.

2 - The immigration rate of the rural people to towns and cities is quite high. Its impact on distribution seems to be important. This increases the proportion of newly emigrated people to the established workers working in organized labor markets. Whereas a great proportion of new migrants find employment in unorganized markets receiving lower wages. This worsens income distribution.

3 - The impact of unions on inequality of earnings seems to be noticeable. There is a sort of compartimentalization in labor markets. According to some studies, the

average income of unionized workers is some 30-40 percent higher than those nonunionized workers.

4 - According to some surveys, the oligopolistic practices in several sectors of the economy give rise to an increase of profits to the detriment of wages.

5 - Due to the law of supply, positions requiring high level competence, efficiency and education yield abnormally high incomes. As the quantity of these kind of people is limited, this creates a bias against equal distribution.

6 - There are rents given rise by import substitution in the country; as a result of those earnings and the possibility of detracting them by certain working groups, a bias against an equal distribution comes into existence.

7- The very high amount of interest incomes especially after 1980 seems to have worsened income distribution.

8 - In Turkey high rates of inflation are a fact of life. This worsens income distribution.

9 - The switching efforts to liberalization of the economy seem to have exerted a deteriorating influence on income distribution. This becomes quite apparent if wage statistics are examined.

10 - There is a fear that privatization efforts will exert an unfavorable influence on wages. Therefore there is a struggle against it.

11 - The fast population increase should make dependency ratio higher; in turn, this is a deteriorating factor of income distribution.

12 - The ever faster increase in the informal sector is a factor which makes income distribution more unequal. It is known that wages are lower in informal sector.

13 - In 1961 the new constitutional law granted all sorts of privileges to unions. As a result, this created inequality in the distribution of labor income.

14 - The ever decreasing share of employment in population gives rise to a bad income distribution.

15 - The increase of more labor intensive commodities in exports could be assured by pushing down labor prices; as a result income distribution did not improve.

16 - The increase of the people who have a high school education created an inequality in distribution.

17 - The impact of high real wages on inflation seems to have created a bad distribution.

C- INTERSECTORAL INCOME DIFFERENCES AND INCOME DISTRIBUTION

The importance of the intersectoral income differences in explaining the income distiribution in Turkey was pointed out and underlined by Derviş-Robinson (1980).

The overall distribution in an economy is a linear weighted sum of the individual group distribution.

$$f\,(y|q)_{i=1} = \sum_{i=1}^{n} W_i \quad f_i \ (y|q)_i$$

Where y refers to income variable, q is vector of parameters characterizing the distribution function, and f reflects a particular functional form characterizing the distribution within group i. The weights w represent population shares and the vector q is a set of all within group parameters q_i. If we do note the mean income of in each group by m_i. the economy wide average income by m and the within group variance by s^2, then overall variance of incomes in a society is given by the formula:

$$s^2 = \sum\nolimits^{n}_{i=1} \ W.s^2_i \ + \sum\nolimits_{i=1} W_i \ (m_i - m)^2_{i=i}$$

Intuitively it is clear that overall inequality in a society is a function of the inequality within specified socioeconomic groups, inequality between these same groups, and finally the numerical weights these groups carry in a society. This is reflected in the formula above, which is essentially a statistical decomposition of the variance. Suppose for an instant that all groups are perfectly homogenous with no within-group variance in income. We thus have:

$$s^2 = \sum\nolimits^{n}_{i=1} \ W_i(m_i - m)^2$$

In this case, overall inequality would increase whenever one group's income moves further away form the economy-wide average and /or whenever the weight of a group characterized by greater distance form the mean increases with respect to the weight of a group closer to the group-wide average.

If, on the other hand, we assume that all groups are characterized by an identical mean income but within group variance is positive, we have

$$s^2 = \sum\nolimits^{n}_{i=1} W_{i.}s_i^2$$

Now overall inequality increases whenever inequality within one group increases and/or whenever the weight of a group characterized by relatively high variance increases relative to the weight of a group displaying lower variance.

In the general case of a different mean income and positive within group variances it is still true that, all other things held constant, an increase in inequality within any one group as well as an increase in the distance between any one group's mean income and the economy wide average will increase the overall inequality, (Derviş - Robinson 1980, p.85)

After a general description of the impact of intergroup earning differences on the distribution of income, the authors dwelling on this fact give figures about the general earning differences in countries having different per capita income and compare them with the Turkish figures.

TABLE XV - 3

THE KUZNETS OR INTERSECTORAL PRODUCTIVITY RATIOS IN 24 COUNTRIES: (I + S)/ A (X)

	1950	1960
Group I ($ 62)	2.14	3.48
Group II ($ 173)	3.03	2.62
Group III ($ 252)	1.95	2.25
Group IV ($ 487)	2.30	1.60
Group V ($ 725)	2.12	1.44
Group VI ($ 1284)	1.79	1.37

Source, Derviş-Robinson (1980) p 87 ; (x) I, industry, S services, A agriculture.

After the examination they conclude that such an extreme difference in labor productivity must have a major impact on overall inequality in Turkey.

The authors try to decompose the impact of the interindustrial causes. They use the following formula;

TABLE XV - 4

LABOR PRODUCTIVITY IN AGRICULTURE AND INDUSTRY AND KUZNETS RATIOS IN TURKEY (1950-1973)

	Value Added Per Worker in Agriculture (TL)	Value Added Per Worker in Industry (TL)	K Ratio
1950	603	2,154	3.57
1963	2347	10,224	4.36
1968	3174	16,154	5.09
1973	8292	35,360	4.26

Source, Derviş - Robinson, 1980, P.89

$s_T = W_{A.}s_A{}^2 + W_{i.}m_I{}^2 + W\ (s_A - s_T)^2 + W_I\ (m_I - m_T)^2$

Where the w_i, m_i and s stand for the shares in the economically active population, the log-mean incomes, and the log-variances of incomes, respectively. The suscripts A, I and T denotes agriculture, industry and the whole economy (Turkey). Writing the share of overall variance due to intersectoral mean income differences as S^X, we have

$$S^X = \frac{W_{A.}\ (m_A - m_T)^2 + W_{I_{ST2}}\ (m_I - m_T)^2}{S_T{}^2}$$

They use the Turkish estimates for the percent of overall log variances due to intersectoral productivity difference and come up with Table XV-5. (Assuming 25 percent higher variances should give us lower bound estimates.)

TABLE XV - 5

PERCENT OF OVERALL LOG VARIANCE DUE TO INTERSECTORAL PRODUCTIVITY DIFFERANTIALS AND LOWER - BOUND ESTIMATES, 1950-1973

	Lower %	**Upper %**
1950	41.8	47.6
1963	62.6	72.3
1968	80.8	94.3
1973	69.2	80.3

Source, Derviş - Robinson 1980

The values obtained for S^X are quite high, and it is clear that the dual structure of the Turkish Economy is a major source of overall inequality (Derviş - Robinson, 1980, p.90)

The impact of earning differences between agricultural and nonagricultural sectors on income distribution as presented by D-R is summarized above. Why were there such a big difference in earnings or Kuznet's K? The explanation of that difference by Hansen is typical (Hansen 1991, p. 469) "because of labor productivity is typically much lower in agriculture than other activities K is usually found above 2."

My explanation of high K in Turkey is much deep-rooted. The traditional explanation is not wrong. Yet the untypically high K should be explained by additional factors in Turkey. These are the labor prices in nonagricultural sectors. It is shown that as a good proportion of exports in those years were of agricultural origin, there was not a pressure on nonagricultural prices to be in line with the relative productivity to nonagricultural commodities, compared to agricultural sectors. It is shown above that rents of a special nature earned in nonagricultural sectors were making nonagricultural prices high. The behavior of wages (see Table XV - 2) could support my assertion. It is quite evident that, in line with rents I have been alluding, they were increasing during pre- 1980 period; after that date we observe a very high decline. What is more interesting and important is the fall in Kuznet's K after the economy turned to outside. According to my theoretical reasoning this was expected, and this has occurred. In 1975 Kuznet's K was 4.42; whereas it went down to 3.28 by 2000.

E - IDEOLOGICAL ASPECTS OF INCOME DISTRIBUTION

As a great proportion of academics in Turkey are left-wing economists, most of the books and/or chapters on income distribution in those books are biased. They all emphasize the low and constantly lowering share of wages in national income in Turkey. On the other hand, the increasing share of capital disturbs them.

Turkish Marxists are still occupied with the squeezing of workers and the distribution of the surplus.

According to those people this distorted distribution gives rise to both economic and social problems. They all impede economic development.

They try to show that although the share of high incomes increases continuously, investments are not increasing, and capacity to produce does not expand. (I feel that this is, to say the least, is an a priori assertion.) In addition, taxing high incomes is not possible, and as a result, this creates a loss of income for the public. In turn, the government binds itself to the necessity of borrowing at high interests which create inflationary pressure. Again, high expenditure by high earning people increases inflationary pressures. Here is one statement by a Turkish Marxist: "Ever increasing strength of high earning capitalists impedes unionization and the use of democratic rights, and endangers democracy in the country. As a result of the deterioration of income distribution after the liberalization efforts, (after 1980) the new urban culture burgeoning within the working classes in the 1970s disappeared and a particular brand of bourgeois ideology in its consumerist as opposed to entrepreneurial form has been strikingly widespread within the ranks of the educated professional groups aspiring to western style and the consumption norms and thereby repudiating vehemently any economic model and political alternative in which protectionism and etatism are likely to play significant role "(Boratav 1989, p. 225).

§ 3 -UNCONVENTIONAL DIMENSIONS IN THE EXPLANATION OF INCOME DISTRIBUTION IN TURKEY

Almost every factor determining income distribution examined in the international literature, and also in the writings on Turkey, which are a replica of what there is in international literature, are mentioned above. But as will be seen below they are not enough to explain the Turkish case. Several different dimensions of income distribution must be taken into consideration before we understand it thoroughly. Moreover, conclusions based on the traditional approach might be unjustified. Some unconventional ideas are mentioned below.

1- Income distribution in Turkey and in countries like it is heavily related to the pattern of growth and development in this country. Actually, the relationship between growth and distribution is known in the literature, i.e., for example the theory of distribution put forward by Cambridge economists. But what I mean is different.

As was explained in this book, a good percentage of growth was given rise by rents in a special sense before 1980. In UATE, rents due to the overblowing of the nonagricultural sectors were on the foreground. The sharing of these rents (which was the pet subject of Marxist economists) would give rise to an inequal income distribution. In my posterior writings to UATE, I tried to show that the bias against labor was also related to the growth pattern of the economy. (The low proportion of TFP.) The relationship between rents and wages is made clear at the beginning of the book. This being the case, we shouldn't say much without understanding the growth pattern of the economy. Again, various factors such as political and ideological within the sectors and intersectoral factors are all intermixed, and it is difficult to separate each from the other.

2- A theory of wage determination is the most important dimension of the theory of income distribution. Wages are explained by the theory of marginal productivity. But as demonstrated above, marginal productivity being the same, if the country has enough natural resources and/or if it has factors of production with exceptional skill and/or if exports based on this is high enough to satisfy import needs, wages can be high. This is known in the literature. They are all factors of micro and macro character. When their impacts are investigated, micro and macro factors are separately studied. I am of the opinion that they should be mixed together. If this is done, the whole theory would be overshadowed by rents in the country.

3- The importance of the interindustry earnings differences in explaining income distribution in Turkey is underlined and carefully analyzed by Derviş-Robinson. This is first noticed by the author in the UATE (1978) (See, p. 283 and 285).

I say the same but I go several steps ahead of them. When they decompose its impact in terms of quantity and prices, they take prices as they are, whereas the crux of the problem is the relative prices between the two sectors. The rest is simple mathematics: the decomposition doesn't mean much unless we understand the factors giving rise to interindustrial earning differences. Actualy, my diognosis proved right.

4- Many scholars try to understand the distribution by means of a struggle among classes. Especially extreme leftists make much ado about it. These Marxist thoughts are criticized in the literature. This approach may modify the theory based on the marginal productivity to a certain extent. But to explain the whole story by means of that theory is irrelevant. If, in the end of the struggle, shares deviate from what is justified by economic factors, it would give rise to all sorts of problems. Moreover, the economic foundation of distribution is not understood by those people.

5- The exchange rate is determined at a level, where the prices of exportable goods should be at the international level. The use of capital in the exporting sector is a determining factor. If more capital is used in the exporting sector, the efficiency of labor would be higher. Therefore a lower exchange rate may be enough to export. But in that case less capital remains for nonexporting or labor intensive goods producing sectors; as a result, labor prices would be lower. All this means that one of the factors determining distribution is the level of the exchange rate and the nature of goods to be exported. If exported goods are more capital intensive, the exchange rate would be lower but labor prices would be lower too. On the other hand, with higher exchange rates less capital intensive but more labor intensive goods are exported; in that case more capital would be available to make labor prices higher in nonexportable good sector. Yet if labor prices get higher in labor intensive sectors of the economy, would't exported goods be more expensive? All I want to show is that there is a tradeoff among labor prices, exchange rates and allocation of capital.

In conclusion it can be said that distribution of income is related to a certain extent on to the nature of exported goods. If they are more capital intensive, the exchange rate would be lower but the share of labor in the national income would be lower. But this could the compensated by the lower exchange rate. On the other hand, if more labor intensive goods are exported, the exchange rate would be higher but as more capital remains for nonexporting sectors, labor prices would be higher. Would that be compensated by higher prices due higher exchange rate? All this would depend on parameters and elasticities. But what is important is to see the above mentioned relationship. In the case of exporting natural resource and skill intensive goods the price of labor is always higher.

6- The analysis of the functional distribution is full of misconceptions. In most analyses agricultural sectors are not separated from nonagricultural ones. It is shown throughout the book that we must go deeper into the problem. Moreover, when it comes to the analysis of nonagricultural sectors, available statistics are used to show the decrease in the share of wages but nothing much is told about factors causing those variations among different jobs and the distribution of the product among the wages of the unskilled workers and rental income.

It is observed that although the share of labor in GNP decreased by almost 50 percent, the size distribution stayed the same. This two contradicting events should be explained.One explanation is a decrease of the segmentation in labor markets. Therefore, the relationship between the segmentation of labor markets and income distribution should be more thoroughly investigated.

7- A very important factor which is significant in explaining bad income distribution in Turkey is the slow productivity increase in the country. The level of productivity increase is an important factor which determines income distribution. It is natural that if there is a productivity increase, workers can easily increase their shares. Otherwise distribution would be based more on the conflict among the owners of production factors.

8- In pre– 1980 years the exports of the country consisted of natural resources intensive goods. In that case the conflict among the sharetakers in nonagriculture could be resulted in paying high wages to skilled workers and union members which were in a sort of monopoly position. This would deteriorate income distribution.

In post 1980 years the huge increase of exports of labor intensive goods should result in lower wages. This had to exert an influence in the direction of bad income distribution. Yet, the decrease in segmentation of labor markets would attenute it.

9- The discrepancy between the fast population increase in nonagricultural sectors and the possible income increase in them is another factor making bad income distribution in those sectors persistent. There is a sharp productivity difference in various subsectors of nonagricultural sectors. But the high productivity in some subsectors does not make low wages in low productivity sectors high., i.e., there is not a factor price equalization rule. In fact, this theorem is one of the main factors explaining very high wage differences. If fastly increasing people working in low productivity sectors such as services and construction received high wages, imports and exports of the country would not be consistent for a sustaining growth.

It should not be forgetten that high rents in the economy were a consequence of the pattern of growth of the country.

10- The improvement in income distribution (2002) should be related partly to the decrease of segmentation due to a better operation of price mechanism, whereas according to Turkish economists the main factor is the decrease of high earnings as a result of the last crisis. This is not wrong but not enough.

TABLE XV - 6
FUNCTIONAL INCOME DISTRIBUTION TURKEY
(SIS) (Proportions)

	2002	2003	2005
Wages and salaries	38.7	41.8	40.5
Entrepreneurial incomes	34.5	32.0	28.8
Property income	9.3	6.2	5.6
Transfers	17.5	20.0	23.0
Total	100.0	100.0	100.0

11- The probably a most important dimension of income distribution in Turkey is the proportional increase of capital and labor in nonagricultural sectors. The growth of capital is around 6 percent; whereas that of labor is 4-4.5 percent. That means that almost the whole increase is absorbed by increasing labor. Nothing much is left for the productivity (technical advance). As a result, there is very little room for the increase of labor income; in general. The improverment I expect in distribution is a tendency in the equalization of wages.

CHAPTER XVI

THE ANALYSIS OF INFLATION AND THE FINANCIAL SECTOR IN TURKEY LEADING TO UNCONVENTIONAL COMMENTS

§ 1 - INFLATION

Inflation has always been a most burdening problem in Turkey. Along with that it is studied by many economists. They are all guided by what there is in the literature. I agree with all of them. Yet I have some unconventional ideas.

In the 1923-1940 period there was no inflation in Turkey.In the war years as result of an excessive issue of currency necessitated by the mobilization of the army, prices increased some 400 percent in 1940-1944 period without much economic impact.Until 1954 prices were rather stable;in the ensuing 4 years prices increased 15 percent annually. In the 60 s the rate of increase was 5 percent.In the 70's the increase of prices speeded up, and by 1980 it was 100 percent. In the first half of 1980, there was relatively lower inflation, around 30-35 percent.But after the mid-1980 s a steady increase of the rate occurred. In the 90 s that continued and the average was around 70 percent.By 2000 it seems to come to an end. First a very short summary of what we have in the literature will be given.

1- An increase in the volume of money (here, M2 is usually meant) seems to be the immediate cause of inflation. In turn, its increase is closely related to the monetary base. There are dozens of econometric studies which support this view.

2- The effects of cost push factors such as inflationary expectations, the level of exchange and interest rates, wages and administered prices such as goods produced or imported by the public sector, all seem to be important. Although the results vary, most regressions and simulations reveal the importance of price expectations, exchange and interest rates as cost push factors.

3- Several economists have demonstrated that the impact of cost push factors is closely related to the existence and degree of a permissive monetary policy (generally motivated by political consideration) which permits the increase in the volume of currency necessitated by cost push factors.

4- Several economists have explored deeper and attempted to discover those factors determining the monetary base. The most common factor was the public deficit, which is influenced by public revenue and expenditure. The significance of the impact of the level of public debt and its interest payments has also been examined.

I agree with the majority of arguments put forward to explain inflation in Turkey. Yet, when the problem is studied unconventionally, it is possible to view the whole problem differently. Moreover, if the Turkish figures are manipulated rather simply instead of by sophisticated econometric methods, we reach different conclusions. Especially when the meaning of money is concerned.

1- Let us see the significant ingredients of money by using a very simple equation. It is P=M-0; here P is the rate of increase of prices, M is that of money, and 0 is that of national income. It is evident that this is nothing but the quantity theory of money. Then I plugged Turkish figures into it. If the price increase predicted by this equation is very much the same as the actual figures, it means that the quantity theory of money is relevant in Turkey. Now the problem is what to use as money volume figures. This may be money issued by the central bank, currency in circulation which I call (Mo) or central bank money + sight deposits, (Ml) or Ml+time deposits(M2) or M2 + deposits in foreign exchange (M3). The expected inflation based on each of those figures is compared with actual inflation figures: the better fit shows that kind of money which is a better factor in explaining inflation. When I did so, I observed that the best indicator for 1950-1975 was MO; M1 was not relevant at all; again M2 was not relevant in that period. But in the period ensuing 1975 MO becomes irrelevant. After 1998 Mo is again relevant.

2- The expectation of economists did not come true in the first period: why? But their method proved to be true in the second period. Why? Before answering that question let me underline the following relationship. When P=M-0 was true, the inclusion of this or that kind of money amounted to that: the velocity of circulation or income velocity of money (V) relating to the kind of money in the equation stayed constant in the period in question. Actually, when several V's are calculated, it is found that in the first period the V of central bank money stayed constant; whereas in the second period the V's of M2 or M3 stayed almost constant. In the first period central bank money only could be used in income payments whereas in the second period all sorts of money could be used in income payments. This was one of the reasons why in the second period M2 or M3 were relevant. Now the difficult problem: would everything depend on the stability of the velocity of money? Would it not be an accounting or accommodating identity, to a certain extent? May be half and half. There are other factors: A very important one is the free movement of various sorts of money among themselves. If they were freely movable among themselves, M2 or M3 could be a better money. But this is not the case in Turkey; therefore M2 or M3 is not one hundred percent reliable. Especially as the move of various kinds of money changes in the short run, to base inflation on one of the money definition would lead us to wrong conclusions.

It is evident that there is a secular increase of V_0: it is expected. It must be due to the emergence of several financial instruments which serve to economize the use of money.

In the pre-1975 years the main factor determining inflation was currency issued by the central bank of Turkey, i.e., money in narrow sense. This could be explained by the existence of the relatively small amount of deposits and the use of central bank money in income payments transactions. But after the emergence of other financial instruments and their gradual use in income payments resulted in a huge increase of income velocity of the central bank money. As velocity of other sorts of money was volatile, the control of inflation by adjusting money volume, which was very difficult anyway, has been difficult. Other factors determining prices such as the exchange rates and interest rates have been influential; moreover, in a country like Turkey to manipulate them was very difficult.

Permissive monetary policy has always been important in Turkey. But its success depends on the controlling ability by the policy makers. When a policy is used to control inflation it is usually a deflationary one but it creates problems for the economy, banking system as well as other businesses. I believe that a very important factor neglected in anti-inflationary policies is the impact of relative prices. It is known in the literature that the most important drawback of deflationary policies is the rigidity of some prices. I try to show that the success of anti-inflationary policies in Turkey depends on the changing relative prices of labor and nonlabor intensive good prices. As this aspect of the problem is not properly investigated, the struggle against inflation would be very difficult.

Here is a short summary.

1- There are various types of money: M0, M1, M2 and M3. In the theory the transferences among them is considered smooth. As a result, the importance of the velocity of circulation of money, which was on the foreground some 70-80 years ago, seems to be diminished. Again, the use of this or that kind money in income payments would make that concept meaningful. If income payments are made by any kind of money, this makes velocity of circulation of money less important. The impact of the changes in automatic increases of money is also related to the fact if there is a transference of various sorts of money among them or not.

2- The second problem is the analysis of the impact of cost push or accommodating-permissive factors. I think that there is another cost push factor which is the change of relative prices. If the monetary authorities are in a position of adjusting relative prices of nonlabor and labor intensive good prices, the impact of monetary factors on inflation would be strong.

My views are tested by the Turkish case and a perfect fit is found. As before 1975 there was little transference possibility among various kind of money and income payments were effected by central bank money (M0) only, it is found that it was the only influential factor on inflation. As after 1980 income payments could be effected by other sorts of money, the impact of M_0 on prices decreased. But as there was a limited transference among various sorts money this could not continue. The importance of the volume of M_0 would emerge again. As the rapid transformation in the financial system slackened in the 2000 s, a close relationship between M_0 and prices is being observed since 1998.

Yet, as the adjustments of relative prices became difficult after 1980, the important of cost push factors seems to have increased.

§ 2 - THE RELATIONSHIP BETWEEN MONETARY STOCK AND PRICE LEVEL

Theoretical arguments, as well as empirical work, suggest that there should be a close relationship between monetary stock and price level in developing countries. In a country where money seems to be the only significant financial asset, and where financial development is in its infancy, it is not difficult to defend such a view, (Friedman 1968, Yenal 1968, Fry 1972 and 1980). In fact, several empirical investigations are made showing the close relationship between the changes of the stock of money and price changes. Two of them will be summarized here, one by Fry (1980) and the other by IBRD (1980)

Fry's conclusion can be conveyed by citing a passage from his recent book

"A regression in (GNP) on in (M) using Turkish data over the period 1950-1977 is bound to produce a high correlation coefficient simply because there are strong upward trends in both variables. One way of eliminating spurious associations of this kind is to conduct the regression in first difference form with the variables expressed as logarithms. First differences give the percentage rates of change (compounded continuously rather than annually) in the variables:

$$\text{In (GNP)}_t = a + b \text{ In (M)}_t \qquad (1.13)$$

$$\text{In (GNP)}_{t-1} = a + b \text{ In (M)}_{t-1} \qquad (1.14)$$

Subtract (1.14) from (1.13):

$$\text{In (GNP)}_t - \text{In (GNP)}_{t-1} = b\ [\text{In } (M_t) - \text{In } (M_{t-1})] \qquad (1.15)$$

or D In (GNP) = b D In (M)

where D stands for the first difference in the variables' value. Note that the constant a disappears. For convenience, (1.16) can be written:

$$GNP = bM^* \qquad (1.16)$$

where "." stands for D In.

The regression estimate of (1.17) for the regression period 1950-1977 (the data observation period is therefore 1968 - 1977) is:

$$GNP = 0.929\ M \qquad (1.17)$$
$$(15.808)$$

$\bar{R}^2 = 0.457$, D.W. = 1.82

Where the figures in brackets are t values. Clearly, the two variables are significantly correlated with one another. The DW coefficient rejects the hypothesis that serial correlation or autocorrelation of the error terms exists." (Fry 1980, pp. 28-29).

After having added a constant term and more important, after having used better estimates of the average money stock for 1969-1976, he comes up with a better equation:

$$GNP = -0.068 + 1.304\ M$$
$$(-1.241)\ (4.929)$$

$R^2 = 0.700$ DW = 2.15

(Fry 1980, p. 29).

One of the dozens of econometric studies on this relationship is that of IBRD.

Now, let us quote IBRD report.

"A more simple analysis also indicates that monetary expansion has been associated with accelerating inflation. Specifically, it appears that the rate of inflation is significantly related to the gap between the rate of monetary growth and the rate of growth of real GNP. For example, over the period 1961-1977, there was on average, an increase in the rate of domestic inflation of 0.8 percent for each 1 percentage point increase in the gap between the rate of growth of M2 and real GNP. For the most recent decade for which complete data are available (1968-1977), a similar relationship obtains showing almost a full 1 percent increase in the rate of inflation for each rise of 1 percentage point in the gap between the rate of growth of M2 and real GNP."

M. Fry, who is one of the most prolific writers on the monetary issues in Turkey, improves his previous regression equations and writes the following one: (Fry, 1988, p. 99).

$$p = (m - u) - \Delta \ln (m)^d$$

where p is the inflation rate, m is the rate of growth in the nominal money supply, u is the population growth rate, and m^d is the real per capita money demand.

It is evident that this is in the same spirit of the previous ones based on the simple equation of exchange, except that the factors determining the velocity of circulation of money are more explicitly included in the equation.

The regression results for 1951-1985 period based on this formula is as follows. (ibid, p.100)

$$p = \underset{(18.413)}{1.096 (m - u)} - \underset{(-5.096)}{2.045 D \ln (y^e)} - \underset{(-5.386)}{1.641 D (d - p^e)}.$$

$$\bar{R}^2 = 0.826 \qquad DW = 1.65$$

where $\ln(y^e)$ is the expected growth in per capita real GNP. d-p^e the real deposit interest rate, d is the nominal deposit interest rate, and p^e expected inflation rate. Fry writes as follows: "The coefficients of the tree variables in that equation all agree with a priori expectations. The coefficient in the rate of change in the nominal money supply is not significantly different from one. (This shows a very high correlation between money increases and price increases in the long run.) The elasticity of money demand with respect to per capita real permenent income is about 2, a figure comparable with elasticities estimated directly in the money demand studies using a broad definition of money. The coefficient of the change in the expected real deposit rate of interest, i.e., -1.64, is also of the same order of magnitudes estimated for Turkey and other developing countries in money demand function." ibid, p. 100

The next problem was to find out factors determining the money volume. Almost all economists found out that the most important factors were credits granted to the private sector and perhaps more important one was those granted to government, and plus the increase of the foreign assets of the central bank. Here there is an example of those type of analyses.

Professor Fry estimates the growth of money supply by means of the following equation (Fry 1988)

M2 = DCp + NDCg + NFA - NOI (p. 90)

where M2 is money broadly defined including time and savings deposits as well as currency in circulation and demand deposits, DCp is domestic credit to the private sector, NDCg is net domestic credit to the government or public sector, NFA is the net foreign asset, and NOI is the net other items.

After writing that equation he estimates various factors determining each items in this equation.

Here is his conclusion: "Those equations explain the behavior of money supply in Turkey during the period 1951-85. Dynamic simulations of this money supply model ...suggest that the stability of this money supply process is fragile. The rapid rise in foreign exchange receipts in the early 1970s causes an explosive in the acceleration of the simulated monetary growth rate. Once inflation gets under way, the feedback mechanism from inflation to monetary acceleration through the widening public sector deficit can also produce explosive monetary acceleration unless foreign exchange receipts fall sufficiently rapidly under a fixed and increasingly overvalued exchange rate. Whether or not Turkey's money supply system is unstable, both postwar inflations were certainly accompanied by increasing instability......Substantial increases in foreign exchange receipts seems to have set the inflationary process in motion twice during the post war period."

In order to improve the analysis, the factors determining the volume of money are investigated from another point of view, and it is found that there is a reliable relationship between the reserve money and the volume of money affecting general price levels. All investigations show that the financial need of the public sector was the most important factor determining the volume of money.

In more sophisticated analyses, several macro-magnitudes are brought together to explain inflation in Turkey. They are centered around the relationship between investments and savings. They had to be the same in the end; but the financing of investments was of crucial importance here. If the ex-ante gap of investments over ex-ante savings were financed by external deficits, there was no problem. But if the public investment saving gap was financed by means of the reverse private investment saving gap, this would cause inflationary pressures by giving rise to an increase of the currency volume and/or by increasing interest rates, the latter factor being much more important in the recent high inflation.

Several economists tried to understand cost push factors such as interest rates, increases in the SEE (state economic enterprises) prices, inflationary expectations, etc. While doing it the permissiveness factor was brought in the foreground.

In the early investigations, the relationship between the permissiveness and import substitution was sought. Now permissiveness is looked into as a factor inducing governments to create the necessary money volume after the increase of cost push factors. Otherwise, the recessions expected might create political drawbacks for them.

Isn't all this like reading a textbook in monetary economics?

§ 3 - THE FINANCIAL SECTOR

The conventional discussions of financial sector are carried out under three headings: financial sector in general, banking and stock markets.

1-The shallow financial sector (1930-1980), which was an integrated part of the import substitution strategy is criticized on proper grounds. Yet the advantages and disadvantages of liberalization of the financial sector after 1980 are not considered the same by the leftist and market oriented economists. While some economists believe that the liberalization has been beneficial, others think just the opposite. According to former the increase of the proportion of the financial sector with respect to GNP (from 30 to over 100 percent) was a sign that financial markets were deepened and savings were increased. On the other hand, economists on the left tried to show that after the liberalization savings did not increase and it had all sorts of harmful effects on the economy. All those discussions are carried out conventionally.

2- After the investigations on conventional ground many economists underline the deficiency in banking: the instability in the development of banking system, the low level of real profits of banks, the increase of the cost of banking due to instability, the low ratio of the equity capital to bank assets, the high level of bad debts, high taxes collected by the government, high duty losses of public banks (not anymore), the high level of necessary liquidity kept by banks, the high share of assets kept by the public banks and all sorts of advantages accorded to them, the small size of banks, etc. They also draw attention to undesired practices in banking after the liberalization of the financial system: the theft and siphoning by private bank owners, the use of bank assets for financing companies belonging to the owners of banks, total guarantee for deposits by the government, etc.

3- The study of the stock market is also conventional. The very high volatility in the market and the inconsistency between the stock market yields and others prevailing in the country are explained by the impact of high sensibility of the stock market to temporary economic conditions and sharp changes in flow in and flow out of foreign funds into the market.

Now my unconventional comments are summarized below.

The important characteristics of financial markets in Turkey call for a different analysis from the traditional one. Here they will be touched upon.

1- After the liberalization of financial markets, negative real interest rates (especially in high inflationary years) were replaced by positive ones. As the continuing deficits of the central government were financed by loans, it pulled interest rates over what they should be if those high deficits of the central government did not exist. Were high interest rates a consequence of continuing inflations due to deficit finance (just remember Fisher's differentiation between nominal and real interest rates) or would a high loanable fund demand create a pressure on it? How should we decompose those different factors? There is not an analysis in this direction.

As the drawing of a liquidity preference curve was impossible under the circumstances the solution of that problem is difficult by using the tools of the traditional theory. As the integration of Turkish financial markets with world markets was quite imperfect due to devaluation and interest rate risks, the whole analysis is made more complicated. Nobody seems to have attempted such analyses.

2- To understand and to judge the deepening of financial markets in national economy (in fact the share of the financial market went up from 30 percent to over 100 percent after they were liberalized) without understanding its characteristics seems to be rising misleading conclusions. The most important mistake is to neglect of the transference of various funds from one to another. In fact if currency, bank deposits, government bonds and stocks and forex deposits are tried to be transferred from one to another in large quantities, all sort of difficult problems would arise. Again, structural problems relating to all financial institutions giving rise to difficulties of that sort are not investigated properly. I am of the opinion that if the unconventional analysis I developed is not understood, that problem cannot be tackled.

3- The study of high interest rates from the point of view of equity is full of misconception. There is no problem in calculating real interest rates of various assets. But when it comes to calculate the share of the total interest paid in the country wrong conclusions are drawn. Let me give an example based on crude figures. If the total interest bearing assets (deposits and bonds) is 100 percent of national income and if their nominal interest rate is 60 percent, the share of interest in national income would be calculated as 60 percent. Several economists make such calculations. In fact, the exact share should be much less than that... Suppose there was some 50 percent inflation; at the end of the year $ 60 would be paid as interest. It is probable that national income would be $ 150 at the end of the year. The rate of interest payments would be 40 percent of national income. Although this figure is much less than 60 percent, 40 percent is also an abnormally high figure. If inflation did not exist and the real interest was the same, say 10 percent, the share of total interests to national income would be 10 percent only. The burden caused by inflation is abnormally high.

But there is an important problem here. In order that the share of interest payments should be 40 percent of national income, interest bearing assets should not lose 50 percent of their real value. Although interest receiving people would have $60, $50 out of which is the loss of the value of their interest bearing assets. Therefore if they are made equal to their previous real value, their volume would increase by $50,i.e.,they should be $ 150. In that case the extra money possessed by interest receiving people is $ 10, which is 6.6 percent of national income ($10/ $ 150, which is equal to real interest rate).

All those calculations are known in the literature. What I say additionally is that in inflationary periods the prices and growth of the share of interest bearing assets is crucial in determining the share of interest in national income.

4- The impact of real interests and inflation seems to be equivocal. Actually we don't observe a fall in investments in Turkey as a result of very high interest rates. Actually if government investments were in question, that was no problem. The inability of interest rates to reduce private investments is a problem to explain.

5-There are high differences among the returns of several assets; they are quite different from each other and the change of differences becomes different in various years. Could that be explained by the traditional literature? I don't think so. The difficulty of transference of various assets among themselves should be one of the main factors in the explication at this abnormal situation.

6- The impact of forex deposits has not been investigated properly. It is shown that after the convertibility year the share of forex deposits in total deposits increased immensely. This is considered to be an undesired development for financial markets. What were its impacts and was it a threat? In fact, the literature on this subject is not satisfactory. Suppose people earn dollars or buy them on the markets. Then they deposit them as forex deposits. Or as an alternative they keep them in their safes. If those dollars are not kept in the safes dollar prices would be determined by the supply and demand originating from operations. If they are kept in safes. But there is a limit to keep them in safes. Abnormal dollar prices resulting from it may be very harmful for the economy. But if it is kept in banks, this does not change anything as long as there are not changes in foreign exchange reserves. On the other hand, when more and more dollars are drawn from banks this might be a problem, especially when foreign exchange reserves of the country are limited.

7-The most important conclusion of my unconventional analysis of financial markets is related to the explanations of high real interest rates prevailing in the country. In the literature it is asserted that this was due, to a great extent, to expectations. Yet, I try to show that one of the reason why expectations are as effective as that is the lack of the transferability of various financial assets among them. Once they are made transferable, this would constitute a buffer against the pressure by expectations.

8- During the pre-1980 years, the banking system as a whole constituted a sort of monopoly as no competition existed from other institutions and markets. Again, as some 6-7 banks carried out close to 90 percent of banking operations, the system operated essentially as an oligopoly. In addition, the control of interest rates and the legal environment, remindful of middle-age practices, strengthened their monopoly and oligopolistic practices. Interest rates were under a very high pressure. Banks were not permitted to pay interest rates above a certain percentage, regardless of the inflation rate. This was quite in line with banks' interest. Although some limitations existed with respect to bank lending rates, these could easily be avoided. As a result, a large spread existed between rates on deposits and lending; on average, interest paid on deposits was 5 percent (I describe the pre-1980 period) but the average interest on non-privileged loans was 15 percent. This spread gave rise to a very important conclusion which was elaborated in my book entitled TÜRKİYE'DE BANKACILIK - BANKING IN TURKEY, 1966. Bankers ignored my important arguments. Without going into too much detail let me explain the bankers' point of view. According to them the spread between deposits and credit rates was caused by taxes on deposits, high compulsory reserves that earned low interest rates, and high banking costs. As a result, high spreads did not allow banks to earn high profits. I tried to demonstrate that this agrument was quite superficial. My ideas on banking (in pre-1980 years) can be listed as follows. (They didn't attract the attention of anybody. An exception is the book antitled "MONEY AND BANKING IN TURKEY" by professor M. Fry, in which parallel views to mines are asserted. I shall summarize this book in the next chapter.)

A. High credit costs were not a result of high banking operation costs, but on the contrary, banking operation costs were made expensive as a result of the financial atmosphere. It is an established fact that in oligopolistic markets the relationship between costs and prices is loose, and firms in those markets tend to increase their cost in order to increase their market shares. This was the main feature of banking system during the pre-1980 years.

B. If in inflationary years interest rates were under pressure, the volume of deposits should decrease. Actually, the multiplier between deposits and currency in circulation went down from 3.24 in 1973 to 2.72 in 1979.

C. If returns on liquid assets (deposits) were kept low, this would give to exceptionally high returns in real assets which were not commensurate with economic conditions (see, Hatiboğlu, Türkiye'de Bankacılık 1966). If the return of monetary assets, which must reflect real conditions, are kept low, the return on cost of real assets (such as houses, land, etc.) should be under pressure (equalization of returns theorem), and they must be low. This implies both high real assets prices and a disrupture of the link between the cost of production and the price of real assets. As a result, a discrepancy between cost and prices appears. This would induce the production of real assets rather than liquid capital which is vital for the smooth operation of the economy.

D. The high cost of banking operations was perhaps unique in the world (around 10 percent of deposits in pre-1980 years). After 1980 a change in the structure of banking costs was observed. In fact, a rather low proportion of banking cost consisted of interest paid by banks before 1980. Now a greater proportion of costs are in the form of interests paid by banks. Yet banking costs are abnormally high in Turkey, and this is not properly studied.

§ 4 - CAPITAL MARKETS IN TURKEY

Under the Ottoman Empire a capital market existed in the country. But after the Republic it went down to an insignificant level. Several efforts were made after 1960 but they did not bring any consequence until the restructuring of the Istanbul Stock Exchange in 1986. From then on we observe a very fast development.

In Table XVI- 1 we see the index of Istanbul Stock Exchange at the end of years. Along with that, the average yield is exhibited in the other column. The average yield is around 60 percent. In this period the average yearly increase of the national income deflator was 60 percent. As a result, the average yearly real yield seems to be around dividents paid, which are rather small.

While the capitilization at the end of 2007 was $ 287 billion it went down to $135 billion in October 10, 2008. The index, which was 55,486 at the end of 2007 went down to 28,496 in October 10, 2008.

TABLE XVI -2
THE COMPOSITE INDEX OF THE ISTANBUL STOCK EXCHANGE
(Year End) (1986 = 100)

	INDEX	Growth Rate %	US $ Based (Jan 1986=100)
1986 (1)	171	70	131
1987	673	393	384
1988	374	-44	120
1989	2218	593	561
1990	3256	47	643
1991	4369	33	501
1992	4004	8	273
1993	20683	516	833
1994	27257	32	413
1995	40025	46	382
1996	97589	243	532
1997 (2)	3541	353	982
1998	2598	-28	484
1999	15209	585	1654
2000	9437	-38	817
2001	13782	46	557
2002	10370	-24	368
2003	18625	79	788
2004	29971	60	1075
2005	39779	33	1726
2006	39117	-2	1620
2007	55486	41	2214
2008	28496	-49	—

(1) Year end figures
(2) 00 is taken out

In order to compare the yield on the stock exchange with the yield of the public securities, a simple calculation can be made. In 1986 - 2008, the average yield of public securities was 70 percent; that of stocks was around the same. The performance of Istanbul Stock Exchange seems to be not too bad in terms of dollars, as well. But the most important problem there is the high volatility in the market. On the other hand, the volatility seems to be related to the rather small size of the market, which is influnced by the capital flows in and out. (Note: The growth rate of the index in terms of dollars is 16 percent.)

The volatility of stock prices is very wide as would be observed in Table XVI-3.

A few comments on the efficiency and future of capital markets in Turkey are listed below.

TABLE XVI - 3
IMKB INDEX in ($)

1990	August 7	1.87
1992	November 25	0.44
1994	January 1	1.37
1994	June 2	0.48
1997	October 8	1.67
1998	October 16	0.71
2000	January 20	3.29
2001	September 28	0.50
2002	January 21	0.95
2002	October 4	0.55
2003	December 31	0.88
2004	December 31	1.70

1- The total capitalization was around $ 287 billion at the end of 2007 (much less, now, as a result of the decrease of stock prices, October 10, 2008.) But it doesn't seem to show the real value of total stocks. It must be stressed that some 30-35 percent of total stocks listed are made public. The rest is kept by the individual owners of corporations. On the other hand, when total capitalization is calculated the 70 percent of stocks kept by owners are also accounted. This overswells the total value of stocks. It is estimated that some 70 percent of circulating stocks are owned by foreigners.

2- As 30 percent of total shares on the stock exchange are public, when stock prices increase old owners offer some of their stocks and as a result, stock prices decrease. In a way there is a limit to stock prices which originates not from the business conditions but from the proportion of stocks kept by the old owners.

3- The most important factor affecting stock prices, in the short run, is the flow of money to and from the stock exchange. As the total value of stocks to be bought or sold on the stock exchange is low compared to flow in and out of money, it seems that this becomes very influencial on stock prices. As result, stock prices seem to be very sensitive to expected changes in interest rates, foreign exchange prices and the government cash needs: they are all volatile.

§ 5 - DISCUSSIONS ON THE BENEFICIAL ASPECTS AND DISADVANTAGES OF THE DEEPENING OF FINANCIAL MARKETS IN TURKEY

It is shown above that shallow financial markets deepened in Turkey after 1980.

According to some economists shallow markets created all sorts of problems for the country and deepening markets have been beneficial in every sense, whereas there are economists who argue that deepening markets have given rise to disadvantageous consequences. Which is true? Before answering, it must be underlined that when the Turkish experience is studied, economists try to use arguments existing in literature. The particular aspects of the Turkish economy did not seem to have attracted their attention.

In this section I shall try to summarize arguments put forward by two economists: M. Fry, who approves the deepening, and Y. Akyüz, an extreme leftlist, who disapproves it.

Arguments Put Forward by M. Fry (Fry, 1995)

Let me start by an econometric research which is repeated by Fry.

Several economists estimated the impact of financial conditions on growth. Here is one of them on 21 developing countries for 1971-1980:

$$YG = 4.35 + 2.40\ (R)$$

$$\qquad (9.12)\quad (3.64)$$

$$\bar{R}^2 = 0.41$$

Here YG growth of national income, R is interest rate (whether it is low or high).

According to that regression equation there is a strong relationship between interest rate and growth.

Fry tests two propositions by means of Turkish data. One is the relationship between the real interest rates and inflation; and the other is the relationship between real interest rates and economic growth. Theoretically it is expected that when the real interest rate rises, this should exert a dampening influence on inflationary pressure. Here is Fry's regression equation for the 1951-1985 period. (p. 208)

$$INF = 1.096\,(MNG) - 2.045\,(YNGE) - 1.641\,\Delta\,(d - p^e)$$

$$(18.413) \qquad (-5.096) \qquad (-5.386)$$

$$\bar{R}^2 = 0.826 \qquad DW = 1.65$$

Here, INF is the rate of inflation, MNG is the rate of growth in per capita M2, YNGE is the rate growth in per capita real GNP, and Δ $(d - p^e)$ is the expected change in real deposit rate of interest. As the coefficient of real deposit interest is negative with 1.641 multiplier, this shows that high real interest rates, by causing higher money demand, dampen the inflationary pressure.

In the case of the impact of real interest rates on national income growth, the regression equation covering the1951-1985 period by Fry is as follows

$$YG = 0.957\,(YGN) + 0.009\,(PPE) + 0.154\,\Delta\,(d - p^e) \text{ (p. 210)}$$

$$(8.585) \qquad (1.304) \qquad (3.039)$$

$$\bar{R}^2 = 0.731 \qquad DW = 1.95$$

Here YG is the growth of national income. YGN is the trend growth in national income, PPE is the actual price level divided by the expected price level. $(d - p^e)$ is the expected change in real deposit rate; as the sign of the last term is positive this shows that high real interest rates affect the growth of national income positively.

Two assertions by Professor Fry are summarized. How significant are they? Although I think that the liberalization of the economy has been and will be beneficial for the economy, arguments by Professor Fry seem to be very simple and naive.

Firstly, let us look into his argument about the dampening effect of expected high interest rates on inflation. Although his regression equation suggests it, the mechanism is much too complex to be understood by this regression calculation.

In the long period covered by the regression equation (1951-1985) many important changes occurred in the economy. In 1951-1975 the only influencial factor on inflation was the currency issued. In the remaining period the impact of money in wider sense became important. All this means that although the level of interest rates could be effective in monetary demand, two different periods, having different characteristics, could not be brought together.

The argument relating to the relationship between interest rates and growth seems to be very naive. In the period under consideration (1951-1985) there are such strong factors affecting national income growth that the impact of interest rates should be totally negligible. As a result, to rely on regression result should not be plausible.

Actually, the impact of interest rates might be effective in the increase of the liquidity of the economy, which in turn, might affect the growth; yet this influence should not be at a degree influencing growth rate even minimally. Then why bother?

After having stated accepted advantages of the financial liberation, Professor Akyüz tries to show that the Turkish experience does not validate them. Here are some tendencies underlined by Akyüz. (Arıcanlı-Tosun 1990)

1- There is no decrease in the holding of marchandise and gold stocks in the economy after the liberalization. This means that an increase in loanable funds (or liquidity) should not be expected.

2- The increase in interest rates does not give rise to an increase in the savings of the more interest receiving sector of the economy. "Clearly, this experience does not conform to the McKinnon-Show paradigm of a portfolio shift from improductive uses to financial resources for fixed capital formation. At best, it can represent a substitution of one type of investment to another" (p. 120).

3- There is no a decrease in the self- financed housing construction.

4- The ever increasing holding of foreign deposits has restricted the efficiency of the economic policy.

5- The increase of high interests channeled a very high proportion of public funds to interest payments; and as a result, public investment decreased.

6- The informal money markets which served the needs of small merchants disappeared, and instead rich corporations had more access to limited funds. In addition, the shift of funds previously possessed by informal markets is a redistribution of income in the sense that money is used now by richer people rather than poor ones.

7- Liberalization restricted the effectiveness of interest and exchange rate policy by rendering the control of money supply difficult under conditions of rapid depreciation of Turkish Lira.

Again he shares the following common belief: "Turkish experience in the 1980 s demonstrates once again the potentially destablizing nature of financial deregulation and capital account liberalization before permanently reducing inflation, ensuring financial dicipline, and eliminating the need for continuous real devaluations (Akyüz 1990, p. 127)."

There are others. In my opinion all the arguments are naive and difficult to support by facts. But what is important is that Prof. Yılmaz does not show any alternative to the financial liberalization. Could the economy move ahead with the financial markets cherished by socialist economists?

I don't think that I can share Professor Akyüz's arguments. A longer and more in depth critique of them is needed. Here some observations in the Turkish economy will be presented, which could be considered as denial of Akyüz's arguments.

1- The years studied by Professor Akyüz were the early ones after the liberalization of the financial markets. In the years following the early years we observe a very significant increase in savings. Actually, in the 1990 s the average savings/GNP ratio was nearly 24 percent, which was much higher when the financial markets were shallow: see the table below:

Year	Savings/GNP
1978	15.8
1986	11.7
1999	29.8
2000	24.7
2001	17.5
2002	19.2
2003	19.3

2- The share of investment to GNP has been around 24 percent, which is again the highest ratio observed in this country after the few years following the liberation.

I don't think that the impact of the liberalization of financial markets on savings and investment ratio to GNP could be denied by naive arguments put forward by Professor Akyüz.

3- The increase of Financial Assets/GNP has been phenomenal; while it was around 30 percent before the liberalization of the economy, it is now almost 100 percent, and this has occurred in less than two decades. Does this mean that an increase of liquidity has not occurred in the country?

4- If foreign exchange reserves do not increase at a proportion equal to the increase of Forex deposits, this means that those deposits are in the monetary system.

5- The recent events and experience suggest that monetary policy seems to have been efficient in the country: just the contrary to Professor Akyüz's assertion.

6- Like all economists on the left, Professor Akyüz is worried about the high interest paid by the government. But it is shown that it is not closely related to liberalization.

7- In recent years a good proportion of real estate financing is made by the banking system.

In the previous pages I tried to give an idea about the controversy between Fry and Yılmaz. Of course, this controversy does not end there. Here I would like to mention one argument put forward by Öniş and Alper against financial liberalization (see, Öniş and Alper 2000).

They show that financial liberalization might be beneficial in the long run. But it may have serious problems. The most important problem is related to the flow in and out of hot capital. There is a relationship between the political capacity of the government and the beneficial aspects of the use of foreign capital flows. Turkey abopted full convertibility in 1989. But the most destructive crises occurred after this date, i.e., 1994, 2000 and 2001. As a result, a relationship should be established between them. They show that current deficits in the balance of payments are lost out of sight when there is a free movement of foreign capital. In Turkey democratic auditing mechanism did not exist. They say that there is delegative democracy in Turkey. It means that the power of a single person is much too strong compared to what was the case in western democracies. Moreover, the relationship with electors depends on fuduciary interest. There is populism. Funds belonging to public are used for the political interest or political parties. The inception of total convertibility in 1989 was related the diminishing popularity of the T. Özal, the political leader of the country in those years. He thought that by full convertibility more foreign capital would flow in and as a result, economic conditions would be improved. Especially the rate of inflation would decrease. But things did not occur in expected direction.

§ 6 - DISCUSSIONS ON PUBLIC FINANCE

One of the economic discussions in Turkey is the impact of the policy of public finance on the economy. Traditionally governments have 3 functions. 1- Traditional government functions such as law, public defense, health, education, etc. 2- Regulation of the economy to create an atmosphere for stability and growth, and 3- to improve income distribution. In performing all those functions public sector needs money and it should be spent properly. Both the level and use of public funds are in question here.

In Turkey all those problems are discussed under two periods: pre and post-1980. Almost every economist who studies the second period in which the country adopted a liberalized economy criticizes the second period and tries to show that almost everything went astray in the second period. Those investigations could be gathered under 3 headings.

1- The anatomy of public revenue. In the criticism directed to the second period main arguments can be summarized as follows.

a) The share of the public revenue in GNP is supposed to have decreased after turning outside. Indeed, if taxes only are considered as the main item of the government revenue, it is true that especially in the early years of liberalization there is such a decrease. If other sources of revenue such as extra budget funds whose importance increased after 1980, and other revenues such as the revenue of regional administration, non-tax revenue, social insurance revenue, factor incomes, privatization income, etc. are taken into consideration, an increase in the share would be observed. Again, when the share of the public revenue to GNP is compared with that of other countries in similar per capita income that was not too much below the average. Again, in last years that ratio seems to increase rapidly. Although there are many calculations in this direction I don't think that an exact figure is determined. For recent years some 30 percent is not a bad estimate. But much more important than that is that the figures relating to national income of pre- and post-1980 should not be compared easily.

b) In the second period, the share of direct taxes seems to be getting lower which is supposed to be against equity. I think that the recent tendency in the world is an increase of indirect taxes.

c) The share of taxes paid by low income taxpayers increased after the switch to a more liberalized economy. This is considered quite natural because in the new era supply side policies have been on the foreground. Tax rates for upper income groups decreased in order that they would save more. Again, all sorts of subsidies are given to high income people. (No, in fact transfers to social insurance institutions are the highest items of the government budgets.) According to adversaries an increase of savings by this way is not obtained. I think it is not investigated properly.

d) It is asserted that all sorts of taxes for capital decreased for the same goal mentioned above. I think this has been beneficial for the development of capital markets.

The anatomy of expenditure

The second aspect of public finance in Turkey is a study of public expenditure. Some views about it are listed below.

a) After 1980 there has been a decreasing trend of expenditures on health and education. Their share to national income seems be decreasing noticeably. Meanwhile expenditure on defense is still high.

b) While the share of current expenditure increases, the share of investments decreases.

c) The deficits in public accounts increase very fast, exponentially. PSBR was in an unbearable level. (It is now almost zero.)

d) Interest on the ever increasing public debt is very high and it constitutes almost 50 percent of the consolidated government budget. (Not anymore.)

The finance of public investments

There are all sorts of calculations regarding the financing of public investments. Until 1980 a great proportion of public investments were secured by public savings. But this has decreased continuously and they are financed by private ones. What is more alarming is the negative level of public savings. To give just an example public savings were some -6.6 of GNP in 2000. Meanwhile public consumption has been increasing continuously.

Criticism of Analyses of Public Finance Policies

My views on the public finance policies are related to my understanding of the economy. The level of national income is greatly under the influence of relative prices. To compare national income figures in two periods does not mean much if this is not taken into consideration.. Again figures relating to government revenue and expenditure have the same character and they cannot be compared with each other without taking the distortion underlined above.

1- The idea that government revenue is low (decreasing with respect to national income) leaves much to be desired. There are several factors here. Especially, there a sharp difference between deflators applying to the government and other sectors in the sense that the prices of government services increased much less than other prices: as a result, the comparison of government revenue with the previous ones must be made very carefully. Actually when figures are examined, it will be evident that the ratio of the total revenue to GNP is not too low.

2- The discussion of the impact of the share of interest paid for the domestic debt on the government budget is full of misconceptions. If the more recent figures are considered, (actually this is the case) the share of interest payments may seem to be around some 40-45 percent of the total government budget expenditure. Actually, the rate should be around 28 percent. The calculation is very simple.

Suppose the real interest rate paid by the government is around 20 percent (average); for the last 10 years, it is even less. And again, suppose that the government domestic debt is some 50 percent of GDP. If government expenditure is some 35 percent of the GDP, the total interest payment for domestic debt would be 28 percent of the government budget rather than 40-45 percent. The government may have paid some 40-45 percent of all its revenue as interest but as a result of time lag, the real expenditure should be around 28 percent of the budget. (There is truth and flaw in this calculation.)

3- There is a decrease in the participation of the government in economic activity. Many services or the production of several goods previously assumed by the government are performed by the private sector now. In the past, when the government produced many goods they were priced cheaply considering their cost of production. As a result, part of the government revenue was used to compensate the losses incurred that way. As the proportion of the factors of production to be devoted to government services is less now, a lower government expenditd compared to the past: if other services are assumed by the government in future, this may increase.

TABLE 1A

RECENT CENTRAL BANK AND GOVERNMENT BONDS INTEREST RATES (%)

	Central Bank	Goverment Bonds
November 2008	16.75	24.15
January 2009	13.00	15.11
April 2009	9.75	12.55

CURRENCY ISSUED AND DEPOSITS IN 2006

(Thousond TL)	
Currency issued	26 815 151
Total deposits	285 487 831

TABLE 1

RECENT INFLATION IN TURKEY

Year	Wholesale Prices Producer	Consumer Prices
1990	52	60
1991	55	66
1992	62	70
1993	58	66
1994	120	106
1995	88	93
1996	76	79
1997	82	85
1998	72	84
1999	53	69
2000	33	39
2001	86	67
2002	31	39
2003	13.9	18.4
2004	13.4	9.3
2005	2.7	7.6
2006	**9.8**	**9.6**
2007	**6.5**	**8.4**
2008	**8.1**	**10.6**

TABLE 2

THE GROWTH OF THE FINANCIAL SECTOR, 1980-2005

	1980	1990	1996	2005
Deposits/Currency	2.85	6.43	17.5	11.33
Stocks/GNP	0.059	0.104	0.22	0.470
Currency/GNP	0.062	0.029	0.021	0.040
Deposits/GNP	0.179	0.184	0.372	0.457
Domestic gov. debt/GNP	0.060	0.145	0.183	0.505
Foreign debt/GNP	0.205	0.390	0.444	0.457
Currency+Deposits+Securities/GNP	0.360	0.462	0.576	1.460

TABLE 3

MONEY VOLUME (YEAR END, TL TRILLION)

	2001	2002	2003	2004
M1	11,073	14,259	21,564	29,469
Currency in circulation	4,801	7,209	10,129	12,446
Current deposits	6,272	7,050	11,434	17,023
M2	46,986	61,195	80,923	109,344
Time deposits	35,913	46,936	59,359	79,875
M3=M2+Forex	104,133	133,450	149,855	185,419
Forex deposits	57,147	72,255	68,932	76,074

TABLE 4
MONETARY ASSETS IN TURKEY

	Billion TL Aug. 2004	% Dec. 2000	% Aug. 2004
I- Money or near money	173,337	43	34
(1) TL	100,754	26	20
(2) Currency in circulation	13,224	2	3
(3) Sight deposit	13,822	3	3
(4) Time deposits	73,707	17	15
(5) Repo	1,870	4	0
(6) Forex deposits	72,583	17	14
II- Securities (Private)	104,166	32	21
(1) Stocks	104,166	32	21
III-Government Securities	214,275	25	42
(1) Gov. Bonds	183,960	23	36
(2) Treasury notes	30,315	1	6
(3) Others	1,019	0	0
IV-Investment funds	14,321	0	3
V- Total	506,100	100	100

Source: Oct 25, 2004, Milliyet.

TABLE 5
A SHORT SUMMARY OF THE ANALYTICAL BALANCE SHEET OF THE TURKISH CENTRAL BANK (TL Trillion)

	2005	2006
Total assets	90,070	116,829
Foreign	72,337	
Domestic	17,732	
Gov. Bonds	19,470	
Other	-3,767	
Total Liabilities	90,070	
Foreign liabilities	51,522	
Domestic Liabilities	28,064	
Central bank money	38,547	
Reserve money	32,696	
Issued currency	19,612	
Bank deposits	12, 898	
Open market operations	4,983	
Government deposits	868	

Source: Central Bank 2005, p.212

TABLE 6
THE PRICES OF INVESTMENT INSTRUMENTS AND RETURN

	Nominal return %					Real return %	
	2007	January 2008	February	February	2 Month	February	2 Month
Bonds	16.59	16.39	16.95	1.27	2.5	-0.01	0.40
Repo	15.75	15.50	15.25	1.08	2.18	-0.20	0.06
1 month deposits	16.13	16.08	15.53	1.10	2.24	-0.18	0.12
3 month	16.14	16.00	15.65	1.11	2.25	-0.17	0.13
6 month	15.75	15.63	15.38	1.08	2.19	-0.20	0.07
1 year	15.53	14.97	15.23	1.07	2.14	-0.21	0.02
Republic gold coin	209.00	230.00	243.85	6.02	16.67	4.66	14.25
Euro	1.7184	1.7441	1.8185	4.26	5.82	2.93	3.63
Dollar	1.1703	1.1736	1.1963	1.93	2.22	0.63	0.10
F.E.Basket	2.2887	2.9177	3.0148	3.32	4.36	2.00	2.20
Investment fund	814.910	804.525	812.320	0.96	-0.31	-0.32	-5.44
A type	522.024	453.493	462.495	1.98	-11.40	0.68	-13.23
B type	1.118.303	1.130.876	1.139.835	0.79	1.92	-0.49	-0.18
IMKB-100	55.538	42.698	44.777	4.58	-19.37	3.52	-21.03
IMKB-30	70.457	53.435	55.489	3.84	-21.24	2.51	-22.86
Financial index	83.822	63.089	62.933	-2.47	-24.92	-3.71	-26.47
Industry index	40.567	33.011	36.002	9.06	-11.25	7.67	-13.08

Source: Sabah, March 4, 2008

TABLE 7
REAL INTEREST (March 2009)

	Numinal Interest	Real Intrest
Island	15.50	10.7
Brazil	11.75	8.15
Turkey	15.25	7.05
N. Zelland	8.25	5.85
Australia	7.25	4.95
Norvey	5.25	4.45
S. Africa	11.00	4.4
Hong Kong	5.00	3
China	7.47	2.97
U.K.	5.25	2.85
Korea	5.00	2.4
Sweden	4.25	1.85
Slovakia	4.25	1.85
India	8.00	1.8
Switzerland	2.75	1.75
Canada	3.50	1.3
Hungary	8.00	1.1
EU	4.00	0.9
Chekoslovakia	3.75	0.85
Japan	0.50	0.5
USA	2.25	-0.45
Egypt	9.50	-2.6

TABLE 8
SOCIAL SECURITY DEFICIT
Social Security Administration Deficits
(Million TL)

	Income	Expenditure	Deficit
2000	8.576	10.987	2.411
2001	13.361	17.831	4.470
2002	20.018	27.982	7.964
2003	27.917	41.336	13.420
2004	34.689	50.622	15.932
2005	41.249	59.941	18.692
2006	53.831	71.867	18.037
2007	56.875	81.915	25.041

CHAPTER XVII
MORE ON INFLATION AND REPRESSIVE FINANCE

§ 1- INTRODUCTION

In chapter XVI, 1 summarized my unconvencianal ideas on inflation and finance, and also I gave a few examples how some well known economists explained factors affecting inflation in Turkey.The second topic was their comments about the repressed finance and the liberalization of it. I extend my writings in that chapter.

In the case of inflation, I survey the writings of several well known writers on inflation in this country.They are a sort of replica of what is found in a textbook on money.All they did was to use the tools existing in books in the Turkish case.The common factor is the importance of money in large sense(M2),deficits in government finance,financing the gap between investments and savings by private sector savings or by money issue and or by foreign capital inflows.Again,the importance of base money in affecting total money is in the foreground.Nothing much is written about the kind of currency which affects inflation in this country.Almost every economist is of the opinion that it is M2, whereas by drawing upon existing figures, I tried to show that the kind of money in question changes from time to time,somtimes MO and sometimes M2.Along with that I explained why it was so,and I focused on factors giving rise to that change.

In the second part of the chapter I tried to summarize very shortly two relevant parts of the book entitled MONEY AND BANKING by Professor Fry, who was the first economist applying modern economic literature on money and banking to the Turkish case.He tried to underline the detrimental effects of the repressive finance policy which was being followed in Turkey when his book was published.In my BANKING IN TURKEY I did the same but he was much more informed compared to me.

Everything written in this chapter supports my writings and comments in Chapter XVI.

§ 2 - ANALYSES BY LEADING TURKISH ECONOMISTS

Professor Celasun, different from pure Keynesians, gives special emphasis to the monetary aspects of the system in creating a pressure on prices. His monetary analysis is parallel to present day writings on this subject. "In Turkey's present institutional setting, the latter processes (monetary supply, author's note) essentially involve the following: (a) the monetary - base expansion as a given function of public sector financing deficit, debt management policies, (i.e., government bond sales), and foreign exchange reserve change; (b) money supply creation as a multiple of monetary-base change affected by currency and reserve-deposit ratios; and (c) increase in commercial bank credit through the credit-to-base multiplier relation. The money supply creation may then be contrasted with the desired money demand implied by real economic magnitudes (and other factors such as expected inflation), and thus the excess demand in the commodity market may be estimated" (Celasun 1980, p. 10).

Along with the aggregation of the several monetary magnitudes, the crucial question here is the definition of desired money demand. As the traditional income velocity concept is not used, how would money demand be defined? It is evident that some cost push factors would be influential in determining it. This will be taken up below. If faith is laid on the Keynesian aggregates, they might be conceived as indices affecting monetary demand. Although he does not say so, the only feasible combination with monetary magnitudes and Keynesian analysis can be sought in this direction and he does so. (See his Tables 1, 2 and 3; their explanations verify this conjecture.) In the tables mentioned the relationship between I (investment) and S (Savings) is investigated for the period of 1973 - 1977 and the lack of savings (especially public savings) is emphasized in inducing monetary expansion. As was shown in those tables, the I-S gap was financed by foreign inflow.

"The rapidly widening savings and financing gaps of the public sector (measured as a proportion of public disposable income and/or investment) created strains in the financial system to affect the required financial transfers from the private sectors. These transfers were effected to some degree by new domestic borrowing (i.e., net increase in the stock of government bonds), and to a large extent by private savings through deficit financing by the Central Bank" (Celasun 1980, p. 17).

We should be very careful that all this analysis leads to monetary expansion and the factors initiating it are conceived as of Keynesian magnitudes. Nothing is said about the relative stability of income velocity of money and Keynesian aggregates. To repeat, what is done is to find the impact of Keynesian aggregates on monetary expansion.

He investigates the overall consequences of financing public deficits on a monetary base. Along with others, Gürsel (1977) and Keyder (1978), he concludes that "the principal contribution to growth of M 1 (currency plus deposits) has come from a monetary base, which is largely under the control of monetary authorities, and exhibits a fairly stable proportion of currency (46 percent), legal reserves (36-37 percent) and excess reserves (16-17 percent) during 1973-77".

The table showing the calculation of monetary base by Celasun is reproduced below. (Table XVI-1)

TABLE XVI - 1

MONETARY BASE (MB) AND NARROW MONEY (M l)

(Billion TL. End-Year)

	1973	1974	1975	1976	1977	1978
Monetary Base (MB)						
1. Net Foreign Assets	13.3	3.8	-16.3	-47.7	-65.1	-88.1
2. Import Deposits	-1.2	-1.0	-1.9	-11.5	-46.5	-70.8
3. Net Domestic Assets						
- Public sector (2)	21.4	29.5	48.4	77.7	138.6	220.7
- Deposit banks	17.6	25.2	40.7	70.1	96.3	125.1
- Other financial institutions	1.4	7.5	14.7	23.5	37.1	42.3
4. Net other items	-3.8	-4.6	-4.6	-9.5	-8.7	-13.2
Total (MB)	48.6	60.6	80.9	102.6	151.6	216.1
Narrow Money (M 1)	69.8	88.7	117.6	150.4	209.1	283.6
Money Multiplier (MI/MB. money)	1.44	1.46	1.45	1.47	1.38	1.31

(1) Figures may not add due to rounding.

(2) Including State Investment Bank.

Source: Central Bank (1979).

(Author's note: The increase of prices in 1973-1978 is approximately 2.7 fold; whereas that of M 1 is 4 fold. If the increase of national income is deducted from that of M 1, both the rate of increase of prices and that of M 1 becomes closer.)

It is evident that according to Celasun's analysis, which can be an example of the monetarist approach to inflation in Turkey, Keynesian aggregates can be conceived only as follow up items. "In sum, it appears that the ex-ante savings and financing gaps projected in the annual programs were in fact unbalanced, and not tested in advance for consistency with the feasible limits to monetary expansion. The inability to take concrete measures to raise public disposable income (via a tax reform, and more efficient SEE performance) and unwillingness to moderate the growth of public expenditure eventually caused massive imbalances in the money and credit system." (Celasun 1980, p. 19).

Professor Celasun believes that along with purely monetary factors there are also non-monetary dimensions in the Turkish inflation.

In order to find the role of both monetary factors and cost push factors he constructs several regression equations. As a cost push factor he introduces (a) inflationary expectations and (b) import-related cost push factors. He expresses the main conclusion as follows. "... the excess monetary growth (or excess demand in the goods market) is a predominant variable explaining price-level changes in conjunction with inflationary expectations." (Celasun 1980, p. 23). His equations imply also that there remain unexplained factors behind price-level changes. Therefore he includes cost push factors. As he does not possess series relating to wages and an index of SEE's administered prices for basic intermediate goods, he introduces the average domestic price of imports. His conclusion is this: "the regression equations show that the domestic price of imports significantly affects the general price level, and its inclusion in the estimation reduces the coefficients of expected inflation" (Celasun 1980, p. 24).

In a more recent analysis (Celasun 1993) Professor Celasun develops his analysis based on the interaction of macroeconomic aggregates. His analysis can be summarized as follows:

1- A closer study of various factors affecting inflation should be carried out. They are exchange rates, interest rates, wages, subsidies and transfers by the public.

2- In order to understand inflation in Turkey the interconnection and the determination of macromagnitudes such as private savings, public savings, private investments, public investments, external deficits, employment, etc. should be investigated. The main cause of the inflation in Turkey is related to this interaction.

3- The most important factor is the level of the public savings. Its low level gives rise to inflation. Again, the deficit given rise by the low public savings is compensated for by high interests, which, in turn, increases deficits. Another way of covering low public savings is foreign deficit. But if it is paid in the long run, this will give rise to inflationary pressures.

4- The demand for reserve money has decreased after the liberalization of the economy. Along with that the dollarization, increasing government bond issues, high inflationary expectations made the same effect, and the velocity of circulation of money increased. This gave rise to a decrease of the public income originating from the segniorage revenues. That means that the necessary deficit financing of the public has increased.

5- During the liberalization period, the dependency on the Central Bank has decreased. The issue of high amount of government negociable debt made it possible. But now its amount is so excessive that this cannot continue.

6- A better public finance policy is necessary in order to control inflation. But its effect is deflationary, and that would give rise to a decrease in the growth of the economy.

Professors Ziya Öniş and Süleyman Özmucur, who rank among the outstanding members of the young generation of economists in Turkey, have produced one of the best studies of Turkish inflation (see Öniş and Özmucur 1987). They have offered a theoretical analysis of inflation in Turkey together with a detailed econometric study of past events.

They have demonstrated that bottlenecks are much more likely to occur in developing compared to developed countries. This is because of the fact that in developing countries the input/output relations are constant. As a consequence, relative price changes become powerless in an adjustment. If there are not necessary inputs, a low supply elasticity would result. The aggregate supply curve would then become steep before reaching full employment income. The most important bottleneck is the lack of foreign exchange.

If the scarcity of foreign exchange leads to an increase in its price, this cost push factor shifts the aggregate supply curve leftwards and the level of national income would decrease. If, on the other hand, the government attempts to combat lower unemployment levels, a permissive monetary policy would be pursued. An increase in currency supply would make it possible to return to the original starting point; yet prices would rise.

This general reasoning has been applied to the import substitution and export orientation situations.

During the first stage of import substitution the rate of income increase is rapid. But in the second stage there is a greater need for intermediate and capital goods. Together with low exports, this results in an increase in foreign exchange prices.

The mechanism outlined above would appear. In addition to the scarcity of foreign exchange other tendencies would foster inflationary pressures. These are the low level of productivity, monopolistic markets, and the financing needs caused by the low prices of goods produced by the public sector. Also, the proportionally less increase of government revenue in inflationary periods would also lead to inflationary pressures.

With reference to the impact of export orientation on inflation the authors initially have examined the favorable consequences of a switch to this policy. This concerns the increase in foreign exchange and productivity, etc. But unfavorable inflationary pressures are also caused. These are a rise in foreign exchange prices, interest rates and in the prices of goods produced by the public sectors. Such cost push factors result in the emergence of the mechanism described above.

This is the theoretical background of the survey conducted by the authors. Verification is then attempted using a sophisticated econometric analysis. As the impact of the monetary base on inflation is quite evident, a substantial proportion of the book is devoted to the analysis of causation. Similar research work has been produced by Celasun (1980), Neftci (1980), Ertugrul (1982), and Olgun (1982).

The causation test is based on the following reasoning: If the present value of Y is estimated more accurately by including past values of X, thus X causes Y. Using this method the authors have obtained the following conclusion:

The relationship between monetary base and price level is very strong. Yet the change in exchange rate seems to be influencing prices as a cost push factor, which in turn, would give rise to the increase in monetary stock as monetary authorities are inclined to follow a permissive monetary policy. This value induces an increase in the price of foreign exchange, and the process continues.

An Analysis Emphasizing the Importance of the Public Debt

In the analysis carried out by (Çiller and Kaytaz 1989), factors influencing inflation are determined within the framework of a model. The parameters of the equations constituting the model are found by a regression method based on past figures and Bayesian statistics.

I shall attempt to unravel the argument presented in this book. In my opinion the explanations offered by Çiller and Kaytaz were not clearly stated.

The main finding of the research concerns the dominant role of the public deficit in determining inflation. The public deficit determines money supply which has an impact on prices. The model is enriched by imagining that domestic and external borrowings would at first reduce the effect of the public deficit, but when the interest and principal require payment a pressure to increase the public deficit is produced which again leads to an increase in money supply and so on.

Ten equations and their parameters were discovered by the regression method based on three months data. Five were identities and the other five were based on regression findings.

The estimates of inflation cover the 1980-1986 period and appear to produce results in line with theoretical expectations. This finding leads to certain conclusions concerning factors influencing inflation.

Equations are self-explanatory. It is quite evident that the GNP deflator depends on money stock (M_3 - Money including every monetary component), exchange rates and the interest rate on credits.

Monetary stock (M_3) depends on the monetary base, previous stock (3 periods prior), GNP and the domestic stock of debt. The monetary base is principally determined by the requirement of public debt, which equals the difference between public expenditure and the public debt. This leads to the conclusion outlined at the beginning of this section.

Reflections on the Use of Keynesian Tools

Most economists in Turkey are prone to use an analysis based on Keynesian tools in monetary analysis as well as when they analyze the development of the country.

Some economists have used these tools naively and others more rigorously.

In naive uses, some statistical tests are conducted without giving much regard to their pitfalls and in most cases, verbal analyses are made using Keynesian concepts such as the effect of a gap between investments and savings causing inflation, the psychological attitude of people, cost push, etc. (See, Ulgener et. al., 1968).

Nothing much should be said about those approaches as they are not backed either by rigorous testing or theoretical reasoning. But on the other hand, the use of the Keynesian approach should be evaluated when it is tested by rigorous analysis. (The best example of this approach is found in Celasun (1980). One rigorous testing known in western countries is that of Ateşoglu (See Ateşoglu 1973 and 1975).

Ateşoglu tried the usability of both Keynesian and monetary approaches in the Turkish case. He tested two standard Friedman-Meiselman equations:

1) $D\,E_t = B_1\,D\,A_t + Y_1 + D\,Z_t + U_{1t}$ — Keynesian Version

2) $D\,E_t = B_2\,D\,M^S + Y_2 + D\,Z_t + U_{2t}$ — Quantity Theory Version

where E_t is the change in induced expenditure in period t, At is the change in autonomous expenditure in period t, $D\,Z_t$ is the change in agricultural income in period t, $D\,M^S$ is the change in money supply in period t. B_1, Y_1, B_2, Y_2 are regression coefficients and U's are random disturbances in period t.

To avoid spurious correlation, due to the strong upward trend in the data, the Keynesian and quantity theory alternative are stated in first difference forms.

Professor Ateşoglu feeds Turkish data for the 1950-1968 period into ordinary least square equations, and for each case he gets excellent fits of almost similar order. In other words, he finds out that both autonomous expenditure and money supply are quite stable, and therefore each can be used to explain the situation in this country.

Nothing much can be said about conclusions reached by the quantity equation version, as they were commented on above. But, his use of the Keynesian version will be criticized here. Before doing that, let us examine his definition of autonomous expenditure which is shown by A. In fact, he tries several alternatives to define A; but they are not much different one from another, if viewed with our purpose in mind. In fact, almost the same conclusions are reached by each of them. Let us take the first definition:

$$A_1 = I+G+(X—I_m) + F$$

$$E_1 = Y —A_1 = (C + B) + D$$

Where A_1 represents autonomous expenditure, E - induced expenditure, I - net investment, G - government consumption. X - exports. Im - imports, F - net factor income from abroad, Y - total expenditure, C - private consumption, B - change in inventory and D - depreciation. His conclusions show that by feeding the amount of autonomous expenditure into the regression equation, we can predict changes in Turkey. But, without discussing the legitimacy of using the Keynesian method in Turkey, one is tempted to think about figures to be plugged in the equation, i.e., G, I, X, Im and F. It will be shown that the actual figures to be found and used for those elements of autonomous expenditure in Turkey are not of a nature to be anything similar to the definition of those terms in industrialized countries. If it is so, there is not any use in expecting significant results from tests of the Keynesian version of monetary relationship. The more satisfactory statistical conclusions may not be beyond coincidence or they may be caused by spurious relationship, which may be the case in some econometric research.

Now, let us start with G.A selection of actual level for G, which may be significant as far as outonomous expenditure is concerned, would be very difficult to decide upon, apart from the difficulties of computing it. In fact, the activities of the government are so intermixed with those of the Central Bank in public financing that it is meaningless to separate one from the other. The government gives subsidies to most agricultural products and/or pays for deficits of state government enterprises which are very important in economic life. For these purposes, the government sometimes uses its budgetary funds, sometimes borrows from the Central Bank and sometimes subsidies and losses are paid by the Central Bank itself. Will these expenditures be included in autonomous expenditure; and if they are, should government expenditures and Central Bank credits (which are not paid back in any case) be lumped together?

Let us look at I. We know that for both government and private investments, the most important factor was the availability of cash and foreign exchange during the period under consideration. Investments in Turkey are not incurred, in most cases, according to economic calculations, but the availability of cash and foreign exchange is the most decisive factor. Then, why treat the surface phenomenon (I) as the autonomous expenditure?

The meaning of exports, X, as an autonomous expenditure is problematic. Almost half of exports were made by the public sector and it is very difficult to separate export earnings from other public sector earnings.

In the case of imports, Im, the problem is much too complex. In fact, there is a very loose relationship between imports and expenditure. That is because of overvalued exchange rates, restriction of imports and the government's fixing of prices of some imported items (such as oil).

When it comes to foreign inflow, F, it also gives rise to problems. The importance of worker's remittances makes any figure relating to F very difficult to interpret (See Hatiboglu 1978, pp. 209-11).

If all elements constituting autonomous expenditure cannot be interpreted unequivocally, how can one expect any conclusion from a regression equation in which these figures are plugged in?

N.B. All commants are for the pre - 1980 period.

The Political Economy of Inflation

Several economists (among them Uygur 1993 and Çubukoğlu, 1993) emphasized the importance of the political impact of the measures relating to the monetary administration. They show that a move to decrease inflation would create unfavorable effects on the level of growth. This is a sort of Phyllips curve effect.

The reasons mentioned are the impact of the decrease of government investments, salaries, wages, and short term foreign exchange inflows on the domestic consumption. Again, the same impact arises as a result of the increase of taxes, and decreases of subsidies.

The decrease of consumption expenditure, and the recession caused by it in the short run would create detrimental effects for the political parties in power and no political party in opposition would support such policies. As a result, in order to control inflation a concensus among political parties as well as other actors such as unions, employers must be created. And economists must influence the public opinion in that direction. Actually, the situation is just on the contrary in the country; a conflict of any kind is the most important characteristic of the country. Again, the restructuring the whole economy and SEE'S and social security institutions should also be emphasized. General public must believe that the difficulties would be short termed and spring would follow winter: this is a sort of the credibility of the government. All those actions can be taken by a government which feels that there are at least 3-4 years ahead of it, during which it will keep its power of governing.

§ 3- VALIDATION OF UNCONVENTIONAL COMMENTS IN TURKEY

Different approaches to explain inflation in Turkey are summarized above. They must be all relevant in a sense. In all of them the impact of money is in the foreground. Usually, the importance of money in a wider sense is emphasized. Cost push factors seem to be important also. This view is validated by all sorts of econometric studies. But if we look into figures rather intuitively, this view cannot be adhered to one hundred percent. There are unknown features of inflation in Turkey. This will be shown step by step.

First, the impact of money. Here the pre-1980 and post-1980 period must be distinguished from each other.

In pre-1970 years the impact of money in the narrow sense, i.e.. currency issued by the central bank, is quite strong. (Tables XVII - 2)

Table XVII - 2
THE RELATIONSHIP BETWEEN
CURRENCY AND PRICE INCREASE (*)

Period	Currency Index (**)	GNP Index	GNP Deflators (Price Index Actual)	Hypothetical Price Index (***)
I	II	III	IV	V
1950-1960	442	184	262	240
1960-1970	297	176	165	168
1970-1980	1,895	164	1,747	1,155

(*) The index for the beginning of each period is taken at 100.
(**) Yearly averages based on the beginning and the end of years.
(***) Column V is calculated by dividing column II by column III.

Table XVII - 3

THE RELATIONSHIP BETWEEN MONETARY STOCK (M2) AND PRICES

Period	Monetary Stock Index	GNP Index	GNP Deflator (Price Index Actual)	Hypothetical Price Index
1950-1960	545	184	262	294
1960-1970	422	176	165	239
1970-1980	1,922	164	1,747	1.171

Those tables are prepared on the basis of the simple equation:

M - 0 = P

Here M is the growth of currency issued by the Central Bank, O is growth of the national income and P is the growth of prices. In column II of the table XVII-2, the currency index, in Column III the index of growth of national income and in Column IV national income price deflators are found. Calculations are made for 10 year intervals. Columns II and III are those factors on the left side of the above equation. Figures obtained when the equation is solved are found in the Column V. If the figures in Columns IV and V are the same, it can be said that the equation, which is a quantity of money equation, reflects the situation, and prices depend on the quantity of money and output changes.

It is evident that in the first and second periods price increases are exactly the same as expected by the crude quantity theory.

On the other hand, if the same calculations are made by money in a wider sense (currency plus all sorts of deposits) (Table XVII-3), we see that there is a wide discrepancy between the actual and expected or predicted inflation. Therefore in the 1950-1970 period inflation could be explained by the increase of currency by the Central Bank.

When we look at the figures for the 1970-1980 period, we notice that the results obtained by this equation are not true either in the case of narrow or wider sense money. Therefore, this suggests that the velocity of circulation of money (V) in narrow money sense was rather stable in 1950 - 1970 but it must have increased and was volatile in the other period, i.e., 1970 -1980. This can be observed in Table XVII-4.

TABLE XVII - 4
INCOME VELOCITY OF MONEY
(Currency Only)

Year	Income Velocity	Year	Income Velocity
1950	10.69	1966	10.50
1951	11.18	1967	10.00
1952	11.51	1968	10.30
1953	11.94	1969	10.95
1954	11.01	1970	10.23
1955	11.50	1971	11.54
1956	11.24	1972	12.72
1957	11.85	1973	13.40
1958	10.50	1974	14.47
1959	11.80	1975	14.30
1960	11.39	1976	14.20
1961	10.65	1977	13.26
1962	11.51	1978	14-45
1963	11.50	1979	15.96
1964	11.05	1980	23.80
1965	10.35		

All this suggests that the key factor of inflation in Turkey in 1950- 1970 period must be the increase of the currency in a narrow sense.

Now let us look at the situation in the 1980-1998 period. Data for that period are found in tables XVII- 5, 6, 7. It must be added that in that period, in addition to M_0, M_1 and M_2 there is M3. Remember that M_0 is currency in circulation M_1 is M_0 plus sight deposits, M_2 is M_1 plus other of TL. denominated deposits and M_3 is M_2 plus foreign currency deposits.

When the table is examined it looks as if none of the definition of money as M0, Ml are able to explain price increases. Prices increased much more than justified by money increase. The worst is M_o.

In the case of M_2 and M_3 there is a much better fit. But this time, although in the previous case, price increases were more than required by the money increase, in this case they were a bit less than justified by money increase.

All those calculations show that velocities based on M_0, M_1, M_2, and M_3 are all unstable in the short and intermediate run..

TABLE XVII-5

MONEY VOLUME AND PRICES

1980 - 1990, 1980 = 100

Type of Money	Money Index 1990 (1980=100)	GNP Index 1990 (1980=100)	GNP Deflator 1990 (1980=100)	Hypothetical Deflator 1990
M_0	5,426	169	4,496	3.211
M_1	4,191	169	4,496	2.480
M_2	8,458	169	4,496	5,004
M_3	16,865	137	1,299 (x)	1,231

(x) 1984-1990

In 1980-1990 period price increases were lower than the hypothetical onces. But in the case of M_2 and M_3 there is a perfect fit between the price increase and the increase of money.

TABLE XVII-6

VARIOUS KINDS OF MONEY AND THEIR INCOME VELOCITY
1990-1998 (Billions of TL)

	M_0	V_0	M_1	V_1	M_2	V_2	M_3	V_3
1990	11.378	34.9	31.399	12.6	71,571	5.55	89,195	4.25
1991	18.546	34.2	47,033	15.1	113.483	5.61	159,453	3.98
1992	30.389	36.3	78,341	14.1	190.736	5.78	306,492	3.6C
1993	51.645	38.6	129.087	15.5	282.442	7.07	473,059	4.22
1994	102,328	38.0	230.847	16.8	630.348	6.17	1.233.358	3.15
1995	189,465	41.5	388,184	20.2	1,256,635	6.27	2.495.183	6.37
1996	319,024	47.2	896.855	16.7	2,944,893	5.08	5.608.502	2.67
1997	610,871	48.1	1,581,210	18.6	5,658,800	4.54	11,144,869	2.63
1998	1,057,863	50.5	2,562.241	20.09	11.423,198	4.68	20,826,990	2.57

Table XVII - 7

INCREASE IN MONEY AND PRICES

1990-1998, 1990=100

The Kind of Money	Increase in Money (Fold)	GNP Increase (Fold)	GNP Deflator (Fold)	Expected Increase in Prices (Fold)
M_0	92.9	1.41	94.7	65.9
M_1	81.1	1.41	94.7	57.5
M_2	159.6	1.41	94.7	113.3
M_3	233.4	1.41	94.7	165.5

M_0	94.7/65.9	= % 1.43
M_1	94.7/57.5	= % 1.65
M_2	94.7/113.3 =	% 0.83
M_3	94.7/165.5 =	% 0.57

It seems that M_2 fares the best.

All these analyses take us to 1998. After 1998 there is a parallelism in the increase of 3 kinds of money as would be seen below. (1998-2006)

The Yearly Increase of Money (%)

M_0	48
M_1	51
M_2	50

In that period the annual increase of prices (a mixt of national income deflators, consumer and wholesale prices) after the deduction of the national income increases was around 43 percent. That means that price increases in this period could be explained by the crude quantity theory of money. What was interesting was the parallelism of increase among various kinds of money, which was quite different in the previous periods.

In 1990-1998 price increases were higher than what the crude quantity theory implies if the increase of M_0 and M_1 are taken as the basis. But if M_2 and M_3 are taken as the basis, price increases are lower from what they should be. The best fit is found between the behavior of M_2 and that of prices.

It is evident that there is a secular increase of V0: it is expected. It must be due to the emergence of several financial instruments which serve to economize the use of money.

The change of M_3 seems to explain price movements in 1980-90 much better. But it is unreliable. It includes foreign exchange denominated deposits. They must be very volatile. Again, what is more important is the nature of foreign exchange denominated deposits. They are like other means of savings such as real estate, gold, stocks and bonds, etc. It is difficult to differentiate their impact from other means of saving; I don't think that they should be lumped together with other forms of money. Actually, in 1990-1998 it looks as if the relationship is cut off between M3 and price increases.

All this amounts to the same conclusion: if the behavior of M3 cannot be predicted, the control of inflation would be very difficult.

After considering all those figures and arguments, it can be concluded that conventional analyses of inflation are not enough to undestand the behavior of general prices in Turkey.

Relative prices must be important in determining the level of general prices. On the other hand, in conventional analyses of inflation that dimension is neglected compleletly. Prior to 1980, the government had a certain amount of power to determine relative prices. As a result, their cost push influence was rather limited. Price movements could be explained by the change of the quantity of money. After 1980,relative prices were under the influence of economic forces. Therefore, the impact of money should be less. Another factor seems to be the use of non-currency money in income payments. As until 1980 almost all income payments were made by currency, its impact on inflation should be higher, and this is the case. But as after 1980 other instruments are used in income payments, the impact of the currency on prices seems to be lessening. Actually nobody seems to have looked into the difference between income payments and non-income payments. This is a very important topic for future research.

Another topic should be the factors determining the velocity of circulation of money and income velocity. The distinction of institutional forces from others would give us a very important clue in the understanding of inflation in Turkey.

§ 4- M. FRY ON FINANCIAL REPRESSION AND THE DYNAMICS OF INFLATION

Financial restriction and repression was an integral part of import substitution policy followed in Turkey in 1930-1980. I have always been against this policy and wrote several books and articles about it and tried to underline various disadvantages of this policy.In those years very few economists,bankers, columnists and politicians used to agree with me. Professor M. Fry came to Turkey to teach in Bogaziçi University (Istanbul) in the 70 s. When he tried to observe what was going on in the financial markets in this country, he was very much upset about what he saw. He wrote several books and articles about financial repression in Turkey and tried to show how this practice was detrimental for the development of this economy.

My critical comments about the repressive policy culminated in my book entitled BANKING IN TURKEY pubished in 1964. Some 10 years after the publication of this book he wrote on the same subjects in this book.Instead of sunmmarizing what I wrote about disadvantages of restrictions on finance, I thought that a summary of Fry would be more pertinent.This was because of the fact that he was better informed of practices in the world and also he was more knowegeable in economics compared to me. Both he and I had a common belief about financial disadvatages of the financial restrictions.

His criticism can be summarized under 9 headings.

1-Financial repression decreases the efficiency of allocation of scarce resources among investments.Firstly, low rates of return for capital decreases the amount of savings.Secondly,as interests are low, this might attract investments to low productivity fields.Thirdly, the size of finanacial system becomes lower relative to nonfinancial economy .All these should retard development.

2-The government sells its debt with low interest;at the beginning inflation gets lower but the cumulative effects would give rise to an increase of inflation.

3-A financial restriction results in segmented markets.Its impact for the operation of the economy has all sorts of detrimental consequences.

4-Falling real money demand after financial repression should create destablizing consequences.

5-The change of interest rates is used to combat against inflation.But this possibility does not exist in repressed financial markets.

6-Repressive financial markets would give rise to degressive tax in the sense that poor people should be more adversely inflicted by this policy in the end.

7-The interest rate regulations in Turkey explicitly prohibit banks from taking compesating balances. However,this is an unenforceable provision,which is evaded by banks and their customers with impunity. Indeed the negative spread between the official loan and deposit rates appear almost as explicit recognition of the fact that loan rate ceilings are unenforceable.

8-As interests are tried to be kept low in this system, this induces capital intensive methods of production and as a result this create unemployment.

Professor Fry examines the dynamics of the inflationary process in Turkey by observing factors inducing the growth of money supply .He also stresses the fact that when a large increase of foreign reserves induces an increase in monetary stock, the effort of the government is not in the direction of the sterilization of it. “Rather than sterilising the effect of higher net foreign assets on money supply,the central bank responded by expanding domestic credit to finance a greater volume of imports of capital equipments and raw materials.Although this reduced rapidly the level of net foreign assets, it sustained the expantionary monetary impulse.The central bank then followed the real bills doctrine toward domestic credit expansion accomadating with a lag in demand pressures generated by the accelerating rise in nominal GNP.

Accelerated monertary growth produced inflation. This,in turn,enlarged the public sector deficit due to the lag in the collection of tax receipts ,erosion of the tax base and price freezes on products of the state economic enterprises.The public sector deficit was financed by further increase in the money supply,thus adding fuel to the inlationary fire.” (Fry 1979, 133-134.)

Another citation from Fry." Turkey’s disequilibrium institutional interest rate system assures that there is always excess demand for institutional credit at the administratively fixed rates of interests.This seems that the nominal quantity of credit is determined solely by supply. Through rediscount and interest ceilings, required reserve and liquidity ratios,the selective credit policy and various informal pressures such as persuading commercial banks to take up unsold government bonds,monetary authorities have had strong influence over the volume and distribution of domestic credit.Furthermore, 50 percent of commercial bank assets are held by the state owned special law banks.These are under the same degree of government control as are the bank assets or the central bank. Therefore, domestic credit expansion is taken here to be determined by by the monetary authorities "ibit 134-135.

CHAPTER XVIII

INTERNATIONAL TRADE

§ 1 - INTRODUCTION

This chapter is a theoretical appreciation of writings relating to international trade in Turkey by Turkish and well known economists in the world. As a traditional economic analysis is used by them, this appreciation is a sort of test of the contemporary economics. In fact, in almost every page of this chapter the same goal is followed. The main theme is an investigation of factors determining exports. As a derivative of that, the writings about the effectiveness of devaluations in promoting exports are viewed by a different way.

§ 2 - CONVENTIONAL WRITINGS ON FACTORS DETERMINING EXPORTS

Factors determining exports in Turkey have been examined for a long time. There were all sorts of arguments around the idea that the elasticity of probable exports was low and as a result, there was not much hope for increasing them. All those arguments pleased leftist economists. They are all referred to and criticized in my previously published books. Along with that, some economists have shown that the idea, i.e., exports consisting of low elasticity goods couldn't be increased, cannot be generalized. In fact, Professor Krueger calculated the export elasticity of some exported goods. She found out that the elasticity for certain goods was not low. (Krueger 1974, pp. 208-211.)

During the post-1980 years, economists (Turkish ones as well) investigated the problem more thoroughly and showed that the outward orientation of the economy had exerted a favorable influence on the increase of exports. They also underlined the importance of high exchange rates and all sorts of other promotionary measures such as credit facilities, exemptions from taxes, etc. for exports. In addition to these the shrinkage of domestic demand, the high demand originating from newly prosperous middle eastern countries (Şenses 1989), etc. have been quite important in the approximately 4 fold increase in exports in a short period of time, 3 or 4 years. Yet, most economists believe that such a dramatic increase in exports was one of the causes of the domestic price increase in Turkey (TUSES - Kazgan 1990). Again, some economists relate the increase in export to the production capacity of those industries which were established during the second generation of the import substitution period.

Several regressions carried out by Turkish economists suggest that the following factors have been instrumental in increasing Turkish exports (Arslan and the Celasun 1993; see Table XVIII-3 and 4). Firstly, the export of agricultural products is related to agricultural production, and, as most exportable products were exported in the pre-1980 period, nothing much should be expected for the increase of agricultural exports. It is also advanced that the possibility of increase lies in industrial goods. Moreover, their conclusions as to the factors influencing exports are exactly the same as what we observe in the literature, namely: the level of production, the level of foreign exchange prices, tax incentives, price levels in the domestic economy and abroad, external demand conditions, and price elasticity of demand for Turkish export goods, etc. (see TUSES - Kazgan 1990, Şenesen 1987, Özmucur 1987). In fact, regressions in Turkey are not different from those existing in the literature. Worth noting is the work of Yotopoulos-Nugent (Yotopoulos-Nugent 1976).Yotopoulos-Nugent research covering 38 countries over the 1949-1967 period included the following variables in their regression equation: increases in domestic income, real exchange rates, changes in the prices of export goods, world demand for export goods, changes in export taxes and, the association with local custom unions. They observed that among them the most important ones were the increase in the national income and real exchange rates. There are, of course, problems in the regression results.

A most interesting and innovating analysis of the huge export increase when the economy turned outward was carried out by Hansen, (see Hansen 1991). Actually, Arslan - Celasun analysis is based on Hansen's original approach to the competitiveness of the Turkish industrial products on world markets.

Hansen brought together the foreign exchange devaluation and the fall in real wages after 1980 to determine the competitiveness of the Turkish industry (See Table XVIII-6-7).

The factors determining imports should also be differentiated for the pre-and post-1980 periods. There are no systematical investigations relating to factors determining imports in the pre-1980 period. One generally shared opinion is as follows: commodities should be imported somehow, whatever their prices are; their prices will have a negligible effect on demand. In fact, the most important factor, however, was the availability of foreign exchange.

When the availability of foreign exchange greatly increased after 1980, it is discovered that import demand had an economic dimension. According to one research work (Arin, 1990) factors determining import demand are as follows: national income, income distribution, the price differentials between the domestic economy and foreign economies, utilization of existing production facilities, the necessity of imports and foreign exchange availability. After the calculation of the regression equations, Arin shows that the elasticity of imports to foreign exchange prices does not exist. (Isn't hard to believe?)

APPENDICE I TO SECTION 2 : ARSLAN AND CELASUN ON FACTORS DETERMINING EXPORTS

A very good analysis of factors determining exports in Turkey is carried out by Arslan and Celasun, 1995. Now let us report on their findings. **(Extracts from Arslan - Celasun article).**

Export performance and cost competitiveness

Recent econometric studies by Arslan and van Wijnbergen (1990) and Uygur (1992) provide strong evidence on the prominent role of real exchange rate policy in Turkey's post-1980 export expansion. In this chapter we will use econometric techniques to throw more light on cost competitiveness as an explanatory factor in export performance.

Before we discuss our regression results, we examine the findings of a constant-market-share analysis (CMSA) undertaken by the OECD (1992) as shown in Table XVIII-3. The OECD analysis attributes the differential growth of Turkish and world exports to a regional composition effect, a product mix effect as a residual, which presumably reflects changes in competitiveness. As expected, the findings show that Turkish exports in 1980-5 was achieved in an inhospitable world trade environment, but benefited quite significantly from changes in regional composition and most prominently from gains in competitiveness. From 1985 to 1987 accelerated world demand coupled with the continuing positive residual effect became the major pull factors. From 1987 to 1990 Turkish export growth lagged world export growth concurrently with losses in Turkish competitiveness as borne out by the price data given in panel B in Table XVIII-3.

TABLE XVIII - 3
EXPORT PERFORMANCE AND WAGE-PRICE MOVEMENTS,TURKEY

	1981-2 / 1979-80	1984-5 / 1982-3	1987-8 / 1985-6	1988-90 / 1987-8
A Constant market share analysis				
Growth of Turkish exports (%)	42.1	14.7	19.1	6.1
Growth of world exports	0.7	3.9	15.8	10.9
Difference	41.6	11.2	3.8	-5.3
Regional composition effect	9.2	-3.9	-3.6	0.7
Product mix effect	-0.3	-0.6	-0.5	-1.3
Residual	34.9	15.1	7.6	-4.8
	1988	**1989**	**1990**	**1991**
B Prices				
1 Nominal				
Export prices (TL)	70	50	34	57
Wholesale prices	70	64	52	57
Unit labour cost (TL)	57	106	71	87
2 Real exchange rate (appreciation -)	5	-7	-14	3
3 Relative cost position of Turkish labour[a]	-4	43	44	38

[a] Real unit labour cost in terms of trade partners' currencies

Sources: OECD 1992 for Panel A and B.l data; authors' calculations for Panel B.2 and B.3 estimates

To focus on the issue of international competitiveness, we have calculated a new time series for real (productivity-adjusted) unit cost of Turkish manufacturing labour expressed in major trading partners' currencies; this series was inspired by Hansen (1991: 415-19). By extending the database of Arslan and van Wijnbergen (1990) to the year 1990, regression estimates (using annual data) are obtained for Turkish exports to the Middle East oil-exporting countries (RXO) and to the rest of the world (RXDC), which are reported in Table XVIII-4.

The regression results confirm the significant price responsiveness of Turkish exports in both trading regions. They are also significantly

TABLE XVIII - 4
REGRESSION ESTIMATES FOR TURKISH EXPORTS, 1975-90
(T-VALUES IN PARENTHESES) COEFFICIENT

A Dependent variable: LRXDC				
1	Constant	-13.17(-5.28)	Adj.R**2	0.89
	LRELP	-1.53C-2.85)	D-W	1.09
	LDCRG	3.10(14.13)	SEE	0.21
2	Constant	-5.09(-3.13)	Adj.R**2	0.90
	LRW	-0.49(-3.11)	D-W	1.37
	LDCRG	3.37(12.08)	SEE	0.21
3	Constant	2.01(0.93)	Adj.R**2	0.95
	LREXR	-1.04(-5.27)	D-W	1.70
	LDCRG	2.36(7.48)	SEE	0.14
4	Constant	-1.79(1.61)	Adj.R**2	0.90
	LRW	-0.63(-3.99)	D-W	1.41
	LDCM	2.02(13.04)	SEE	0.20
5	Constant	7.08(5.06)	Adj.R**2	0.90
	LREXR	-1.15(-6.08)	D-W	1.72
	LDCM	1.37(8.92)	SEE	0.13
B Dependent variable: LRXO				
6	Constant	12.00(3.89)	Adj.R**2	0.95
	LREXR	-4.54(-18.45)	D-W	1.36
	LORM	2.17(4.90)	SEE	0.27

Key:

LRXDC = Log of real exports to countries other than Middle East oil-exporting countries

LRELP = Log of relative prices (Turkish export prices over nine developed country import prices)

LDCRG = Log of nine developed country real GDP growth
LRW = Log of real unit cost of labour in trade partners' currencies
LREXR = Log of real exchange rate (depreciation down)
LDCM = Log of nine developed country real import growth
LRXO = Log of real exports to Middle East oil-exporting countries
LORM = Log of real imports of Middle East oil-exporting countries
Source: *Based on extended database of Arslan and van Wijnbergen 1990*

elastic to real income (or import) growth in both areas. The analysis verifies the very favourable impact of the import explosion in the oil-exporting countries in the early 1980s in the aftermath of the 1979 oil-price shock, especially in the context of flat demand in OECD countries as was also shown by the CMSA estimates.

These regression estimates underline the central role of real exchange rates in Turkey's export performance in the 1980s. The findings also strongly support our contention that wage competitiveness has been a crucial factor in Turkey's exporting process as it explains, together with the OECD income effect, about 90 percent of the variations in the 1976-90 sample period.

In these regressions, we have not been able to incorporate export subsidy variables because of data limitations for the pre- 1980 period. However, Uygur's (1992) study provides helpful evidence on the subsidy effects based on regressions using quarterly data for more recent periods. Uygur reports that direct export incentives had a moderately significant impact in the earlier phase of the export drive, but their influence tended to disappear in the latter part of the 1980s.

The present analysis provides additional support to the available cross-country evidence that an appropriate exchange rate is an essential ingredient of 'successful' industrial exporting (Helleiner 1994). As Helleiner aptly emphasizes, the exchange rate is basically a macroeconomic policy instrument, and should preferably not be subsumed under the heading of trade policy. (Strictly, trade policy is concerned with the structure of external incentives namely import tariffs and restrictions, and export subsidies.) In the Turkish context, we have shown that real wage reduction and real currency depreciation moved in tandem to ensure the competitiveness of Turkish exports in the 1980s.

Appendice II to Section 2: B. Hansen's Original Research

AN INTERESTING EXPLANATION OF THE UPSURGE OF EXPORTS AFTER 1980

It is shown that after Turkey turned outward in 1980 an unbelievable upsurge of exports occurred. There are various explanations of this very important development. Professor Bent Hansen, who wrote a very comprehensive and important book on the recent history of the Turkish economy, (Hansen 1991), has an original approach to explain it.

Before examining the figures, let me throw a blick on his conclusion. He shows that, along with others, the change is not related to a transformation in the structure of the economy. Rather, it is an end result of a change in the structure of the prices and wages. This change, by increasing competitive power of the Turkish endustry, has given rise to the upsurge of exports.

Professor Hansen starts with the an examination of the distribution of exports among countries. Table XVIII-5 shows it.

The Table is very indicative. Exports both to developed and devoloping countries increased very fast; but it seems that export increases in developing countries is much faster. Exports to developing countries in constant prices increased by 55.3 percent in 1980-1984; whereas the ratio to developed countries is 25.1 percent. Figures relating to export volumes are shown in Table XVIII-5.

Here two fundamental factors leading to it must be underwritten. The first is a high devaluation, i.e., approximatively 50 percent. The second factor is the increase of petroleum prices which were beneficial for some developing countries.

TABLE XVIII - 5

THE VALUE OF EXPORTS AND ITS DISTRIBUTION AMONG SEVERAL COUNTRIES

(The Rate of Increase)

Year	Developing Count. 1980 ConstantPrices	Developed Coun.	All Countries
1962-70	12.1	3.8	5.2
1970-80	14.2	-1.4	2.2
1980-84	55.3	25.1	31.5

The Proportion of the Total Increase

%

	(Developing)	(Developed)
1962	4.8	94.3
1975	15.9	76.8
1980	24.1	58.9
1984	47.0	48.2

Based on Hansen (1991) Table: XII-4

Hansen goes further by investigating the share of increase of the volume of sales and prices. A summary can be made by drawing upon various tables depicted by Hansen. (See Tables XII-5 and 6; here Tables XVIII-6-7)

It is quite clear that exports to developing countries consisted of goods the prices of which did not increase much; yet, the increase of volume was much more significant. On the other hand, the situation for developed countries was just contrary. Then he investigates the causes of this observation. Here is his conclusion:

At the beginning period profit margins for goods which were exported to developing countries were very high; Turkish exporters preferred to decrease them in order to increase exports. Another reason might be the sale of lower quality goods to developing countries, whereas higher quality goods might have been sold to developed countries.

The most interesting analysis of Hansen is perhaps his emphasis of low wages in the explanation of exports.

In 1965-1977 the productivity of labor increased annually by 4.7 percent, whereas the increase in real wages were 6.8 percent. This development greatly reduced the competitiveness of the Turkish industry. But in 1977-84 productivity increased annualy by 2.3 but real wages decreased annualy by 10.4 percent. This made competitiveness stronger. In addition, as real foreign exchange prices increased in this period, it made it stronger still. When those two factors are brought together the Table XVIII-7 could be compiled. It is apparent that the relative cost position of Turkish manufacturing went down to 49.9 in 1984 while it was 133 in 1979.

TABLE XVIII-6

PRICE AND VOLUME OF EXPORTS TO DEVELOPING COUNTRIES RELATIVE TO EXPORTS TO DEVELOPED COUNTRIES BY COMMODITY GROUP AND REGION, 1970 AND 1984

(annually chained Fisher indexes)

	By commodity group						By regions		
								Oil exporters	
Category	Food and food products	Agricultural raw materials	Minerals and metals	Semi-manufactures	Finished manufactures	Total	Middle East	With capital surplus[a]	Other
Price									
1970	100	100	100	100	100	100	100	100	100
1984	64	89	48	38	40	58	56	70	51
Volume									
1970	100	100	100	100	100	100	100	100	100
1984	169	256	10,230	1,094	205	1,040	1,165	2,817	2,507

Does not include mineral fuels and commodities, not elsewhere stated.
a. United Arab Emirates, Libya, Kuwait, Saudi Arabia, and Brunei.
Source: Hansen, Table 12.8

TABLE XVIII-7

COMPETITIVENES OF MANUFACTURING INDUSTRY, 1962-84

Year	GDP[a] per unit of labor (thousands of lira)[a]	Nominal wages (lira per day)[b]	Real wages in terms of GDP[a] (1965=100)	Nominal wage costs per unit of GDP[a] (1965=100)	NEER units of trade partners' currency per lira[c] (1980=100)	Wage costs Per unit of GDP[a] in trade partners' currencies (1965=100)	Trade partners' WPI (1965=100)	Relative cost position of Turkish manufacturing (1965=100)	Wage bill (percent of GDP)[d]
1962	10.1	20.0	92.7	106.7	908.5	105.6	94.2	112.1	38.5
1963	11.3	18.7	83.9	88.7	902.0	87.1	95.2	91.5	32.5
1964	12.0	24.7	109.6	110.5	914.9	110.1	98.0	112.4	36.2
1965	12.9	24.0	100.0	100.0	918.3	100.0	100.0	100.0	36.8
1966	14.1	27.1	107.4	103.4	934.7	105.2	102.7	102.4	36.2
1967	14.7	30.5	117.4	111.2	975.7	118.8	104.4	113.8	38.0
1968	15.6	33.3	126.1	114.4	1,020.8	127.1	107.2	118.6	37.4
1969	16.7	n.a.	n.a.	n.a.	1,023.7	n.a.	111.9	n.a.	n.a.
1970	16.3	44.1	151.3	145.1	847.4	133.9	122.5	109.3	35.9
1971	16.9	54.5	153.6	173.2	594.7	112.3	123.8	90.7	34.9
1972	17.2	58.1	147.8	181.0	598.7	96.4	127.7	75.5	35.1
1973	18.4	63.7	136.3	185.5	576.2	116.4	147.9	78.7	34.4
1974	19.1	86.6	138.5	243.1	585.2	154.9	184.2	84.1	31.9
1975	20.0	114.6	164.3	306.7	569.7	190.3	196.9	96.7	37.5
1976	21.2	138.2	177.0	349.6	538.0	204.8	208.1	98.4	38.4
1977	22.3	205.4	212.9	493.9	466.3	250.8	221.1	113.4	44.7
1978	22.9	312.3	187.5	732.6	309.3	246.8	229.9	107.4	40.8
1979	22.2	537.8	170.6	1,299.1	237.9	336.6	253.1	133.0	38.4
1980	21.3	888.4	127.5	2,234.5	100.0	243.3	288.4	84.4	30.7
1981	22.5	1,276.5	132.0	3,039.6	77.1	255.3	317.5	80.4	29.6
1982	23.2	1,587.8	125.1	3,676.4	57.9	231.9	341.0	68.0	29.7
1983	24.3	2,083.4	124.9	4,649.3	46.8	237.2	366.2	64.8	24.3
1984	26.1	2,724.3	110.6	5,608.1	32.7	199.8	400.8	49.9	20.2

In this table GDP means GDP at factor cost in manufacturing.
n.a. = Not available.
a. Manufacturing, at 1968 factor cost.
b. Manufacturing, not including pension and social security contributions.
c. Nominal effective exchange rate = NEER.
d. Manufacturing, at current factor cost.
Source: Hansen, Table, XII-16

§ 3- UNCONVENTIONAL COMMENTS ON WRITINGS ABOUT FACTORS DETERMINING EXPORTS

A good sample of writings about factors determining exports in Turkey are summarized above; my comments about them are presented below.

1- All regressions between exports and factors supposedly determining them cover both the pre-and post -1980 periods. I have strong objections to that procedure. The impacts of all variables, which affect exports, in regression equations in those different periods are different. Firstly let me remind that the most strategic variable is, of course, real exchange rates. In pre-1980 period the significant problem was the overswollen prices in nonagricultural sectors.. As long as they were so high the change in real exchange rates would not be efficient; whereas in post 1980 period as nonagricultural prices were more in line with the realities of the country, real exchange rates would be efficient in promoting exports. Then how could we lump together observations in those two periods?

In addition, in post-1980 years the impact of increases of real exchange rates on exports (real rate calculated by deflating nominal rates by relative inflation at home and abroad) was increased by a relative fall of labor intensive goods prices vis-a-vis capital-skill-natural resources-import intensive goods, whereas that factor did not exist before 1980, as a result, the impacts of changes of real exchange rates on imports were not so noticeably felt.

2- According to my unconventional approach to measuring income over time, the main factor determining the level of exports is the relative prices of goods in Turkey and in its trade partners. This is simply commonsense, and all scientific and econometric work indicates it. Can we satisfy ourselves with that? Definitely not. Let me elaborate upon that point.

The relationship between the exchange rate and the export level is rather equivocal. If a regression between exports and real exchange rates is made, a very important dimension would be lost from sight. In fact, when in order to find the real exchange rate the nominal rate is deflated by the change in general prices, the impact of relative prices of labor intensive and nonlabor intensive goods on exports would not be distinguished, whereas this is very important. On the other hand, if an attempt is made to establish a relationship between wage levels in terms of foreign currency and export increase, the relative impact of the wage levels and the change of the foreign exchange cannot be distinguished again.

If labor price and general price changes are the same, the country would not export less competitive goods but the terms of trade would have to deteriorate. In that case the exports of competitive goods would increase, but at what cost?

A methodology should be determined to separate the impact of foreign exchange from that of lower labor prices.

The relative prices of exported goods in Turkey and the prices of those goods abroad (in foreign money) are determined by their absolute prices in TL and the exchange rate. But nobody has perceived the meaning that there is a relationship between absolute prices and the exchange rates. It is evident that if absolute prices remain the same but the exchange rate changes, the relative prices of the Turkish export goods will have to change. But as the mechanism of the relationship between export goods prices and the level of the exchange rate is not understood, we cannot decompose the factors giving rise to export. This is quite evident in the approaches put forward by many economists.

To put it in a nut shell, we cannot lump together the level of the exchange rate and absolute prices. It is shown that other things being the same, if we change the exchange rate, absolute prices will change and/or if we change absolute prices, the exchange rate will change. The end result may be the switch of exports from the production of commodities having less to more competitive advantages, or vice versa. Suppose we increase the exchange rate. In that case, goods having less competitive advantages will become exportable but the change in the exchange rates may give rise to a change in absolute prices. Everything depends on goods, the prices of which will have to change. If the relative prices of the production factors used in the production of the previously competitive goods decreases, it is not necessary that exports should switch to less competitive goods. If, on the other hand, the prices of factors of production previously used in the production of the less competitive goods decreases, then exports will have to switch to the production of less competitive goods.

The gist of the argument is that the approach which reflects the present state of the literature doesn't cover this important distinction. It is important because by using the methodology of the literature we would not understand the real factors behind the increasing exports.

3- Some economists emphasized the cross impact of increasing real exchange rates and the fall of wages after 1980 but they did not attempt to separate the contribution of each. That relationship would lead to a tradeoff between real wages and real exchange rate. If real wages are reduced more, less increase in real exchange rate would be needed (vice versa) to promote exports. It is not difficult to see the tradeoff. But nothing was done to quantify it and to find out its consequences.What is more important is the impact of nonagricultural sectors to exports.The impact of exchange rates could not be isolated from that fact.In other words,if the share of nonagricultural sectors did not increase and if they were not opened to exports,the impact of the decrease of labor prices along with the increase in real foreign exchange rate would not be strong as we observe.

4- The most interesting analysis is perhaps the emphasis of low wages in the explanation of exports.

In 1965-1977 the productivity of labor increased annually by 4.7 percent, whereas the increase in real wages were 6.8 percent. This development greatly reduced the competitiveness of the Turkish industry. But in 1977-84 productivity increased annually by 2.3 percent but real wages decreased annually by 10.4 percent. This made competitiveness stronger. In addition, as real foreign exchange prices increased in this period, it made it stronger still. When those two factors are brought together it is apparent that the relative cost position of Turkish manufacturing went down to 49.9 in 1984 while it was 133 in 1979.

I have a strong objection to that conclusion. Throughout this book I tried to show that the productivity increase in pre -and post- 1980 years should not be compared. Those in pre-1980 years are related to higher relative prices of labor intensive goods, whereas those in post -1980 years are related to more genuine factors. As a result, the impact of those productivity increases should not be considered the same.

5- A very important observation relating to Turkey reveals the importance of my contention. The yearly increase of exports in 1979 to 2000 is 12 percent in terms of dollars. Yet the average share of exports to national income was around 13 percent (all in dollars) until 2002, and there were very little fluctuations around that figure. We know that in that period the growth rate of national income in terms of constant TL is around 4 percent. How can we bring together those two conflicting ratios? Is it only the calculation of the rate of increase of exports in nominal terms (mominal dollars) but that of growth of national income in real terms? One alternative in our case is to calculate the level of national income in terms of dollars as higher. This would mean that there is either an undervaluation in exchange rates or a drastic change in relative prices. If so, this problem should be looked into very carefully.

6- Another topic analyzed is the investigation of the impact of devaluations in two periods (pre -and post- 1980). In fact, all sorts of tools of the literature relating to the analysis of devaluations are used in those two periods. In the first subperiod the main problem was related to rents earned in the nonagricultural sectors of the economy. In that case the tools of the traditional analysis could not be used. But in the second subperiod the main problem is the possibility of decreasing relative prices of labor intensive commodities. If so, different analyses should be sought.

§ 4 - ARGUMENTS AGAINST MEMBERSHIP TO THE EU

Economists on the left have always been against membership to the EU. I shall try to summarize their arguments. Before Turkey turned outward, opponents of the EU had three main arguments. 1- The level of national incomes in Turkey and Common Market countries were very different. As that of Turkey was very low, the opponents were trying to show that high income countries would exploit the low income country. 2- As after the association, more foreign capital would be invested in Turkey, this would be against the interest of Turkey. According to them, foreigners would invest in fields which would not be of a nature to improve techniques in the country. 3- After the membership, the liberalization of the economy would give rise to high inflation.

Here is a short list of recent arguments against membership.

1- The reason why Turkey was accepted as an associate member to Common Market in the early 1960 s was to strengthen it against Russia which was a danger during the cold war years. As that is over now, European countries are not enthusiastic to make Turkey a full member.

2- Although Turkey was made a member of the Custom Union in 1995, there was no sign to accept it as a full member in the agreement, whereas a custom union has always, historically, been a first step in the political union. While all previously participating countries were granted all sorts of financial aid, Turkey has not: in this sense Turkey's situation is unique.

3- By being a member of the Customs Union, Turkey gave away its privilege of adopting an independent international trade policy. It is in a position to adopt the common custom union tariff. And this is without the privilege of enjoying several advantages of being a full member of the Community. That loss of independence is especially important in carrying out economic relations with Russia and its associate countries. As a result of that limitation, Turkey cannot import raw materials necessary for its industry with zero custom duty. Again, as the EU has given all sorts concessions to various countries, Turkey is in a position to do the same.

4- Turkey is not represented in political institutions of the EU. Yet, it has to conform with all sorts of rules, regulations and policies of the EU.

5- In the case of agricultural commodities, Turkey's position has been weakened after the Custom Union. Although agriculture is not included in custom union agreement, it is believed that agricultural products would enter Turkey easily with low duties. On the other hand, as they receive all sorts of subsidies in the EU countries, the competition of Turkish agriculture would be very difficult. That would be quite detrimental to Turkish agriculture; actually it has been the case.

6- All sorts of financial aid previewed in the agreement is vetoed by Greece. But as Turkey is nowhere in the decision mechanism, the aid is not received.

After reviewing all those disadvantages, let us ask the question: would it be beneficial for Turkey to be a member? As I am in favor of a liberal economy my answer is in the positive. Advantages of more trade are well known. Moreover, the discipline to the economy is the most important aspect of the membership. Access to capital and especially to advanced technology is very important for Turkey.

But I must make it clear that my preference for the coming years is not for a full membership but to strengthen the custom union with EU. As wages are very low in Turkey compared to EU countries, they cannot be adjusted by a flow out of workers to those countries. Suppose several million workers found employment in those countries. And suppose as a result of diminishing supply of workers in Turkey, wages increased in this country. This would induce high imports but as Turkish exports are labor intensive goods (and they could not be made technology intensive ones in a short time) they would not increase. And this would create problems in Turkey. The flow of Turkish workers would create a problem for EU countries: everybody knows it; but my argument is more important than that. It is apparent.

§ 5 - ARGUMENTS AGAINST THE FAVORABLE IMPACTS OF EXCHANGE RATES ON EXPORTS

It is shown above that according to several investigations by various economists, one of the factors determining exports in Turkey was relative prices of commodities in Turkey and abroad, in other terms real exchange rates, whereas there has been an adverse attitude toward devaluations by which exchange rates were changed. Below there are some arguments put forward to show why devaluations are not efficient. Those argument are summarily listed below. (They are expressed under three headings.)

1- All arguments based on elasticity calculations are put forward to show that devaluations are inefficient in Turkey. This will be taken up later; yet, it is stressed in this book that the future of exports are related mainly to relative prices and a better use of the abundant production factors., i.e., labor. In turn, at this stage this depends on the price of labor. The elasticity of the exported goods in the pre-1980 era may be low; but this is irrelevant. Actually, most of the exported goods were natural resource intensive goods, the production of which could not be increased anyway. Therefore, the actual increase should be expected in the export of other goods.

2- An illogical argument about the effect of low elasticity of Turkish export commodities put forward by an extreme leftist Turkish economist is summarized below.

Professor Kazgan (1988) has referred to a World Bank calculations relating to the income elasticity of imported goods in Turkey. The figures are as follows:

Period	Income elasticity of imported goods
1965 - 70	1.7
1970 - 75	1.8
1975 - 80	1.3
1984 - 87	2.5

She then refers to domestic income elasticity figures for industrial goods probably to be exported. These figures are 1.1 for textile and leather products and 1.4 for glass and ceramics. From these figures, generalizations are made for all export goods. Let us ignore the illogical nature of this procedure. The economist in question then makes a number of plausible assumptions concerning the income increase in Turkey (5 percent per annum) and in the world (4 percent per annum). She deduces (believe it or not) that as a result of this increase of income in Turkey imports will rise by 12.5 percent annually (0.05 multiplied by 2.5, the income elasticity of imported goods). This may be plausible, but what about the increase of exports? Here, the argument (believe it or not) is as follows: If income increases by 4 percent worldwide, Turkish exports would rise by 4.8 percent, annually again (4 percent multiplied by 1.2 percent, income elasticity of Turkish exports). If we compare export and import increases, we observe that imports will rise by 12.5 percent but exports only by 4.7 percent. Given these figures the economy is doomed to failure. That argument will be criticized in Section 8 below.

3- There are other arguments to show that nothing much could be achieved by manipulating the exchange rate; therefore the level of exchange rates would be ineffective to promote exports. Here are some of them; those arguments are put forward in the pre-1980 years (see UATE pp. 291-302).

It must be made clear that my views about devaluation in the 1970's were rather crude and naive; yet they were not wrong.

Inconclusive Arguments Against Devaluation (Extracts From UATE)

There has always been a misbelief against devaluation of currency as a balancing instrument of foreign trade deficits in Turkey. The source of this misbelief comes from a static evaluation of the Turkish situation. Attention is partly drawn to the fact that there was not any commodity stocks to be exported if devaluation were made, and partly to the supply and demand inelasticity of existing export goods. This point was studied when export pessimism was examined. It was shown that the belief about export pessimism in Turkey is unfounded to a great extent.

In this section other inconclusive arguments advanced against devaluation are examined. (Extracts from UATE.) (All those arguments will be criticized in Section 8 below)

a) There is a widespread opinion in Turkey that devaluation would cause important increases in the prices of goods and services. This contention is based on the price increases of imported inputs of industry and on the relationship of prices to each other, i.e., if some prices increase, the others follow suit. Each contention is worth studying carefully.

It can be shown that the proportion of the cost of imported inputs (priced by official rate of exchange) in the selling price of many goods is very low. On the other hand, imported goods purchased directly by consumers are very limited, and the market price has little relation to the cost of importing due to import restrictions. Petroleum products are excepted, but even in petroleum products prices the relation between the prices paid by consumers and the import price of petroleum products is loose because of variable taxes levied by the government.

The second contention with respect to the parallel movements of prices is not true to a great extent and it can be shown that general price level is determined by the issue of currency in Turkey.

It should also be pointed out that the effect of past devaluations on the price level has been very limited and the high price increases occurred not after devaluations, but before. In fact, past devaluations exerted a stabilizing effect on prices.

b) Many politician-administrators and economists claim that Turkey should import a certain amount of goods with no regard to the price of currency, and that very high import prices are not a factor acting in the direction of decreasing imports. It should be pointed out that this argument is not connected with the low elasticity of imports. The point that is stressed by this argument is the import needs of Turkey as a developing country. If the country is determined to develop, it should import a certain amount of commodities.

It is easy to see that this argument is inconclusive. The mere desire to import more does not mean very much if the country does not find means of financing its imports.

c) In Turkey there is a strong belief that devaluations are recommanded by interest groups and speculators; it is advanced that these groups will draw high profits from devaluations, and poor sections of the country will lose from an eventual devaluation. The argument should be completely reversed. If a devaluation is made, exports prices will certainly increase, and, as a great proportion of export commodities are produced by peasants, i.e., the poorest section of the population in the country, their income will increase. But, it is advanced that if export prices increase, only intermediaries and capitalists will profit from that, not the peasants themselves. This contention does not seem to be true in view of the fact that either a great proportion of agricultural exports is handled by the government or the price paid to farmers is regulated by the government. On the other hand, a probable devaluation would decrease rents earned in the country by industrialists and importers by pricing imported goods much above their costs. A devaluation definitly decreases such rents.

d) Another argument against devaluation is the fact that a devaluation is a temporary measure, and after sometime a new devaluation will have to be made; if so, the argument goes, instead of a devaluation other measures should be taken up in order to improve the balance of payments. If devaluations after the Second World War are considered, one may conclude that this contention is right. After each devaluation the balance of payments situation improved somewhat, and then deteriorated again, and the need of another devaluation was felt. But this argument is connected with an inflationary and import substitution policy followed in Turkey rather than devaluations themselves. Why should we blame the previous devaluation for the present one?

If inflation did not occur and if an import substitution policy was not followed and if the productivity difference between agriculture and nonagricultural sectors did not remain as before, the need for a new devaluation would not perhaps be felt. Moreover, economists disfavoring devaluations do not offer any arguments which can be used to show that with an overvalued currency such as the Turkish currency, payment problems of the country would be solved.

e) Some economists, maintaining that a devaluation is not needed, mention the fact that there is no great difference between official exchange rates and free market rates in the mid-70 s. According to them, if equilibrium rates of Turkish currency were much less in terms of foreign currency, the free market rate of the currency would also be much less than the official rate; in fact, it is not. This argument is inconclusive, like others.

In 1958 the free market rate of the currency was over 9 TL to a dollar, while the official rate was 2.80. At that time invisible earnings were very low. But in the 70 s invisible earnings were very high because of workers' remittances. In such a case, if a great proportion of imports are paid for by government allocated foreign exchange and if workers' remittances are very high compared to imports for which official foreign currency is needed, there is no reason why official and free market rates should be much different from each other, and the difference does not show in any way the degree of devaluation needed.

f) Economists arguing against devaluation in the mid-70's pointed out the fact that the spectacular increase in the 1974 and 1975 imports were caused by fourfold increases in petroleum prices and the ensuing price increases in Turkey's trade partners. It is argued that if the great excess of imports over exports is caused by import prices, the efficiency of a devaluation in bringing imports and exports into balance is very limited.

If this argument is closely examined it will be seen that the influence of import price increases in creating an excess was very limited. The price increases of export commodities were not much less than those of imported commodities. The deterioration of terms of trade can explain only a small proportion of the great excess. In 1976, the increase of imports was at a rate equal to only 8.7 percent. The rate of increase seems to be decreasing. But, if part of the transfer orders waiting are added to the 1976 figures, import demand can be calculated to be some 17-18 percent heigher than 1975 imports. Still much less than 1974 and 1975 increases.

A fundamental criticism can be directed at this kind of reasoning. The demand for imports cannot be judged simply by actual import figures because of various import controls and restrictions. To some extent, import levels are determined by the import finance available in the country. The estimates based on historical import trends do not mean very much. What is important in Turkey is the factors which cause steady import increases. Among them are the swelling of incomes having high import propensity and the establishing of an industry based on imported inputs.

Conclusion as to the Devaluation

The level of Turkish currency with respect to foreign currencies should not be thought of as a price equilibrating balance of payments. If the reasoning all through this book is true, the level has a close connection with the level of national income: national income growth would be high or low when the exchange rate is fixed at one level or another. The kind of growth, which has occurred in Turkey, has been closely related to the level of foreign exchange rates. Rents earned in that period could not have been earned if the level of foreign exchange had been higher than the levels which have prevailed in the past.

§ 6 - THE NEGATION OF IRRELEVANT ARGUMENTS

1- The expectation of Professor Kazgan is negated by facts. Let us look at Kazgan's figures seriously.

According to her expectations, exports would have been $ 27.2 billion and imports $ 117 billion; whereas they were $ 85 and $ 137 (billion) by 2006, respectively. Those figures are calculated by the relative expected increase of exports and imports by Professor Kazgan. It means that Professor Kazgan tried to exaggerate the impact of income elasticities in order to belittle the operation of market forces.

The trick here is to take the domestic income elasticity and the demand elasticity of exported goods as the same. But as first year economics students know, the sale potential of an export good depends on income elasticity, price elasticity and its share of world exports.

If the share is small (say less than 10 percent) and the degree of differentiation is not too great (which applies to almost all future Turkish exports), a small price decrease would give rise to a huge sale increase. If Turkey maintains the same price for exported goods, it is quite natural that exports will scarcely increase. But this is a continuation of the import substitution policy. Once the country switches to an outward oriented policy, the price of exported goods must fall. If so, the argument becomes more than illogical. In fact at beginning years of the century exports became $ 85 billion, much higher than the Kazgan figure.

2- Negation of Other Arguments

Although those arguments were commented upon above (in UATE), a few notes could be added:

a- The inexistance of commodities for export arguments were true to a certain extent in pre-1980 years simply because all exports consisted of agricultural products; and not only could their production not be increased, but their world demand was also limited, whereas in post-1980, Turkey could export various labor intensive commodities originating from nonagricultural sectors, which did not exist in pre-1980 years.

b- The idea that after an increase in exchange rates, prices will also increase is a false perception. Everything would depend on the monetary and fiscal policies of the government. If the government is willing to keep relative prices the same because of political reasons and /or ignorance, inflation would follow devaluations. Again, if we stick to import substitution policy, it is quite natural that all prices would increase uniformly after a devaluation. The problem is to perceive what was going on and to take measure to decrease labor prices. If so, that argument would be irrelevant.

c- The argument as to the impossibility of reducing imports is irrelevant. Goods and services can be imported if the country has necessary funds to finance them. If the operation of the economy requires a greater amount of imported goods (more than its capability), this means that there is a structural disequilibrium, which should be corrected.

d- The idea that devaluations are desired by interest groups has no scientific content; therefore it is not worth commenting on.

e- The idea that devaluations would have temporary consequences is based on the view that the price of less competitive goods could not be made lower after devaluations. If so, it can be concluded that there is a mismanagement and /or a structural disequilibrium which should be corrected.

f- The balance of payments problems in Turkey in the 1970 s is attributed to high petroleum prices. This can be partially true. But the main problem is somewhere else as explained throughout this book.

g- It is evident that if money is devalued, the external debt of the country would increase. But I think that this is a short term impact and it would be corrected after the increase in exports and the growth of the economy.

h- It is true that lower exchange rates are a sort of subsidy for import intensive investments. But that could be sustained when the industry was protected. Again, like all subsidies, they should be financed anyway. If they are not, this would give rise to difficult problems.

§ 7 - THE EXPLOSION OF EXPORTS AND IMPORTS IN RECENT YEARS

The increase of exports in the last 4 years has been phenemonal. In the 1994-2000 period the yearly increase of exports (in dollars) was around 8 percent. But that has been 20-21 percent after 2000. In 1984-2000 the share of exports in GNP was 14 percent, except for a few years. In a way it was stabilized around that figure. But a phenemonal upswing has taken place since 2000. It went up over 20 percent. What was the reason and would that high figure continue?

I would like to explain the factors giving rise to the upswing,

1 - In the first year of the upswing, there was some 30 percent depreciation of the currency.

2 - As a result of high depreciation of the currency, dollar figures of national income decreased.

3 - Those two facts gave rise to an increase in the shares of exports to GNP.

4 - Although in terms of the calculation made by means of general prices, the real value of the currency was restored to its previous level, this was not so when it was calculated in terms of real wages. As they got lower after the depreciation, the real value of the currency was lower compared to its value in 2000.

5 - The value of Dollar vis-a-vis Euro got lower; this could be one of the reason for a proportion of the increase in exports.

6 - Long years of experience and the decrease of domestic demand must have been effective in the increase in exports.

7- It is advanced that one of the reasons why exports increased so fast after 2003 was the rapid increase of productivity in Turkey.According to an estimate, while the increase of wages was 8.5 percent,the increase of productivity was 21 percent in 2003-2006.

8- The increase of the cost of energy was less than what it was in the world in 2003-2006.

9- As the Turkish currency was appreciated in this period the liability (foreign debts) of the private sector decreased.

10- The increase of the share of low priced import goods in exports was shown as an important factor in the increase of exports.

11- The price of exported goods increased in this period.

12- The income increase of the EU countries is shown as another factor.(See Kumcu 2007.)

When the future trend of exports is considered, I think that an export volume of some 18-19 percent of national income could be sustained.

The present problem is the very high current account deficit. If very high foreign investments do not occur in the recent future, it seems to give rise to serious problems. A part of the problem is related to the way of covering a higher balance of payment deficits. The impact of huge invisible revenue, such as tourism income, workers' remittances, hot money and the money earned by narcotics transit is of the sort factor giving rise to national income increases without exerting the same influence for the future net foreign cash flow.

§ 8- THE DISCUSSIONS OF CURRENT ACCOUNT DEFICITS

The ever existing current account deficits in 2004-2008 and along with them measures to be taken to attenuate them have given rise to hot discussions in recent years.

The majority of economists are of the opinion that a current account deficit which was equal to some 8 percent of GNP (this is the case) should create acute problems for the economy.It is more so if it was financed by hot money,which was the case.Once the fragile character of financial markets were thought of, a danger loomed ahead. Economists asserting the dangers of hot money mention also its harmful impact on the exchange rates which were overvalued; in fact, many firms preferred to replace labor by machinery which was made cheap as a result of low import prices. Another argument on the same line is the ever increasing imports of consumer and intermediate goods which,in turn,should deviate demand from the domestic market to foreign goods while creating a depressive effect for it.

Those economists who think that it was not as dangerous as was alleged are of the opinion that a great percentage of hot money belonged to the Turkish citizens who were financing their businesses. Moreover, according to them, the present state of the Turkish economy would probably continue in the sense that, forget about an outflow of hot money, more foreign capital would be induced to inflow to the economy. In addition ,the present level of foreign reserves ($ 80 billion) and floating exchange rates should be a buffer against a danger which could give rise to a huge outflow of money.

I feel that as long as a sharp change in the economic policy and world economic conditions do not occur,a serious danger is not on the horizon,at least for 2007 to 2009.

Another line of discussion is related to the close relationship between interest rates and the exchange rate, which is supposed to be undervalued.It is asserted that if interest rate is allowed to decrease, that would make exchange rates higher, which, in turn, should induce more exports and discourages imports.This would decrease the current account deficits.Lower interest rates would also discourage the inflow of hot money;all this would attenuate current account deficit pressures on the country.

There are some economists who argue that lowering interest rates should not be a cure for current account problems. It is asserted that in recent years,nominal interests decreased by some 50 percent points and they are under 20 percent recently; yet the real value of the Turkish currency, interests for deposits and loans might not be affected due to the risk perception of the country by foreign investors. Another argument on the same line is the relationship between interest and current accounts. It is advanced that exports are not so elastic to the exchange rate; whereas imports are very elastic to the economic growth of the economy, which would be induced by lower interst rates. Those economists show that one of the reasons why exchange rates were getting lower was the shift of the money previously invested in foreign money to the Turkish currency,and this should be considered beneficial for the economy. If so, why should not measures be taken to reverse that tendency?

My response to all these arguments is that nothing much could be done without understanding my unconventional ideas about the level and growth of national income. In addition, if the dynamic effects of the long year inflow of foreign money is felt, structural adjustments could take place. In turn, the need for foreign money could be less; as a result current account deficits may decrease.

The explanation of economists about the ever existing balance of payments deficits in Turkey is not satisfactory at all. The inability of price changes to bring out an equlibrium or to get rid of a disequilibrium is expected when there is a structural problem. It may be efficient in the long run but it may take long time and also it may cause troubsome problems. But what is the structural problem here? I tried to identify it. Before 1980 it was the inability to create export possibilities of the nonagricultural sector as a result of swollen prices there and also the fixing of exchange rates according to the needs of agriculture. This was solved by taking out the overswollen prices in that sector after 1980. Yet the aridity of imports due to long years of import subtitution policy gave rise to a very high import demands when the pressure on it was taken out. Therefore exports could not catch up with import increases. How could this problem be solved after 1980?I tried to show that the structural problem after 1980 was to cover balance of payments deficits by invisible transactions such as tourism, workers' remittances, narcotics revenue, etc. Moreover, the possibility of obtaining foreign debt was of the same character. They all made labor prices higher which, in turn, was making exports difficult and induced high imports.

§ 9- IMPORT CONTENTS OF EXPORTS

Another discussion raging in recent days is related to the import contents of exports. It is advanced that the very high volume of exports is not as high as it seems to be, and again, even if they are so high, they were not so beneficial for the economy as it was thought.

There is no doubt that there is a noticeable increase in the import content of exports. But that observation should not be exploited in order to show that high exports were caused by the high import content, and again this has not been beneficial for the economy. It should be underlined that that argument is generally stressed by left wing economists (they are abound) who are against the full operation of free markets. In other words, even if the free operation of markets has given rise to higher exports, they are not as high as thought; again even if they are high, it was not harmful to the economy.

The following statistics are presented in order to show the huge share of imports in exports.

THE PROPORTION OF EXPORTS IN THE MANUFACTURING INDUSTRY (%)

1997	2002	2005
15.5	28.4	34.5

IMPORTS FOR MANUFACTURING INDUSTRY/PRODUCTION VALUE (%)

1997	2002	2005
32.9	37.6	58.9

I do not think that the above figures are as meaningful as they seem. Some 90 percent of Turkish exports consist of industrial commodities. At present, the industrial sector is some 25 percent of the total economy. If imported inputs consist of 60 percent of the production of industrial sector, this amounts to some 15 percent of national income. As imports are some 33 percent of national income I8 percent of imports are demanded for other purposes. Isn't a very small figure? What is more important is that some 35 percent of the manufacturing industry is exported. A greater percent of imports are used to sustain the growth of manufacturing. Could that be true? Moreover, 8 years ago (1997), when the proportion of imported inputs in exports was much smaller, the deficits were as high as they are now. Isn't that a coutradiction?

The arguments which are asserted by those economists are false and this fact indicates the credulity of those left wing economists. I do not know whether they believe in these arguments or not. But it is certain that their ideology induces them to stick to such arguments. Let us scrutinize some of their arguments. They argue that while the economy was growing some 7 percent only, exports increased 17 percent during recent years. According to them this is not beneficial for the economy. They do not think that the growth of national income is determined by all sorts of factors and a very close correlation should not be sought between the growth of national income and the increase of exports. The increase of exports should definitely contribute to the increase of national income. Yet a very close correlation between the growth rates of each of them should not be sought. There is another argument put forward by those left wing economists: there is not a relationship between the growth of industry and exports. It is shown that while in 1989 the share of industry was 23.1 percent of GNP that of exports was 10.7 percent. Those figures are compared with those of 2004. In that year the share of the manufacturing industry was 20.4 percent but that of exports were 22.3. Believe or not, it is jumped to the conclusion that the growth of exports has been an impediment to the development of the industry. I do not think that I should even attempt to show how stupid that argument is.

Many economists compare the speed of exports and imports and underline the ever greater gap between them occurring every year recently and conclude that the growth of exports has not been beneficial to the economy. I think that what is important is the access of technical progress to the economy. This has been known ever since Adam Smith. Along with its short term benefits, long term ones would be felt if market forces are allowed to persist and an intelligent economic policy follows it. Those figures should not be interpreted in a void.

I think that all alleged or critical appraisals are marginal and the important development is the increase in international trade. The factual research of economists going back to several years ago suggests that almost every country, which has had great trade volume, has developed fast. The increase of efficiency and the propagation of new ideas have always been important. Yet, the ever increasing balance of payment problems forestalls serious problems for the future years. How are we going to solve that problem? Three measures seem to stand out: the increase of the real exchange rate, a decrease in the growth rate of national income and a decrease in labor prices. They all are of a character to give rise to undesired results for masses of people, as a result they are politically difficult to adopt. Yet deep rooted changes in the structure of the economy might be beneficial in solving this difficult problem..

THE PRESSING CURRENT ACCOUNT PROBLEMS

Although the arguments relating to the fact that the continuing foreign capital inflows might delay the harmful effects of ever increasing current account deficits, the majority of economists are of the opinion that it should create acute problems for the country in the near future. Among these economists is R. Mundell, who visited Turkey recently, and presented an excellent and detailed paper dealing with the recent future of the Turkish economy. It would be quite illuminating to sum up his thoughts.

After having shown the success of past governments in dealing with the ever lasting instability in the economy, especially high inflations lasting for the last 30 years, he underlines the fact that the fall of the inflation rate from over 50 percent to below 10 percent was an end result of tight fiscal and monetary policies that were adopted. Yet, he stresses the fact that by keeping interest rates very high and creating an atmosphere assuring stability in future, an overvaluation of the Turkish currency would be inevitable. The world financial markets should also be taken into consideration. As a result of high liquidity in world markets, high interest rates in Turkey would attract a large amount of funds to this country. This has been the case. It was again natural that a highly valued currency should create high current account deficits. He validates his assertions by drawing upon the experience of several countries in the recent past. He exhibits the Turkish data which is quite in line with his expectations.

In order to cure the problems he recommends that the Turkish Central Bank should interfere with the market by buying foreign exchange so that their prices become higher which, in turn, should lessen current account deficits. In fact this was his only recommendation. But several arguments could be raised against this policy. It is shown that this would make the volume of currency in circulation higher and, in turn, that would create a pressure on prices. Moreover, if the money were drawn from circulation by a costly inverse repo operation it would make interest rates higher, which are very high anyway. This is all common sense. But there is a more serious problem. This is the impact of higher exchange rates on imports and exports. The past experience shows that their impact on imports has not been so very powerful unless national income decreases as a result of high devaluations. As a result, everything would depend on the behavior of national income. He and everybody writing on this very important issue do not consider that fact properly. Here comes my innovation in economics.

It is shown above that in order to understand the behavior of national income, the growth should be studied under level and growth effects. But this distinction does not exist in the literature. One way to observe and understand that distinction is to compare the growth rates of national income in constant prices currency in lira and in foreign exchange, let us say in dollars. It is calculated that the growth rate, which includes both level and growth effects during the last 55 year period (1950-2005) is 4.3 percent in Tl, constant Turkish money, but in constant dollars it is 4.5-4.8 percent. This is my measurement of the over or undervaluation of foreign currency, whereas according to the calculation of Mundell there seems to be a some 75 percent overvaluation of the Turkish currency vis-a-vis dollars in the 2001-2005 periods. According to my calculation based on the differences of national incomes measured in dollars and Tl, the overvaluation is much less. I think that in the 1979-2005 periods (at the end of 2005) some 20 to 25 overvaluation may have existed in the Turkish currency. This should be taken out by administering exchange rates properly. The remedy is to create conditions which would induce a decrease in the level of national income. The only way to do it is to decrease the price of labor. In fact, devaluations could coincide with the decrease of labor prices. But this should be manipulated very carefully.

TABLE 1
INTERNATIONAL TRADE IN TURKEY ($ MILLION)

Years	Exports FOB	Imports CIF	Deficits
1950	263	286	23
1951	314	402	88
1952	363	356	193
1953	396	533	137
1954	335	478	143
1955	313	498	185
1956	305	407	102
1957	345	397	52
1958	247	315	68
1959	354	470	116
1960	321	486	147
1961	365	537	172
1962	361	622	241
1963	368	688	320
1964	411	537	126
1965	464	572	108
1966	490	718	228
1967	523	685	162
1968	496	764	268
1969	537	801	264
1970	588	948	360
1971	677	1,171	494
1972	885	1,563	678
1973	1,250	2,150	900
1974	1,532	3,777	2,245
1975	1,401	4,739	3,338
1976	1,906	5,128	3,222
1977	1,700	5,700	4,000
1978	2,288	4,599	2,311
1979	2,261	5,064	2,803
1980	2,910	7,909	4,999
1981	4,703	8,933	4,230
1982	5,746	8,842	3,096
1983	5,727	9,235	3,508
1984	7,135	10,757	3,615
1985	7,958	11,343	3,385
1986	7,456	11,104	3,648
1987	10,190	14,157	3,968
1988	11,662	14,135	2,673
1989	11,627	15,762	4,135
1990	12,960	22,302	9,342
1991	13,598	21,038	7,440
1992	14,914	22,890	7,976
1993	15,345	29,448	14,103
1994	18,106	23,270	5,164
1995	21,637	35,709	14,072
1996	23,082	42,453	20,403
1997	26,246	48,657	22,411
1998	26,974	45,921	18,947
1999	26,508	40,692	14,184
2000	27,372	53,982	26,658
2001	31,334	41,399	10,065
2002	36,659	51,554	15,495
2003	46,878	68,876	21,858
2004	62,800	97,200	34,380
2005	73,000	116,000	43,000
2006	85,309	137,449	52,140
2007	**107,000**	**176,000**	**69,000**
2008	**132,500**	**201,000**	**68,500**
2008 Jan-March	**33,136**	**49,177**	**16,041**
2009 Jan-March	**24,507**	**28,625**	**4,119**

TABLE 1 A

Foreign Trade by Economic Activity (2007)

Million $

Exports	107,213
Agriculture forestry	3,725
Fishing	158
Mining and quarrying	1,661
Manufacturing	101,023
Others	646
Imports	170,057
Agriculture	4,641
Fishing	31
Mining and quarrying	25,314
Manufacturing	133,933
Others	6,139

TABLE 2
INTERNATIONAL TRADE IN TURKEY

Years	Exports/Imports	Exports/GNP
1977	0.30	0.0590
1978	0.50	0.0430
1979	0.45	0.0344
1980	0.37	0.0499
1981	0.53	0.0810
1982	0.65	0.1073
1983	0.62	0.1124
1984	0.66	0.1482
1985	0.70	0.1613
1986	0.67	0.1280
1987	0.72	0.1515
1988	0.81	0.1641
1989	0.74	0.1455
1990	0.58	0.0872
1991	0.65	0.1020
1992	0.64	0.0894
1993	0.63	0.0924
1994	0.79	0.1350
1995	0.61	0.1357
1996	0.54	0.1440
1997	0.54	0.1363
1998	0.59	0.1366
1999	0.65	0.1414
2000	0.51	0.1400
2001	0.77	0.213 (x)
2002	0.71	0.189
2003	0.68	0.194
2004	0.64	0.228
2005	0.63	0.202
2006	0.62	0.212
2007	**0.64**	**0.169**
2008	**0.52**	**0.177**

(x) Mostly due to the shrinkage of GNP as a result of 2001 February devaluation.

TABLE 3
FOREIGN DEBT ($ BILLION)

	2001	2002	2003	2005	2007 June
Total	113.9	130.4	145.8	165.516	226,3
Long-long term	97.5	113.9	122.8	128.322	-
Public	46.4	64.0	70.3	68.717	72,3
Central Bank	23.6	20.3	21.5	13.367	15,5
Private sector	27.5	29.6	31.0	46.239	138,5
Financial	4.8	4.6	5.0	13.485	41,5
Non-financial	22.7	25.0	26.0	10.614	97,0
Short term	16.4	16.4	23.0	37.2	-
Public	0.0	0.0	0.0	0.0	-
Central Bank	0.8	1.7	2.9	2.8	-
Commercial Banks	8.0	6.3	9.7	16.674	-
Others	7.7	8.4	10.5	17.605	-
Debt/GNP	0.791	0.714	0.610	0.460	-

Source: Central Bank Report 2005, P.216. 2007 figures include both short and long term debts.

TABLE 13
FOREIGN FINANCING NEEDS AND SOURCES ($ BILLION)

	2003	2004	2005
1. Current Accounts	-8.037	-15.451	-22.852
2. Error and omissions	5.043	2.982	1.983
3. Financing needs (1+2)	-2.994	-12.469	-20.890
4. Total financing (1+2+3)	2.994	12.469	20.890
5. Capital accounts (net)	6.367	22.745	44.339
Direct investments	1.195	1.711	8.603
Portfolio Invest.	2.569	8.070	13.709
Gov. bonds	1.509	1.959	3.417
Securities purchased by foreigners	2.623	7.250	11.603
Securities purchase by nationals	-1.386	-1.139	-963
Credits (IMF excluded)	2.837	13.775	20.415
Government	-2.194	-1.163	-2.165
Banks	1.975	5.642	9.116
Long term	-40	2.295	6.413
Short term	2.015	3.347	2.703
Other sectors	3.056	9.296	13.514
Long term	587	4.787	9.721
Short term	288	341	359
Commercial	2.181	4.168	3.434
Deposits	1.368	393	489
Others	-1.602	-1.289	-489
6. IMF Credits	-50	-3.518	-5.353
7. Reserve Change	-3.323	-6.673	18.117
Banks	724	-5.849	-270
Official	-4.047	-824	-17.847

Source: Central Bank Report 2004, p. 59 and 2005 p. 55

TABLE 5
FOREIGN HOT MONEY IN TURKEY (US $ MILLIONS)

	2002	2004	2007/7	2008/3
Securities	6,362	20,891	94.078	
TL government bonds	1,839	6,121	34.890 (*)	28.262
Forex government bonds	160	1,144		
Eurobonds (Turkish Issue)	870	1,279		
Stocks	3,450	12,264	59.188	47.162
Others	43	83	-	
Deposits	1,843	2,761	4.007	4.723
Total	8,205	23,652	98.455	80.147

(*) Total government bonds
Source: Hurriyet, November 22, 2004 plus 2007.

TABLE 6
GROSS INTERNATIONAL RESERVES
($ Million)

	Gold	Central Bank	Banks	Total
1997	1,124	18,419	7,625	27,168
1998	1,012	19,721	8,625	29,506
1999	1,011	23,177	9,569	33,757
2000	1,006	22,172	11,007	34,185
2001	1,032	18,778	10,325	30,144
2002	1,279	26,807	9,980	30,051
2003	1,279	31,324	9,089	41,681
2004	1,635	36,006	16,039	53,678
2005	1,915	50,518	16,234	68,656
2006	**2,372**	**60.845**	**27,503**	**90,741**
2007	**3,123**	**73,319**	**9,024**	**108,224**

Source: Central Bank Annual Repart (2005) p.213

TABLE 7

OFFICIAL AND EXPECTED DOLLAR RATES ACCORDING TO SLIDING PAG METHOD

	Official Rate (TL)	Expected Rate (TL)	Official Rate/ Expected Rate
1950	2.80	2.80	1.00
1957	2.80	4.18	0.67
1969	9.00	6.79	0.59
1979	36.05	36.64	1.00
1985	518.3	279.11	1.86
1990	2,607	1,889	1.38
1995	45,704	25,816	1.77
1998	260,040	136,353	1.91
1999	416,086	209,995	1.99
2000	623, 685	297,193	2.09
2001	1,220,921	478,489	2.84
2002	1,415,150	633,950	2.23
2003	1,433,300	743,525	1.93
2004	1,400,000	891,900	1.76
2005	1,350,000	909,738	1.48
2006	1,400,000	922,090	1.52
2007	1,200,000	1,041,660	1.16
2009	1.6 NTL (*)	1.104	1.44

(*) 000,000 is taken out, new Turkish lira

TABLE 8

BALANCE OF PAYMENTS
Millions of Dollars

	2002	2004	2005	2006
Current Accounts	-8,036	-15,604	22,852	-31,316
Trade Balance	-14,010	-23,878	-32,576	-39,934
Exports (FOB)	47,253	63,167	73,122	91,555
Luggage	3,953	3,880	3,473	–
Imports (CIF)	-69,340	-97,540	-116,048	-131,484
Invisibles Equilibrium	10,504	12,784	14,004	13.539
Invisibles	17,945	22,928	25,854	–
Tourism	13,203	15,888	18,152	14
Invisibles Expenditure	-7,4411	-10,144	-11,850	–
Investment Equilibrium	-5,557	-5,637	-5,748	–
Interest Payments	-4,579	-5,637	-5,012	–
Current transfers	1,027	1,127	1,468	1.687
Workers remittances	729	804	851	1.111
Finance Account	3,095	13,337	20,869	34.052
Reserves	-4,047	-824	-17,847	-6114
Errors and omissions	4,941	2,267	1,983	-2736
(Tourism income-Foreigners, $ millions)			13.929	

TABLE 9
The Increase of Foreign Debt of Industrialists
($ Million)

	2001	2002	2003	2004	2005	2006	2007
Total Foreign Debt ($ million)	113,592	129,671	144,266	160,760	168,716	205,548	247,200
Public Sector	47.129	64.534	70.844	75.668	70.414	71.590	73.359
Central Bank	24.351	22.003	24.373	21.410	15.425	15.678	15.801
Private Sector	42.112	43.135	49.049	43.682	82.877	118.280	158.039
The Share of Various Sectors (%)	41.5	49.8	49.1	47.1	41.7	34.8	29.7
Public	21.4	17.0	16.9	13.3	9.1	7.6	6.4
Private	37.1	33.3	34.0	39.6	49.1	57.5	63.9

Source: Sabah, April 1, 2008

CHAPTER XIX
THE DETERMINATION OF EXCHANGE RATES

§ 1 - INTRODUCTION

There are numerous shortcomings in the analyses of the determination (or fixing) of exchange rates in Turkey. Actually, these analyses may be divided into two categories. Those by popular Turkish economists and those produced by internationally well-known economists.

Writings by popular Turkish economists have remained influential even after 1980, although in recent years works contributed by distinguished economists have attracted attention, too.

Between 1940 and 1980 the Turkish currency was overvalued. But my views about this overvaluation differed from other economists. According to others, by correcting this overvaluation Turkey would not be able to solve the continuing problem of balance of payments. This was because of insufficient goods to be exported, their low demand elasticity, the protectionary policies of prospective importers, the inflationary effects of devaluations, etc.

Many economists and businessmen and the public in general shared this belief. But absolutely no reference was made to the equilibrium exchange rate.

More eminent economists (some of them are the members of the staff of the World Bank) have contended that by fixing the exchange rate at a proper level exports could be promoted and Turkey would finally solve its balance of payments problems which had hindered the effective operation of the economy since the 1930 s.

Turkish administrators have accepted this argument and adopted such a policy since 1980.

Nevertheless, the proper level of foreign exchange needed to be estimated. In two serious studies have tackled this subject. These works by Professor Krueger and by Dervis-Robinson are critically examined below.

TABLE XIX - 1
OFFICIAL AND EXPECTED $ RATES ACCORDING TO THE SLIDING PEG METHOD

	Official Rate (TL)	Expected Rate (TL)	Official Rate/ Expected Rate
1950	2.80	2.80	1.00
1957	2.80	4.18	0.67
1969	9.00	6.79	0.59
1979	36.05	36.64	1.00
1985	518.3	279.11	1.86
1990	2,607	1,889	1.38
1995	45,704	25,816	1.77
1998	260,040	136,353	1.91
2001	1,360,000	478,483	2.84
2002	1,415,150	633,950	2.23
2003	1,450,000	729,000	1.98
2004	1,400,000	801,900	1.76
2005	1,350,000	909,738	1.48
2006	1,400,000	922,090	1.52
2007	1,200,000	1,041,660	1.16
2009 April	1.6 NTL	1.10	1.41

Table XIX-1 reveals the following observation: although the exchange rates between 1950-1957 and 1960-1969 were overvalued in the mid-years, when the 1950 figure is compared with the 1979 figure, its value was the same at the beginning and the end of the period, 1979. Between 1979 and 1985 the currency was devalued by some 50 percent, and except for a short period between 1990-1993: it had kept its value (what it was in 1985) in the following years. In 2001 there was a sharp increase as a result of the devaluation; but by 2002 the currency almost restored to its previous real value. Again, the multiplier was around 1.98 by 2003, the same as the pre-devaluation value. Why? This is answered below. All those figures are based on a calculation of the sliding peg method, the change of prices in the US and in Turkey.

Almost everybody is of the opinion that the Turkish currency, whose value was stricktly controlled in 1950-1979, was overvalued. It is evident that if looked at through sliding peg spectacles, this was not so. Yet, what was important was a lack of understanding of what was meant by the genuine value of the currency. Another problem is to interpret the meaning of a 50 percent devaluation after the 1980 devaluation.

§ 2 - KRUEGER AND THE EXCHANGE RATES

Professor Krueger has demonstrated that during the period in question (pre 1980 years) real exchange rates decreased systematically. This conclusion is based on tables showing real exchange rates from 1950 to 1978 which are reproduced below. Her calculations are made according to the sliding peg method. This requires some explanation.

The sliding peg method is based on a very simple idea. It is assumed that the exchange rate at the year of commencement was the equilibrium rate, and if this equilibrium is distorted as a result of relative inflations, adjustments are made in order to compensate for them.

According to Krueger, external shocks may lead to shifts in the demand and supply curves and therefore the equilibrium rate may change. By shifts, she means those caused by the exploitation of North Sea oil, etc.

Krueger's basic conclusion is that there is a need to depreciate the country's exhange rate at approximately the same rate as the relative inflations between it and the rest of the world. According to Krueger, this is why the sliding peg method may be employed (Krueger 1978. p. 39).

Examining Krueger's tables with respect to Turkey (Tables XIX-2, 3 and 4) it seems that at the end of each period, the real value of the exchange rate is much more than that at the start of the period. Here, the conclusion is straightforward. Turkish currency was overvalued at the end of each period. This discouraged exports and resulted in the downsloping trend.

Let us examine her calculations more precisely (see Tables XIX-2, 3 and 4). In order to do so. a few definitions are first required. These are reproduced below. (For Krueger's tables see Krueger 1974, pp. 34, 172 and Krueger 1979, p. 98).

TABLE XIX- 2

NOMINAL and PLD - EERs, 1953 to 1957

	1953	1954	1955	1956	1957
	A. Nominal EERs (TL per dollar)				
Sales of foreign exchange					
Traditional exports	2.80	2.85	2.89	2.91	2.94
Nontraditional exports	3.92	4.48	4.50	5.00	5.00
Tourists and invisibles	2.80	2.80	2.80	5.75	5.75
Capital account	2.80	2.80	2.80	2.80	2.80
Purchases of foreign exchange					
Capital goods imports	3.22	3.48	4.02	4.72	5.97
Consumer goods imports	5.60	6.09	6.37	6.54	7.47
Tourists and invisibles	2.80	2.80	2.80	5.25	5.25
Capital account	2.80	2.80	2.80	2.80	2.80
	B. PLD -EERs (1958TL per dollar)				
Sales of foreign exchange					
Traditional exports	5.83	5.28	4.82	3.93	3.26
Nontraditional exports	8.16	8.30	7.50	6.76	5.55
Tourists and invisibles	5.83	5.18	4.66	7.77	6.39
Capital account	5.83	5.18	4.66	3.78	3.11
Purchases of foreign exchange					
Capital goods imports	6.71	6.44	6.70	6.38	6.63
Consumer goods imports	11.67	11.28	10.62	8.84	8.30
Tourists and invisibles	5.83	5.18	4.66	7.09	5.83
Capital account	5.83	5.18	4.66	3.78	3.11

Notes: a) Capital goods import rate taken as the machinery and equipment rate.

b) PLD - EERs were computed by dividing the nominal NER by the home goods wholesale price index (1958=100).

c) Capital account sales of foreign exchange does not include capital repatriated by Turks after 1956, which was subject to the TL. 5.25=$ 1 exchange rate.

Definitions and Concepts

It will simplify the exposition if some terms can be defined. There are, first, a series of concepts relating to exchange rates. These, and their definitions, are:

Nominal exchange rate (NER) - the number of local currency units paid per unit of foreign exchange brought from or sold by the Central Bank.

Parity exchange rate - the exchange rate registered with the IMF.

Effective exchange rate (EER) - the number of local currency units paid or received when buying or selling one unit's worth of foreign currency value of a good. In the case of an import subject to a 10 percent duty and 5 percent wharf tax. the EER would be 1.15 times the NER.

TABLE XIX - 3

IMPORT EERs and PLD-EERs by END-USE CATEGORY of IMPORT, 1960 to 1969 (TL PER DOLLAR C.I.F.PRICE)

	Capital Goods	Intermediate Goods	Imports Competing with Domestic Production	Consumer Goods
EERs				
1960	12.11	13.25	21.22	18.66
1961	12.55	13.25	21.22	18.66
1962	12.54	13.12	18.96	15.78
1963	12.99	13.57	19.41	16.23
1964	12.99	13.57	19.41	16.23
1965	15.50	14.79	23.01	17.75
1966	15.50	14.79	23.01	17.75
1967	15.29	15.27	23.46	18.20
1968	12.26	16.15	21.98	18.79
1969	13.16	17.05	21.98	19.69
PLD-EER				
1960	10.35	11.32	18.13	15.95
1961	10.54	11.13	17.83	15.68
1962	10.03	10.49	15.17	14.70
1963	9.84	10.28	14.70	12.30
1964	10.14	10.60	15.16	12.68
1965	11.48	10.96	17.04	13.14
1966	10.61	10.13	15.76	12.16
1967	10.09	9.65	14.85	11.52
1968	7.52	9.91	13.48	11.64
1969	7.44	9.63	12.96	11.12

Notes: a) For defimitions of categories of imports, see Appendex A.
b) PLD-NERs are 1958 TL perdollar c.i.f. price.

TABLE XIX - 4

NOMINAL, REAL, AND PPP EXCHANGE RATES, 1963 TO 1978

	NER (1) (TL/$US)	PLD NER (2) (1964 TL/$US)	PPP PLD NER-U.S. (3) ((2)/1963 US$)	PPP PLD NER Germany (4) ((2) /1963 DM)	PPP PLD NER 7 countries (5) ((2) /7 currencies)
1963	9.00	9.20	9.22	2.32	8.85
1964	9.00	9.00	9.03	2.31	8.77
1965	9.00	8.07	8.34	2.10	7.87
1966	9.00	8.05	8.51	2.13	7.88
1967	9.00	7.59	8.08	1.98	7.27
1968	9.00	6.79	7.42	1.68	6.34
1969	9.00	6.48	7.41	1.81	6.34
1970	9.00	10.05	11.81	2.99	10.28
1971	14.85	7.80	9.49	2.69	8.44
1972	14.15	6.78	8.69	2.48	7.47
1973	14.15	5.34	8.04	2.47	6.51
1974	13.99	4.07	7.27	2.39	5.65
1975	15.15	4.00	7.82	2.26	5.02
1976	16.66	3.81	7.78	2.48	4.46
1977	19.44	3.57	7.73	2.68	4.43
1978*	25.25	3.17	7.41	2.44	4.12

Sources: Exchange rates to U.S. dollar from **International Financial Statistics**
Price series: Line 63a (or, if unavailable, Line 63) of **International**

Financial Statistics.

Trade weights: 1976 data from Direction of Trade Annual 1970-76.

NOTE: The seven largest trading partners, and their shares were:

Germany (31.1 %); United States (14.8 %); Italy (13.1 %); United Kingdom (12.9 %); Switzerland (10.8 %); France (10.1 %); and Japan (7.2 %). Share were calculated by summing imports and exports.

(*) Estimates for 1978 are for the month of June.

Premium-inclusive EER - the amount a buyer or seller of one unit of foreign exchange would be willing to obtain the right to buy or sell. The concept or premium, which is the excess value of a right to transact international business earned by the holder of a license, is discussed further below.

Real, or price-level deflated (PLD) EER - the EER deflated by the domestic price level. The appropriate indicator of the domestic price level is the price of home, or nontraded goods, since that index is not as influenced by exchange rate policy as are alternative price indices. However, in many circumstances, lack of availability ot a reliable index of home goods prices has led researches to rely upon other price indices. For research on a particular country, this is not crucial to the analysis.

Purchasing-power-parity (PPP) EER- the real EER adjusted for (1) the rate of inflation in the rest of the world, and (2) in a multicountry world, for any alterations in the exchange rates of the country's trading partners.

Undoubtedly, Turkish currency was overvalued vis-a-vis foreign exchange especially at the end of each period. As a result, devaluations occurred at that time, i.e., in 1958, 1970, and a substantial one in 1980.

Problems with Krueger's argument are presented below.

1 - Although at the end of each sub-period the real exchange rate was lower than when compared to that at the beginning, no decreasing trend was evident. The value of the real exchange rate at the end of the period (1978) was virtually the same as it had been at the period's commencement (1950).

2 - In her first book (1974) Krueger based her calculations on figures which did not correspond with reality. Moreover, in her 1978 publication there is a serious discrepancy in Table 1 (here Table XIX-4) which is impossible to be explained.

This discrepancy concerns the figures of columns (3-4) and 5. Before 1970 there are no problems. Taking the figures in column 3 first, that for 1969 is 0.80 of 1963 . In column 4 the figure for 1969 is 0.78 of 1963, and in column 5, it is 0.72 for the same year. Evidently the figures of column 5 are closely related to those of 3 and 4.

In column 3 the figure for 1978 is 0.63 of that of 1970. The corresponding figure for column 4 is 0.82. We would expect the figure in column 5 to be similar but it is actually 0.40, clearly impossible. There could not be such a huge difference between price levels and exchange rates in the remaining five countries. (Moreover, when examined carefully, it does not seem to be a printing mistake.)

3 - There is an even more fundamental criticism of Krueger's method. I contended that there was a shift, but this was not an external one like the one taken into consideration by Krueger. In my opinion it was connected to an endogenous and systematical event (similar to serial correlation as known in econometrics). If economic development was based on import substitution, equilibrium prices of

foreign exchange would rise continuously and systematically for sometime.

Suppose that after devaluation the country continues to export the same goods. If this devaluation is to succeed, more of those goods should be exported. In order to promote the production of these goods the factors of production should be shifted to exporting sectors. This is possible if their income increases. If so, the new exchange rate should be in excess of the previous rate regardless of relative inflation rate.

If, on the other hand, previously import substituted goods are sold abroad, the exchange rate should systematically increase again irrespective of relative inflation rates. This is for the simple reason that the relative prices of import substituting goods to exported goods were high in comparison with the same relative prices abroad. If so, their export would necessitate a continuously increasing real exchange rate. (More in depth criticism is found in Section 3 below.)

4 - There is one more reason why the sliding peg method is not applicable to Turkey. In the pre-1980 era (Krueger's writings were based on what occurred in this period) almost 70 percent of Turkish exports consisted of four agricultural products (tobacco, cotton, hazelnuts and raisin). The prevailing rates were fixed on the saleability of these four products. Hence, how may we determine exchange rates by the sliding peg method and expect that exports would increase because of this? Without any exogenous shift the depreciation of money should be in excess of relative inflations.

To conclude. It was not possible to determine the exchange rate by using the sliding peg method in pre-1980 years. This would only provide an idea about the change of the level of the real exchange rate, but should not be accepted as a basis for fixing the exchange rate.

§ 3 - THE FOUNDATION OF THE CRITICISM OF THE TRADITIONAL APPROACHES

Now, I would like to comment about Krueger's more substantial contention which, to a certain extent, might be considered similar to mine. But before doing it let me quote her. 'There is therefore a strong assumption that exchange rate should move to offset differentials in inflation rates; that they might also move for other reasons, is not denied by that statement." (Krueger 1979, p. 34)

"A devaluation which raises the real price of foreign exchange will generally result in an increase in domestic prices of tradable goods by the full proportion of devaluation and the prices of home goods by less than the proportion of devaluation...

The price level compatible with the prevailing money supply will therefore increase, but by less than the proportion of devaluation" (Krueger, 1979. p. 36)

"An exchange rate will remain a market clearing rate only as long as the demand and supply for home goods as a function of their relative prices remains unaltered at a fixed exchange rate." (Krueger. 1979, p.38)

I think that those sentences are very illuminating and they gave me an impetus to study deeply the determination and the impact of exchange rates. My main challenge is based on the change of prices of labor and nonlabor intensive goods. To a certain extent it is similar to her contention of the impact of devaluation on tradable and nontradable goods. In fact, she says that the prices of tradable goods are related to the exchange rate but those of nontradable goods are not: they are independent of the exchange rate. I say the same but I ferret out my contention. According to Krueger, once the prices of tradable goods increase after a devaluation, the prices of nontradable goods would depend on domestic demand determined by the money volume, which, in turn, would depend on the remaining demand volume left after the increase of the prices of importable and exportable goods. That is true. But there is more to it. I try to show that the relative prices of tradable goods with respect to foreign goods is under the influence of the productivity in producing them in the home and the foreign country. But those of the home goods are not under the influence of those forces. Moreover, the nature of exported goods, which are a proportion of tradable goods, would be influential on their prices. If they are labor intensive, the impact of exchange prices would be different compared to the case when export goods are not labor intensive. My main and important difference from the literature is not to consider the prices of nontradable goods under the influence of domestic demand determined by the money volume only. If this is the starting point, the determination of exchange prices should be considered to be quite different from the literature, that of Krueger's being an example.

The changes of exchange rate in developing countries exhibits different dimensions compared to those in developed countries. It would be necessary to summarize that divergence which is very meaningful in the understanding the Turkish economy.

When the real exchange rate is calculated in a developed country an adjustment of the nominal rate by means of the relative inflations in home and foreign countries could do the job. But in developing countries like Turkey, it is necessary to take into consideration the change in relative prices of labor and nonlabor intensive commodities... In the traditional literature instead of labor and nonlabor commodities, tradable and nontradable goods are used. As a result, in this summary, the latter ones will be considered first.

First a very simple mathematical background information will be given. Writing them I am inspired by Balassa (Balassa, 1987).

The demand for the country's export goods is shown by X^F. It depends on the competitive power of the country in question. In the literature it is supposed to be related to the relative prices of tradable goods in the two countries. P^F_T shows the prices of tradable goods in the foreign country and P^D_T is used for the prices of tradable goods in the home country. Then the following equation could be written:

$$X^F = f\,(R.P^F_T \,/\, P^D_T \,;\, Y^F\,)$$

R in this equation is the nominal exchange price and Y^F is the level of national income in the foreign country. The equation is very simple. Export demand is determined by the relative prices of tradable goods in the domestic and foreign countries and the level of national income in the foreign country.

The supply of exports (X^D) is supposed to depend on relative prices of tradable and nontradable goods in the home country (P^D_T and P^D_N) and the capacity of exports (CD). That can be expressed in the following equation:

$$X^D=g(P^D_T/P^D_N;C^D)$$

In these two equations, both the competitive power of the country and relative prices of tradable and nontradable goods are taken into consideration. In the first equation the exchange rate adjusted by the relative prices of tradable goods and in the second one the relative prices of tradable and nontradable goods are taken into consideration.

In the first equation, exchange rates reflect relative prices of tradable goods and/or exchange rates are adjusted according to them. If this is the case, the international index of competitiveness is always one (1). That means that the exchange rate is at a level where the price of domestic and foreign prices of tradable goods are always the same. This is called one price rule. Of course, price differentiations, etc. should create a difference; yet theoretically or at least as a reference point, the one price rule can be accepted.

The following conclusion can be drawn from the above explanations.

1- According to the first equation, the exchange rate in full competition, depends on the relative prices of tradable goods.

2- The ratio between tradable and nontradable goods is crucial in determining the supply of export goods. For example, if the relative prices of tradable goods with respect of nontradable goods prices decreases, more nontradable goods would be produced (they would become tradable) and as a result, their supply would increase.

This means that the supply of tradable goods will increase along with a decrease in the prices of tradable goods. If previously nontradable goods become tradable ones after their prices become lower, according to our first equation, the nominal exchange rate has to decrease as a result of one price law. But as a result of lower domestic prices, the real exchange prices will not be changed due to one price rule... Let us remember the formula by which real exchange rates ($\bar{R}$) is derived. (Let us not confuse this with the previous equation. In the present one P^D_T is the home prices and P^F_T is the foreign prices.)

$\bar{R} = R . (P^F_T / P^D_T)$ ($\bar{R}$ is the real exchange rate)

In the considered case, P^D_T is lower now but for the realization of the one price law R should be made lower as well. The only way to estimate the level of $\bar{R}$ is to deflate R by a price index in which the change of the prices of nontradeable goods should have a higher weight. If the deflation is affected by general prices, the one price law would make real exchange prices to stay where they were. If what is written above is true, another factor additional to those determining real exchange prices will be added: relative prices of tradable and nontradable goods. Actually, as in my case the crucial factor creating the difference between tradable and nontradable goods is the impact of labor and nonlabor intensive goods, the strategic factor becomes the relative prices of nonlabor and labor intensive good prices.

I shall give give an example in order to clarify the argument asserted above.

Let us suppose that one basket good could be bought for $ 50 in the US;whereas the same basket is bought for 100 Lira in the developing country.We suppose that there are no transportation costs,no customs duties and no intervention to trade.In that case $ 1 should be equal to 2 lira.We consider the real value of the dollar as 1 , 2(50/100)= 1.Now let us suppose that in order to export more,the Lira is devalued and it is made $ 1=4 Lira.Again, we suppose that in the basket there are two kinds of good,the first is labor intensive and the other is nonlabor intensive one; 50 percent of the basket was nonlabor and the other 50 percent was labor intensive goods. Before the devaluation only nonlabor intensive goods were exported. After the devaluation the price of nonlabor intensive goods increased proportionally to the devaluation rate and it becames 100L; whereas labor intesive ones stayed the same,50L.In that case according to our formula the real value of the dollar is 1.33, 4(50/150)=1.33.That means that the real value of the dollar is 33 percent higher.In other words,if we use a deflator based on all prices this is the expected figure.But I suppose that after the devaluation nonlabor intensive goods became exportable.In that case, the real value of the dollar is now much higher than 1.33 if all exported goods are labor intensive now: it is 2 , 4(50/ 100)=2.

In the considered case P^D_T is lower now but for the realization of the one price law R should be made lower as well. The only way to estimate the level of $\bar{R}$ is to deflate R by a price index in which the change of the prices of nontradable goods should have a higher weight. If the deflation is affected by general prices, the one price law would rnake real exchange prices stay where they were. If what is written above is true, another factor additional to those determining real exchange prices in the literature will be added: relative prices of tradable and nontradable goods. Actually as in my case the crucial factor creating the difference between tradable and nontradable goods is the impact of labor nonlabor intensive goods, the strategic factor becomes the relative prices of nonlabor and labor prices.

§ 4 - THE DERVIS - ROBINSON APPROACH TO EQUILIBRIUM RATE

A most detailed analysis of the equilibrium exchange rate is carried out by Derviş and Robinson. They present the problem as follows: «The major question to be explored in this section is what would have happened if Turkey had pursued a flexible exchange rate policy during the 1973-77 period. Would the equilibrium or shadow exchange rate have had to depreciate at a rate only equal to the difference in inflation rates between Turkey and its trade partners? How did the price rise affect the equilibrium rate? How different would performance have been?» (Derviş-Robinson 1978, p. 47). (See also Derviş, de Melo and Robinson 1981).

The authors take into consideration both reserve position and capital inflow (normal debt and worker's remittances). On the other hand, they take the structure of Turkey's tariffs as given and assume that there is no quantity restriction.

Then by using their basic model (TGT) they explore «what value market clearing or equilibrium exchange rate would have taken if it had been allowed to move to equilibrate the supply of and demand for foreign exchange» (Ibid, p. 50-51). Their results are shown in Table XIX-5.

TABLE XIX - 5

EQUILIBRIUM EXCHANGE RATES, 1973-77

	Equilibrium Rates	Official Rates
1973	10.4	14.0
1974	14.7	13.5
1975	17.8	14.5
1976	20.5	16.0
1977	28.2	18.2

After having found the equilibrium rate they analyze the increase in that period. They decompose the change in the equilibrium exchange rate that occurred between 1973 and 1977 as follows:

Differential Inflations	32 %
Oil price Rise	12%
Other Factors	56 %
Total	100 %

Other factors «include some of the indirect effects of the oil crisis, such as changes in world market demand for Turkish exports, particularly textiles, as well as workers remittances, both in part, but not wholly, due to the deflationary impact of the oil crisis» (p. 55).

The Impact of Exchange Rate Change on the Sectoral Growth

A portion of D-R's work is devoted to a more detailed analysis of sectoral growth in order to discover the tempo of import substitution/expansion and technological advance.

Although they emphasize the importance of relative prices on sectoral development, their attention is focused on the impact of the level of exchange rates. According to D-R, severe import restriction greatly stimulates import substitution, whereas high exchange rates create incentives in favor of export oriented activities.

D-R examine the effect of a devaluation not on the basis of a clear-cut distinction between tradable and nontradable goods but on the share of goods in export-imports/value added and substitution elasticities.

They show that the slower growing sectors are those which are technologically more advanced and that their development corresponds to the intensification of industrialization which constitutes a major objective of Turkish development policy (p. 122). Therefore, it is obvious that a successful devaluation cannot be considered as a policy option.

Hence, a better policy package that reconciles the need for expanding export earnings with the desire to emphasize development of basic intermediates and capital goods is sought. This appears to be a high exchange rate policy with a 50 percent increase in the subsidies accorded to non-traditional exports.

A Criticism of D-R Approach

In my opinion the importance of the distinction between tradable and non-taradable goods should always be emphasized. In the above brief examination of R-D this distinction is also made use of; so how does my analysis differ?

According to my analysis, the relative prices of exportable, import substituting and nontradable goods are instrumental in determining the value of the national income when measured by one of the three categories. This, its turn, would create a difference between its value when measured in dollars and constant Turkish Lira. If these values are known, a prediction could be made concerning the economy and, in particular, the future growth of the national income, inflation rate, income distribution, foreign debt, etc. In short, a better strategy could be followed. Unlike other economists, this book is concerned with determining these crucial values.

It is very difficult to agree with some of the assumptions of D-R. In finding the equilibrium exchange rate the tariff structure is kept stable but quantity restrictions are eliminated. I believe that it is impossible to make such an assumption in a developing country such as Turkey. The tariff structure and quantity restrictions that existed in the base year were only a coincidence; it had no economic rationale: the balance of payments situation as well as the requirement of industry of that year required such a structure. As they change rapidly the structure must change accordingly. Therefore it is impossible to stick to the same structure.

Secondly, the authors consider different items of foreign exchange supply (export earnings, foreign capital inflow and workers' remittances) on the same footing. This conventional problem can be objected to on several grounds. Workers' remittances were some 70 percent of exports in this period. That made a much larger quantity of imports possible without forcing larger amounts of exports. This has meant a greater allocation of resources to import substitution.In the end, a distortion is created in the economy. It is apparent that the authors have included foreign earning creating activities, such as workers remittances on the same footing as, for example, exports.

Thirdly, the authors do not take into consideration the effects of import substitution on the exchange rate. As more import substituting industry is created, it requires higher exchange rates for their product being exported. It is well known that the rate of import substitution increased enormously in that period. Therefore, an equilibrium exchange rate should have been much higher than what is found by the authors.

In a World Bank Staff Working Paper entitled A General Equilibrium Analysis of Foreign Exchange Shortages in A Developing Economy (No 443-January 1981),

Derviş - de Melo - Robinson examine the effects of three alternative methods of solving a foreign exchange shortage. They offer a theoretical framework first and then they apply it to the Turkish situation. According to them a foreign exchange shortage can only be solved at the cost of diminishing the national income. Among the three methods they study, the effect of a devaluation on the national income is less harmful than the others. According to their calculations, the decreasing effect of a devaluation attempted in order to cure an exchange situation, which is rather substantial, on the national income is - 0.3 to - 0.4 percent, whereas my method suggests that it should be much higher than that.

CHAPTER XX

THE SWITCH TO OUTWARD AND GLOBALIZATION POLICIES

§ 1 - INTRODUCTION

When Turkey left long time adopted import substitution policy and turned to an outward oriented one, it was expected that all economists on the left would criticize the new policy by well trodden ideological arguments. But more interestingly several well known economists, both Turkish and international, drew attention to problems to arise after the switch. (*)

It was shown that for a country like Turkey this change of policy would give rise to all sorts of problems. According to them, in the end, the country would have to consider if it should adopt previously used protectionary policies again. The worsening conditions in Turkey after the switch would probably support the ideas of those economists.

In this chapter all those arguments will be summarized firstly, and then their validity will be questionned. The main problem, i.e., should not Turkey turn to outside, will be adressed in view of worsening conditions in the country right after the switch, and it will be shown that this issue should not be discussed if factors determining growth in Turkey are not properly understood, which is the case,as-shown throughout this book.

Before listing summarily the arguments against the switch to outward it would be useful to talk about very widespread belief that many countries left import substitution policy in fashion and switched to export promotion after 1970s.

Liberal economic policies and almost full operation of price mechanism was a rule in most countries until the 1929 crisis. Yet after the crash and ensuing deep and long years of depression, many economists believed that if left to itself, the economy would not restore itself and state intervention to the economy and the use of fiscal

---

(*) In two books published in UK several internationally known economists criticized the outward orientation policy of Turkey.

policies would be necessary. Yet, the inability of that policy to get rid of the crisis ensuing high petroleum prices in the 1970 s induced a great majority of economists to show the beneficiary aspects of a market economy and globalization. All sorts of research work was carried out especially under the auspices of the World Bank.

It is an interesting question whether Turkey turned outside because of the change of world opinion about import substitution or was it related to unsurmountable problems given rise by import substitution policy in this country.

Many economists are of the opinion that for a developing country like Turkey the operation of maket mechanism cum globalization would create all sorts of problems. According to them the use of market mechanism, where there are all sorts of bottlenecks and technical rigidities, is not feasible. They think that once the price mechanism is used to cure difficulties, its impact would be inflation rather than an increase of production. According to them the idea that economic efficiency could be induced by foreign competition and whenever domestic prices are more expensive than foreign prices, those commodities should be imported is wrong. They put forward all sorts of arguments (some of them wrong, others too theoretical) to support their thesis. Let me give an example: should the country import sugar when sugar prices decrease suddenly due to changing world conditions?

§ 2 - THE STUDIES RELATING TO THE SWITCH TO EXPORT ORIENTATION

A summary of all arguments against the switch to export orientation strategy after 1980 may be collected under 4 headings: 1- Worsening economic conditions after switching to export orientation. 2- The temporary character of the improved trade position. 3- Arguments based on the low elasticity of Turkish exports. 4- The inoperability of the classical theory based on the static comparative advantages of the country.

1- WORSENING CONDITIONS AFTER SWITCHING TO EXPORT ORIENTATION

Several economists trying to crticize the switch to export orientation contend that as a result of the switch, all sorts of unfavorable results occurred in the country. They are listed below:

a- Income distribution has worsened as a result of the recession in the economy and real wages decreased by at least 40 percent.

b-Several economists investigating factors causing inflation have found out that among cost push factors causing inflation higher exchange rates and higher interest rates are important culprits. On the other hand, higher exchange rates and interests are closely related to the switch.

c- In import substitution era, interest rates were suppressed and as a result, they were low. After 1980, as a result of the free operation of price mechanism and the liberalization of the financial system, they went up. High interest rates discourage private investments and give rise to huge government deficits, which, in turn, pull up inflation.

e- The switch gave rise to a deterioration of external terms of trade. After 1980 they decreased by around 25 percent. In order to increase exports, an unprecedented increase in the real exchange rate took place, and as a result, terms of trade deteriorated.

f- Many economists believe that the switch was recessionary simply because consumption expenditures were restricted, public expenditures decreased, investments were cut off.

g- Frequent devaluations give rise to unfavorable expectations for interest rates, exchange rates, and prices. They reduce confidence, which is detrimental to stability. Again, an economic policy consistent with local conditions would be difficult to follow.

h- An inflow of foreign funds is difficult when there is a continuous expectation for devaluation.

2- THE TEMPORARY CHARACTER OF THE IMPROVEMENT

a- According to several economists, the improvement in the balance of payments and the increase of exports are of temporary character. After the switch, investments decreased and no new investments were incurred to support the export increase.

b- All export increases originated in the old import substitution industries. No new capacity was created to support the export expansion.

c- Moreover, there was not any increase in productivity, on the contrary, it decreased.

d- It was fragile in the sense that there is a danger of a capital flight from the country.

e- As there was not a financial infrastructure in the country, the expanding export performance could not be sustained.

f- According to several economists, without establishing competitive free markets and creating a proper legal structure all measures to sustain a high export volume would not be enough.

g- For a successful export orientation

(i) the impact of the political pressure on the economy should be low;

(ii) capital markets should be developed.

(iii) Budget deficits should be made smaller.

(iiii) A better tax system should be introduced, and tax evasion should be avoided.

(iiiii) Provison of collective goods by the government should be promoted.

(h) The increase of investment after export orientation was due to generous capital inflows and an upsurge in government investment.

There was not a significant increase in savings, just the contrary it decreased; (even non-communists think so).

i - Structuralist arguments were used: nothing much could be achieved by devaluations.

j- The improvement observed was related to the policy with respect of SEE's, which induced them to increase prices rather than productivity increases: this was a temporary relief.

k- In the implementation of the liberalization of the economy extra budget funds were heavily used. It is expected that they would create problems in future.

l- The policy concerning lay-offs made labor cost fixed, which, in turn, made the economy competitive; but there was not a supply response. Again, the deterioration of income distribution would have to create problems in future.

m- The improvement in trade deficits may have been caused by reduced investment rather than by an expenditures switching.

n- Exports staggered after 1983. Actually the easy stage seemed to have passed; in future an increase in exports is not expected.

o- The increasing foreign debt and interest rates would increase the indebtedness of the public sector; it would reach a very high level, and as a result, this policy could not be sustained.

p- Nothing much could be done by depressing the economy.

3 - ARGUMENTS BASED ON THE LOW ELASTICITY OF TURKISH EXPORT GOODS

Arguments with respect to the low price elasticity of goods exported by developing countries were quite common in the literature. They are all applied in the Turkish case. This is reported and criticized in Chapter XVIII.

4 - THE INOPERABILITY OF THE CLASSICAL THEORY OF INTERNATIONAL TRADE IN DEVELOPING COUNTRIES

Many arguments favoring international trade are based on the Ricardian theory of comparative costs. All those arguments are refuted especially by the leftist economists.

It is shown that the Ricardian theory is based on statical conditions, whereas technological development would lead to changes in comparative advantages of a developing country like Turkey, where comparative advantages lie in agriculture and natural resource - labor intensive goods, the labor value added of which is rather low. If it is adopted, this amounts to a relative impoverishment of the country as time passes.

In addition, according to some economists, if recent trends in world trade are taken into consideration, there is no hope for export orientation for the country.

The main counter argument against the classical theory and/or neo-classical one is this: the worsening of conditions after the opening of the economy is related to the characteristics of developing countries.

In developing countries in addition to the adverse effects of monopolies, there are all sorts of bottlenecks relating to production and technology. The production and distribution systems would not give rise to an appropriate atmosphere for the working of the market economy. The problem in those countries is not the working of the market mechanism but the rigidity of production and distribution mechanism. A demand increase would give rise to price increases rather than to production of goods. As there are not perfect competition and numerous producers, the increases of prices may not induce production.

The policy of export orientation, in a sense, is to restrict domestic demand in order that exports should increase. But there is an assumption here: the possibility of the increase of production. In fact, that does not exist in developing countries. Again, it is supposed that when the public economy is minimized, this would be replaced by the private one: according to anty-market economists this does not exist.

§ 3 - THE COUNTER ARGUMENTS

All those arguments against the switch to outward orientation will be commented in more detail below. Although some of them are relevant, others are naive and many of them are irrevelant. Retrospectively, when all those books and articles written in 1980s and 1990s are read now, the impression one gets is mixed and controversial.

The export increase has not been temporary: it has been 15 percent yearly.

But the main question was different. Could the old closed economy with the minimized operation of the price mechanism be sustained without a shift to export orientation? Theoretically with a better policy without turning outward, things could be improved: now the question. Why was the case so? Are there any country which did so without switching outward? Along with the switching, a more balanced and well-planned policy could follow it. Yes, it is done so in some countries. But would the structure (political, technical, educational) allow the same in Turkey? The most important consideration as reported in this book several times, in Turkey, the past heritage in the economy which was not appropriate to select a different path. Economists who contributed to make a public opinion created an illusion that the past growth rate was 6.4 percent: actually it was some 4-5 percent. According to my opinion the only way to correct the illusion was the present path: the switch to export orientation.

Some arguments put forward against the switch are summarized above. What are my unconventional thoughts? I think that a quantitative comparison of favorable and unfavorable arguments is not possible. Each argument might have sense and a balance cannot be found. My preference is definitely export orientation, even if I am aware of undesired consequences which have occurred after the switch. I do think that the most destructive consequence of the inward looking and import substituting policy has been an unsustainable increase of national income; and present economic difficulties are created by that swollen national income. For me there is no doubt about it. Difficult problems confronting Turkey after the adoption of export orientation are related to previous policy and this is not discussed in Turkey. I also firmly believe that the previous policy could not be followed any more.

Before expressing my views about it I would like to give a table showing what occurred in Turkey after she turned outward. It is obvious that except for an increase of exports every economic indicator deteriorated. Should not Turkey turn outward? It should!

TABLE XX - 1

The Level of Some Economic Indicators after the Switch (In the Middle of Period)

	1930 - 1980		1980 - 1998
Growth rate	6%		4%
Inflation	10 %		60 %
Agricultural growth	3 %		1%
Industrial growth	9 %		6 %
Domestic debt / GNP	-		17 %
PSBR	0.5 %	(1964-1974)	7 %
Foreign Debt/GNP	20 %	(1960-1980)	40 %
Interest/Budget	12 %	(1980-1988)	28 % (1989-1998)

Source: Kazgan 2000, pp, 453-458

Now let us look into the table showing that the performance of the economy has deteriorated after switching to export oriented policy. This is of a nature of giving a false perception. It is shown throughout this book that in pre-1980 period the growth rate was not 6 percent but it was only 4 percent. The same is true of the industrial growth. In the case of reduction of agricultural production from 3 percent to 1 percent I should say that the agricultural growth after 1980 is not 1 percent; it is 1.1 percent. Again, 3 percent growth in agriculture in pre-1980 years was related to the opening of uncultivated areas to agricultural production. In fact, after that process ended, agricultural production increases slowed down. There is no dispute that there is a huge increase in the indeptedness of the government; but this is not related to the switch of the policy.

Now my counter arguments will be listed:

1- The undesired effects arguments put forward by economists are listed above: are they related to the switch to the liberalization of the economy or are they ad hoc fallacy arguments? If all those undesired after-effects were inevitable, I believe that they were, and there is no need to scrutinize them. Even so, let us see their substance.

a- The deterioration of income distribution is not quite accentuated as alleged by the economists. Actually, according to figures about size distribution of income, whatever worth they are, it has improved. It is certain that real wages decreased after the liberalization of the economy; but this might be an indication of a decrease in the segmentation in the labor markets. Moreover, if for the operation of the economy a decrease in wage rates was necessary, there was no harm in it.

b- The higher interest rates are an end - result of the financial liberation. Before the reforms, real interest rates were below zero. After them the real rates are around 20-25 percent, which is high but they are caused by the public sector deficits and inflations; yet, what is more important is the fact that they did not give rise to a decrease of the private investment. (The present real rate is 7 percent) Again, it is shown that its impact both on government finance and income distribution is less than what is generally believed. In Turkey the availability of liquid funds is more important than their prices: actually, the existence of liquid funds is secured by the liberalization of the financial sector.

c- It is true that there is an upward shift in the secular inflation rate after the liberalization of the economy. But the rate in 1977-1979-1980 was very high. Cost push factors such as ever increasing nominal exchange rates, high interest rates and inflationary expectations are not an integral part of the switch. Actually, after the initial exchange rate increase the necessary adjustments could be made by decreasing wages rather than by continuing devaluations. Actually, this is one of the main contentions of this book. As explained in this book, social and political pressure are very important factors giving rise to inflation. Arguments about the increasing effects of the liberalization on the government expenditure are not so strong as other contributing factors to it, such as the expenditure policy of the governments.

d- Arguments about the recessionary effects of the shift due to a decrease of private expenditure continued a few years, but in a rather short time both consumption and investment expenditure turned back to their trend level, even above it.

2- All arguments based on elasticity calculations are irrelevant. It is stressed in this book that the future of exports are related to relative prices and a better use of the abundant production factors, i.e., labor. In turn, at this stage this depends on the price of labor. The elasticity of the exported goods in the pre-1980 era may be low; but this is irrelevant. Actually, most of the exported goods were natural resource intensive goods, the production of which could not be increased anyway. Therefore, the actual increase should be expected in the export of other goods.

3- A host of arguments put forward by extreme leftists are not worth criticizing. But arguments against the classical theory of trade must be criticized. To repeat shortly, they are related to the operation of the price mechanism and also on outmoded Marxist ideas. The ideological ones were related to the colonization of the country by the capitalist powers, and IMF being a representative of them. More scientific ones are related to the irrelevance of comparative cost and domestic resource cost ideas as they depended on static conditions, the new protectionary tendencies by developed countries, the irrelevance of the monetarist measures to control of the economy, etc. I don't want to comment about them because they are all a replica of what is found in the literature, and again, their refutation are even found in simple textbooks. Yet one of them should be taken seriously.

This is inoperability of the classical theory and the fact that it is based on statical conditions. It is not wrong that the Ricardian theory depends on statical conditions. But in the short run, there is no other way to increase exports. This should be the starting point; but if the country follows an appropriate economic policy and if technical progress is induced, more skill and techniques intensive goods could be made exportable. Could that be done by an import substitution policy? The Turkish experience shows that this has not been possible; but on the other hand, the post-1980 experience reveals that a passage from the export of labor intensive to more techniques intensive goods could be secured more easily.

§ 4 - INWARD AND OUTWARD LOOKING INDUSTRIALIZATION

Strategies to promote industrialization can be grouped under two headings: import substitution and export promotion (inward and outward orientation).

In the import substitution strategy the goal is to produce the previously imported goods in the country. It is preferred by the administrators of the country on the ground that the whole economic structure in the country is changed in order to create an industrial structure similar to those in developed countries. It is thought that in that way the economic dependency of the country in question to foreigners would be diminished: self sufficiency is a passion. Moreover, in the after war period it was believed that the establishment of an industry would necessitate less foreign exchange, and new taxation possibilities would arise.

It is mentioned in several parts of this book that Turkey had adopted an inward looking industrialization strategy until 1980 but after that date the country has turned outward. In this chapter the arguments of economists favoring and disfavoring inward-outward looking trade strategies are summarized. Again, the emergence of SEE's which were the most important instruments of the inward looking industrialization strategy, is summarized.

Now, conventional arguments for and against the inward looking industrialization will be summarized.

1- After the 1929 depression the decline of primary goods prices, among them agricultural goods, was felt so bitterly in many other developing countries besides Turkey that the probability of a new depression induced many developing countries to set up industry.

2- The dependence of export earnings on a limited number of goods has always created a danger of wide fluctuations of the country's export earnings due to the caprices of international markets for primary products. Turkey has felt this unfovorable effect and tried to industrialize in order to diversify its export goods.

3- The disadvantages of an industry established by foreign capital created an atmosphere which favored the setting up of a national industry. Once it was decided that a national industry should be established, the economic aspects of the industrialization (cost and return) were relegated to the background, and attempts were made to establish an industry at any cost. If it was public, the low level of its return was no great problem, especially in the short run; if it was private, it could be protected in many ways.

4- The difficulty of finding some strategic goods (goods produced by the war industry in particular, especialy during war times) intensified the desire of politician - administrators of the country to set up an industry. The conflict between Turkey and Greece in the 1970 s, occasioned by the Cyprus crisis, caused great problems because of a sharp cut in the supply of war goods by the U.S. There are intentions to establish a war goods industry.

5- Industry has a value of its own. It has been believed in this country that industrialization is a way of life, and it is a prerequisite of economic development.

6- The employment-creating effect of industrialization has always been stressed in Turkey as in other developing countries. It is supposed that the labor absorption of industry is much greater than that of agriculture, and for the employment of an ever increasing population the establishment of industry is necessary.

7- The high difference of value added per working laborer between agriculture and nonagricultural sectors has always induced industrialization in Turkey. In fact, value added per working person in industry has been some five times higher than agricultural value added. As shown in this book a great proportion of income growth in Turkey was caused by this great difference between agricultural and nonagricultural value added per working population.

Several methods have been used for the promotion of industry in Turkey, but never in the history Turkey had the idea of promoting industry by purely socialistic methods and industrializing the country solely by state action gained momentum. There have been some dispersed writings, especially by intellectuals, as to the necessity of an industrialization to be realized by socialistic methods. According to socialist thought, industrialization and therefore economic development in a developing country can only be achieved by the overall state ownership of industry and by state action alone. But in the history of the country the private sector has always been given a chance to participate in the industrialization of the country.

Methods used for industrialization were various: among them were the establishment of industrial concerns by the state, the drafting of economic plans promoting particular industries (such as the plans of the 30 s), overall plans favoring industrialization (such as the five-year plans of the post 1960 period), piecemeal measures taken under development plans. The variety of forms of the latter is wide enough to constitute the subject matter for a book. To gain some idea of them, it is worth mentioning the following: protection of industry against import competition, overvaluation of the currency, import restrictions and prohibitions, exemptions of taxes, differential taxes and tax holidays, price controls, foreign exchange licensing favoring some industries, public channeling of official aid, special measures favoring foreign investment in selected areas, etc.

All these methods have been used in Turkey: the degree of emphasis on each has changed from time to time.

A short summary of problems which seem to have been created by industrialization in Turkey in the period 1950 - 1980 are summarized below.

a- The industry seems to be a capital intensive one. The degree of absorption of labor by the industry is low and the high level of unemployment is probably a consequence of industrialization in Turkey along with the high rate of population growth.

b- The size of industrial firms is very small, and they are far too numerous. This form of industrial organization puts an upward pressure on the cost of industrial goods.

c- The cost of industrial products was very high compared with the products of other sectors. This fact can be proved by the degree of protection accorded to industrial goods in the form of quotas, import prohibitions, import duties and subsidies in that period. Also the high difference of value added on labor input in the industrial and agricultural sectors is a proof of the high cost character of industry.

d- Capacity utilization seemed to be low in industry.

e- Industrialization in Turkey seems to have caused an inequal distribution of income. Research on income distribution in Turkey shows that it is very unequal. It can be said that the rents created in industry is one of the main causes of highly inequal uncome distribution in Turkey.

f- Industrialization had increased import needs of the country to an excessive degree. In fact, the ratio of imports to national income in Turkey was below international standards, if the trade balance deficits are taken as a proxy of high level of imports. As a great proportion of these imports are intermediate and capital goods for industry, the excessive amount of trade deficit could be attributed to industrialization.

g- The cost of industrial goods is ever increasing, and the infant industry argument for industrialization has not proved right in Turkey.

h- A great proportion of the country's scarce resources are allocated to industries producing goods for domestic demand. This allocation has hindered proportional development in other sectors.

i- When the intensity of government intervention increases, uncertainity in the country increases, and this could be harmful for the economy.

j- High bureaucracy would make the operation of the market economy less efficient.

k- Conditions in the country may not give rise to a higher absoption of labor compared to capital. The artificial cheapness of capital would give rise to this conclusion.

1- The importance of competition is emphasized in export orientation strategy. That would induce competition and monopolists could not dominate the market. There is a pressure from external competition.

m- The Turkish experience should reveal how inefficient the replacement of imported inputs by domestically produced ones had been in 1968-1973 period. In fact, as the total imported inputs for industrial products was 10.2 percent of the production in 1968, it was 14.1 percent in 1973. That increase was noticeable especially for the production of intemediate and investment goods. (Korum 1976)

§ 5 - DISCUSSIONS ON INDUSTRIALIZATION IN TURKEY

Some research works give the impression that the growth of internal demand was the main dynamic force influencing industrial growth (Table XX-2) (see Celasun 1980 and 1983, Korum 1977, Çiller 1976).

The research methodology and the conclusion of the economists who conducted those analyses do not seem to reflect the reality of Turkey. This research can be criticized on several grounds. I would like to mention one interesting conclusion, i.e.,

TABLE XX -2

THE SOURCES OF GROWTH OF INDUSTRY IN TURKEY (%)

	1963-1968	1968-1973	1973-1977
The growth of domestic demand	83.6	81.8	100.4
The expansion of export	4.9	16.3	-1.0
Import substitution	8.3	-1.4	0.6
Technical change	3.2	3.3	-

Source: Celasun 1980, p.8.

the share of import substitution in the growth of industry was found to be very low, especially during the last part of the 1960 s and the 1970 s. This conclusion seems to be connected with the level of imports. If the level of actual imports are determined by the availability rather than by economic reasons, the peculiar conclusions about the share of import substitution is inevitable but it is irrelevant. The clear evidence is the decrease of import substitution in 1968-1977. During that period there was a spurt in imports due to the workers' remittances and convertible deposits. Since actual imports were higher relative to expected imports, import substitution was calculated to be lower compared to the previous period in all 4 calculations I am aware of.

Two main factors giving rise to industrial growth are the increase in inputs and productivity. If the growth in the value added in industrial sectors is divided by additional workers in industry, this shows a productivity increase.

There is a very important difference between the productivity increase in the pre-1976 and post-1976 periods. The gross value added of the industrial sector per working population in industry increased by 6.2 percent in 1966-1976. According to Krueger-Tuncer (Krueger-Tuncer 1982 a and b) the productivity increase to be ascribed to labor in 1963-1976 is 2.1 percent, whereas for 1976-1985 the productivity increase was 0.6 percent (Ozmucur 1988). According to another research paper there was a decrease in productivity by 0.3 percent for 1976-1988 (Uygur 1990). Yet another research work shows that the productivity decreased by 0.6 percent in 1975-1985 (Türel 1990).

There are various explanations for the decrease. According to Krueger-Tuncer. a decrease in productivity was inevitable. The reason was the increasing use of resources in high cost and less efficient fields of import substitution (Krueger-Tuncer 1982).

According to another research, the factors were as follows (Türel 1990): 1- The shift of the industry to less productive areas, 2- the decrease in the scale, 3- the decrease in productivity when the scale increases, 4- the low rate of wages, the increase of inducements to exports, and real devaluation must have decreased productivity, 5- the deflator in previous years based on low prices of imported goods was wrong. (To me they are all irrelevant.)

According to the unconventional approach expounded in previous chapters the conclusion about the causes of productivity decrease by all researchers should be considered irrelevant, or at least they fail to indicate one of the main factors giving rise to the productivity decline. What is it?

The increase in the productivity in the first period is closely related to the overvaluation of industrial goods. Again, the decrease in productivity is related to the decrease in the overvaluation of industrial goods.

We know that in the post-1976 period real wages of organized labor decreased by about 50 percent. This means that relative prices of industrial goods must have decreased relative to the prices of other sectors; this is the result of the fact that a large percentage of organized labor (the wage decrease is there) is in industry. Actually, the yearly increase in the nonagricultural sector is now around 5.5 percent. The previous high increase in industry was related, to a certain extent, to the overvaluation of industrial goods. I believe that without analyzing relative prices nothing much can be said in this subject. Although I didn't thoroughly analyze the growth of industry, my hunch is that the maximum growth rate in future should be around 6 percent.

§ 6 - THE CRITICISM OF IMPORT SUBSTITUTING STRATEGY BY KRUEGER

Professor A. Krueger (1974, 1979, 1981, 1982) studied Turkey's highly inward looking (anti-trade) development strategy and criticized it by means of conventional arguments.

Professor Krueger and other economists following her (especially IBRD) try to demonstrate two things. Firstly, they show the disadvantages of relying on import substitution. Secondly, they try to demonstrate that if Turkey had promoted trade based on comparative advantages, both her exports and national income would have been much higher. They do this by analyzing the consequences of inward looking industrialization. This is done under two headings: micro and macro consequences.

I will try to summarize that analysis very shortly below; but before attempting this I want to make it clear that although I have always been against inward looking industrialization and although I have always emphasized the advantages of trade based on comparative advantages, I believe that it is not possible either to demonstrate the disadvantages of import substitution or the advantages of trade by the method used by Krueger and other economists writing on the same lines.

Krueger points out two micro consequences of this policy; they all create problems for the economy and hinder a healthy development. Two of them relate directly to trade; therefore they will be taken up here.

Micro consequences of an inward looking policy

1 - Domestic Resource Cost

Domestic resource cost is a concept devised to measure distortions caused by import substitution. It is based on a belief in comparative advantages. Without using this concept, there were some attempts to find out the comparative advantages of Turkey (Aker 1967). In Aker's study, comparative advantages are measured by comparing historical trends of cost in several industries. If the cost in one industry shows decreasing trends compared with import prices, that industry is considered as having comparative advantages.

Professor Krueger tries to measure the opportunity cost of the inward looking strategy by means of domestic resource costs.

One of the distortions caused by inward looking industrialization and trade regimes based on heavy protection of industry is the misallocation of resources, and misallocation of resources can be measured by what is called domestic resource cost (DRC). DRC is a figure showing the resource cost of producing various commodities. «If one activitiy has a DRC twice as high as another, the implication is that had the first activity not been undertaken and had the resources been employed in the second activity, these resources would have produced twice as much foreign exchange earnings or savings as under the existing allocation» (1974, p. 218). Extensive research has been done by Professor Krueger on this subject; the results show the great variance of DRC's in the production of nearly 100 commodities. Moreover, the relative levels of DRC's are very much the same as expected: goods produced by the industries established for the production of goods substituting imports are very high compared with industries which would probably have comparative advantages.

IBRD fully adapted this concept and based all its recommendations on it (IBRD 1980).

2 - Excess Real Costs of the System

Quite parallel to theoretical expectations, the conclusions reached by Professor Krueger's comprehensive research show that this strategy has several real costs. She examines them under 5 headings: (1) enterepreneurial time and energy; (2) additional clerical staff required to handle paperwork; (3) expenses, such as airplane trips to the capitol, associated with obtaining import licenses; (4) costs associated with the effects of the regime on inventory level; and (5) excess capacity resulting either from inability to obtain imports or from incentives to overbuild resulting from the trade regime.

As the first three costs are extremely difficult to quantify, she makes some estimates about the last two costs.

Macroeconomic Effects of the Inward Looking strategy.

Professor Krueger analyzes the macroeconomic effects of inward looking and outward looking strategies by trying to find out the probable effects of both strategies on value added, job creations and imports.

Professor Krueger carried out extensive reserch in order to find out the effects of the misallocation of resources on growth, import requirements and employment. The goal of the research is explained by Professor Krueger as follows. «The two growth alternatives represent identifiable allocation patterns. They both give heavier weight than the plans did to those industries where Turkey apparently has the greater comparative advantage. Both patterns imply at least as rapid a growth of the overall manufacturing sector as was envisaged by the policy makers. Thus, if the hypothetical alternatives had enabled more rapid growth of manufacturing income,and employment, those alternatives would presumably have been preferred to the actual pattern oriented toward import-substitution. Several questions are relevant: taking the amount of investment in manufacturing as given, how did the rate of growth of manufacturing value added compare with that which would have occurred under 'moderate import substitution' (MIS) or 'balanced export promotion and import substitution' (BEPIS) with the same total investment when value - added is evalued at Turkish prices? Further, how does the actual growth rate compare with that which would have been experienced under the two alternatives evaluated at world prices? Then what would have been the import content of investment and how does that compare with the actual import contents? What would intermediate goods imports have been, compared to what then actually were? And what would employment in manufacturing have been?» (1974, p. 250).

Professor Krueger collects data on the relative ICOR's, import coefficients and employment provided per value added in different industrial sectors and with the use of historical data she tries to see the effects of two alternative strategies and compares the results with actual figures.

The conclusions of Krueger are shown in her Tables XXI - 3, 4, 5, 6, 7. Some of them are summarized below: (Tables, XX - 3, 4, 5, 6).

TABLE XX - 3

FIRST FIVE YEAR PLAN (FFYP): INCREASE IN VALUE-ADDED AT TURKISH AND INTERNATIONAL PRICES UNDER ALTERNATIVE ALLOCATIONS OF INVESTMENTS

(INCREASE FROM 1962 IN MILLIONS OF 1961 TL) (INDUSTRY ONLY)

Value added at Turkish prices			Value added at international prices		
FFYP	**MIS**	**BEPIS**	**FFYP**	**MIS**	**BEPIS**
5,641	5,926	8,523	3,397	4,309	6,198

Table XX - 4

ICOR'S FOR THE MANUFACTURING SECTOR

	Plan	MIS	BEPIS
FFYP	1.85	1.70	1.18
SFYP	1.89	1.73	1.28

TABLE XX - 5

IMPORT REQUIREMENTS UNDER ALTERNATIVE GROWTH STRATEGIES (millions of TL)

	Capital Goods	Intermediate Goods
FFYP(1961 prices)		
Plan	3656	1911
MIS	3332	1214
BEPIS	2778	1423
SFYP (1965 prices)		
Plan	8966	4321
MIS	7909	3383
BEPIS	7888	4076

TABLE XX - 6

NEW JOBS CREATED BY ALTERNATIVE INVESTMENT PLANS

(THOUSAND OF JOBS)

FFYP			SFYP		
Plan	MISS	BEPIM	Plan	MISS	BEPIM
197.1	233.8	335.3	428.0	520.9	640.4

Professor Krueger's calculation is based on a simple model reproduced below (Krueger 1974, p. 241).

e_j employment per million TL of value added in the jth sector

k_j the ICOR of the jth sector in value-added terms

m_j imports of intermediate goods per unit of output of j

n_j imports of capital goods per unit of investment in j

q_j ratio of Turkish value-added price to world value-added price of j

v_j ratio of value-added to output at Turkish prices in j

The variables for which estimates were derived, under each of the three growth alternatives, are:

E_j^i employment in j under the ith allocation strategy

I_j^i investment in j under the ith allocation strategy

IVA_j^i value added in the jth sector at world prices

K^i ICOR in value-added terms for all manufacturing

M_j^i intermediate goods imports in the jth sector under the ith strategy

N_j^i capital goods imports for investment in j under the ith strategy

P_j^i output in the jth sector at Turkish prices

V_j^i value-added in j at Turkish prices under the ith strategy where i superscript refers to alternative allocations. These are denoted by

a the allocation in the plan

b BEPIM

m MIS

Under any allocation pattern, by definition:

$$E_j = e_j V_j \quad (1)$$

$$V_j = I_j / k_j \quad (2)$$

$$P_j = V_j / v_j \quad (3)$$

$$IVA_j = q_j V_j \quad (4)$$

$$M_j = m_j P_j \quad (5)$$

$$N_j = n_j P_j \quad (6)$$

and totals for all manufacturing sectors can be obtained by summing the both sides of each equation over j.

Letting the period for which output patterns are observed be denoted by a superscript 0,

$$I_j^b = \sum_k I_k^a [V_j^0 / \Sigma V_k^0] \quad (7)$$

$$I_j^m = \sum_k I_k^a [k_j V_j^0 / \Sigma V_k^0 K_k]. \quad (8)$$

Recent Writings by Krueger on the Turkish Economy

Professor Krueger has continued to write on the Turkish economy and employed her findings as references in her extensive contribution to international economic literature. Many economists working on development and trade in semi-industrialized countries have referred to her writings.

Two papers by Krueger (with B. Tuncer as co-author) were published in prestigious American journals:

1 - An Empirical Test of Infant Industry Argument, American Economic

Review, 1982.

2 - Growth of Factor Productivity in Turkish Manufacturing Industry, Journal of Development Economics, 1982.

Both papers were further examples of views Krueger initially expressed in 1974.

The first paper examined the infant industry argument and documented that input-output relations in protected industries remained constant. It had been expected that inputs would decrease vis-a-vis output. In that case one was able to conclude that protection had led to the expected result and that industry could survive without protection.

The results of this paper's research on a large proportion of the industry revealed that the Turkish case is somewhat different. The input-output relationship appeared to remain constant throughout the whole period. Therefore, the policy of protection was unsuccessful. The cost to the economy was too great.

The second paper studied the productivity increase in the Turkish industry. Observations were made concerning the relationship between value added and input in various industries. Attempts were made to discover the relative impacts of input and productivity increases. According to an examination of the Turkish economy between 1963-1976 - a period of import substitution - the average productivity increase only totalled 2.10 percent while the rate of growth of industry amounted to 12.2 percent. The conclusion was again the inefficiency of the import substitution strategy.

§ 7 - CRITICISM OF IMPORT SUBSTITUTION ARGUMENTS

Critical appreciations of import substitution by Krueger are reported above (Section 5). This reappraisal can be contrasted with the unconventional one presented in this book. My approach requires that although the switch to export-led growth was necessary, national income had to decrease rather than increase as adduced by economists. Almost half of this book is devoted to the explanation of this fact. To repeat very shortly: the changes in the valuation of goods in the traditional analysis do not exist. When the country switches to export-led growth the prices of services and along with that those of labor intensive goods decrease with respect of capital-skill-technology-import intensive goods. It is shown that this would give rise to a decrease in national income.

But this is also a conceptual definition of national income, and it doesn't reflect the actual computations properly. It is shown in several chapters above that apart from the impact of the probable increases of imports and their prices, the actual level of national income must converge with the level determined by the new valuations of goods. Actually after Turkey switched to export led growth, the growth rate of the economy decreased. Its mechanism is explained in the various chapter above.

It is quite apparent that the method used by Krueger is very simple. Her conclusions are based on the fixitity of the following ratios:

1 - ICOR's are constant in each industry (her k);

2 - The employment ratio to value added is constant in each industry (her e);

3 - Input/output coefficients are constant in each industry (her v);

4 - Import coefficients are constant in each industry (her m);

5 - Import of capital goods per unit of investment is constant in each industry (her n);

6 - The ratio of Turkish value-added prices to world value added prices are constant in each industry (her q).

I must say that it is unfortunate that such a renowned economist has adopted such a simplistic approach. I am in favor of such a switch in policy. Turkey had to switch to export orientation on account of the problems caused by import substitution. But I have attempted to demonstrate that this switch to export orientation was not a rose without thorns (a Turkish saying). A switch to exports has been necessary but the specific problems of Turkey should also be addressed. If this had been more carefully studied, it would have been realized that the least troublesome of a number of alternative strategies could have been selected. The experience of the Turkish economy in the post-1980 period has clearly indicated how Krueger and her associates at the World Bank and IMF were mistaken, and how tragic such a mistake can be.

The dramatic improvement of the Turkish economy after its switch to export orientation in the 1980s at first sight seems to have provided a total vindication of those recommendations for such a strategy found in economic literature (see, for example, Derviş 1987, Balassa 1983). But significantly, the hostile response of the Turkish public to this policy in March 1989 has led to an unexpected collapse of this strategy. What is then wrong with Krueger's strategy?

The constancy of all six of the parameters enumarated above is crucial. As soon as they are considered constant in each industry, the shift among them should work wonders: shift from import substitution to export orientation and then all your macroeconomic magnitude would change in the desired direction! But is it possible for all these parameters to remain constant?

The work of Krueger and other model builders to prove the inefficiency of inward looking industrialization and the advantages of export orientation is based on the fixity of relative price ratios of labor and nonlabor intensive goods during the import substitution and export orientation years of the economy. In Turkey, as has been noted, after 1980, a strategy of export orientation was adopted.

I have demonstrated in UATE (1978) and in other chapters of this book that if Turkey is to increase its exports without suffering from inflation, worsening income distribution and increasing foreign debt, the price ratio of nonlabor to labor intensive goods should increase. As is noted, the most important characteristics of an inward looking industrialization are the relatively high costs of industrial goods having no comparative advantages, and the more likely monopolistic market structure produced by such a strategy. If an outward oriented strategy is adopted, a relative decrease in the prices of labor intensive goods should be expected.

The model builders assume that input output ratios (Krueger's v) would remain the same before and after the switch to export orientation. But it can be demonstrated that a switch should bring about a systematic change in input output ratios. The technical coefficients may stay constant but the prices of inputs and outputs may alter. If so, they will have to change. We know that if the value of intermediate goods inputs are deducted from the total production, the remaining figure is the value added. If the value added for the exportable goods remains the same or even falls in terms of foreign currency, the value added for labor intensive goods should be reduced. Although the technical input coefficients are the same, the relative value of labor intensive goods to nonlabor intensive ones would decrease. If so, the value in the production of labor intensive goods should decrease, which means a charge in input/output ratios, Krueger's v.

Krueger's study about industrialization attracted several criticisms. Left winged economists who have stuck to inward looking industrialization tried to put forward all sorts of arguments against export orientation. They are taken up above.

Although I am against inward looking industrialization, I put forward a very serious argument against that of Krueger.

CHAPTER XXI

MARKET ECONOMY OR SOCIALISM

§ 1 - THE ECONOMIC SYSTEM

After the establishment of the Republic, Turkey continued its reliance on the market economy even under the pressure coming from its neighbor, i.e., Russia. It was not only a political pressure but as years went by, many Turkish educated people among them writers, literary people, artists, economists, etc, carried on a very strong battle against the proponents of the market economy, favoring socialism or communism. Their arguments were based on controversial issues such as the stinging capitalism, which existed for the benefit of a tiny proportion of the population, the personal distaste and dissatisfaction because of their (educated people) lower material welfare compared to some noneducated people, and the lack of operability of the price system in a developing country like Turkey rather than on scientific arguments.

It cannot be negated that there was a humanistic flavor in the belief of some leftists. Their persistence in favoring communism continues even after the fall of communism at the end of 1980s.

Atatürk, the founder of the Turkish republic, who might have been tempted to adopt the Russian communist regime, did not do so perhaps because of his firm belief in the achievement of western countries under capitalism.

It is an indisputable fact that Ottoman Turkey was exploited economically by the imperialist countries of the West, and it was then broken into pieces politically. It could be expected that the elite, struggling against the West, might have adopted an economic system different from theirs. And that was at a time when the socialist thought was developing on the premises that capitalism and imperialism was intermixed.

The economic system could be discussed under two headings. One is the discussion of the advantages and disadvantages of an economic system based on private property and better operation of price mechanism. The other topic is a study of the operation of state economic enterprises.

In the first case opponents of a capitalist system argue ideologically rather than dwelling on economic dimensions. They usually forget about advantages of a more open system based on the operation of price mechanism.

The advantages and disadvantages of the operation of state owned economic corporations are also discussed. Some favor them, but others state their disadvantages. There is no doubt that at the beginning they were indispensable and performed important functions in the development of the economy. But nowadays their disadvantages are discussed; they are: 1- The difficulty they give rise to the operation of the price system. 2-The lower efficiency existing in state enterprises . 3- The burden on government finance. 4-The incompatibility with the more open economy.

When the Turkish left defended its thesis in the pre-1980 years they used to base their arguments on theoretical ones in favor of a socialist economy as well as on the world experience of those years. Although serious problems of a mixed economy started to emerge in those years, problems given rise by a globalized economy did not exist then.

According to those economists the in pre-1980 years the priority of the government was fast growth and a better distribution of income. But after the adoption of the globalization policy, they were replaced by a desire of a fall of the share of public sector in the economy and a globalization policy without any regard to previously targeted goals. After 1980 all efforts were concentrated on a restriction of the area of maneuvering of governing people. The behavior of the economy would be shaped by the movement of capital, structure of financial markets and the operation of price mechanism. It is shown that while the share of international trade was 17 percent of GNP before, it went up over 40 percent after 1980. While discretion was the main tool of the economic policy in pre-1980 years, it has been replaced by price mechanism. Corruption, siphoning and theft, high interest payments, more public deficits, the increasing strength of giant international companies, increasing reflection of adverse world economic conditions on the national economy, an undesired flow in and out of hot money have been an integrated part of globalization. The ability of the government to govern the country has been greatly restricted.

§ 2- THE CRITICISM OF THE MARKET ECONOMY AFTER A GLOBALIZATION POLICY WAS ADOPTED

Until 1980 when a closed economy depending on planning and a heavy state intervention prevailed, arguments against the market economy were rather old fashioned and also they were mixed with ideology. After the market orientation in 1980, more liberalized economic policies were adopted . All those people in favor of a planned economy and the lovers of socialism tried to mix their old arguments with their alleged disadvantages of globalization. According to them the deterioration in the economy after 1980 supported their opinion.

In this section, their way of thinking and arguments will be summarized. Although some problems of the Turkish economy disappeared after the export orientation and a better operation of market economy set in, new difficulties emerged and the economy deteriorated somewhat.

What were the beneficial characteristics of the inward looking planned economy, which they call national state?

1- The main function of the previous state was to protect the rights and security of individuals; whereas under the new winds of globalization, the main goal of the state is to protect the interest of capital owners and international monopolies.

2- In the old regime the government had previously targeted goals in line with the interest of a high proportion of citizens, which was a fast growth and a better distribution of income; whereas now the economy is governed by the movements of capital and prices.

3- In the old regime the flow of capital in and out was restricted; whereas now it flows freely in and out, and it gives rise to instability in the economy.

4- In the old regime, the government was in a position to take measures to improve worsening conditions; whereas now the area of maneuvering of the government is restricted, and macroeconomic policies are not used efficiently any more.

5- A better practice of rules and regulations was possible before; whereas under globalization and market economy theft is a rule and the country is a mafia economy. Ethical values are lost in that regime.

6- Although there were monopolies in the old regime, they belonged to the state and as a result of the discretion relating to consumers, the price policy was more in line with the poorer section of the economy. Moreover, monopoly profits belonged to the state itself. But under the new regime international monopolies and dominating classes are exploiting people.

7- In the old regime the impact of the worsening of world conditions was restricted; whereas now the economy would be affected as soon as the world economic conditions deteriorated.

8- In the old regime it was possible to take all sorts of measures against unfair foreign competition, whereas after the adoption of GATT rules, nothing much could be made.

9- In the old regime a proactive economic policy based on local conditions, needs and opportunities could be adopted.

10- In the old regime the minimum wage of poor workers was tried to be kept intact; whereas under the new regime when difficult problems were encountered, they were solved by flexible wages.

11- In the old regime higher wages could sustain a high demand; again, high wages would enhance the efficiency of workers. But as they were made flexible, the emergence of an under-capacity becames a rule.

12- In the old regime when a public deficit existed, it was covered by new taxes. But under the new regime public deficits are covered by loans. As a result of increasing interest to be paid by the government, the most urgent state functions are not performed efficiently.

13- In the old regime the production capacity was parallel to the needs of an equitable distribution; whereas in the new regime as income distribution worsens, the old capacity set-up for the needs of the poor section of the economy could not be used properly.

14- In the old regime the newly established industry was protected against foreign competition, whereas now many enterprises are confronted by difficult conditions; as a result they cannot exist anymore.

15- In the old regime unjust protection of some companies was not a rule, whereas under the new regime all sorts of incentives and subsidies are accorded to a few privileged companies and that deteriorates the government accounts.

16- In the old regime an harmonization of the interest of every section of the economy was tried to be achieved, whereas now the interest of a few minority groups is protected against the masses of people.

17- Last but not the least let us read the summary of these arguments: private losses are nationalized and public benefits are privatized.

Some of the arguments which are in favor of a closed planned economy are summarized above. There are others, there is no end to them.

Being in favor of a more market oriented economy, what do I say?

As repeated in several sections of this book, the problem is not a selection between white and black. A lot depends on the circumstances and the resources of the country in question, both natural and human. Yet what is wrong in all those arguments is the impossibility of explanation of the deterioration of the Turkish economy in the sense that the share of TFP was unbelievably low under the old regime. Although a better picture emerges in the old regime when pre -and post-1980 performances are compared, I tried to show that this was an illusion and a very superficial observation.

What I am trying to say is that the old regime could not be sustained, and again the present problems of the economy are a heritage of the old regime. As repeated several times, both the growth and the level of national income in the old regime is an illusion. It is obtained at the cost of creating all those problems encountered by the economy after it adopted a more open market economic policy. If this is not agreed, it is not possible to defend the new regime.

Many economists dwell upon the loss of efficiency and productivity in the old regime, and beneficial aspects of competition in the new regime in introducing productivity. Moreover, it is believed that when there is more protection and more interference by political institutions, populism (or popularity) would be in question. When there is a planned economy it is impossible to avoid interference by politicians. The defense of economists favoring the planning and closed economy is that the unfavorable consequences are not related to the logic of the system but to the mismanagement of the administrating people. To me this is misplaced.

It's impossible to separate the system from the people practicing it. It is in the character and nature of humans to benefit from the position they possess.

Moreover, a lot has been done to replace the market by plans designed by people, yet its success has been limited. There is more: many arguments asserted by anti-market economists are mixed with ideology, while some of them are wrong and at least very superficial or inconsistent. Again, the use of factual observations to defend an anti-market regime is very naive. I don't want to extend and justify my views anymore simply because they're even written in textbooks. My original thesis is the impossibility of arguing on the basis of the past figures relating to the level of national income and its past growth. In other words those economists assert their arguments without understanding the operation of the Turkish economy. In addition, I believe that their competence in economics is very limited.

§ 3- A MARXIST INTERPRETATION OF ETATISM

There have always been intellectuals with socialist tendencies in Turkey, but it was only after the 60 s that their ideas spread through every segment of the country: universities, political parties, workers' unions, government employees and artisans. It is not even rare to meet peasants or employers who are influenced by these ideas.

Even a short history of socialist thought and its impact on various segments of society is beyond the scope of this book. Yet, a complete silence on these views would constitute an important gap in this work. Therefore, a compromise is found by summarizing part of a book concerning Etatism by one of the most prominent and perharps of the ablest Turkish Marxists (Küçük, 1975). In the book, economic development is studied with special reference to Turkey and an analysis of the Turkish economy from a Marxist point of view is conducted.

Dr. Küçük thinks that the existence of an economic system essentially based on private enterprise is connected with the ever-continuing existence of dominant classes. However, the slogan of a nation without classes has been repeated, even taught in primary schools, since the beginning of the Turkish Republic. Dr. Küçük thinks that there have always been classes in Turkey. The power of the dominant classes was above the power of the founders of the Republic and that of administrator-politicians.

He gives several examples to verify this view. They are listed below. In the 20 s the Parliament did not approve a bill allowing for the establishment of solely state-owned enterprises. The bill had to be changed in order for it to be approved by the Parliament. The relevant article as to the goals of establishments to be founded according to this law was expressed as follows: "(a) To manage industrial concerns to be given to the possession of the government until they are transferred to companies to be established; (b) to participate in the management of industrial concerns." (p. 229) It is apparent that the Parliament allowed for state-owned establishments if they were eventually transferred to the private sector.

The second example is Ataturk's inability to materialize an agricultural reform (mostly redistribution of land), a move strongly opposed by the big land owners.

In 1932 the same Parliament approved a bill allowing for government ownership and management of the "Sanayi Bankası" (The Industrial Bank), but a year later this institution was abolished and its assets were transferred to Sümerbank. According to Küçük, this fact is highly illustrative. The solely state owned new institution, Sümerbank, had the function of granting credits to the private sector along with its other functions, i.e., the establishment and management of industrial firms. This fact is interpreted by Dr. Küçük as follows: "State management of indurstry would be allowed if it created conditions for the flourishing of the private sector. A bureaucracy as such, and a state based on such a bureaucracy is not feasible. What is feasible is this: either bureaucracy is not dominant or it is under the control of other dominant powers. In other words, bureaucracy is effective at a rate permitted by the dominant classes, as everywhere in the world, not only in Turkey."

As another example of the dominance of industrialists he refers to the Economic Congress of Izmir and interprets the resolutions taken at thes Congress as follows: "Industrialists decided that a law (Encouragement of Industry) should be extended and national industry should also profit from this law, a desire different from that of the industrialists of our days." (p.233).

The new Law of Encouragement of Industry was issued by the Parliament. The comment by Dr. Küçük: "The Parliament works for the dominant classes and issues laws which create incentives for the prospering private enterprises."

Etatism is viewed as a materialistic process by the author. The interests of developed countries lie in the backwardness of underdeveloped countries, and this means their remaining as agricultural countries. Etatism was considered a defence mechanism, because industrialization was necessary. But why should the state be active in industrialization? He presents an explanation based on materialism by showing that technical structure required large enterprises and this could be realized only by the state.

The following quotation is an example of the same line of thought. "At a time when there was harmony of classes the effort of the government was to foster the birth or continuation of classes of possession; the prices of products of the soil were supported in order that land owners should profit, and the construction of state projects was left to private persons." (p.238)

Another quotation: "The fundamental feature of the 1923-1929 period was a spreading of the process of a firm establishment of capitalism in the society with the collaboration of the state." (p.240)

It is even advanced that a tax called the dime was abolished in order to establish a contact between agriculture and the market! According to Dr. Küçük, the first bank of the Republic, İş Bankası, the capital of which belonged mostly to the founders of the Republic, among them Atatürk, was founded in order to grant credit to private persons. Again, Dr. Küçük advances the view that the Free Party, which was founded in 1930 by the order of Atatürk as an opposition party to the ruling Republican People's Party, was a piece of the example of class dominance. Let us quote again: "Etatism emerged as a reaction to the crisis of 1929. The goal was to industrialize and to create industrialists. In order to measure the reaction of other classes to this policy and to keep it in reliable channels the establishment of a new party (Free Party) was attempted. This attempt brought forth an adverse public reaction, and when public unease had reached a high level the party was closed." (p.244-245)

Dr. Küçük shows that state aid did not foster the development of private industry as much as desired. A portion of foreign capital was still operating, but new concessions were not allowed. Another quotation: "The system of Economie Dirigée was being discussed. Etatism was included in the program of the Republican People's Party, the party in power. The condition that government participation in industry should be limited to fields into which private industry was reluctant to enter was suspended. Several articles of The Law of Encouragement of Industriy were changed so that private persons could profit from this law." (p.246)

Dr. Küçük has a very different interpretation of the price control law, called the National Protection Law, issued during the Second World War. "This law was not against the development of private firms. On the contrary, the regulation of procurement of their raw materials and distrubution of their products was put into order by means of this law. The profits of the private firms were increased and were guaranteed. Moreover, the law legalized compulsory work and the work day was increased to thirteen hours." (p.247)

Dr. Küçük quotes a scholar in order to support his ideas: "The hostility against capitalism in Turkey is quite different from that in other countries: a detestation of the foreign capital bottleneck, which had other motives concealed beneath business motives... Free enterprise, rent of land or interest, which all constitute essential ingredients of capitalism, were not considered as means of exploitation." (p.250)

Comments on the line of reasoning by Dr. Küçük:

A summary of the analysis of the formative years by Dr. Küçük has been given above. His analysis of the later periods is exactly the same. The analyses of other Marxists (they proliferate) are also exactly the same. The same Marxist tools are used, the same conclusions are always drawn, as is the case anywhere in the world. However short the space devoted to reflecting the Marxist analysis may be, it can show the line of reasoning. Everything which has happened in the country is interpreted to support Marxist views. There may be some bits of truth in the Marxist explanation, but the author of this book does not agree with the whole of the main arguments by Marxists, some of which have been quoted above. It should also be added that anything that has ever occurred in the country is explained by the Marxist idea: that it has occurred simply because the dominant classes wanted it to.

§ 4- AN EXTRACT FROM DOĞAN AVCIOĞLU

In the 60 s and 70 s, Doğan Avcıoğlu was very active in conveying international socialist thoughts to Turkey and to propogate them in journal articles (especially in a weekly periodical entitled YÖN). He gathered his thoughts in a two volume book entitled "Türkiye'nin Düzeni (The Order in Turkey)" (1968-1972). According to his closest assistant, Hasan Cemal, who gave up socialistic ideas and has become a well known journalist, he was in close contact with the military and wanted to get it involved in a socialistic revolution (see, Cemal 1999).

The best way to reflect the main ideas expressed by Avcıoğlu is to give an extract from his book entitled "Türkiye'nin Düzeni". In fact, in a 750-page book, he strolls around the ideas expressed in the summary of his book and gives examples and quotations to verify his ideas. Here is a short translation of the summary.

"I tried to show that investigations going back to the Ottoman Empire suggest that Turkey could have been a highly industrialized country and along with that one of the comtemporary civilized nations of the world. This has not been the case and this was simply because of the fact that it was hindered by imperialism. In a country under a heavy influence of imperialism the road to development by means of capitalistic methods is stopped. Capitalism under imperialism does mean colonialism and exploitation rather than development in the sense of an increase of welfare.

The investigation of our history and scientific research reveals that the first and the most important condition for selecting an independent road to development is to get rid of foreign hegomony. Economic independence is not a desire but it is a must for development.

The Turkish nation, which gained independence after the Republic in 1923, tried to create an independent developed country by establishing a national capitalism. Yet, the elite in business, which was supposed to be nationalistically inclined, became to be intermediaries of western capitalism instead of establishing factories. Actually, a few factories established in order to produce consumption goods were dependent on western companies in procuring spare parts and technology.

Political independence was not consolidated by economic one. As a result, the trend was reversed in the Tanzimat (the era opened as result of the first westernization effort of Ottoman Empire which took place in 1836), and westernization and the development was based on foreign loans and capital. Today, Turkey adopts an American type of development model. The government is transfering a huge amount of capital to private sector in order to make them stronger. Engineers and administrators trained by means of possibilities provided by the state are employed by the private sector now. Private companies are using the capital and know-how provided by foreign capitalists. The government allows private companies to earn enormous money by import restrictions and evasion from taxes.

It is necessary to set up a balance sheet of the development methods which were used during the last 20 years. Although large sums of money provided by the government was used by private companies, an industrialization has not been materialized. The established industry has been an artificial monopoly producing consumption goods which are demanded and enjoyed by rich people.

This industry is dependent on foreign countries for procuring its machinery, equipment, spare parts, raw materials and technology. While it was not in a position to export, its development increased import needs. Its total export revenue is not even equal to its import needs. If enough foreign loans are not found, that industry is doomed to failure.

In privileged markets, capitalist classes are becoming rich and prosperous. Although they earn some one third of national income, they do not make necessary investments. They waste investible funds by luxurious consumption. There is a contrast between their luxurious expenditure and the waste and the misery of large masses of poor people. Social problems are getting worse everyday.

An agricultural country like Turkey is not in a position to feed itself. Shanty towns are growing unbelievably. Unemployment is increasing every year. Foreign debts are becoming burdersome. In villages the difficulties of villagers working as employees and as small farmers are becoming insupportable. They have difficulties in feeding themselves. Meanwhile the feodal leaders and usurpers are living a prospherous life on the deposits left by the serf order of the ancient times.

Both town captialists and feodal leaders of villages are against reforms to solve those difficult problems: they hinder the road to development. It is time to bring an end to that at a time all countries are in a competition for growth.

Nationalist revolitionaries should play a part in comtemporary Turkey. Ever since the mid-1800's they struggled to stop that tendency which would make the country a colony. They wanted to create a civilized and independent country. But this was not reached and what was the worse, we are not on the way to achieve that. It is possible that undesired conditions in the past had a part to play in that outcome. As a result, we must learn the teachings of economics and recent history better in order to receive the necessary lesson.

The problem boils down to that: what to take and what not to take from the West. In fact, Atatürk had suggested an answer to that: in order to westernize the first condition was to become independent... Once the independence is obtained what to do was a revolutionary movement (he meant a military coup, author) to bring about a change in the order. Westernization is not possible when the country is an sattelite of western capitalists; but it would be possible by changing the old order by means of revolution.

The sultanate and khaliphate should be replaced by a laic administration, which is a part of a rational and scientific world concept."

§ 5- THE SOCIALIST IDEOLOGY IN 2004

The evolution of socialist thoughts in Turkey is definitely the subject matter of a book. In this chapter it is overviewed by giving a short summary and by touching upon the writings of the two socialist economists above. But if I try to underline briefly how the present system (outward oriented) is attacked, I can give a better idea by summarizing an article by a well known Turkish Marxist. In order to so I shall try to summarize a newspaper article by one of the best known economists, i.e., Professor Deniz Gökçe, who is market mechanism minded.

The article appeared in AKŞAM dailypaper on December 11, 2004. This article is a sort of reaction to an article published in The International Herald Tribune on Dec. 5, 2004. One of the coauthors of that article is Professor Erinç Yeldan of Bilkent University, Ankara. He is a well known left minded academician. The title of the article is IS TURKEY THE NEXT ARGENTINA? It is written that the success of Turkey is praised in international literature. But people who know Argentina well would not be trapped by that assertion. The situation in Turkey is quite parallel to that of Argentina. When the Argentinian currency was overvalued, hot money invaded that country; as a result, the industrial understructure of that country cracked down; yet employment increased. Like the present situation in Turkey, the increase of GNP was 9.5 percent. But interest rates and external debts were increasing, exchange rates were free, and money was overvalued. Privatization was giving rise to unemployment, and subsidies to agriculture were decreasing. Although hot money inflow to the country was high, foreign investments were low; as a result, no employment was created. Now they ask: was the present situation in Turkey exactly the same? In fact, the high income growth in Turkey is supported by current account deficits, which are not its cause but they are an end result of high income growth; as a result, a high growth rate is unsustainable. They stress the point that although there is high income growth, unemployment increases. Real interests are very high, and government debts are increasing. Then they add: after the interest rate increase in the US, hot money would leave Turkey. And this would mean a deep crisis in Turkey. In fact, under the burden of the present government debt, this is inevitable. In addition, 6.5 percent surplus after non-interest payments in the government, the budget should not allow for human and capital investments.

According to Professor Gökçe, Professor Yeldan is one hundred percent wrong. In fact, the import of investment goods in Turkey has been $ 12.5 billion since the beginning of 2004. Export and import levels have been phenomenal in the last year, $ 62 billion and $ 90 billion, respectively. Again domestic debt of Turkey is decreasing rapidly with lower interest rates, especially in external borrowings. According to Professor Gökçe, his assertions are all ideological: what could we expect from somebody who is against liberalization policies?

Now the decision: are the assertions and expectations of Professor Yeldan based on a good economic analysis or on ideology? I think that some of his observations are not wrong, yet his reasoning seems to reflect his socialist ideology. Economic analysis is used to support the socialist ideology. This is how left-minded Turkish economists are!

§ 6 - SOCIAL DEMOCRACY IN TURKEY

A summary of my writings about the discussion of the advantages and disadvantages of adopting an economic system based on the operation of the price mechanism and the impact of the switch from inward to outward orientation is found above.

In 2001-2002, the Turkish economy was shaken by a most destructive economic crisis; contrary to practices during previous crises, backward steps to a more controlled and planned economy were not taken. In fact, under present conditions and the existence of firmly established institutions since 1980, (i.e., after the economy turned outward) and in view of the impact of the global economy, to go back to the pre-1980 era seems to be impossible. Except for chauvinistic and extreme rightist-leftist political parties, all moderate rightist-leftist parties are trying to advance on the post-1980 path. Yet social democrats and along with them many economists are trying to find a way to apply the principles of social democracy.

In the past, social democracy in this country was interpreted as statism (etatism) in the sense that of a big share of industrial production should be carried out by state economic enterprises, and a tightly controlled economy with an aggregative plan or without it. As the operation of price mechanism and requisites of being a part of a globalized economy would not allow it, intellectual efforts and eyes of economists turned to european sort of democracy. Now well trained economists try to interpret social democracy as it was practiced in Western countries.

What are the main principles of social democracy? Let us list them.

1- The state should intervene in the economy not under the guise of establishing and operating economic enterprises and by adopting economic plans but it should not let wild capitalism exists. It should establish a legal framework for economic activities and as a result theft, siphoning and unfair competition are avoided.

2- The state should use discretion for a fair distribution of income by subsidies, taxes, etc. Again, the operation of trade unions should be promoted.

3- When it comes to subsidies to various economic activities, their impact on productivity should be thought of, and again the state could distribute subsidies to the extent that its financial reserves would permit. In a way, the state could not give what it has not.

So far, so good. On the face, those principles of the social democracy seem to be fine. But could they be applied in Turkey under present conditions?

In a fragile economy in the midst of the deepest crisis, how would the state afford those social goals? Actually in an economy like the Turkish one, which has had such a poor record in the productivity (it is shown that productivity increase in Turkey during the last half century was almost nothing), should turn all its efforts and means to promote productivity. Tradeoff between productivity and equity is well known. But in the Turkish case it is more than that. Many problems confronting this country have arisen as a result of government spendings not related to promoting productivity. What I try to say is that principles of social democracy should be consistent with the conditions of this country.

§ 7 - THE STATE ECONOMIC ENTERPRISES AND ETATISM

In the economic development of Turkey after the foundation of the Republic, the role played by the state owned economic enterprises has been very important. The following passage from the UATE would provide an idea of the reasons for their introduction, (pp. 17-19)

"Etatism

In the early years of the Republic, economic problems of the country were given a great priority. Atatürk, the founder and uncontestable leader of the country, expressed the importance he attached to the economy of the country in a speech he delivered at the Izmir Economic Congress, which took place in 1923. The economic development of the country was considered an absolute necessity; and every measure would have to be taken to achieve this goal. The transition to Etatism began under these circumstances. A short summary of the causes which induced the country to adopt Etatism is given below.

1-Historical causes

Turkey's exploitation by imperialist powers during the Ottoman reign was very severe. The founders of the republic were determined to wipe out imperialism:

capitulations, foreign concessionary companies, the dominance of foreigners in industry and commerce; the importation of almost all industrial goods, exports consisting solely of agricultural products were all thought to be effects or signs of imperialism.

The founders thought that the exclusion of foreigners from the economy was necessary in order to bring an end to the dominance of foreigners. But who would replace foreigners ?

2- The private sector was very weak.

The replacement of foreigners leaving the country by the private sector was impossible in the formative years of the Republic. Turkish nationals had no experience, knowledge, financial resources or desire to enter industry and commerce. During the Ottoman reign, commercial activities of some importance and such industry as existed were left to foreigners. Even if the private sector had the necessary experience for these activities, the only financial resource owners apart from foreigners were large land owners, who were reluctant to enter industry and commerce. Moreover, incentives for private individuals did not exist as capital investments conducive to the development of the country did not promise immediate profits. Although satisfactory profits might have been obtained in years to come, the private sector was not ready to wait (and probably risks its assets) for long years.

3- The operation of the price mechanism was not conducive to an economic takeoff.

The inadequacy of the price mechanism to start and to promote economic development had been discussed ever since the first scientific writings on economics. Although the founders of the Republic were not, perhaps, familiar with the economic literature on this subject, they felt that the operation of the price mechanism would not be conducive to the mobilization of economic resources for a quick economic development. The discussion of problems such as economies of scale, indivisibility of factors of production, external economies, inability of prices to reflect the relative scarcity of goods, the speed of adaptability of the economy to signals coming from the market, etc:, were beyond the reach of the administrators and academicians of the country. Yet, they had a feeling that the mere operation of the price system was not conducive to a quick economic takeoff.

4- The founders did not want to adopt a socialist system such as that of the Soviet Union.

As was shown above, conditions for an effective participation of the private sector in economic development and an efficient working of the price mechanism did not exist in Turkey. It would therefore be thought that the alternative to the private sector and the price mechanism would have been the adoption of a socialist system such as the Soviet Union's. However, even the existence of close relations between the Soviet Union and Turkey during the War of Independence and the years following it, i.e., the Soviet Union's substantial financial and political aid to Turkey, did not induce the founders to adopt such a system; the thought was not even given serious consideration.

Private property, free enterprise, economic freedom of individuals have been in the foreground since the first days of the Republic. It was thought that the system of Etatism would remedy the lack of participation of private enterprise in economic development and the inefficiency of the price mechanism to mobilize economic resources without adopting a kind of socialism.

The intervention of the government in economic affairs in the first years of Etatism was in the form of founding state economic enterprises and regulation of foreign exchange markets. But, as years passed by, the intervention intensified to such a degree that nothing much is left of the price mechanism in the 1970 s. Yet the private sector is thought to be the backbone of the economy. Would such a complex system of price intervention and full operation of the private sector coexist, and if it coexisted what kind of problems would arise? A full account of abnormalities given rise to by such a coexistence is presented in this book." (UATE, pp. 17-23)

After reading what was written in UATE a few words should be added. Firstly, a few words about the definition of state economic enterprises (SEE). Those are business units owned by the State; their activities must have impacts on the economic and social life of the country. Although they are owned by the State, goods and services produced by them are not freely offered to public. It is stressed by several economists, (see, Okyar 1978 and Aysan 1979) that they should be considered in two categories. One is those serving to general public, such as social security organizations, electricity, water, PTT, railways, employment agencies, etc. Others are selling all sorts of goods and services like any business company. The latter ones should be organized as private companies, profit motive being in front. In fact, in their inception it is understood that they should organize their activities according to market conditions. As they are established on the principle of profitability, that is expected. Again, as their establishment was due to a lack or an insufficiency of private funds, they are supposed to exist temporarily. In the end, their activities would be taken over by private companies. They would be transferred to private sector when they reach a satisfactory profit level. Yet, it is stressed by various writers that in their establishment there are political and social considerations.

The activities of SEE's are discussed in detail be various economists. I would like to underline two conferences held where they are discussed in depth.

1- Conference Board 1965: Aren, Arnon, Hanson, Parsons, Okyar, Yaşa. Soysal: 2- Hiç, 1979: Kerwin, Okyar, Singer, Iren, Aκgüç, Korum, Manisalı, Ekin, Tuncer.

(A short summary of the discussions in (1) is found in the Appendice to § 7. below.)

A lot is written about their advantages and disadvantages. Their main advantages and their historical necessity are summarized above. A few more can be added to them (see, Korum 1979). It is shown that the plant size of SEE's is much bigger than similar firms in private sector. Again, it is known that technological potentials of big plants are higher. Now, as the optimum economic plant size increases the production is shifted from consumer goods to intermediate goods industry. On the other hand, it is found that public consumption goods industries are becoming intermediate goods industries. That means that their development is in desired directions.

Debates regarding the privatization of public enterprises began in the 1950 s; however, there was not much action until the 1980 s. In recent years, a great number of them were privatized. Unions and the Left have opposed it; and they have been quite successful. In the end, a privatization law was issued by Parliament in October 1994.

The waste caused by the public sector and as a result, its pressure on the government budget has been enormous.

One economist writes as follows: "Part of this delinquency of the government is to be attributed to its treatment of the state industrial enterprises. Because of the political expediency, as well as economic policy, it constantly interfered with their alleged autonomy, as in determining their prices, and it frequently mismanaged their affairs, as in not providing for the completion of many of their projects." (Singer 1978, p. 302).

The above passage suggests that if left to themselves, they could have been much more instrumental in the development of the country. The belief is based partly on their necessity in the economic life and partly on their inner administrative structure.

Part of the importance of the state economic enterprises is based on their inner administrative structure. It is stressed by several economists that they used a relatively advanced form of administration and more advanced production techniques. This was related partly to their less fear from losses and readier access to capital funds. This was true in the early years of the Republic.

State economic enterprises have additional advantages. One is related to their location; they could be established in the more backward regions of the country, where private firms were much less disposed to go. Again, the same administrative and technical staff who had a wide experience in them have later constituted the leading managers of the emerging private sector of the country.

Problems with the management of those institutions can be listed as follows.

1- There has been a large turnover of top and middle personnel. This has been partly due to the activities of changing governments in preferring to employ top level administrators favoring their political party and partly due to the higher salaries offered by private enterprises.

2- It is a visible fact that state economic enterprises have always employed more personnel than they need. This is partly a government policy to create employment for those who would otherwise be unemployed, and partly it is due to political pressure to employ more personnel sharing the views held by the party in power.

3- A great problem created by their operation was concerned with their decision as to the determination of the prices of goods and services they produce. Every government uses a price policy which attracts more votes for its party, and these prices are controlled in order to attenuate ever existing inflationary pressures. But the negative difference between the cost and revenue of these institutions compelled governments to go to the Central Bank, as a result of which more money was printed, and that contributed to inflations. Moreover, necessary financing for those institutions was not found; even, in some cases, some capital investments were not completed withim the scheduled time.

4- The coordination of the activities of various state enterprises constituted an important cause of the inefficiency of the whole system. Several institutions were established and/or the task was given to different ministries in order to control/ coordinate and raise both the individual and common efficiency of the state economic enterprises; but none of those efforts were successful.

5- When the lack of autonomy of those institutions came together with the classical weaknesses, such as the non-existence of incentives and a slow functioning bureaucracy, their operations caused great problems.

APPENDICE TO § 7 - THE CONTROVERSY ON SEE'S IN 1966

This section is a summary of discussions which took place at an international seminar organized by The Conference Board in Istanbul in 1966.

The main theme was as follows.

1 - Is mixed economy a historical necessity? If so, is mixed economy a temporary-trasitionary system or is it going to stay forever? Is it a pragmatic solution? Has it got rules and principles?

2 - Should there be a competition between private and public enterprises? If it should be, should it be on equal conditions?

3 - What are management problems of SEE's and is productivity low in those enterprises?

According to some economists the mixed economy is a transitionary state in the shift of the market economy to socialism; in the end, socialism would be a permanent system. This was the opinion of Turkish Marxists. Just the contrary opinions were expressed by several economists stating that the existence of a mixed economy had not anything to do with the shift to socialism.

Economists defending the first line of thought tried to support their thesis by a well known reasoning that factors which transfered feudalism to a capitalist order were the same as those which would transfer capitalism to socialism by means of mixed economy; and it was trasitionary. According to those economists, productivity was the same both in state and private enterprises. If it were different, one of them could not be permanent.

According to economists opposing socialism, if the economy turns out to be a socialist economy, the state would be dominant in the whole economy but this would amount to a sort of limitation of the freedom of individuals. They think that the state exists for the welfare of individuals; therefore it is not a goal but a vehicle only. It is a fact that individuals are sacrificed for the state from time to time; but this is wrong. The state could interfere with the economy for the benefit of individuals only. According to them, the mixed economy in Turkey emerged as a result of a historical -structural necessity; therefore it should be considered pragmatic

The width of SEE's is limited by managerial and technical constraints. On the other hand, the width of private sector is constrained by the entrepreunial capacity and risk taking desire of private people. As a result, when a development model is chosen, the mix of public and private enterprises should depend on objective criteria rather than on ideological ones.

It is claimed that the mixed economy model is an end result of pragmatic considerations. The goal is to get rid of difficulties confronting the economy. Yet, in the Turkish case it is difficult to say whether it is related to ideological factors or to pragmatic ones.

Once a coexistance of private and public enterprises is considered a fact of life, the problem is to establish a borderline between them. Yet, according to some economists the determination of a borderline is not logical. The main guide is the necessity of the existence of SEE's dictated by conditions or constraints.

Different thoughts about the future of SEE's are expressed in the conference. Here are two extremes. Firstly if the development of public enterprises is detrimental to private ones, the former ones would be dominant in the end. But on the other hand, it is claimed that as private ones are more productive and aggressive, they would be final winners.. All that means that they cannot coexist together. At the time when the discussion took place it was difficult to side with one or another. But the prevalent ideas at that time was that the following criteria could be taken into consideration for the establishment of SEE's. 1-The high level investment for establishing and running them. 2-The difficulties of seeing the future. 3-The risk involved. 4-Ignorance. 5-The lack of desire on the part of private investors to enter a certain field. 6-The low level of expected profits. 7-The importance of the field (or sector) from the point of view of the economic development of the country. It is discussed whether or not a borderline could be drawn. But when all these criteria are brought together, this seems to be very difficult.

The above is a very short summary of what is discussed in the seminar in question. Retrospectively when it is viewed in 2008, let us see what has happened since.

Until the 1980's SEE's continued to grow and their share in the national economy increased continously. But toward the end of 1980 s the trend reversed and they started to shrink. Why? Although the discussion was timely and relevant in those years, it is evident that several factors reducing their importance were not perceived. Was it because of the changes in ideological views? Was it because of the fact that their missions had come to an end? Did they perform their mission and they had to leave their place to private companies? Was it because of the fact that the private enterprises had the technical and managerial capacity? Was it becacuse the productivity of the private sector overpassed that of the SEE's? Was it because the price mechanism was more efficient now under new world conditions?

All these questions are worthy of being asked. I think that along with that the financial position of the state weakened as a result of new functions it has assumed.

§ 8- THE RECENT WORLWIDE RECESSION AND THE FATE OF PRICE MECHANISIM (OR CAPITALISM)

The probability of a worldwide recession originating in the US as a result of the bubble given rise by an extraordinary expansion of the financial superstructure along with the innovation of new tools has been very delightful for many left wing economists and ones which were not properly educated in economics.Left minded people were not happy when the socialist ideology collapsed after 1980's.Many socialists and badly educated people think that this is the end of capitalism based on the operation of price mechanism

There is no end to the writings of economists and journalists-columnists on the expected crisis.It is evident that they are a replica of what is written in the West.All I am going to do in this final section of this book is a short summary of writings by well known economists and journalists in this country.

The general perception is that it is closely related to the working of price mechanism and the greediness of players in this game. Again, many of them are of the opinion that things would be different in the future after a tight control of the price mechanism by all sorts of regulations and interventions by governments.Many people believe that the transfer of private companies to the state is against the philosophy of the price mechanism and capitalism.

The opinion of extereme leftists is more pronounced.They are happy to see the disorder given rise by the capitalism philosophy;especially because their past criticism of this system has proved right.They believe that the dominant ideology (laissez faire, laissez passer)has brought false solutions and created disorder rather than wealth and this crisis is an example only.According to them disorder is everywhere in economic life.They think that the traditional teaching of economics should be changed and economics will be taught by different textbooks. Again they think that the problem is not so simple in the sense that when problems arise the government would intervene and once it is solved capitalism would come back.The remedy is the change of the whole order and that capitalism should not return any more.According to them capitalism is a system based on inequalties.There is not equity in this system.High risk,high leverage and as their by-product inequality are musts for capitalism.They are all detrimental to an equitable society.

Left wing economists and those who are not educated properly believe that the aim of the economic system is the production of goods and services satisfying the needs of people.People cannot eat or draw satisfaction from financial operations.It is acceptable that profits could be earned in the production of goods and services. Yet when capitalism created a huge financial superstructure(with no use for human happiness); it made the earnings for people engaged in it very high.Why wouldn't capitalist institutions take this advantage? The main motive in capitalism is to earn more and more money.The financial system is enlarged to an extent that it had not any relation to the real economy.The relation between the real economy and finacial markets is cut off.

I do not think that a high percentage of well educated economists and writers are recommending adopting a socialist system. Most of them are of the opinon that a properly organized and planned government intervention to the economy and the creation of necessary regulation would solve the problem.

I am quite confident that price mechnism and capitalism will subsist more vigorously in future.The present problem will be solved at the cost of more inflation and lower incomes of some countries.

An in-depth analysis of the recent recession is beyond me.But I think that the behavior of people creating the big bubble in financial markets are quite in line with the philosophy of capitalism. On the one hand, the huge balance of payment deficits in the dominating economy needed funds to compensate for it. Yet people were not saving enough to solve the problem.The reason was that huge funds existing in the world searched fields of investments.As a result, why would they save more and decrease the pleasure of drawing from high incomes?And the financial institutions or sectors accomodated by creating new tools and means.

It is evident that there is a correlation between the size and operations of financial markets and the economic development of the country. Everybody knows that it is not possible to develop without a good monetary system.Finance is about the same.lt sustains the production level and contribute to its growth.People cannot consume finance but yet for the permanent flow of goods and services it is necessary.The problem is the harmony of both the real and financial sectors.But in this complex world one hundred percent harmony is difficult to achieve. Could that be solved by government interevention and by more and more regulation? Here is the difficult problem.More regulation, more intervention would make price system less efficient. There is always risks in economic life especially when innovation is in question. Interventions and regulations would make risks lower but this would also make efficiency lower.When you try to avoid inequality you must decrease risk but, in turn, this a deterrent for development.

INDEX

T

U

V

W

Y

Akgüç, Ö., The Development of the Public Sector in Turkey's Mixed Economy, in Hiç 1979.

Aksoy, A., *Structural Aspects of Turkish Inflation*, IBRD, 1982

Aksoy, A., Wages, Relative Shares and Unionization in Turkish Manufacturing, in *Özbudun-Ulusan*, Holmes and Meier, New York, 1980.

Akyüz, A., *Money and Inflation in Turkey*, SBF, Ankara, 1983.

Akyüz, Y., Financial System and Policies in Turkey in the 1980's, in Arıcanli-Tosun, 1990.

Alper, E ve Öniş Z., Finansal Küreselleşme, Demokrasi Açığı ve Yükselen Piyasalarda Yaşanan Sürekli Krizler, Doğu Batı Dergisi, 2001.

Anand, Ritu, Ajay Chhibber and Sweder Van Bergen, External Balance in Turkey: Can they be reconciled? in Arıcanlı-Tosun, 1990.

Aral, S., Social Mobility in Turkey, in *Özbudun-Ulusan*, New York, 1980.

Aren, S., Karma Ekonomide Planlama ve Gelişme, Conference Board, İstanbul 1965.

Arıcanlı, Tosun and Rodric Dani, Eds. *The Political Economy of Turkey: Debt, Adjustment and Sustainability*. St. Martin Press, New York, 1990.

Arıcanlı, Tosun, The Political Economy of Turkey's External Debt: The bearing of Exogenous Factors, in Arıcanlı-Tosun, 1990.

Arın, T., İthalatın Evrimi, 1981-1990, Dış Ticaret ve Ödemeler Dengisi, in Kazgan-TUSES, 1990.

Arslan, I., Celasun, M., Sustainability of Industrial Exporting in a Liberalized Economy: The Turkish Experience, in Helleneir, G.K. (ed), Manufacturing for Exports, in the Developing World, Routledge, London, 1995.

Ateşoğlu, S., *Comparison of Keynesian and Quantity Theory Models: The Case of Turkey*, 1950-1963. University of Pittsburgh, Doctoral Thesis, 1972.

Avcıoğlu, D., Türkiye'nin Düzeni, 2 Volumes, 1968 and 1972, İstanbul.

Aysan, M., Özellikle Bankalar ve Kamu İktisadi Teşekkülleri Açısından Kurumsal Yapıda Yeni Düzenlemeler, in Conference Board 1978.

Balassa, B., *The Purchasing Power Parity Doctrine:A Reappaisal*, JPE, 1964.

Balassa, B., The Role of Exchange Rate Policy in Achieving the Outward Orientation of the Turkish Economy, *World Bank Reprint Series No 181*, 1981.

Balassa, B., Outward Orientation and Exchange Rate Policy in Developing Countries: Turkish Experience, *The Middle East Journal*, 1983.

Balassa, B., The International Monetary System and Exchange Rate Policies in Developing Countries, *IBRD, Discussion Paper*, 1987.

Balassa, B., Effects of Exchange Rate Changes in Developing Countries, IBRD Discussion Paper 291.

Baysan, Tercan, C. Blitzer, Turkey's Trade Liberalization in the 1980's and Projects of its Sustainability, in Arıcanlı-Rodric, 1990.

Bergsman, J., Commercial Policy, Allocative Efficiency and X Efficiency, *QJE*, 1974.

Berk, M., Public Policies Affecting the Distribution of Income among Cotton Producers in Turkey, in *Özbudun-Ulusan*, New York, 1980.

Beyarslan, A., *Türkiye'de Gelir Dağılımı ve Ücretlerin Seyri*, Ankara 1982.

Bilkur, Ş., Revenue National et Defense National de la Turquie en 1947 et 1948, Ankara.

Boratav, K., 1980'li Yıllarda Gelir Dağılımı: Bir Makro Analiz, *Yeniden Dağıtım Mekanizmaları*, Boratav-TUSES, 1990.

Boratav, Korkut, Inter-Class and Intra-Class Relations of Distribution under Structural Adjustments: Turkey During 1980's, in Arıcanlı-Rodric, 1990.

Bronfenbrenner, M., *Income distribution Theory*, Macmillan 1971.

Buchanan, J.M. et al, *Toward a Theory of Rent-Seeking Society*, Texas University Press, 1980.

Bulutay, T., Tezel, Y., Yıldırım, N., Türkiye Milli Geliri 1923-1948, Ankara, 1974.

Burk, M., Strategies for Optimum Employment Maximization and Economic Growth in Turkey, in *Miller 1971*, AID, Ankara, 1971.

Carliner, G., 1990'lı Yıllar için Ekonomik Kalkınma Stratejileri, in *TUSIAD* 1990.

Celasun, M., Prospective Growth of Non-agricultural Employment in Turkey, in *Miller 1971*, AID, Ankara, 1971.

Celasun, M., *Perspectives of Economic Growth in Turkey, 1973-1977*, ODTU, 1972.

Celasun, M., Real and Monetary Aspects in the Turkish Economic Planning, *METU, Studies in Development*, 1980.

Celasun, M., *Sources of Industrial Growth and Structural Change*, IBRD, 1983.

Celasun, M., Income Distribution and Domestic Terms of Trade in Turkey 1978-1983. *METU, Studies in Development*, Volume 13, No:1-2, 1986.

Celasun, M., General Equilibrium Model of Turkish Economy, *METU Studies in Development*, 1986.

Celasun M., Income Distribution and Employment Aspects of Turkey's Post-1980 Adjustment, *METU, Studies in Development*, 1989.

Celasun, M, Rodrik, D., Debt, *Adjustment, and Growth*: Turkey, Edited by Sachs, D. and Collins, S., N.B.E.R., 1989.

Celasun, M, (a) Gelişen Ekonomilerin Dış Kaynak Kullanımı, Finansal Krizler ve Türkiye Örneği, 2001, Doğu Batı, 2001.

Celasun, M. (b) Ekonomilerde Uzun Dönemli Büyüme, Enflasyon Süreci ve IMF Destekli Programı, Doğu Batı, 2001.

Celasun, M., 2001 Krizi, Öncesi ve Sonrası: Makroekonomik ve mali Bir Değerlendirme, in Küreselleşme, Emek Süreçleri ve Yapısal Uyum, İmaj Yayıncılık, Ankara 2002.

Cemal H., Kimse Kızmasın, Kendimi Yazdım, Doğan Kitapçılık, İstanbul 1999.

Chenery, H., Patterns of Industrial Growth, *American Economic Review*, 50, 1960.

Chenery, H., Syrquin, M., Patterns of Development, Oxford University, Press, 1975.

Chenery, H., Türkiye'nin Gelişmesine Karşılıklı Bakış, in *Türk Ekonomisinin Dışa Açılma Sorunları*, Conference Board, 1979.

Chenery, Hollis; Robinson Sherman, Syrquin, Moshe, *Industrialization and Growth: A Comparative Study,* Oxford University Press, 1987.

Cillov, H., Türkiye Ekonomisi, Istanbul, 1972.

Conway, Patrich, The Impact of Recent Trade Liberalization Policies in Turkey, in Nas-Odekon 1988.

Çiller, T., *Türk Sanayiinin Büyümesinin Kaynakları: İthal İkamesi, İhracat ve İç Talep,* Boğaziçi Üniversitesi, İstanbul, 1976.

Çiller, T., Kızılyallı, D., *Dış Borçlar,* TUSIAD, 1987.

Çiller, T., Kaytaz, M., *Kamu Kesimi Açıkları ve Enflasyon,* ITO, Istanbul, 1989.

Conway, Patrick, The Record on Private Investment in Turkey, in Arıcanlı-Rodric, 1990.

DPT (State Planning Department), *Gelir Dağılımı,* 1963.

DPT, *3. 5 Yıl Planı Makro Modeli,* 1973.

DPT, *GelirDağılımı,* 1976.

DPT, *1-6.5 Yıllık Planlar* (Development Plans)

DPT, 8 Beş Yıllık Kalkınma Planı Nüfus, Demografi Yapısı, Ankara 2001.

Danielson, M., Keleş, R., Allocating Public Resources in Urban Turkey, in *Özbudun-Ulusan,* New York, 1980.

Demirgil, D., Factors Affecting the Choice of Technology in Turkey and the Implication for the Level of Employment, in *Miller 1971,* AID, 1971.

Denison, E., *Why Growth Rates Differ: Postwar Experience in Nine Western Countries,* Washington Brooking Institution, 1967.

Denison, E., *Accounting for United States Economic Growth,* Brooking Institution, Washington, 1974.

Derviş, K., Robinson, S., H., The Foreign Exchange Gap, Growth and Industrial Strategy in Turkey: 1973-1983, *The World Bank Staff Papers,* 1978.

Derviş, K., Ekonomide Bunalım ve Çözüm Seçenekleri, *Bulgu,* 1978

Derviş, K., Robinson, S., The Structure of Income Inequality in Turkey: 1950-1973, in Özbudun-Ulusan, New York, 1980.

Derviş, K. et al., *General Equilibrium Models for Development Policy,* New York, 1983.

Diaz-Alejandro, C.F., Exchange Rate Devaluation in a Semi-Industrialized Country, M.I.T. Press 1965.

Eldem, V., Türkiye Milli Geliri, İktisat Fakültesi Mecmuası, Istanbul, 1948.

Ekin, N., Türkiye'de Yapay İstihdam ve İstihdam Politikaları, İstanbul 2000.

Ergüder, Ü., Politics of Agricultural Price Policy in Turkey, in *Özbudun-Ulusan,* New York, 1980.

Ertuğrul, A., *Kamu Açıkları, Para Stoku ve Enflasyon,* YKB, İstanbul, 1982.

Faik, B., Matbuat, Basın, Medya, Doğan Yayıncılık, İstanbul 2002.

Fry, M., *Finance and Development Planning in Turkey,* Brill, 1972.

Fry, M., Türkiye Ekonomisinin Dışa Açılması için Para Politikası, *Türkiye Ekonomisinin Dışa Açılma Sorunları*, Conference Board, İstanbul, 1979.

Fry, M., *Money and Banking in Turkey*, Boğaziçi Üniversitesi, İstanbul, 1980.

Fry, M., *Money Interest and Banking in Economic Development*, John Hopkins University Press, 1988.

Fry, M., Maxwell, Money Supply Responses to Exogenous Shocks in Turkey, in Nas-Odekon 1988.

Fry, M., Maxwell, Money, Interest, and Banking in Economic Development, London, 1995.

Gökçe D., Akşam, Dec. 11, 2004.

Gökçe, D., Büyüme Tuş Etti., Akşam, July 26, 2007.

Hagen, E.E., The Economics of Development, Irwin, 1975.

Hansen, Bent, *The Political Economy of Poverty, Equity and Growth: Egypt and Turkey*, Oxford University Press, New York, 1991.

Hamurdan, Y., *Türkiye'de İstihdamın Yapısı ve Yönlendirilmesi*, DPT, 1976.

Hatiboğlu, Z., *Türkiye'de Bankacılık, Institute of Business Economics*, Istanbul, 1966.

Hatiboğlu, Z., *Cumhuriyet Rejiminde Türkiye Ekonomisinin Gelişmesi*, Istanbul, 1973.

Hatiboğlu, Z., *An Unconventional Analysis of the Turkish Economy*, Aktif Büro, Istanbul, 1978.

Hatiboğlu, Z., *Growth and Rents in Developing Countries*, Istanbul, 1979 A.

Hatiboğlu, Z., *Explorations in Development Economics*, Istanbul, 1979 B.

Hatiboğlu, Z., *Rents, Development and Economic Analysis*, Beta, Istanbul, 1983.

Hatiboğlu, Z., *Comments on Conventional Economics in the Light of the Turkish Experience*, Institute of Business Economics, Istanbul, 1990.

Hatiboğlu, Z., *A Theory of Growth and Its Validation by the Turkish Experience*, Istanbul, 1990.

Hatiboğlu, Z., *An Unconventional Analysis of the Turkish Economy and Beyond*, Istanbul, 1992.

Hatiboğlu, Z., *Gelişme ve Türkiye İktisadı*, Beta, Istanbul, 1993.

Hatiboğlu, Z., *Economic Theory and the Turkish Experience*, Istanbul, 1995.

Hatiboğlu, Z., *Conventional and Unconventional Economic Analyses*, Istanbul, 2002.

Herschlag, Z. Y., *Turkey, An Economy in Transition, Van Keulen, The Hague*, 1958.

Hiç, M., Turkey's and Other Countries Experience with the Mixed Economy, Editor, İstanbul, 1979.

IBRD, *Turkey: Prospects and Problems of an Expanding Economy*, 1974.

IBRD, *Turkey: Policies and Prospects of Growth*, 1980.

IBRD, *Turkey: Industrialization and Trade Strategies*, 1982.

IBRD, *World Development Report*, 1982.

IBRD, *World Development Report*, 1992.

IBRD, *Country Report, Turkey 2000.*

Kazgan, *G., Ortak Pazar ve Türkiye*, Istanbul, 1973.

Kazgan, *G., Dışa Açık Büyüme*, 2. Edition, Altın Kitaplar, İstanbul, 1988.

Kazgan, G., Türkiye'nin Cari İşlemler Bilançosu ve Dış Borçları, *Dış Ticaret ve Ödemeler Dengesi*, Kazgan-TUSES, 1990.

Kazgan, G., Önder, İ., Kirmanoğlu, H., Tuncer, N., *Türkiye'de Gelir Bölüşümünü Bozan Etkenler ve İyileştirilmesine İlişkin Politikalar*, TOBB, Ankara, 1992.

Kazgan, G., *Tanzimattan XXI Yüzyılına Türkiye Ekonomisi*, İstanbul, 1999.

Kepenek, Y., Altıntaş, M., Alpaslan,I., Şenses, F., Türel, O., Yetkiner, H., *İstihdam Politikaları*, Kepenek-TUSES, 1990.

Kepenek, Y. and Yentürk, N., *Türkiye Ekonomisi*, İstanbul 2001 (The last edition)

Keyder, N., Money, Theory, Policy Application, *METU, Studies in Development*, 1986.

Kongar, E., *Türkiye'de Gelir Dağılımı*, Kongar-TUSES, 1989.

Korum, O., The Mixed Economy in Turkey, (1930-1975) in Hiç 1975.

Korum, O., The Structural Interdependence of Public and Private Sectors in the Turkish Manufacturing Industry, in Hiç 1975.

Korum, U., *Türk İmalat Sanayii ve İthal İkamesi: Bir Değerlendirme*, SBF, Ankara, 1977.

Köklü, A., Türkiye'de Para Meseleleri, Ankara 1947.

Kravis, J.E., Kenessey, Z., Heston, A., Summers, R., *A System of International Comparisons of Gross Products and Purchasing Power*, John Hopkins Press, 1975.

Kravis, J. E., Heston, A., Summers, R., *Real GDP per Capita for More than One Hundred Countries*, E. J., 1978.

Kravis, I. B., and R. E. Lipsey, *Towards an Explanation of National Price Levels*, Princeton University Press, 1983, N. J.

Krueger, A., (b) Political Economy of Rent Seeking Society, AER, 1974.

Krueger, A., (a) *Foreign Trade Regimes and Economi Development: Turkey*, Columbia University Press, 1974.

Krueger, A., Ekonominin Dışa Açılmasında Kambiyo Kuru Politikası, *Türkiye Ekonomisinin Dışa Açılması Sorunları*, Konferans Heyeti, Istanbul, 1979.

Krueger, A., and B. Tuncer, Estimates of Total Factor Productivity Growth forthe Turkish Economy, World Bank Development Research Department, 1980, Washington, .C.

Krueger, A., Tuncer, B., *An Empirical Test of Infant Industry Argument*, AER, 1982.

Krueger, E., Exchange Rate Liberalization and Economic Stability: Turkish Experience, in Nas-Odekon 1988.

Kumcu, E., İstikrar Arayışları, İstanbul 2002.

Kuran, T., Internal Migration: The Unorganized Urban Sector and Income Distribution in Turkey, in *Özbudun-Ulusan*, New York, 1980.

Kuyucaklı, N., *Türkiye İktisadı*, BETA, 1986.

Kuznets, S., *Modern Economic Growth*, Yale University Press, 1966.

Kuznets, S., The Gap: Concept, Measurement, Trends, in *the Gap between Rich and Poor Nations*, Edited by Ranis, G., MacMillan, 1972.

Kumcu, E., İhracat Artışının Nedenleri, Hürriyet, July 6, 2007.

Kuznets, S., Problems in Comparing Recent Growth Rates for Developed and Less Developed Countries, *EDCC*, January 1972.

Küçük, Y., Planlama, Kalkınma ve Türkiye 1975, İstanbul.

Little, I., Scitvosky, T., Scott, M., *Industry and Trade in some Developing Countries: A Comparative Study*. OECD, London, 1970.

Mann, Ch., The Effects of Government Policy on Income Distribution, in *Özbudun-Ulusan*, New York, 1980.

Mardin, Ş., Turkey: The Transformation of an Economic Code, in *Özbudun-Ulusan*, New York, 1980.

Miller, D., *Labor Force and Employment, Essays on Labor Force and Employment in Turkey*, AID Ankara, 1971.

Myint, H., *Economic Theory and Underdeveloped Countries*, Oxford University Press, 1971.

Mumcuoğlu, M., Political Activities of Trade Unions and Income Distribution, in *Özbudun-Ulusan*, New York, 1980.

Nas, Tevfik and Odekon Mehmet, Eds, *Liberalization and the Turkish Economy*, Greewood Press, New York, 1988.

Neftçi, S., *An Analysis of Inflationary Dynamics in Turkey*, IBRD, 1980.

Okyar, O., Mixed Economy in Turkey (1930-1975) in Hiç 1979.

Olgun, H., Türkiye'de Ödemeler Dengesi, Para ve Enflasyon, 1963-1976, ODTU, Ankara, 1982.

Oyan, O., Kamu Gelirleri Sistemi Reformu Üzerine, in *Önder-TUSES* 1990.

Oyan, O., Kamu Maliyesi ve Bölüşün İlişkileri, in *Boratav-TUSES* 1990.

Önder, İ., Şenatalar, B., Görgün, S., Falay, U., Oyan, O., Akbulut, E. T., *Türkiye'de Kamu Kesimi Ekonomisi,* TUSES, 1990.

Önder, İ., Konsolide Bütçe Kamu Harcamaları, in *Önder-TUSES* 1990.

Önder, İ., Arın, T., Akbulut, E., Karakaş, E., *Türkiye'de Kamu Harcamalarının Gelişimi*, TUSES, 1989.

Örgüt, İ., Economic Policies, Investment Decisions and Employment in Turkish Industry, in *Miller 1971*. AID, Ankara, 1971.

Öniş, Z., Özmucur, S., Exchange Rates, Inflation and Money Supply in Turkey, *Boğaziçi Üniversitesi Research Paper,* 1986.

Öniş, Z., Stabilization and Growth in a Semi-industrial Economy: An Evaluation of the Recent Turkish Experiment, 1977-1984, *METU Studies in Development*, 1986.

Özbudun, E., Income distribution as an Issue in Turkish Politics, in *Özbudun-Ulusan*, New York, 1980.

Özbudun, E., Ulusan, A., *The Political Economy of Income Distribution in Turkey,* Holmes and Meier, New York, 1980.

Özdeniz, S., Education and Income Distribution in Turkey, in *Özbudun-Ulusan*, New York, 1980.

Öncü, A., Chambers of Industry in Turkey: A Inquiry into State-Industry Relations as a Distributive Domain, in *Özbudun-Ulusan*, New York, 1980.

Özmucur, S., *An Economic Model for Turkey 1965-85*, TUSIAD, 1986.

Özmucur, S., Öniş, Z., *Türkiye'de Enflasyon*, ITO, Istanbul,1 987.

Özmucur, S., *Milli Gelirin Üç Aylık Dönemler İtibariyle Tahmini, Dolarla İfadesi ve Gelir Yoluyla Hesaplanması,* İstanbul Ticaret Odası, 1987.

Özmucur, S., Öniş, Z., *Enflasyon Sorunu ve Türkiye'de Enflasyonu Önleme Politikaları*, TUSES, 1989.

Pamuk, Ş., Ottoman Empire and European Capitalism, 1920-1913, Cambridge University Press, 1987.

Reynolds, C.H., Financial Planning with Macroeconomic Planning for Efficient Foreign Debt Management in LDC, *External Debt and the World Economy,* (Ed. Wionczek, M.S.), 1978.

Rittenberg, Libby, Financial Liberalization and Savings in Turkey, in Nas-Odekon 1988.

Rodric, Dani, Some Policy Dilemmas in Turkish Macroeconomic Management, in Arıcanlı-Rodric 1990.

Rodric, Dani, External Debt and Economic Performance in Turkey, in Nas-Odekon 1988.

Rodric, D., Premature Liberalization: Özal Decade in Stabilization and Aftermath, Eds: Bruno et al, MIT Press, 1991.

Sachs, J. and Larain F., Macroeconomics in the Global Economy, New York, 1993.

Sarç, Ö. C., Türkiye Ekonomisi, Akbank İstanbul, 1980.

Sayan, S., Demorafik Gelişmeler ve Türkiye Ekonomisi, Doğu Batı Dergisi, Ankara 2001.

Selçuk, F., Alaca Karanlık Kuşağı, Doğu Batı 2001.

Singer, M., The *Economic Advane of Turkey*, Turkish Economic Society, Ankara, 1978.

Singh, S. K., *Development Economics,* Lexington Books, 1975.

Solow, R. M., *Technical Progress and Productivity Change*, RES, 1957.

Şenatalar, B. Önder, İ., Oyan, O., Seviğ, V., *Türkiye'de 1980 Sonrası Vergi Politikası,* Şenatalar-TUSES, 1990.

Şenesen, Ü. et al., *Türkiye Ekonomisi için Bir Ekonometrik Model*, ITO, 1986.

Şenses, F., Gelişme İktisadi ve Türkiye'nin İktisadi Gelişmesi, *METU, Studies in Development*, Ankara, 1983 (The review of UATE by Hatiboğlu)

Şenses, Fikret, An overview of Recent Turkish Experience with Economic Stabilization and Liberalization, in Nas-Odekon 1988.

Şenses, F., The Nature and Main Characteristics of Recent Turkish Growth in Export of Manufacturing, *The Developing Economies*, XXVII-1, 1989.

Şenses, F., Türkiye'de Gelir Dağılımı, Gelirin Yeniden Dağılımı ve İşgücü Piyasaları, in *Boratav-TUSES* 1990.

State Institute of Statistics (SIS), Yearly Statistical Bulletins

State Institute of Statistics (SIS), Income Distribution, 1994, Ankara.

Stiglitz, T., *Globalization and its Discontents*, Norton, 2002.

Syrquin, Moshe, Productivity growth and Factor Reallocation, in Chenery, Industralization and Growth, 1986.

Taylor, Lance, Turkish Experience: Summary and Comparative Notes, in Arıcanlı-Rodric, 1990.

Tezel, Y., Turkish Economy Development, 1975-50. Policy and Achievements, Cambridge University, 1975.

Tuncer, B., The Regulatory Role of theGovernment in the Turkish Economy, in Hiç 1979.

Türel, O., *Sanayileşme, Nereden, Nereye, Nasıl*, Kuruç-TUSES, 1990.

Türel, O., Faktör ve Mal Piyasalarındaki Diğer Politika Öğeleri, in *Boratav-TUSES* 1990.

TUSIAD, *Mali Aracı Kurulumlar*, Istanbul, 1982.

TUSIAD, *Gelir Dağılımı*, 1986.

TUSIAD, *An Econometric Model for Turkey*, 1965-1984, Istanbul, 1986.

TUSIAD, *1988 Yılına Girerken Türkiye Ekonomisi*, 1988.

TUSIAD, *Piyasa Ekonomilerinde Endüstriyel Kalkınma Stratejileri*, 1990.

TUSIAD, *21.Yüzyıla Doğru Türkiye: Geleceğe Doğru Bir Açılım Stratejisi*, 1991, 2 Volumes.

Ulusan, A., Public Policy Toward Agriculture an Its Redistributive Implications, in *Özbudun-Ulusan*, New York, 1980.

Uygur, E., *Policy, Productivity, Growth and Employment, 1960-1989 and Prospects for the 1990*, (not published), 1990.

Uygur, E., *İktisat Söyleşileri*, Bilgi Yayınevi 1991.

Üstünel, B., Kalkınmanın Neresindeyiz? Ankara, 1962.

Yeldan, E., Türkiye Ekonomisi 2000-2002 Krizinin Yapısal Kaynakları Üzerine, Doğu-Batı, 2001-2002.

Yeldan, E., Küreselleşme Sürecinde Türkiye Ekonomisi, İletişim Yayınevi, İstanbul, 2002.

Yotopoulos, P., Nugent, J., *Economics of Development*, Harper and Row, 1976.

The Reviews of An Unconventional Analysis of the Turkish Economy by Z. Hatiboğlu:

1) *The South African Journal of Economics*, 1978-4.

2) *The Journal of Economic Literature*, March 1979.

3) *The Economic Journal 1979*, March 1979.

4) *The Middle East Journal*, 1979-1.